Armies of the Napoleonic Wars

Armies of the Napoleonic Wars

Edited by
Gregory Fremont-Barnes

Pen & Sword
MILITARY

First published in Great Britain in 2011 by
PEN & SWORD MILITARY
An imprint of
Pen & Sword Books Ltd
47 Church Street
Barnsley
South Yorkshire
S70 2AS

ISBN 978-1-84884-067-6

A CIP catalogue record for this book is
available from the British Library

Typeset by Concept, Huddersfield, West Yorkshire
Printed and bound in England by the MPG Books Group

Pen & Sword Books Ltd incorporates the Imprints of Pen & Sword Aviation, Pen & Sword Maritime, Pen & Sword Military, Wharncliffe Local History, Pen & Sword Select, Pen & Sword Military Classics, Leo Cooper, Remember When, Seaforth Publishing and Frontline Publishing

For a complete list of Pen & Sword titles please contact
PEN & SWORD BOOKS LIMITED
47 Church Street, Barnsley, South Yorkshire, S70 2AS, England
E-mail: enquiries@pen-and-sword.co.uk
Website: www.pen-and-sword.co.uk

Contents

List of Plates vi
List of Contributors viii
Preface xi

Introduction 1
1. The French Army *by Gregory Fremont-Barnes* 14
2. The Russian Army *by Alexander Mikaberidze* 36
3. The Austrian Army *by David Hollins* 57
4. The Prussian Army *by Oliver Schmidt* 98
5. The British Army *by Gregory Fremont-Barnes* 127
6. Armies of the Confederation of the Rhine *by John H. Gill* 150
7. The Spanish Army *by Charles Esdaile* 188
8. The Portuguese Army *by Malyn Newitt* 212
9. The Army of the Duchy of Warsaw *by Jarosław Czubaty* 230
10. The Army of the Kingdom of Italy *by Frederick C. Schneid* 244

Further Reading 254
Index 264

List of Plates

1. French Dragoon trooper and sapper.
2. French Dragoons in action at Nancis, 1814.
3. French lancer, 1812.
4. French carabinier.
5. French cuirassiers charge over the breastworks of the Great Redoubt at the Battle of Borodino, 7 September 1812.
6. Polish lancers of the Imperial Guard reaching the Spanish guns at the summit of the pass at Somosierra.
7. French cuirassiers awaiting the order to attack at the Battle of Wagram, 5 July 1809.
8. Marshal Michel Ney.
9. Marshal Joachim Murat.
10. Grenadiers of the Imperial Guard relaxing in their quarters.
11. French line infantry at Vitebsk during the campaign of 1812.
12. Marshal Ney leading French grenadiers during the retreat from Moscow in late 1812.
13. Cossacks.
14. General Bagration's infantry ferociously defend the *flêches* at Borodino, 7 September 1812.
15. General Kutusov.
16. Austrian cuirassier and dragoon, 1812.
17. Austrian gunners and artillery officer.
18. Hungarian grenadier and Tyrolean chasseur, 1812.
19. Austrian line infantryman and Chasseur à Cheval, 1812.
20. Prussian foot artilleryman and horse artillery officer, 1812.
21. Cuirassier and infantryman of the Prussian Royal Guard, 1812.
22. Chasseur, fusilier and fusilier officer of the Prussian Royal Guard, 1812.
23. Lancers of the Prussian Royal Guard, 1812.
24. Prussian infantry of the line, 1812.
25. British infantry at the Battle of Talavera.
26. British infantry and gunners repulsing a French sortie during the siege of Ciudad Rodrigo, January 1812.

27. British dragoons charging French infantry and guns at the Battle of Salamanca.
28. Wellington and his staff at the Battle of Waterloo, 18 June 1815.
29. Napoleon addressing Bavarian troops at Abensberg, 20 April 1809.
30. Saxon cuirassiers charging Austrian infantry at Dresden, 27 August 1813.
31. Line infantry from Saxony and Württemburg, 1812.
32. Bavarian Royal Guard and officer of artillery, 1812.
33. Italian Gendarmerie d'Elite.
34. Italian Guard Carabiniers.
35. Italian troops of General Pino's 15th Division, part of Eugène's IV Corps, advancing into Russia, 1812.

List of Contributors

Dr Jarosław Czubaty has been a lecturer at the Institute of History, University of Warsaw since 1986. His main field of research is Polish history and the history of Central and Eastern Europe between 1795 and 1850, particularly the Napoleonic period in Poland. His interests focus on the role of the army in Polish society and the development of political ideas. His recent publications include: *Wodzowie i politycy. Generalicja polska 1806–1815* (*Commanders and Politicians: Polish Generals 1806–1815*) (1994) and 'Glory, Honour and Patriotism: Military Careers in the Duchy of Warsaw, 1806–1815', in *Soldiers, Citizens and Civilians: Experience and Perceptions of the Revolutionary and Napoleonic Wars, 1790–1820*, ed. A. Forrest, K. Hagemann and J. Rendall (2009).

Charles Esdaile has been a member of the staff of School of History at the University of Liverpool since 1989, and was awarded a personal chair in 2004. As the author of numerous books, articles and conference papers on the Napoleonic epoch in general and the Peninsular War in particular – his most well-known works, perhaps, are *The Wars of Napoleon* (1995); *The Peninsular War: a New History* (2002); and *Napoleon's Wars: an International History* (2007) – he is recognised as a world authority in this field and regularly attends scholarly meetings on the subject in destinations that have ranged from Poland to the USA. At the moment he is working on a study of the French occupation of Andalucia in the period 1810–12.

Gregory Fremont-Barnes holds a doctorate in Modern History from Oxford University and serves as a Senior Lecturer in the Department of War Studies at the Royal Military Academy Sandhurst. He has published numerous books on the military and naval history of the eighteenth to twentieth centuries, with a focus on the Napoleonic period. His edited works include, besides the present work, the three-volume *Encyclopedia of the French Revolutionary and Napoleonic Wars* (2006) and the two-volume *Encyclopedia of the Age of Political Revolutions and New Ideologies, 1760–1815* (2007). His books on the Napoleonic era include *The French Revolutionary Wars* (2001), *The Peninsular War, 1807–14* (2002), *The Fall of the French Empire, 1813–15* (2002), *Trafalgar 1805* (2005), *Nelson's Sailors* (2005), *Nelson's Officers and Midshipmen* (2009) and *Napoleon Bonaparte* (2010).

John (Jack) H. Gill is an Associate Professor in the faculty of the Near East – South Asia Center for Strategic Studies, part of the National Defense

University in Washington DC. Specialising in military history of the Napoleonic period, his publications include *With Eagles to Glory: Napoleon and His German Allies in the 1809 Campaign* (1992) and *A Soldier for Napoleon: The Campaigns of Franz Joseph Hausmann, 7th Bavarian Infantry* (ed.) (1998), as well as chapters, articles, papers and lectures presented to the Society for Military History, the Consortium on the Revolutionary Era, the German Studies Association and the Napoleonic Historical Society. His most recent publications are the first two volumes of *Thunder on the Danube* (2008), a projected three-volume history of the 1809 Franco-Austrian War.

David Hollins was born in Aberdeen, Scotland, in 1962. After graduating from University College London with an LLB (Hons), he trained as a maritime solicitor and then worked in commercial shipping. After completing an MBA and financial exams, he now works in London. He has written seven books related to the Austrian Army for Osprey and has been a frequent contributor to Napoleonic magazines. He has also contributed to two encyclopedic works on the period and is currently researching Napoleonic military espionage.

Dr Alexander Mikaberidze is assistant professor of European history at Louisiana State University in Shreveport. After working for the Ministry of Foreign Affairs of Georgia (1996–2000), he taught European and Middle Eastern history at Florida State and Mississippi State Universities and lectured on strategy and policy for the US Naval War College. He has written and edited eight books, including two award-winning books, *The Russian Officer Corps in the Revolutionary and Napoleonic Wars, 1792–1815* (2005) and *The Battle of Borodino: Napoleon versus Kutuzov* (2007). His latest publication is *Napoleon's Great Escape: The Battle on the Berezina* (2010).

Malyn Newitt was born in 1940. He taught at the University of Rhodesia, 1962–65, and at the University of Exeter, 1966–98. At Exeter he served as Deputy Vice Chancellor (1995–98). In 1998 he was appointed the first Charles Boxer Professor of History at King's College London. He retired in 2005. His speciality is Portuguese colonial history and, in particular, the history of Mozambique and the Indian Ocean. He is author of fifteen books on Portugal and its empire, including *History of Mozambique* (1995), *A History of Portuguese Overseas Expansion* (2004) and *Portugal in European and World History* (2009).

Oliver Schmidt was born in 1964, and lives in Heidelberg, Germany, as a private scholar, with his main interest the French Revolutionary and Napoleonic Wars. He was editor of the historical journal *Circulaire* for several years and has published numerous articles on the Prussian Army, as well as a book entitled *Prussian Regular Infantryman 1808–15* (2003).

Frederick C. Schneid is Professor of History at High Point University in North Carolina. He received his PhD from Purdue University studying under world-renowned military historian Gunther E. Rothenberg. Schneid has published extensively on the Napoleonic era. Among his books are, *Soldiers of Napoleon's Kingdom of Italy: Army State and Society, 1800–1815* (1995); *Napoleon's Italian Campaigns, 1805–1815* (2002); and *Napoleon's Conquest of Europe: The War of the Third Coalition* (2005). He co-edited *Conscription in the Napoleonic Era: A Revolution in Military Affairs?* (2009), and contributed the chapter 'Command and Control' in *Fighting Techniques of the Napoleonic Age* (2008). In 2008, he published 'Kings, Clients and Satellites in the Napoleonic Imperium' in the *Journal of Strategic Studies.*

Preface

This volume seeks to describe the armies of the principal belligerents during the period 1803 to 1815, recognising that to include all participants would require a considerably larger study. In examining a particular army of which he can speak with authority, each contributing author has adopted his own approach, for no template has been imposed that would require uniformity across chapters. Freed from these constraints, each historian has therefore been able to provide a different perspective, and thus, while one chapter alludes to the conduct of a particular force on campaign, another delves into the political context in which another army fought. Some chapters cover such issues as recruitment or higher command; others do not. Some plunge into particular detail about organisation and structure, while others place greater emphasis on describing the various arms of service and their respective functions. What emerges is a study, prepared from the perspective of those with expert knowledge of their respective subjects, that sheds important new light on ten fighting forces whose participation in the Napoleonic Wars is broadly set out – for the sake of establishing a contextual framework for understanding them – in the Introduction that follows.

It remains only for me to acknowledge my debt to all the contributing authors, whose unique perspectives on Napoleonic armies will doubtless continue to stimulate debate within a subject of enduring interest to scholars and students alike. Many thanks in particular to Alexander Mikaberidze, John H. Gill and Frederick Schneid, who generously supplied images for the book.

Gregory Fremont-Barnes
30 March 2010

Introduction

The Napoleonic Wars represented a renewal of the major conflict that had begun in April 1792 between France and a varying host of individual belligerent states and coalitions, finally coming to a short-lived conclusion in March 1802. When fighting resumed in May 1803 after a fourteen-month period of uncertain peace, it initially involved only Britain and France. As the dominant naval power, Britain naturally reverted to its time-honoured strategy of re-imposing its blockade of the major French ports such as Rochefort, Brest and Toulon, and preying on French commercial shipping. The French, at the same time, resumed the construction of shallow-draught transports in preparation for a cross-Channel invasion of England. Over the subsequent months the main construction area around Boulogne grew substantially, as did the concentration of troops established in camps there. Napoleon understood that in order to facilitate an invasion it was vital to distract a large proportion of the Royal Navy's ships, so that the Channel was clear for his highly vulnerable invasion craft. Napoleon, who was ignorant of naval strategy and failed to appreciate that the principles that applied to warfare on land did not necessarily apply to those at sea, devised many plans of varying complexity.

None of these was in fact carried out until April 1805, when Admiral Villeneuve emerged from Toulon, linked up with a Spanish fleet at Cadiz and sailed for the West Indies, with Vice Admiral Nelson in pursuit. In June Villeneuve then returned to European waters, unintentionally falling in with a British squadron off Cape Finisterre on 22 July 1805; the engagement was indecisive in itself, but it obliged Villeneuve to make for Cadiz instead of the Channel. In any event, the Brest fleet had been unable to evade the blockade and was still in port. Villeneuve, with thirty-three ships of the line, then received orders to sail for the Mediterranean, to aid in diversionary operations in Italy. Nelson, however, with twenty-seven ships of the line, intercepted him off Cape Trafalgar on 21 October, achieving a decisive victory over the Combined Fleet (as the united French and Spanish fleet was known) and ending all possibility of a French invasion for the remainder of the Napoleonic Wars. Immensely important though the Battle of Trafalgar was, it did not affect the vital operations then being simultaneously conducted on land, for Napoleon had, by the time of the battle, already changed his plans, temporarily abandoning his scheme for a landing on the English coast in order to free up the Grande Armée, as his main force became known, for operations against the Austrians and Russians.

WAR OF THE THIRD COALITION (1805)

William Pitt, the British prime minister, was instrumental in organising the Third Coalition, which came to fruition on 11 April 1805 with the conclusion of an Anglo-Russian alliance, to which Austria acceded on 9 August. Sweden, a comparatively minor power, joined the coalition shortly thereafter. Napoleon broke up his invasion camp at Boulogne at the end of August and marched for the Danube in order to confront Austro-Russian forces. At the same time, an Austrian army under General Mack, who had no knowledge that the French were moving east, invaded Bavaria, a French ally, on 2 September.

Archduke Charles, meanwhile, advanced into Italy to confront the French forces there under Marshal Masséna, while further east a Russian army under General Mikhail Kutusov slowly advanced through Poland to assist the Austrians in Moravia. The Austrians were shocked to discover that Napoleon had made such remarkably rapid progress, crossing the Rhine on 26 September and reaching the Danube on 6 October. In the course of this march, the French had moved in a broad arc around Mack's army near Ulm, cutting his lines of communication and isolating him from reinforcement. After a feeble attempt to break through the cordon at Elchingen on 14 October, Mack surrendered his entire force of 27,000 men on 17 October, making the encirclement at Ulm one of history's greatest strategic manoeuvres.

With Mack's force neutralised, Napoleon advanced on and occupied Vienna, forcing the Russians back at Dürnstein on 11 November and Hollabrunn on 15–16 November. In Italy, Masséna was victorious at Caldiero, forcing Charles to return back across the Alps, though detached formations from the principal French forces prevented him from linking up with the main Austro-Russian army, for which Napoleon set a trap. By moving north of the Austrian capital to expose his lines of communication, Napoleon tempted Kutusov to sever these lines. The ploy worked. As the Allies attempted to envelop the French flank at Austerlitz on 2 December, Napoleon launched his forces through the Allied centre, dividing it and crushing the enemy left, making Austerlitz one of Napoleon's greatest victories. Two days later Emperor Francis surrendered, and Kutusov, with Tsar Alexander attached to Russian headquarters, promptly withdrew his forces east. Peace between France and Austria was reached on 26 December at Pressburg, where Francis agreed to cede territory to France and her allies in both Germany and Italy.

WAR OF THE FOURTH COALITION (1806–7)

Although Austria withdrew from the coalition after Austerlitz, Britain and Russia remained at war with France. The Fourth Coalition came into being in the autumn of 1806 after a breakdown in Franco-Prussian relations, largely the result of Napoleon's failure to cede Hanover (formerly a hereditary possession of George III) to Prussia, as promised, and of the establishment of the Confederation of the Rhine – a new political entity replacing the Holy Roman Empire (abolished in 1806) consisting of various German states all allied to, or dependent on, France. Prussia had remained neutral during the 1805 campaign – in hindsight a grave strategic error on its part – but with the growing influence of France in German affairs it threw in its lot and, together with its ally, the Electorate of Saxony, declared war.

The Grande Armée, situated in northeast Bavaria, prepared to invade Prussia; the Prussians were commanded by the Duke of Brunswick, a veteran of the wars of Frederick the Great. With remarkable speed the French began their advance on 8 October, achieving complete surprise. Marshal Lannes, in a minor action at Saalfeld on 10 October, defeated a small Prussian force and killed Prince Louis Ferdinand of Prussia, while the main French army turned the Prussian left flank while making for Berlin. Napoleon fought part of the main Prussian army under Prince Hohenlohe at Jena on 14 October. Hohenlohe's command was, however, merely a small force meant to protect Brunswick's rear; Napoleon's numerical superiority predictably told, and Hohenlohe was routed. At Auerstädt, a short distance to the north, on the same day, Davout, who had been sent to cut Prussian communications, encountered the main Prussian force under Brunswick. There the odds were rather different, with Davout outnumbered by a force more than twice the size of his own. He managed to hold on, however, and when Bernadotte arrived, the tide turned decisively in the French favour, with the Prussians routed there as well, and the Duke of Brunswick mortally wounded.

The destruction of Prussia's main army effectively spelled the end of resistance, and the remainder of the campaign consisted of the French pursuit of small contingents, virtually all of which eventually put down their arms, and the capture of fortresses. Berlin itself fell on 24 October, and the last major force to hold out, near Lübeck, surrendered a month later. A small Prussian contingent managed to make contact with the Russians in Poland, into which Napoleon immediately proceeded, taking Warsaw in an effort to prevent the Russians from assisting their vanquished allies.

Adhering to the principle that the key to victory lay in confronting and decisively defeating the main enemy force, Napoleon sought out the Russian army under General Bennigsen, the first encounter taking place on 26 December at Pultusk, where the Russians were bruised but nothing more. The rival armies went into winter quarters in January 1807 amid bitterly cold temperatures, but the campaign resumed the following month, when Bennigsen began to move and Napoleon went in pursuit. Though outnumbered and caught in a blizzard, Napoleon reached the

Russians at Eylau, where on 8 February the two sides inflicted severe losses on one another with no decisive result. Bennigsen withdrew, but with appalling losses and atrocious weather, Napoleon declined to follow. Both sides returned to winter quarters to recover from the carnage, with the renewal of hostilities planned for the spring.

Bennigsen and Napoleon each planned to assume the offensive, but when Bennigsen advanced first, he was stopped at Heilsberg on 10 June. At Friedland four days later the decisive encounter of the campaign took place, with Bennigsen foolishly placing his army with the River Alle at his back. The Russians resisted enemy attacks with magnificent stoicism, eventually collapsing. With no route of escape, the campaign was over. Tsar Alexander, his army in tatters, and accompanied at headquarters by Frederick William III of Prussia, requested a conference to discuss peace. The three sovereigns concluded the Treaty of Tilsit between 7 and 9 July, putting the seal on Napoleonic control of western and central Europe. Frederick William was humiliated, having given up those portions of his Polish possessions originally taken during the partitions of Poland more than a decade before to the newly established Duchy of Warsaw, a French satellite state. To the Confederation of the Rhine, Prussia ceded all its territory between the Rhine and the Elbe, most of this forming the new Kingdom of Westphalia under Napoleon's brother Jerome. A French army of occupation was to remain on Prussian soil until a huge war indemnity was paid. Russia was required to enter into an alliance with France against Britain and to recognise the Duchy of Warsaw. With Russia and Prussia knocked out of the war, only Britain remained to face France, now at the height of its power.

WAR OF THE FIFTH COALITION (1809)

The Fifth Coalition hardly justified its name, for when Austria once again chose to oppose France, it did so without allies to assist it on land. Britain, of course, carried on operations at sea and offered substantial subsidies and loans as it had since 1793, but it could do little more on land than send an expedition in July to Walcheren Island, off the Dutch coast, where disease soon rendered the whole affair a disaster and obliged the British to withdraw in October. Nevertheless, the Austrians had some reason to be hopeful, for in fielding a sizeable army in the spring of 1809, they took advantage of the absence from central Europe of large numbers of French troops who had been diverted to serve in operations in Spain. Yet, with misplaced optimism, they underestimated Napoleon's ability to muster his forces and concentrate them quickly, for by the time the Habsburg armies were ready to fight, the French had shifted reinforcements from the Iberian Peninsula to meet this revived threat.

The main Austrian army under Archduke Charles invaded the principal member of the Confederation of the Rhine, Bavaria, which also had to contend with an Austrian-inspired revolt in the Tyrol, a region formerly under Habsburg control. At the same time, Archduke John crossed the Alps to invade northern Italy, repulsing Eugène de Beauharnais, the Viceroy of Italy and a staunch ally of France, at Sacile on 16 April. When Napoleon arrived from Spain, he moved immediately to the offensive, crossing the Danube and defeating an Austrian force at Abensberg on 19–20 April before turning on Charles, then under observation by Davout. Charles struck first, confronting Davout at Eggmühl but failing, despite overwhelming numerical superiority, to defeat him, as a result of Napoleon's arrival with his main force. French exhaustion from three days' engagements (at Abensberg, Landshut and Eggmühl) denied them the opportunity to pursue Charles. However, they managed to storm and seize Ratisbon on 23 April, and three weeks later French troops occupied Vienna without a shot being fired.

Charles, meanwhile, concentrated his army on the north bank of the Danube. Napoleon ordered pontoon bridges constructed to span the river to Lobau Island, and then to the other side, where troops positioned themselves in the villages of Aspern and Essling. On 21–22 May the two sides fought bitterly for possession of these villages, but the French refused to be dislodged. However, with the single French bridge unable to allow substantial numbers of reinforcements to be fed to the north side of the river, Napoleon withdrew his forces to the opposite bank, marking out Aspern–Essling as the Emperor's first defeat. Napoleon intended to re-cross the Danube and confront Charles for a second time, but he knew he must first develop another plan to do so. Meanwhile, on the Italian front, Archduke John was obliged to withdraw back over the Julian Alps, followed by Eugène, who was successful at Raab on 16 June and subsequently moved to link up with the main French army on the Danube.

Hoping to defeat Charles before he could be reinforced by Archduke John, Napoleon re-crossed the Danube on the night of 4–5 July. The Austrians offered no resistance to the crossing, but on the 5th and 6th heavy fighting took place at Wagram, where Charles attempted to isolate Napoleon from his bridgehead. This manoeuvre, however, failed; the Austrian centre was pierced, and Charles was obliged to retreat, albeit with very heavy losses suffered by both sides. Austria could no longer carry on the war: Vienna was under enemy occupation, the main army had been beaten, though not destroyed, and Russia had not joined the campaign as Austria had hoped. Francis duly sued for peace on 10 July and three months later signed the Treaty of Schönbrunn, by which he relinquished large portions of his empire to France and its allies and promised to adhere to Napoleon's Continental System, by which the Emperor sought to impose an embargo on the importation of British goods to the Continent and the exportation of continental goods to Britain in an effort to strangle its economy.

THE PENINSULAR WAR (1807–14)

Quite separate from the other campaigns waged in Europe, the Peninsular War, fought in the Iberian Peninsula, constituted the principal theatre in which Britain could at last contribute substantial land forces to the war against Napoleon. Portuguese and above all Spanish resistance, involving both regular and guerrilla forces, over time contributed much to the diversion of French troops from other theatres of conflict, and to the continual drain on French manpower. After the Treaty of Tilsit and the introduction of the Continental System, only Portugal continued to defy the ban by accepting British imports. In an effort to close this final avenue of trade, Napoleon sent troops through Spain and Portugal, taking advantage of the opportunity to impose his will on the Spanish, as well.

In November 1807 General Junot began his march through Spain, entering Lisbon in December. The Royal Navy evacuated the Portuguese royal family and transported it to Brazil, while the Provisional Government left behind sought assistance from Britain. Napoleon then revealed his full intentions, when in March 1808 Marshal Murat entered Spain at the head of a large army, occupied Spanish fortresses and disarmed their garrisons under false pretences, and deposed both King Charles IV and his son Ferdinand, who were replaced by Napoleon's brother Joseph, backed by pro-Bonapartist elements in Madrid. The French occupation was never fated to go smoothly; on 2 May the populace of Madrid rose up in revolt, and the spirit of resistance soon spread throughout the country, where guerrilla bands began to spring up and prey on French detachments, couriers and isolated outposts. The regular Spanish armies fought a number of pitched battles against the French in 1808–9, but they were generally defeated, sometimes disastrously. Spanish resistance also manifested itself in a number of epic sieges in which civilians played a prominent part, most notably that at Saragossa, northeast of Madrid, where in the summer of 1808 the inhabitants managed to stave off repeated French attempts to storm the city. The one significant Spanish success in the field came at Bailen, in Andalusia, where on 19 July 1808, General Dupont surrendered an army of 23,000 men, causing shock waves across Europe and destroying the myth of French invincibility.

The war in the Peninsula took on an entirely different character from August 1808, when a British expeditionary force led by Lieutenant General Sir Arthur Wellesley (later the Duke of Wellington) arrived in Portugal and defeated Junot at Vimeiro on 21 August, thus securing a foothold for the British army. By the Convention of Cintra, senior British commanders granted the French generous terms, which allowed them to be transported home with their weapons in British ships. Wellesley alone was cleared by the court of inquiry that convened in London and cashiered the generals responsible for what in Britain were considered the disgraceful terms agreed at Cintra.

With Portugal cleared of French troops and British reinforcements arriving under Lieutenant General Sir John Moore, an opportunity now offered itself for an offensive into Spain. Moore, with promises of Spanish support, therefore advanced in the autumn of 1808. When Spanish support failed to materialise, however, Moore faced numerically superior forces under Napoleon himself, who had arrived in Spain determined to drive the British out of the Iberian Peninsula once and for all. He occupied Madrid on 4 December and pursued the British commander, obliging Moore to make a long, punishing retreat through winter conditions to Corunna (and another, smaller column to retreat to Vigo) on the northwest Spanish coast. The diversion of French attention toward the retreating British columns gave the Spanish armies a much-needed respite. Believing Moore at risk of imminent defeat at the hands of Marshal Soult, and with war looming with Austria, Napoleon left for France. Moore was harassed for much of the journey, but on reaching Corunna he turned to face Soult before evacuating his troops onto Royal Navy transports. Moore died in the ensuing battle, but his ragged army was saved, and by that time Lisbon had been sufficiently fortified to prevent the French from retaking it. Saragossa, however, finally surrendered, after a second enormously costly siege in February 1809.

Wellesley returned to Portugal in command of the army there, to be supplemented by Portuguese forces re-organised on the British model by Marshal Beresford. Soult invaded Portugal in the spring of 1809, but Wellesley ejected him after fighting at Oporto, on the River Douro, on 12 May. Exploiting his success, Wellesley crossed the border into Spain to co-operate with the Spanish commander, General García de la Cuesta, who in the event failed to assist Wellesley at Talavera on 28 July, when he came under attack by Marshal Victor and Joseph Bonaparte. The Anglo-Portuguese narrowly held off the French, as a reward for which Wellesley was raised to the peerage as Marquis Wellington, finishing the Peninsular War as the Duke of Wellington. Meanwhile, the Spanish armies showed themselves to be incapable of confronting the French, who defeated them comprehensively at Ocaña on 19 November. Unable to take the war into Spain, for the moment Wellington concentrated on defending Portugal, where Lisbon was established as an easily accessible base at which supplies and troops could be landed from Britain, and which held complete command of the maritime route from home. Wellington ensured that the defences could sustain an attack on any scale by ordering the construction of a line of impregnable fortifications, known later as the Lines of Torres Vedras, across the peninsula on which Lisbon was situated.

Masséna opened the campaign of 1810 with yet another French invasion of Portugal, in July, but he was defeated at Busaco on 27 September by Wellington, who then withdrew behind the protection afforded by the completed Lines of Torres Vedras. Masséna followed him, but upon discovering the Lines made one attempt at penetrating them before realising that they were unassailable. He therefore camped his troops before the Lines for the remainder of the year and into 1811, with very little food to be foraged or requisitioned in the area, as a result of Wellington's scorched earth policy. The French also sought to capture Cadiz, in the far south of the country, where the Spanish had established an alternative capital to occupied Madrid. At Cadiz a small British force under Sir Thomas Graham repulsed the French at Barrosa on 5 March, securing the port city's safety. Masséna fought Wellington at Fuentes de Oñoro on 5 May, while to the south Beresford's Anglo-Spanish army beat Soult, himself seeking to aid French troops besieged at Badajoz. Losses were very heavy on both sides, and though Soult was unable to relieve the garrison, the fortress remained in French hands and thus prevented Wellington from taking the war into Spain. The French were successful elsewhere; in the south, Marshal Louis Suchet captured Tarragona on 28 July and Valencia on 9 January 1812.

The campaign of 1812 opened with Wellington assuming the offensive, seizing the border fortresses of Ciudad Rodrigo on 19 January and Badajoz on 6 April, the latter taken only after the British storming parties suffered tremendous losses in a series of desperate assaults. Notwithstanding the heavy price paid for possession of these towns, Wellington could at last carry the war into Spain, where he scored a decisive victory over Marshal Marmont at Salamanca on 22 July. Wellington occupied Madrid for a short time in August, but with the failure of his assault on Burgos as a result of inadequate siege equipment, he was obliged to retreat as far as Portugal. Nevertheless, large numbers of French troops had been withdrawn for the Russian campaign, and years of guerrilla warfare had taken a heavy toll on both French strength and morale.

In 1813 Wellington was enabled to return to the offensive, routing Joseph's army at Vitoria on 21 June, thus ending Bonapartist rule and forcing the French from most of the country to a narrow band of territory in the extreme north. Wellington continued to drive the French before him, taking San Sebastian and Pamplona and fighting his way through several passes in the Pyrenees to invade France herself. He defeated Soult, first at Orthez on 27 February 1814, and again in the final major action of the war, on 10 April at Toulouse, where news had not yet arrived that Napoleon had already abdicated in Paris a few days earlier. The Peninsular War had not only brought to the fore one of Britain's greatest commanders, it had drained French resources over the course of many years, thus making an important contribution to Napoleon's ultimate downfall.

THE RUSSIAN CAMPAIGN (1812)

With the Continental System eventually cutting hard into the Russian economy and Alexander growing increasingly concerned about the presence of the Duchy of Warsaw on his borders, war between Russia and France became inevitable. Napoleon, gathering a massive army of unprecedented size and composed of every nationality from his Empire, pushed across the Niemen River with over 500,000 men on 22 June 1812. The two main Russian armies, one under General Barclay de Tolly and the other under Prince Bagration, found themselves unable to resist a force of this size, and withdrew east, uniting at Smolensk on 3 August. Unable to outflank his opponents, Napoleon chose to engage them first on 17 August at Smolensk, where he took the city by storm, and again at Valutino two days later, where he scored a minor success, the Russians simply withdrawing deeper into the interior and obliging the French to extend their increasingly vulnerable lines of communication even further.

The Russian commander-in-chief, Barclay de Tolly, was replaced by Kutusov, who on 7 September made an extremely hard-fought stand at Borodino, where rather than attempting any elaborate manoeuvres to envelop the stationary Russians, Napoleon launched a simple front assault against prepared positions held by troops committed to defend 'Holy Russia' with the utmost determination. The battle degenerated into a horrendous bloodletting with no decisive result. Kutusov withdrew east, the exhausted French unable to pursue in the short term. The Russians made no further attempt to defend Moscow, which the French entered on 14 September. Nevertheless, much of the city was almost immediately destroyed by fire – probably deliberately set by the Russians – though enough remained of Moscow to provide shelter for Napoleon's dwindling army for the month that the Emperor chose to remain there, all the while hoping that the Tsar would sue for peace. Alexander sent no such overtures, and by the time Napoleon began his retreat on 19 October – owing to his inability to supply the army over an otherwise potentially lengthy period of occupation – winter had nearly arrived.

The story of the retreat from Moscow is well known: snow soon began to fall, and the army, harassed by Cossacks and suffering from hunger, cold and lack of horse transport, disintegrated into a mass of fugitives, most of whom could offer little or no resistance to the increasingly vengeful Russians. The entire path of the army was strewn with bodies, abandoned equipment and the spoils of war. On 24 October the Russians caught up with the corps, mostly Italians, under Eugène de Beauharnais at Maloyaroslavets, inflicting a serious blow, and when the army finally reached Smolensk, it was hardly worthy of the name. Stragglers and camp followers were regularly butchered by the Cossacks, and discipline and morale gradually collapsed. Kutusov cut off part of the Grande Armée at Krasnyi on 16–17 November, though Napoleon managed to rescue it, and the whole struggled on to the Berezina River. There, engineers, working under the most difficult circumstances, managed to throw two makeshift bridges across the river, enabling thousands to cross, while what units could be cobbled together fought on the east bank to hold back the attacks of the regular Russian army. Eventually the bridges had to be set on fire by the French to slow the enemy's pursuit, yet leaving thousands to be captured or killed on the Russian side of the river. Fewer than 100,000 survivors eventually reached the Niemen at the end of December, when the Russians halted their pursuit of an army that had dissolved into a mere rabble. The Grande Armée had effectively ceased to exist, but Napoleon had already ventured ahead to Paris to assemble a new army.

THE CAMPAIGN IN GERMANY (1813)

However immense the losses suffered by Napoleon in Russia, his extraordinary administrative skills enabled him to rebuild his army by the spring of 1813, though neither the men nor the horses could be replaced in their former quality or quantity. The Sixth Coalition, which had been formed by Britain, Russia, Spain and Portugal in June 1812, now expanded as other states became emboldened to oppose Napoleonic hegemony in Europe. The Prussian corps, which had reluctantly accompanied the Grande Armée into Russia, declared its neutrality by the Convention of Tauroggen on 30 December 1812, and on 27 February 1813 Frederick William formally brought his country into the coalition by the terms of the Convention of Kalisch, signed with Russia. The Austrians remained neutral during the spring campaign, with Count Schwarzenberg's corps, which had covered the southern flank of the French advance into Russia, withdrawing into Bohemia.

By the time the campaign began in the spring, Napoleon had created new fighting formations from the ashes of the old, calling up men who had been exempted from military service in the past, those who had been previously discharged but could be classed as generally fit and those who, owing to their youth, would not normally have been eligible for front-line duty for at least another year. With such poorly trained and inexperienced, yet still enthusiastic, troops Napoleon occupied the Saxon capital, Dresden on 7–8 May, and defeated General Wittgenstein, first at Lützen on 2 May and again at Bautzen on 20–21 May. Both sides agreed to an armistice, which stretched from June through July and into mid-August, during which time the French recruited and trained their green army, while the Allies assembled larger and larger forces, now to include Austrians, Swedes and troops from a number of former members of the Confederation of the Rhine.

When the campaign resumed, the Allies placed three multi-national armies in the field: one under Schwarzenberg, one under Blücher and a third under Napoleon's former marshal Bernadotte. The Allies formulated a new strategy, known as the Trachenberg Plan, by which they would seek to avoid direct confrontation with the main French army under Napoleon, instead concentrating their efforts against the Emperor's subordinates, whom they would seek to defeat in turn. The plan succeeded: Bernadotte drubbed Oudinot at Grossbeeren on 23 August, and Blücher won against Macdonald at the Katzbach River three days later. Napoleon, for his part, scored a significant victory against Schwarzenberg at Dresden on 26–27 August, but the Emperor failed to pursue the Austrian commander. Shortly thereafter, General Vandamme's corps became isolated during its pursuit of Schwarzenberg and was annihilated at Kulm on 29–30 August.

The end of French control of Germany was nearing. First, Bernadotte defeated Ney at Dennewitz on 6 September; then Bavaria, the principal member of the Confederation of the Rhine, defected to the Allies. The decisive battle of the campaign was fought at Leipzig from 16–19 October, when all three main Allied armies converged on the city to attack Napoleon's positions in and around it. In the largest battle in history up to that time, both sides suffered extremely heavy losses, and though part of the Grande Armée crossed the River Elster and escaped before the bridge was blown, the Allies nevertheless achieved a victory of immense proportions that forced the French out of Germany and back across the Rhine. A Bavarian force under General Wrede tried to stop Napoleon's retreat at Hanau on 30–31 October, but the French managed to push through to reach home soil a week later. Napoleon, his allies having either deserted his cause or found themselves under Allied occupation, now prepared to oppose the invasion of France by numerically superior armies converging on several fronts.

THE CAMPAIGN IN FRANCE (1814)

Convinced that he could still recover his vast territorial losses, Napoleon chose to fight on against all the odds, rejecting offers from the Allies that would have left France with its 'natural' frontiers: the Rhine, the Alps and the Pyrenees. French forces were under pressure on several fronts. Wellington's Anglo-Portuguese and Spanish forces stood poised along the Pyrenees; the Austrians were already operating in northern Italy; and several armies were making seemingly inexorable progress from the east: Schwarzenberg approaching from Switzerland, Blücher through eastern France and Bernadotte from the north through the Netherlands. To oppose these impressive forces, Napoleon possessed little more than a small army consisting of hastily raised units, National Guardsmen and anyone who had somehow avoided the call-ups of the past. Somehow, at least in the initial stages of the campaign, the Emperor managed to summon up the kind of energy and tactical brilliance for which he had become renowned during the Italian campaigns of 1796–7.

In swift succession he drubbed Blücher at Brienne on 29 January, at La Rothière on 30 January, at Champaubert on 10 February, at Montmirail on 11 February, at Château-Thierry on 12 February and at Vauchamps on 14 February. Napoleon then turned to confront Schwarzenberg at

Montereau on 18 February, before again fighting Blücher, at Craonne, near Paris, on 7 March. Yet, however many enemies he could repel in turn, Napoleon could not be everywhere at once, and his corps commanders, despite the continued enthusiasm for battle displayed by the troops themselves, could not achieve the same results in the field as the Emperor. The French could not stand up to the numbers facing them at Laon on 9–10 March, and though there were still successes in March such as at Rheims on the 13th, there were also setbacks such as at Arcis-sur-Aube on 20–21 March. Schwarzenberg then defeated two of Napoleon's subordinates at La-Fère-Champenoise on 25 March, before linking up with Blücher on the 28th.

The Allies were now very close to Paris, where Joseph Bonaparte had failed to make adequate provision for the capital's defence. After token resistance at Clichy and Montmartre on 30 March, Marmont refused to fight on, and the Allies entered the capital the following day. At a conference with his marshals, Napoleon found himself surrounded by men finally prepared to defy him; the troops, they declared, would listen to their generals, not the Emperor. With no alternative, Napoleon abdicated unconditionally on 11 April and, by the terms of the Treaty of Paris, took up residence on Elba, off the Italian coast, while the Bourbon line in France was restored under King Louis XVIII.

THE WATERLOO CAMPAIGN (1815)

Napoleon was not content to remain on Elba and manage the affairs of his tiny island kingdom. Landing in France in March 1815 with a small band of followers, he marched on Paris, gathering loyal veterans and adherents from the army as he went, including Ney, whom the king had specifically sent to apprehend the pretender to the throne. Allied leaders were at the time assembled at Vienna, there to redraw the map of Europe, which had been so radically revised by more than two decades of war. The Seventh Coalition was soon on the march, with effectively the whole of Europe in arms and marching to defeat Napoleon before he could raise sufficient troops to hold off the overwhelming numbers that the Allies had now set in motion toward the French frontiers. With the speed characteristic of his earlier days in uniform, Napoleon quickly moved north to confront the only Allied forces within reach: an Anglo-Dutch army under Wellington and a Prussian one under Blücher, both in Belgium. Napoleon could only hope to survive against the massive onslaught that would soon reach France by defeating the Allied armies separately; to this end he sought to keep Wellington and Blücher – who together outnumbered him by 2:1 – apart.

On 16 June, after a rapid march that caught Wellington, then at Brussels, entirely off guard, Napoleon detached Ney to seize the crossroads at Quatre Bras, then occupied by part of Wellington's army, while with the main body of the Armée du Nord he moved to strike Blücher at Ligny. Ney failed in his objective, and though on the same day Napoleon delivered a sharp blow against the Prussians, the crucial result was that the two Allied armies lay apart. Having detached Marshal Grouchy to follow the Prussians and prevent them from linking up with Wellington, the Emperor launched a frontal assault on Wellington's strong position around Mont St Jean, near Waterloo.

The hard-pressed Anglo-Allied troops held on throughout the day, gradually reinforced by elements of Blücher's army that managed to leave Wavre while Grouchy, busily engaged there with a Prussian holding force, refused to march to the sound of the guns at Waterloo. The French made strenuous attempts to dislodge Wellington's troops, who in turn showed exceptional determination to hold their ground, and as the Prussians gradually made their presence felt on the French right flank, the battle began to turn in the Allies' favour. In a final gamble to break Wellington's centre and clinch victory, Napoleon sent forward the Imperial Guard, but when his veterans recoiled from the intense, point-blank musket and artillery fire they received on the slope, the rest of the army dissolved into a full-scale rout.

With no possibility of retaining power, Napoleon abdicated in Paris a few days later. By the second Treaty of Paris, the Bourbons were restored to the throne, France was reduced to her pre-1792 borders, forced to support an army of occupation and pay a sizable indemnity. As for Napoleon, his hopes of obtaining permission to reside in Britain were dashed; on surrendering himself, he was taken as a captive to spend the remainder of his life on the remote South Atlantic island of St Helena, where he died on 5 May 1821.

Chapter One

The French Army

Gregory Fremont-Barnes

Apart from the German Army of the Second World War and the Union and Confederate forces of the American Civil War, one may assert with confidence that more ink has been spilt to describe the French Army of the Napoleonic Wars – and, specifically, its principal component, the Grande Armée – than any other fighting formation in history. Works by Elting, Forrest, Haythornthwaite and Rogers, to name but a few, have shed considerable light in general terms, while dozens of other authors have explored virtually every conceivable aspect of the subject, from weapons and commanders to tactics and uniforms; from unit histories and command structure to battlefield studies. Nevertheless, the organisation of the principal arms of the French Army – infantry, cavalry and artillery – has remained less well documented, the detail often spread across numerous campaign histories rather than analysed as a discreet subject in its own right. This chapter therefore seeks to examine this neglected aspect of French forces in the decade between Austerlitz and Waterloo – at regimental, brigade, division and corps level, throughout the Napoleonic Wars.

Having said this, as this treatment must compete here for precious space beside studies of the other principal fighting forces of the era, it must necessarily restrict its parameters accordingly, and thus confines itself to the regular units of the French Army, as well as of the Imperial Guard, excluding thereby the various provisional, National Guard and foreign units which at different stages of the wars composed part of the Emperor's forces.

INFANTRY

Infantry was organised into regiments, which for both the line (*Régiments d'Infanterie de Ligne*) and light regiments (*Régiments d'Infanterie Légère*) were identified by number and type, i.e. 1ère de Ligne, 4eme Légère. Infantry of the line was composed of centre companies, known as *fusiliers*, light companies, known as *voltigeurs*, and elite companies composed of *grenadiers*. *Légère* battalions (usually styled simply *léger*) were structured similarly, although the centre companies were known as *chasseurs* and the elite companies termed *carabiniers*. At the start of the Austerlitz campaign the regular infantry were organised into 89 regiments of the line and 26 light. From 1805 until the end of the 1807 campaign, infantry of the line consisted of 1 *voltigeur*, 1 *grenadier* and 7 *fusilier* companies. Light battalions consisted of 1 *voltigeur*, 1 *carabinier* and 7 companies of *chasseurs*. On paper a company held a strength of 123 men, but in reality this figure was usually not met, even at the opening of a campaign. With an average field strength of 80 men per company, typical battalion strength therefore stood at 720 men. Line regiments were numbered from 1 to 122, though the following were unused in the period to 1807: 31, 38, 41, 49, 68, 71, 73, 74, 77, 78, 80, 83, 87, 89, 90, 91, 97, 98, 99, 104, 107, 109 and 110. *Légère* regiments were styled 1 to 31, with several unused numbers: 11, 19, 20, 29 and 30.

During the course of the campaigns of 1805 and 1806, most of the Grande Armée served in Moravia and Saxony, respectively, with casualties replaced by the creation of new formations, which the Emperor made possible by a number of expedients, including increases in infantry regiments in the form of a third battalion and an increase in the strength of infantry companies to 140 men each. In fact, while third battalions were added to infantry regiments – a strength reached by the end of 1806 – the other measures did not come to pass. Many regiments during the campaign against Prussia in fact contained 4 battalions, but at this time most regiments contained 2 battalions, each of 8 companies, with typical battalion strength at 640 officers and other ranks. While operating in Prussia and Poland at the end of the year, the Grande Armée consisted of forty-seven regiments of line infantry and fourteen of *légère*. By this time 18 infantry regiments had 4 battalions instead of the standard 3. Moreover, by detaching a company from each of the third battalions of regiments operating in Germany, eight provisional battalions were formed. Once they reached Poland they were disbanded, their men distributed among other battalions to make up losses. For service in the rear on garrison duty and for security functions, Napoleon ordered the formation of another twenty provisional infantry regiments.

Increased strength was achieved by deploying units from allied armies, including those of the Kingdom of Italy, the Duchy of Warsaw, the Kingdom of Holland and the Confederation of the Rhine. Replacements for losses came in the form not simply of recruits, but by shifting completely French formations from Italy, which apart from the British landing in Calabria in the summer of 1806 remained quiet of conventional fighting. Garrisons in Italy duly furnished two divisions of infantry, totalling eight regiments, while troops garrisoning Naples were moved north to replace them. Further divisions were formed by denuding port garrisons across France and across the Empire, with replacements acquired from reserve forces and conscripts.

During the period between the end of the Friedland campaign and the war against Austria (i.e. the summer of 1807 to the spring of 1809), Napoleon sought to re-organise and enlarge his armies, a process that began after the conclusion of peace with Russia and Prussia at Tilsit in July 1807. Line infantry regiments were recast to contain four field battalions and a depot. Each battalion was reduced from nine companies to six, with the strength of each company unaltered. Thus, a field battalion consisted of 4 *fusilier* companies, 1 of *grenadiers* and 1 of *voltigeurs*. The depot battalion contained four *fusilier* companies. Napoleon's decree of 18 February 1808 laid down the basis for this new system of infantry organisation, the first seven articles stipulating:

1. Our regiments of infantry of the line and light infantry will in future be composed of a staff and five battalions; the first four will be designated war battalions and the fifth the depot battalion.

2. Each war battalion, commanded by a *chef de bataillon* having under his orders an adjutant and two regimental sergeant-majors, will be composed of six companies, of which one will be grenadiers, one light infantry, and four *fusiliers*, and all of equal strength.

3. Each depot battalion will consist of four companies. The Major will always be attached to this battalion. A Captain, designated by the Minister [of War] from three candidates selected by the Colonel, will command the depot battalion under the orders of the Major. He will at the same time command one of the companies. There will be in the depot an adjutant and two regimental sergeant-majors.

4. The strength of the staff and that of each company of grenadiers, of *carabiniers* [in a *légère* regiment], of light infantry, or of *fusiliers* is to be as follows:

Staff	
Colonel	1
Major	1
Chefs de Bataillon	4
Adjutants	5
Quartermaster/Paymaster	1
Paying Officer	1
Eagle Bearer	1
Surgeon Major	1
Assistant Surgeons	4
Assistant Adjutants	5
Regimental Sergeant-Majors	10
2nd and 3rd Eagle Bearers	2
Drum-Major	1
Corporal Drummer	1

Company	
Captain	1
Lieutenant	1
2nd Lieutenant	1
Sergeant-Major	1
Sergeants	4
Quartermaster Corporal	1
Corporals	8
Grenadiers, Light Infantry-men or Fusiliers	121
Drummers	2
	140

Bandsmen (including 1 Bandmaster)	8
Master Craftsmen	4
	—
	50

Thus, the strength of each regiment will be 3,970 all ranks, of which 108 will be officers and 3,862 NCOs and men.

5. There will be in each war battalion four sappers who will be chosen from the grenadier company of which they will continue to form part, and there will be a corporal who will command all the sappers of the regiment.

6. In battle the grenadier company will be on the right of the battalion and that of the light infantry on the left.

7. When the six companies are present with the battalion it will always march and act by divisions. When the grenadiers and light infantry are absent from the battalion it will always manoeuvre and march by platoon. Two companies will form a division; each company will form a platoon; each half company a section.[1]

This process of re-organisation proceeded slowly and did not reach its conclusion until 1809, in the months just preceding the campaign against Austria. Regiments situated in distant garrisons were naturally the last to be affected by these reforms. Even after a fourth battalion was created, it was not uncommon for a regiment to be divided such that some of its battalions served in one theatre while others operated elsewhere. In cases of pressing need, the depots sometimes were required to form new battalions. As well as adding a fourth battalion to infantry regiments, the army increased in size between Tilsit and the commencement of the Austrian campaign as a result of the growth of the Empire, drawing in other nationalities and converting reserve or provisional units into those of the line. Thus, at the start of the campaign, while the army was simultaneously engaged in Spain and Germany, the regular infantry consisted of 100 regiments of the line and 26 *légère*. Most infantry regiments by this time consisted of the regulation 4 battalions plus a 4-company depot, giving it a full complement on paper of 108 officers and 3,862 men, though 3 line regiments (the 26th, 66th and 82nd) boasted 6 field battalions as well as a depot. Light infantry regiments had in almost all cases 4 battalions, though the 32nd had only 3 plus a depot. Light battalions remained organised on the basis of 9 companies. With the increase in *Régiments de Ligne,* the numeric sequence of these formations was simply extended rather than assigning troops to vacant numbers. Growing numbers also dictated that new regiments include – or be wholly composed of – foreign troops, as indeed proved the case with the first one created (the 113th Line), raised in northern Italy.

In 1810, after the conclusion of the campaign against Austria, the army consisted of 105 line infantry regiments and 23 *légère*, though by the end of 1811 this had been increased to 114 of the line and 25 *légère*, for a total of 139 – made possible by the annexation of Holland and areas of northern Germany, and by raising new units in the territories of French allies. Line infantry regiments were numbered up to 129, with their light counterparts to 33. With the incorporation of the Dutch Army into the French the 123rd to 126th line regiments were created, as well as the 33rd Light Infantry. All these new units contained four battalions, in conformity with other entirely French regiments. The 112th Line was raised in Belgium, while Piedmont produced the 31st Légère and the 111th Line. Finally, parts of northern Germany annexed to the Empire supplied the 127th, 128th and the 129th Regiments of the line. In 1811, with war looming against Russia, Napoleon ordered the creation of fifth battalions for line and *légère* regiments, as well as the attachment of two to four 3lb guns to each regiment, though these changes could not be completed before the invasion began in June 1812, such that many regiments crossed the Niemen still composed of two to four battalions with no attached regimental artillery.

For operations in Russia some regiments of line and light infantry had reached the specified total of 5 battalions, such as those in Davout's superb I Corps, consisting of 5 infantry divisions, each of 3 or 4 brigades. 1st Division had 15 battalions, 2nd Division 17, 3rd Division 18 battalions, 4th Division 14 battalions and 5th Division 20 battalions. II Corps contained 3 infantry divisions: 6th Division had 4 brigades with a total of 12 battalions; 8th Division had 2 brigades with 16 battalions; thus, in this case, some regiments were composed of only 3 or 4 battalions, not the officially established 5. The 9th Division contained 3 brigades of Swiss and Croatian infantry, with 17 battalions all told. III Corps, under Ney, contained 3 infantry divisions. The 10th contained 3 brigades, totalling 16 battalions; the 11th consisted of 3 brigades with a total of 18 battalions, some of these Portuguese and Illyrian; and the 25th Division contained 3 brigades of Württemburg infantry – a mixture of line, *jägers* (rifles) and ordinary light infantry, for a total of 18 battalions.

The infantry of IV Corps, under Prince Eugène, Viceroy of Italy, consisted of the Italian Guard of 6 battalions, plus 3 divisions of mixed French, Italian and Dalmatian infantry. The 13th Division contained 3 brigades of French and Croatian line and light infantry, totalling 16 battalions. The 14th comprised 3 brigades of French and Spanish infantry, for a total of 12 battalions; and the 15th Division contained 3 brigades of Italian and Dalmatian line and light infantry, 13 battalions in all. The infantry in V Corps, under Poniatowski, was entirely Polish, drawn from the Duchy of Warsaw and arrayed in 3 divisions. The 16th and 17th Divisions contained

2 brigades each of 4 regiments (12 battalions), but while the 18th Division also contained 2 brigades, these had only 3 regiments instead of 4, for a total of 6 battalions per brigade. The infantry of IV Corps under Gouvion St Cyr, was entirely Bavarian, organised into 2 divisions, with the 19th containing 2 brigades, totalling 8 regiments of line and light infantry – 13 battalions altogether. The 20th Division, of 3 brigades, contained 9 line and light regiments, with 15 battalions in total.

General Reynier's VII Corps, composed entirely of Saxons, contained 2 divisions of infantry, each of 2 brigades. Those of the 21st Division had 11 battalions of line and light infantry, as well as *grenadiers*. The 22nd Division was composed of 7 battalions of mostly *grenadiers*, but also light infantry. The infantry of Prince Jérôme's VIII Corps, all Westphalian, was divided between 2 divisions. The 23rd contained 2 brigades with 6 regiments of line and light infantry, totalling 13 battalions, while the 24th Division had but 1 brigade, of 3 battalions of Guard infantry, 1 battalion of light infantry and 2 battalions of the line. The infantry of Victor's IX Corps consisted of 3 divisions. The 12th Division had 3 brigades containing 6 regiments of French line and light infantry, for a total of 7 battalions, while the 26th Division had 3 brigades containing 11 regiments of Berg, Baden, Hesse-Darmstadt and Westphalian infantry, totalling 22 battalions. The 28th Division comprised 2 brigades of Polish and Saxon infantry, organised into 5 regiments of 13 battalions all told.

The infantry component of Marshal Macdonald's X Corps consisted of 2 divisions: the 7th, of 3 brigades, consisted of Polish, Bavarian and Westphalian line – 5 regiments of 16 battalions in total. The 27th Division, of 3 brigades, was formed entirely of Prussians: 17 battalions belonging to various combined regiments, plus an unattached *jäger* battalion. XI Corps, under Augereau, contained 5 divisions of infantry. The 30th had 3 brigades of 3 provisional regiments, totalling 22 battalions. The 31st, of 2 brigades, contained 4 provisional regiments, with 14 battalions all told. The 32nd Division, of 2 brigades, contained various French, German and Italian regiments, for a total of 18 battalions. The 33rd, of 3 brigades, contained 4 regiments of Neapolitan marines, *vélites* and line infantry, totalling 10 battalions. The 34th Division, of 5 brigades of French infantry and various nationalities drawn from the Confederation of the Rhine, totalled 11 regiments, in all containing 28 battalions.

Despite his massive losses in Russia, by the opening of the spring campaign in April 1813 the Emperor had assembled in Germany twelve corps of infantry (dubbed 'Marie-Louises' or teenaged conscripts), with an increase of two later in the year, mostly by incorporating French allied units. Most corps comprised three infantry divisions and a brigade of light cavalry. The rest of the corps served on detached duty somewhere in Germany other than the main theatre of operations, in Italy, or in garrisons elsewhere. French and Italian forces in Italy under Eugène totalled 3 corps,

2 French and 1 Italian, of which the former contained 2 divisions of 11 or 12 battalions each. The Italian corps infantry comprised 2 divisions, as well as 3 battalions of the Italian Guard in reserve. At the smaller structural level, Napoleon increased the number of line and light infantry regiments by another 22 by incorporating National Guard (*Garde Nationale*) cohorts and drafting in 6 regiments of sailors. All regiments now contained 4 battalions, each averaging about 500 men strong. After the disastrous Battle of Leipzig in October, Napoleon's army retreated to the Rhine. With the defection of practically all his allies, his forces then consisted almost exclusively of French troops, whose numbers and quality were bolstered by drawing heavily upon veteran forces from Spain and the call-up of ever younger recruits for the defence of home soil. In terms exclusively of regular infantry, at the end of the year the army contained six corps, all understrength and exhausted.

For the campaign of 1814 the order of battle changed regularly, with the composition of line units varying greatly as new conscripts were added to existing units and ad hoc formations composed of National Guards and other elements bolstered numbers. In the main theatre of operations east of Paris (as opposed to those operating against Wellington in the south), the Emperor could still deploy five infantry corps in February, when the fighting began, plus several reserve divisions of the National Guard. Most regiments contained only one or two battalions, usually far below regulation strength and containing a high proportion of green troops. Quite apart from Napoleon's immediate forces in eastern France, Soult maintained a force of six infantry divisions around Bayonne, in the south of the country. Eugène continued to maintain a force in Italy in 1814, while Augereau led five infantry divisions at Lyons. General Maison had a small corps in Holland and Suchet still commanded more than 30,000 infantry in Catalonia. When the Allies reached Paris and Napoleon abdicated, the French Army still contained, at least in theory, 130 regiments of the line and 32 of *légère*.

For the Waterloo campaign in 1815 the army had at its disposal – though it could not deploy all of these for operations in Belgium owing to other commitments, particular frontier defence – ninety regiments of line infantry and fifteen of light. Most regiments contained two battalions, though some had three. Line regiments were numbered up to 111, but with some of these lying vacant. *Légère* regiments were numbered 1 to 15. No foreign units served in the campaign apart from the 2nd Swiss. Napoleon deployed five infantry corps in Belgium. I and II Corps, under d'Erlon and Reille, respectively, each contained 4 infantry divisions, each of 2 brigades, each of 2 line or light infantry regiments or a combination of both. III, IV and VI Corps contained only 3 infantry divisions each, but in other respects resembled the organisation of I and II Corps, i.e. 2 brigades per division, each of 2 regiments. Altogether, about 77,400 infantry (including that of the Imperial Guard) fought on 18 June: 53,400 at Waterloo and 24,000 at Wavre.

CAVALRY

Heavy cavalry consisted of *cuirassiers* and *carabiniers,* of which both were almost always consolidated to form a cavalry reserve. The former were mounted on large, heavy set horses with the purpose of performing the charge in battle, taking advantage of their size for the sake of shock action. Officers and troops wore the metal *cuirass,* which protected their chest and back, as well as a helmet. *Carabiniers,* also mounted on heavy horses, were the elite form of *cuirassiers,* starting their existence with only a breastplate, but after 1809 acquiring a double *cuirass.*

Light cavalry consisted of hussars, *chasseurs à cheval, chevau-légers* (later *chevau-léger-lanciers*) and dragoons, the last of which actually qualified as medium cavalry. Hussars were elite light cavalry modelled on Hungarian units which had shown particular skill in raiding and skirmishing during the campaigns against Frederick the Great in the mid-eighteenth century. The *chasseurs,* the mounted equivalent of the light infantry, constituted the standard form of lightly mounted troops and were the most numerous form of cavalry. The *chevau-légers* performed the same function as *chasseurs,* but in 1810 were converted into lancers. Four years later a similar type of unit, the Eclaireurs (Scouts) and Gardes d'honneur, had a brief existence. Dragoons could perform a dual function, fighting mounted or on foot; indeed, they began their existence, long before the Napoleonic Wars, as mounted infantry who employed horses for speed of movement. By the Austerlitz campaign, however, nearly all dragoons served in a mounted role and seldom fought on foot.

Cavalry regiments were led by a colonel, with a second-in-command holding the rank of major, who carried out administrative functions. From 1801 each cavalry regiment had an elite company which always stood on the right end of the line as the cavalry's counterpart of the *grenadier* company in the infantry. The elite company served as the senior company of the two in the 1st Squadron. From September 1803 the number of dragoon regiments was increased to 30, and 2 years later 24 of these consisted of a mixed pattern of 3 mounted squadrons and 1 dismounted, with each squadron composed of 2 companies. Out of these 24 regiments Napoleon could create, if necessary, a corps consisting entirely of dragoons, with 3 mounted divisions and 1 dismounted. The former contained 2 brigades of 3 regiments each, while the dismounted squadrons were detached from regiments to create the dismounted division. The dismounted squadrons, removed from the regiments amalgamated into the mounted brigade, were consolidated into a battalion composed of 6 companies. This created a mounted division of 2 battalions, which together formed a regiment. Thus, a dismounted division comprised 3 regiments, to which were assigned ten pieces of artillery in support. From 1808 eight sappers were attached to each dismounted regiment.

Cavalry divisions typically consisted of 2 or 3 brigades, each of 2 regiments, plus a complement of horse artillery. The dismounted dragoon division in 1805 consisted of 2 brigades, each of 4 battalions, in turn of 8 companies each. Each of the 6 army corps contained 1 division of light cavalry; that is, hussars and *chasseurs à cheval*, in each of the 6 corps operating on the Danube, with the cavalry reserve, under Marshal Murat, composed of 2 *cuirassier* divisions, 4 dragoon divisions and 1 dismounted dragoon division. Horses drawn from the latter formation were employed to increase numbers in other cavalry units, bringing them up to full strength. Later in the campaign the dismounted dragoons received captured horses and resumed their mounted function.

The following year, in the campaign against Prussia, the organisation remained more or less the same: Napoleon deployed 6 army corps, each with a division of cavalry attached, and the cavalry reserve, with Murat again in command, comprising 2 heavy divisions – that is, *cuirassiers* and *carabiniers* – 4 divisions of dragoons and 2 brigades of light cavalry. In 1805 the cavalry of the line consisted of 2 regiments of *carabiniers*, 12 regiments of *cuirassiers*, 30 regiments of dragoons, 10 regiments of hussars and 24 regiments of *chasseurs à cheval*. On campaign only a proportion of these took the field in the main theatre of operations; thus, at end of 1806 the army's complement of cavalry in Prussia and Poland amounted to 2 regiments of *carabiniers*, 12 of *cuirassiers*, 10 of dragoons, 18 of *chasseurs* and 9 of hussars. For service in the rear on garrison duty and for security functions, a further eleven regiments were established from a mixture of conscripts and seasoned troops drawn from regiments still in Germany. At the same time, in order to bolster numbers required for the coming campaign of 1807 in Poland and East Prussia, completely French formations were shifted from Italy.

In August 1806 each *cuirassier* regiment was increased by a fourth squadron, giving a regiment the following composition of officers and men: regimental headquarters contained 1 colonel, 1 major, 2 *chefs d'escadrons* (adjutant-majors), 1 paymaster-quartermaster, 1 surgeon-major, 1 *aide major*, 2 *sous-aides majors*, 2 *adjutants-sous-officiers*, 1 corporal-trumpeter, 1 veterinary surgeon and 6 *maîtres* (tailor, saddler, cobbler, breeches-maker, armourer and spur-maker). Each company consisted of 1 captain, 1 lieutenant, 1 *sous-lieutenant* (second lieutenant), 1 *maréchal-des-logis-chef*, 4 *maréchaux-des-logis*, 1 *fourrier*, 8 corporals, 82 troopers and 1 trumpeter. This amounted to a total strength of 820 men and 831 horses. Light cavalry regiments generally boasted a slightly higher establishment. Thus, a hussar regiment of 1807 consisted of 4 squadrons of 2 companies each, with a regimental staff of 7 officers and 12 men and each company comprising 4 officers, 124 men and 129 horses, giving a total regimental strength of 43 officers, 1,000 men and 1,055 horses. In the same year the new system of organisation for dragoons stipulated that each regiment should consist of 4 squadrons of 2 companies each, with each company comprising 4 officers and 123 troopers. Some regiments even reached a strength of 5 squadrons, in which case they boasted approximately 1,200 effectives.

In 1809, during the campaign against Austria, the army's cavalry force consisted of 2 regiments of *carabiniers*, 12 regiments of *cuirassiers*, 30 regiments of *dragoons*, 26 regiments of *chasseurs à cheval* and 10 regiments of hussars. Most of the provisional cavalry formed for service in Spain had by this time been absorbed into the army, though six dragoon and one provisional *chasseur* regiments saw service in the campaign against Austria. In the following year, with the addition of units incorporated from the Dutch Army, French cavalry were increased to include the newly formed 11th Hussars and 14th Cuirassiers. Recruitment in Belgium (technically part of France) produced the 27th Chasseurs à Cheval, while from Piedmont came recruits creating the 21st Dragoons and the 26th Chasseurs.

Apart from increasing the number of cavalry regiments in expectation of war with Russia, Napoleon ordered various changes, particularly within the light cavalry arm. Thus, appreciating the efficacy of lancers, Napoleon converted six regiments of dragoons (1st, 3rd, 8th, 9th, 10th and 29th) into the 1st to 6th Chevau-léger-lanciers in June 1811, while two Polish regiments were numbered the 7th and 8th regiments. A ninth regiment, bearing that number, was later created by converting the 30th Chasseurs à Cheval. All such regiments contained 4 squadrons. With these changes implemented, the cavalry now consisted of 2 regiments of *carabiniers*, 14 of *cuirassiers*, 24 of dragoons, 11 of hussars, 25 of *chasseurs* and 9 of lancers.

During the Russian campaign each infantry corps contained a contingent of cavalry, with remaining mounted units forming the Cavalry Reserve. I Corps, under Davout, had 2 brigades of light cavalry, totalling 16 squadrons of *chasseurs* and lancers. II Corps, under Oudinot, contained 2 cavalry brigades, also of *chasseurs* and lancers, with 20 squadrons in all. Ney's III Corps consisted of 4 brigades of light cavalry: the first brigade (these were named, not numbered) contained 7 squadrons of French hussars and lancers; the second had 8 squadrons of Württemburg mounted *jägers* and *chevau-légers*; the third consisted of 8 squadrons of *chasseurs*, and the fourth brigade contained 4 squadrons of Württemburg *chevau-légers*, with 4 squadrons of mounted *jägers* transferred to II Cavalry Corps in April. The cavalry contingent in Eugène's IV Corps was organised into 2 brigades and totalled 18 squadrons of French and Italian *chasseurs*. Poniatowski's IV Corps contained 3 brigades of Polish *chasseurs*, lancers and hussars, totalling 5 regiments of 20 squadrons in all. Gouvion St Cyr's VI Corps contained 2 brigades of Bavarian *chevau-légers*, organised into 4 regiments for a total of 16 squadrons. The Saxon cavalry of Reynier's VII Corps consisted of 1 brigade containing 3 regiments of *chasseurs* and hussars, totalling 16 squadrons. The Westphalian cavalry of Prince Jérôme's (later General Junot's) VIII Corps consisted of Westphalian hussars, Guard *chevau-légers* and Garde du Corps, totalling 12 squadrons. The cavalry of Victor's IX Corps was organised into 2 brigades of Berg, Hesse-Darmstadt, Saxon and Baden *chevau-légers*, hussars and lancers, totalling 14 squadrons. The Prussian cavalry of Macdonald's X Corps comprised 2 brigades of hussars and dragoons, totalling 16 squadrons. Integrated within the infantry divisions of Augereau's XI Corps were Würzburg *chevau-légers* and Italian Gardes d'honneur and *vélites*, totalling 5 squadrons, but the principal mounted contingent of this corps consisted of 4 squadrons of dragoons drawn from 8 different regiments.

The Grande Armée in Russia contained 4 cavalry corps: Nansouty's I Cavalry Corps was composed of 1 light and 2 heavy divisions. The 1st Light Cavalry Division contained 3 brigades of French, Polish and Prussian hussars, lancers and *chasseurs*, for a total of 9 regiments (many understrength) – 28 squadrons in all. The 1st Heavy Cavalry Division contained 3 brigades of *cuirassiers* and lancers, with 4 regiments of 15 squadrons altogether. The 5th Heavy Cavalry Division, of 3 brigades, contained 4 regiments of 15 squadrons in total. Montbrun's II Cavalry Corps, like Nansouty's command, was also composed of 1 light cavalry division and 2 heavy. The 2nd Light Cavalry Division consisted of 3 brigades of French, Polish and Prussian *chasseurs*, hussars and lancers, organised into 6 regiments totalling 23 squadrons. The 2nd Heavy Cavalry Division, of 3 brigades, contained 3 regiments of *cuirassiers* and lancers, with 15 squadrons altogether. The 4th Heavy Cavalry Division consisted of 3 brigades of *carabiniers*, *cuirassiers* and lancers, organised into 4 regiments for a total of 15 squadrons. III Cavalry Corps, under Grouchy, contained 1 light and 2 heavy brigades, the 3rd Light Cavalry Division comprising 3 brigades of 6 regiments of French hussars and *chasseurs*, 2 regiments of Bavarian *chevau-légers* and 1 regiment of Saxon light cavalry, totalling 28 squadrons. The 3rd Heavy Cavalry Division, later attached to II Corps, contained 3 brigades of mostly *cuirassiers*, but also lancers, with 12 squadrons of the former and 3 of the latter. The 6th Heavy Cavalry Division, of 3 brigades, also contained *cuirassiers* and lancers, organised into 3 regiments of the former and 1 of the latter, totalling 15 squadrons. IV Cavalry Corps, under Latour-Maubourg, consisted of 2 divisions: the 4th (Polish) contained 2 brigades – 6 regiments of lancers for a total of 18 squadrons – while the 7th Heavy Cavalry Division, organised into 2 brigades, consisted of Saxon, Polish and Westphalian regiments, totalling 18 squadrons.

The cavalry (and the horses involved in transport and other services) suffered such horrendous losses in 1812 that neither their former quality nor numbers could be restored during the remaining years of the conflict, notwithstanding the re-building of regiments on the basis of units withdrawn from Spain. Thus, for the spring campaign of 1813 the Emperor could deploy only four – later increased to five – weak cavalry corps, an expedient made possible by incorporating into most of the previously all-French corps men from foreign contingents. In addition to these purely mounted formations, each infantry corps (including the two French operating in Italy under Eugène) contained a light cavalry division of varying size, but even collectively these never proved adequate to the task of combat, much less reconnaissance or that all-important post-action function: pursuit. During 1813 only three new mounted units, known as Eclaireurs and armed with lances, were formed, each regiment containing 4 squadrons of 200 men. Although attached to the Guard, this light cavalry was not technically part of it. After its decisive defeat at Leipzig and withdrawal to the Rhine, the army contained only four weak cavalry corps and one division of provisional cavalry.

There were six cavalry corps – much of them composed of regiments recently recalled from Spain – in the field when the 1814 campaign began in February, plus several provisional regiments attached to various divisions. At the same time, in the south of the country, Soult possessed a single division of cavalry. In Italy, Eugène maintained a small mounted contingent, as did Suchet in Catalonia. By the time of Napoleon's abdication in April, the army in theory still possessed 91 regiments of line cavalry, but nothing like this number actually remained operational, and of those in the field none reached official strength – virtually all fell well short of it – which for an hussar regiment comprised a staff of 8 officers and 12 men, and each company consisting of 4 officers and 74 men, giving a regimental total of 40 officers and 604 men.

At the start of the 1815 campaign the army consisted of the following regiments ready to take the field: 2 of *carabiniers*, 12 of *cuirassiers*, 6 of lancers, 20 of dragoons, 10 of hussars and 12 of *chasseurs*. Most of these units contained 3 squadrons, though some of the heavy regiments comprised 4. Of the 5 infantry corps deployed at Waterloo 4 contained a division of light cavalry: in I Corps, the 1st Cavalry Division contained 2 brigades, the first with 1 regiment of hussars and another of *chasseurs*, the second with 2 regiments of lancers. The cavalry division of II Corps, designated the 2nd, also contained 2 brigades, the first of which consisted of 2 regiments of *chasseurs* and the second with 2 of lancers. Vandamme's III Corps contained the 3rd Cavalry Division, again of 2 brigades, the first of 2 regiments of *chasseurs*, but the second having only 1 regiment, also of *chasseurs*. IV Corps, with its 7th Cavalry Division, comprised 2 brigades, with 1 regiment each of hussars and *chasseurs* in the first brigade and

3 regiments of dragoons (a fourth being detached to 9th Cavalry division just before Waterloo) in the second brigade. VI Corps, under Lobau, had no attached cavalry. As with the old Grande Armée, the Armée du Nord contained several independent cavalry corps. I Corps, under Pajol, comprised two divisions: the 4th contained 2 brigades, the first of 2 regiments of hussars and the second with only 1 of the same. The 5th Cavalry Division, also of 2 brigades, contained 2 regiments of lancers in the first, and 1 of *chasseurs* in the second. II Cavalry Corps, under Exelmans, comprised 2 divisions of the same composition: each of 2 brigades; these, in turn, of 2 regiments of dragoons. III Cavalry Corps contained the 11th Division, with 2 brigades, each of 2 regiments of dragoons and *cuirassiers*, respectively, while IV Cavalry Corps contained 2 divisions, each of 2 brigades, each in turn composed of 2 regiments of *cuirassiers* – furnishing 8 regiments in total. All told, about 19,000 French cavalry (including that of the Imperial Guard) fought on 18 June: 15,600 at Waterloo and 3,500 at Wavre.

ARTILLERY

During the first three campaigns of the Napoleonic Wars – that is, from Austerlitz to Friedland – artillery of the line consisted of 8 regiments of foot, each regiment sub-divided into 22 companies, and 6 regiments of horse artillery, with each regiment consisting of 6 to 7 companies. On paper, foot companies boasted a strength of 4 officers and 116 gunners, while horse companies comprised 6 to 7 companies. Foot batteries, of 6lb or 8lb pieces and 5.5in howitzers, normally were attached to infantry divisions, whereas their heavier counterparts, composed of 12lb guns, usually formed part of corps artillery or the army's reserve. Horse artillery companies had ninety-six gunners serving six 4lb or 6lb guns. A fluctuating amount of horse artillery was always attached to cavalry divisions. During this period the artillery also included 16 siege batteries, 15 battalions of artillery train, 2 battalions of *pontoniers*, 5 battalions of sappers, 9 companies of miners, 17 companies of artillery workers and 10 regiments of veterans. Train battalions and *pontonier* battalions were composed of six to ten companies, respectively. These companies, in turn, consisted of 1 officer and 140 men at full strength; 1 company of artillerists was required to serve a battery of 6 field pieces and 2 howitzers.

During the next period of the Grande Armée's active campaigning, in 1809, artillery units consisted of the following: 6 regiments of horse artillery, 8 regiments of foot artillery, 13 train battalions, 16 artillery worker companies and 4 artisan companies. Horse artillery regiments contained 6 companies and a depot, apart from 1 that had 7 companies. Foot artillery regiments contained twenty-two companies and a depot. The train battalions consisted of six companies each during times of peace, the figure doubling during wartime. There were also 2 engineer battalions, 2 miner battalions, 5 battalions of sappers, 2 *pontonier* battalions, 8 companies of pioneers and 6 engineer train companies. The engineer and miner battalions each contained 5 companies, while sapper battalions had 9 companies. The *pontonier* battalions contained a total of 16 companies, each of approximately 200 men. The actual number of guns deployed in the field amounted to 152 at Aspern-Essling and 617 at Wagram, respectively, including those of the Imperial Guard.

In the period between Austria's defeat in 1809 and the Russian campaign three years later the artillery was increased by the addition of Dutch units, so creating the 9th Foot Artillery Regiment, the 14th Train Battalion and the 17th and 18th Artillery Worker Companies. Companies of horse artillery were formed into the 1st Horse Artillery Regiment. Prior to the invasion of Russia the Emperor ordered a re-distribution of artillery throughout the army, to the extent that each infantry regiment was to have 2 3lb guns attached; each infantry division was to receive a horse-artillery battery consisting of 4 6lb guns and 2 howitzers, as well as a foot battery of 6 6lb guns and 2 howitzers; and every corps was to receive 2 12lb batteries of foot artillery, each consisting of 6 12lb guns and 2 howitzers. Light cavalry divisions were to receive a 6lb horse battery and each heavy cavalry division was to have two 6lb batteries of horse artillery. Thus, apart from the guns of the Imperial Guard and regimental artillery, the artillery reserve consisted of 60 12lb guns, 214 6lb guns and 106 howitzers, organised into a total of 51 batteries of foot and horse. Nevertheless, these reforms were not complete by the time of the 1812 campaign, so that some infantry regiments marched into Russia without their allotment of artillery, while many divisional artillery batteries had 8lb instead of 12lb pieces.

The structure of line artillery remained the same as before during the campaigns of 1813–14, but with numbers of guns deployed in the field reduced as a consequence of the loss of nearly every piece of ordnance in Russia and, above all, the chronic shortage of horses – a resource considerably more difficult to replace than hardware. Nevertheless, at Lützen (2 May) the Emperor had 210 guns (apart from those of the Imperial Guard), rising to an impressive 476 (again, excluding those of the Guard) at Bautzen only 3 weeks later. When Napoleon abdicated in April 1814, the army, on paper at least, contained 9 regiments of foot artillery, comprising 26 to 32 companies each, and 6 regiments of horse artillery, each of 6 companies. There were also 27 squadrons of artillery train. The Bourbons implemented reforms during their brief period of restoration, but when the Emperor returned in 1815 and formed the Armée du Nord for the campaign in Belgium, about 8,500 artillerists, train personnel and drivers, transporting and serving 342 guns, were available for all the nation's needs, including the defence of the frontier against the slowly approaching Russian and Austrian armies far to the East – quite apart from the Anglo-Allied and Prussian forces already in Belgium. At Waterloo and Wavre, Napoleon deployed 246 and 96 pieces of artillery (including that of the

Imperial Guard), respectively, the distribution at the former as follows: 5 batteries of foot and 1 of horse in I and II Corps, respectively; 4 batteries of foot and 1 of horse in III, IV and VI Corps, respectively; and 2 batteries of horse artillery attached to each of the 3 cavalry corps.

THE IMPERIAL GUARD

Infantry

At the start of the Austerlitz campaign the infantry of the Imperial Guard (Garde Impériale) consisted of three infantry regiments, the Grenadiers à Pied, the Chasseurs à Pied and the Marins (actually seamen, not marines, as popularly believed). Between 1805 and 1807 *grenadier* and *chasseur* regiments contained two field battalions and one of *vélites* (new recruits). Each *grenadier* and *chasseur* field battalion consisted of eight companies, with eighty men per company. The *vélite* battalion contained only 5 companies, each of 172 men. In April 1806 a second regiment of *grenadiers* and of *chasseurs* was added to the establishment of the Guard. In September both *vélite* battalions forming part of the *grenadier* regiments were consolidated into a regiment of Fusiliers-Grenadiers. At the end of 1806 the two *vélite* battalions forming part of the *chasseur* regiments were joined to form the regiment of Fusiliers-Chasseurs. These two new regiments later became known as the Young Guard. Since the *vélite* battalions remained unchanged, the organisation of the *grenadier* and *chasseur* regiments continued to consist of two battalions. The newly formed Fusiliers-Grenadiers and Fusiliers-Chasseurs were composed of 2 battalions each, themselves composed of 4 companies of 120 men.

According to a decree of 16 January 1809 the Imperial Guard was to be composed of six regiments: *grenadiers, fusiliers-grenadiers, tirailleur-grenadiers, chasseurs, fusiliers-chasseurs* and *tirailleurs-chasseurs*. Each regiment was to consist of 2 battalions, each of 4 companies of 200 men. By the time of the campaign against Austria in the same year, the Imperial Guard truly merited its name, for many of its units were foreign. In April the infantry consisted of the following units:

Grenadiers
Fusiliers-Grenadiers
1st and 2nd Tirailleurs-Grenadiers
1st and 2nd Conscrit-Grenadiers
Chasseurs
Fusiliers-Chasseurs
1st and 2nd Tirailleurs-Chasseurs
1st and 2nd Conscrits-Chasseurs
Veteran Company (*c.* 160 men)
Vélites de Turin (1 btn)
Vélites de Florence (1 btn)

The *grenadiers* and *chasseurs* consisted of one regiment of each, with second regiments established in 1811. Battalion organisation remained as before. The regiments of *tirailleurs* had been formed in Spain in late 1808 from selected conscripts. The Conscrits-Grenadiers and Conscrits-Chasseurs were changed to Tirailleurs-Grenadiers and Tirailleurs-Chasseurs, respectively, after the formation of new units of conscripts in Paris in early 1809. All *tirailleur* regiments contained 2 battalions each of 4 companies, with each company numbering approximately 125 men.

Between the end of the campaign against Austria in 1809 and the beginning of the invasion of Russia in June 1812 the Guard underwent various changes, including second regiments added to the *grenadier* and *chasseur* regiments in 1811 by the drafting of men from the line and from the regiments of the Young Guard. The Tirailleurs-Grenadiers and Tirailleurs-Chasseurs were re-designated as the 1st and 2nd regiments of Tirailleurs and Voltigeurs, respectively. In 1811, the Conscrits-Grenadiers and Conscrits-Chasseurs were re-named the 3rd and 4th regiments of Tirailleurs and Voltigeurs, respectively. A fifth and sixth regiment was added to each, as well. Men drawn from forestry work and gamekeepers were assembled to form a regiment of Flanquer-Grenadiers and one of Flanquer-Chasseurs, with both units organised on the same basis as the *tirailleur* and *voltigeur* regiments. At this time the Marins were increased to three battalions. In 1810, as a result of the dissolution of the Dutch Army with the annexation of Holland into the French Empire, the Imperial Guard expanded to include a third regiment of *grenadiers*, fashioned from the Dutch Grenadiers and Honour Guard regiment. A unit known as the Pupilles of the Guard, the sons of veterans and amounting to nine battalions, was added in 1811, serving as a training unit.

The Imperial Guard was divided at this time into three classes: the Old, Middle and Young, in descending order of prestige and commensurate pay. The Old Guard, the most senior of these formations, consisted of the following infantry units: 1st Regiment of Grenadiers; 1st Regiment of Chasseurs; NCOs of the 2nd Regiments of Grenadiers, Chasseurs and Fusiliers; and a company of veterans. Middle Guard infantry consisted of the 2nd Regiment of Grenadiers, the 2nd Chasseurs, the 3rd (Grenadier) regiment and an artillery train. The Young Guard supplied regiments of *voltigeurs* and *tirailleurs, flanquers*, Pupilles and a wagon train.

On the eve of the invasion of Russia the basic structure of Guard infantry remained as before, with the troops distributed in 3 divisions, each of 2 brigades, for a total of 12 battalions in the 1st Division, 10 in the 2nd and 10 in the 3rd. Attached to the Guard were three battalions of Italian and Spanish infantry and engineers, as well as a division of the Vistula Legion (Poles), for a total of twelve battalions. Losses were immense, with the muster rolls of 10 October and 25 December revealing the scale of the disaster that befell the senior regiments of Guard infantry:

Regiment	Strength on 10 October	Strength on 25 December
1st Grenadiers	1,385	407
2nd Grenadiers	1,152	273
3rd Grenadiers	753	41
1st Chasseurs	1,546	463
2nd Chasseurs	1,364	287

In early 1813, after the catastrophe of the Russian campaign, Napoleon re-classified the infantry of the Guard to include the 1st and 2nd Grenadiers, a Veteran company, Fusiliers-Grenadiers, the 1st to 7th Tirailleurs-Grenadiers and an instruction battalion, based at Fontainebleau, consisting of 4 companies of 200 men each. The *chasseurs* formed two regiments, the 1st and 2nd, plus the Fusiliers-Chasseurs, the 1st to 7th Voltigeurs-Flanquers and four battalions of Pupilles. Depot companies were re-organised at this time, with 1 depot company for the 2 grenadier regiments, 1 for the Fusiliers-Grenadiers and 2 for the regiments of Tirailleurs-Grenadiers. A similar procedure was to be followed respecting the *chasseurs*, with each depot company consisting of approximately 300 men.

The Guard infantry was also re-organised: the 3rd regiments of Grenadiers and Chasseurs, respectively both formerly units of the Dutch Royal Guard, were disbanded and the men re-distributed among the 2nd regiments of Grenadiers and Chasseurs, respectively. These were classified as Middle Guard units, but with the officers and NCOs holding Old Guard status. Re-structuring also affected the regiments of Flanquers, Fusiliers-Grenadiers and Fusiliers-Chasseurs, which though they continued to contain 2 battalions, now had only 6 companies of 120 men each. Yet if the senior regiments of the Guard contracted in number, those of the Young Guard expanded considerably, with the *voltigeurs* and *tirailleurs* raised to a strength of thirteen regiments each. The 7th Tirailleurs were created from two battalions of Pupilles, and the 7th Voltgieurs were formed from conscripts and veterans serving in Spain. The 9th Tirailleurs were established from the Pupilles based at Versailles. Cohorts and conscripts of the National Guard supplied the men for the remaining thirteen regiments of *voltigeurs* and *tirailleurs*.

For the 1813 campaign in Saxony, the Imperial Guard was organised into four divisions, of which the infantry component was as follows: the 1st Division, of three brigades, with the first brigade containing the 1st Grenadiers, the 1st Chasseurs and the regiment of *fusiliers-grenadiers*. The second brigade consisted for two and half regiments of *voltigeurs* and one of *tirailleurs*. The third brigade comprised three regiments of *tirailleurs*. The 2nd Division contained three brigades of infantry, of which the first brigade contained the 2nd Chasseurs, the 2nd Grenadiers and the regiment of *flanquer-chasseurs*. The second brigade comprised the *fusilier-chasseur* regiment and a regiment of *voltigeurs*. The third brigade had one regiment each of *voltigeurs*, *tirailleurs* and *flanquer-grenadiers*. The 3rd Division – not worthy of the name – contained 1 brigade of 3 regiments of *voltigeurs*, while the 4th comprised 3 regiments of *tirailleurs*. In the course of the campaign another brigade of three regiments of the Young Guard was added to each of these divisions. At the start of the fighting in April, battalions of the Young Guard stood at nearly full strength, as were the *fusilier* and *flanquer* battalions of the Middle Guard. But notwithstanding the amalgamation of the 3rd Grenadiers and Chasseurs into the ranks of the 1st and 2nd regiments, respectively, these four units still stood at half to two-thirds official strength.

Further changes in organisation took place during the summer armistice, with the Guard then consisting of four divisions of the Young Guard and one of Old Guard. The 1st and 2nd Young Guard divisions comprised 2 *fusilier* regiments and 2 *flanquer* regiments (of the Middle Guard), respectively, in addition to the normal allocation of 5 regiments each of (Young Guard) *voltigeurs* or *tirailleurs*. The 2nd and 3rd Divisions of the Young Guard contained five regiments of *voltigeurs* or *tirailleurs*, but no *fusiliers* or *flanquers*. The division of Old Guard contained the 1st and 2nd regiments of Grenadiers, the 1st and 2nd Chasseurs, both sets of regiments allocated into separate brigades, plus two battalions of Italian Vélites. Further re-organisation took place after the Battle of Dresden, when the infantry was increased in strength by shifting men from the 2nd Chasseurs and Grenadiers to the first regiment of each of the aforementioned units, and by transferring men from the Young Guard to the 2nd Chasseurs, 2nd Grenadiers and the Italian Vélites. By these expedients the battalions of the 1st and 2nd Grenadiers, the 1st and 2nd Chasseurs and the Italian Vélites rose to a strength of 800 men. Expansion within the Middle Guard occurred as a result of adding a battalion of the Saxon Guard and one from the Westphalian Guard. The Old and Middle Guard now had a division each, bolstered by four divisions of the Young Guard. The Old Guard division comprised the two grenadier regiments and the two *chasseur* regiments. The division of the Middle Guard contained the 2 *fusilier* regiments, 2 of *flanquers* and 2 battalions of Italian Vélites, plus 1 each of Westphalian and Saxon Guard. After Dresden the Young Guard contained 22 regiments organised into 4 divisions, each containing from 4 to 6 regiments. In concrete terms this represented, at Leipzig in October, approximately 30,000 infantry. In November, with the arrival at the front of the 12th Voltigeur and 12th Tirailleur regiments, the Young Guard was re-organised into six divisions, each of four regiments.

When the army crossed the Rhine at the end of 1813 it contained, apart obviously from line infantry and cavalry, six divisions of Young Guard infantry and two divisions of Old Guard infantry. For the campaign of 1814, in which Napoleon relied more heavily than ever before on the

Imperial Guard, the *tirailleur* and *voltigeur* regiments of the Young Guard were increased to nineteen each. When operations began in February, the infantry composed one division of the Old Guard (which also incorporated Middle Guard units) and three divisions of the Young Guard. At the time of his abdication in early April, Napoleon had forty regiments of Middle and Young Guard infantry, and four of the Old Guard.

Upon his return from exile on Elba, the Emperor rapidly began to reassemble his army to confront Wellington and Blücher in Belgium. Quite apart from the forces available to defend the frontiers of France against other Allied armies, the formation of the Armée du Nord took precedence. When the campaign opened in June the Guard infantry consisted of 4 regiments of *grenadiers* and 4 of *chasseurs*, plus 1 company of *Marins*. The 1st and 2nd Regiments of these units held Old Guard status, while the 3rd and 4th were classed as Middle Guard. All units had two battalions apart from the 4th Grenadiers, which had only one. The Young Guard consisted of sixteen regiments, divided equally between *tirailleurs* and *voltigeurs*. Each regiment had two battalions, but only the first four regiments were ready for the field when the campaign began.

At Waterloo the infantry of the Guard consisted of a division under Drouot, including the 1st to 4th Grenadiers, all of 2 battalions, the 1st to 4th Chasseurs, also with 2 battalions each, the 1st and 2nd Tirailleurs and the 1st and 2nd Voltigeurs, of 2 battalions each. The first and second regiments of *grenadiers* and *chasseurs* were classed as Old Guard, the third and fourth as Middle Guard, and all the *tirailleurs* and *voltigeurs* constituted Young Guard. In all, Imperial Guard infantry at Waterloo amounted to 22 battalions with a strength of 14,000.

Cavalry

In 1805 Guard cavalry consisted of the Chasseurs à Cheval and the Grenadiers à Cheval, the former comprising 5 squadrons of 200 men each. The Grenadiers were the Guard equivalent to the *carabiniers*, though they never wore a *cuirass*. They had only 4 squadrons of 200 men each. Both the *chasseur* and *grenadier* regiments contained four companies of *vélites*, with each company of 100 men; that is, 200 men in each squadron. The Chasseurs also received an attached squadron of Mamelukes at this time. A Guard dragoon regiment was formed in April 1806 with an initial strength of a single squadron, but by the following year the regiment had increased to 4 squadrons of 200 men each, achieved by reducing the number of *vélites* assigned to the other cavalry regiments to 1 squadron of 250 men. In 1807 the Guard Dragoons were re-designated the Empress Dragoons. In March of the same year the 1st Chevau-Légers, consisting of Poles, was created, also consisting of 4 squadrons of 200 men. During the campaign of 1809 the cavalry of the Guard consisted of the following units: Grenadiers à Cheval; Chasseurs à Cheval; Empress Dragoons; Chevau-

Légers Polonais; Company of Guides (attached to HQ for the protection of Marshal Berthier, the Emperor's Chief-of-Staff); Mamelukes (a squadron attached to the Chasseurs); and the Gendarmes d'élite (two squadrons).

Each regiment consisted of 4 field squadrons and a depot squadron, with each squadron having a paper strength of 248 men. During peacetime the first 3 regiments contained a *vélite* squadron of 240 men. In 1810, with the French absorption of the Dutch Army, the hussar regiment was converted into the 2nd Chevau-Léger Lanciers. In December 1809 the Lancers of Berg joined the Guard with a strength of four squadrons.

With, on the eve of the Russian invasion, the division of the Imperial Guard into Old, Middle and Young, the cavalry consisted of the following units: Grenadiers à Cheval, Chasseurs à Cheval and Mamelukes, the 1st (Polish) Chevau-léger Lanciers (as a result of arming the existing Chevau-Légers Polonais with lances), the Empress Dragoons and the Elite Gendarmes. The Middle Guard cavalry was composed of the 2nd (Dutch) Chevau-léger Lanciers. The Young Guard had no cavalry. Just prior to the invasion, two new units were admitted into the Guard from the Duchy of Warsaw: the Chevau-léger Lanciers of five squadrons and a unit of Lithuanian Tartars, also armed with lances. A squadron of Tartars was assigned to each Guard cavalry regiment serving in Russia. A number of existing Guard units was strengthened at this time, with the Chasseurs à Cheval being increased to six squadrons and the Polish 1st Chevau-léger Lanciers to five. The 2nd (Dutch) Lancers were enlarged to ten squadrons. No changes were made to the structure of Guard cavalry for the campaign in Russia, where the mounted force consisted of nine squadrons of cavalry plus a company of Mamelukes, with various foreign mounted units (Portuguese and Italian elite cavalry) consisting of seven squadrons. At the beginning of 1813 the Emperor expanded the Guard cavalry through the creation of twelve new regiments, five of which constituted Young Guard equivalents of existing cavalry regiments of the Guard. Specifically, two regiments of Young Guard lancers were formed, together with *chasseurs à cheval*, all given an establishment of 5 squadrons of 200 troopers each, while the *grenadiers à cheval* and the dragoons of the Young Guard comprised 6 squadrons of 300 men. Four more Young Guard regiments, known as Gardes d'Honneur, were established. Many of the aforementioned newly created regiments did not reach the front until the summer, and hence did not take part at Lützen and Bautzen, both fought in May.

Before the start of the spring campaign, in an effort to increase their numbers to full strength, the senior regiment of the Guard drafted men from French and Polish line regiments, though paper strength was never reached, leaving the cavalry with the following approximate returns: 1st (Polish) Lancers (530 men); 2nd (Dutch) Lancers (700 men); Chasseurs à Cheval (750 men); Grenadiers à Cheval (550 men); Empress Dragoons (550 men); and Gendarmes d'elite (50 men). The Lanciers de Berg also served in the Guard, but with the disbanding of the 3rd Lancers its troopers were absorbed into the 2nd (Dutch) Lancers. Like the infantry of the Guard, the cavalry was re-organised and increased over the summer armistice, though sometimes only on paper. Thus, theoretically, the Chasseurs à Cheval was composed of 8 squadrons of 200 men, while the 1st Lancers was increased to 5-squadron strength, each also of 200 men. The 2nd Lancers now numbered 10 squadrons of 200 men. With the arrival of the five Young Guard regiments with their senior counterparts, the cavalry was re-organised into three divisions, as follows.

The 1st Guard Cavalry Division comprised the Lanciers de Berg, the Dragoons of the Young Guard and the 2nd Lancers of the Young Guard. The 2nd Division contained three further Young Guard regiments: the 1st Lancers, the Chasseurs à Cheval and the Grenadiers à Cheval. The 3rd Division comprised several regiments of the Old Guard: the Polish Lancers, the Chasseurs à Cheval, the Empress Dragoons and the Grenadiers à Cheval. In all, the Guard cavalry present at Leipzig in October numbered about 8,000 officers and troopers. One final alteration was made, after the Battle of Dresden, when a squadron of Gardes d'Honneur was attached to each of the three Guard cavalry divisions.

When the campaign of 1814 opened in February, however, Napoleon had only 2 Guard cavalry divisions in the field, consisting of 4 regiments by the time of his abdication in April, plus the Polish contingent and 4 regiments of Gardes d'Honneur attached. When the Emperor returned from Elba he formed 5 cavalry units: the Empress Dragoons of 7 squadrons; the Grenadiers à Cheval of 6; the (Red) Lancers of 5 – formed from the 2 Guard lancer regiments of the pre-Restoration era; the Chasseurs à Cheval of 6 squadrons with a small detachment of Mamelukes; and 2 companies of Gendarmes d'élite. In all, this force amounted to 18½ squadrons totalling 4,500 officers and troopers.

Artillery

The first artillery regiment of the Guard was formed in 1806 and comprised four batteries with a squadron of attached *vélites*. Each battery had 4 6lb guns and 2 howitzers, the whole crewed by a company (squadron) of approximately 100 officers and men. The Foot Artillery Regiment was established in 1808 with an initial strength of four batteries. During the following year, in the campaign against Austria the Guard artillery consisted of 1 horse artillery regiment, 1 foot artillery regiment, 1 artillery worker battalion and 1 train battalion. At the same time the horse artillery contained 3 squadrons, with each consisting of 2 companies and a depot. The Foot Artillery Regiment had 4 companies and a depot, while the Train Battalion contained 6 companies. Foot artillery regiments increased to 8 batteries in 1810 and to 9 2 years later, each battery being equipped with 6 pieces of artillery, either 6 or 12lb guns, and 2 howitzers. Trains, that is, the horses, limbers, drivers and ammunition caissons that formed part of the artillery, were organised into 2 battalions, with 1 company attached to each battery. In 1810 a battalion of sappers was formed, together with a wagon-train battalion.

In 1811 the Foot Artillery Regiment of the Guard was increased to nine batteries, giving a total of seventy-two pieces. A total of five batteries from the line were organised to serve as an artillery reserve. No changes were made to the Guard artillery for the campaign against Russia. In the 1813 campaign, the artillery was distributed between the four newly formed Guard infantry divisions. The 1st Division contained 3 foot batteries of the Old Guard, 2 Young Guard foot batteries and 2 Old Guard horse batteries. The 2nd contained 2 Old Guard foot batteries, 2 Young Guard foot and 1 Old Guard horse battery. The 3rd and 4th Divisions contained foot batteries of the Young Guard. After the armistice each Guard division contained a varying number of guns, but generally one battery per brigade. By the end of the year each Guard infantry division had two foot batteries attached, while cavalry divisions had one or two horse batteries.

For the campaign of 1813 the artillery of the Old Guard was organised into 2 regiments: 1 of 6 batteries of foot, armed with 12lb guns, and another containing 6 6lb batteries of horse. The Young Guard received a new regiment in the early months of the year, containing 14 foot batteries of 8lb guns. In operational terms, the Imperial Guard deployed 202 guns at the Battle of Leipzig. By the time of the Emperor's abdication in April 1814 the artillery of the Guard had been reduced to 1 regiment of Guard foot artillery, of 6 companies, 1 horse artillery regiment, also of 6 companies, and 1 Young Guard regiment, of 14 companies. The Guard artillery also contained 6 squadrons of artillery train. During the Waterloo campaign the Guard artillery contained 12 foot batteries, each of 6 12lb guns, 4 horse batteries of 6 6lb guns each and 1 train squadron of 8 companies.

NOTE

1. C.G.L. Saski, *Campagne de 1809 en Allemagne et Autriche* (3 vols, Paris, Berger Levrault, 1899; repr. Solihull, Helion & Co., 2009), vol. i, p. 68.

Chapter Two

The Russian Army

Alexander Mikaberidze

In September 1815 Bergères-lès-Vertus, a small town in Champagne, was a sight to behold. Over 150,000 men, all in parade uniforms, were deployed in various formations on a vast field near the town. Around noon, the soldiers marched past Tsar Alexander I of Russia and his entourage with thundering shouts of 'hurrah' and music. The scene was indeed breathtaking, the triumphal conclusion to the titanic struggle between two opposing worlds and a showcase of Russian military might and success. Only three years before, Europe had watched in suspense as Emperor Napoleon led over 500,000 men into Russia. However, within six months, the once-mighty Grande Armée was destroyed, thousands of its soldiers killed, captured or frozen in the vastness of Russia. The Russian Army emerged victorious from the depths of the East and marched all across the Continent to the heart of France. There were many victories and defeats along the way, but in September 1815, few would have questioned whether the final victory over Napoleon could have been possible without the Russian Army.

The Revolutionary period was one of great activity for the Russian Army since Russia was at war for virtually the entire period from the late eighteenth to the early nineteenth century. Specifically, the Russian Army participated in the six campaigns against France in 1799, 1805, 1806–7, 1812–14, three Russo-Turkish wars covering 1769–74, 1787–91 and 1806–12, the annexation of the Crimea in 1783–84, two Russo-Persian wars in 1796 and 1804–13, two Russo-Swedish wars in 1789–91 and 1808–9 as well as in two partitions of Poland in 1792–95 and annexations of the principalities in Georgia and the northern Caucasus.

RECRUITMENT

Sustaining such a military effort required enormous financial investment and mobilization of human resources. Able to draw on a population of almost 40 million by the late eighteenth century, Russian sovereigns acquired conscripts from a servile population that included serfs, peasants and townspeople. Every year the sovereign or the Senate acting in Imperial name issued a decree (*ukaz*) specifying a levy to be raised. The number of recruits fluctuated with the military needs and each decree described how many individuals were to be recruited from a given number of men, what procedures to be followed and which groups to be exempt. In 1724, the system was modified and levies were imposed based on the number of souls, not households. While under Peter the Great all estates had to provide specified levy quotas, although later the system gradually changed. In 1736, new regulations allowed nobles to keep one son at home to take care of the family property; other male children could study until the age of 20 when they had to be enlisted in the army for twenty-five years. After 1737–39, clergy and merchants were exempted from recruitment if they paid a special fee. Finally, in 1762, Tsar Peter III promulgated the Charter of Liberties which abolished mandatory military service for the nobles. Thereafter, the burden of recruitment fell heavily on serfs, townspeople and peasants. In total, between 1705 and 1825, there were over 90 levies raised, yielding over 4,000,000 men for the Russian armies. During the period 1805–15, Russia raised levies every year except in 1814, drafting over 1,200,000 men.

In time of emergency, Russian sovereigns often issued heavier levies or resorted to militia mobilizations. During the 1806–7 campaigns in Poland, Tsar Alexander issued a special levy for 'temporary internal militia' (*vnutrenneya vremennaya militsiya*) and assigned quotas (1 per 100 souls) to 31 provinces organized in 7 regions throughout the Empire. Townsfolk, as well as state and landlord peasants aged between 17 and 50, were eligible for recruitment. Landlords were required to provide recruits within two weeks of a decree being issued and supply each recruit with 3 rubles, provisions for three months, and some weaponry. Although the levy called for a 612,000-men strong militia, both local and central authorities soon became concerned about arming such a large number of peasants who could turn against the authorities. Therefore, the levy quota was significantly reduced and, in the end, some 200,129 men were raised for militia service. The heaviest levies were held in 1812, when in response to Napoleon's invasion, Russia issued three emergency levies within six months calling for over 400,000 men, excluding militia.

Age limits for recruits were initially defined at 15 to 30, but they were eventually raised by five years. Catherine the Great increased the minimum age requirement to 17. During the Napoleonic Wars, age requirements went through various changes: the maximum age for recruits was raised to 36 in 1806, age limits were defined at 19 to 37 in 1808, the minimum age was lowered to 18 in 1811 and the maximum increased to 40 in 1812. In practice, officials often ignored regulations and accepted underage boys or older men. Regulations regarding height also gradually evolved, starting with 2 arshins and 4 vershkis (5 feet 3 inches) in the 1730s. During the Napoleonic Wars, requirements were lowered in 1805, 1808 and 1809 by ½ inch, in 1806 and 1811 by 1 inch and in 1812 by 2 inches. Shorter

Table 1.1 Levies During the Napoleonic Wars

Levy	Year	Levy quota	Recruits: Expected	Recruits: Actual
73rd	1802	2 per 500 souls	52,523	46,491
74th	1803	2 per 500 souls	60,379	54,855
75th	1804	1 per 500 souls	–	38,437
76th	1805	4 per 500 souls	–	110,000
	1805 (2nd call-up)	–	–	58,205
77th	1806–1807 (militia recruitment)	5 per 500 souls	612,000	200,129
78th	1808	5 per 500 souls	118,300	38,906
79th	1809	5 per 500 souls	82,146	60,000
80th	1810	3 per 500 souls	–	94,589
81st	1811	4 per 500 souls	135,000	120,000
82nd	1812	2 per 500 souls	70,000	166,563 (82nd and 83rd)
83rd	1812	8 per 500 souls	181,585	
84th	1812 (November)	8 per 500 souls (1 per 50 souls in Lifland)	167,686	–
85th	1813	8 per 500 souls (1 per 50 souls in Estland)	–	200,000
86th	1815	1 per 500 souls (Ukraine, Bessarabia and Georgia exempt)	–	33,417

men were usually recruited anyway and assigned to garrison duty or the navy. Soldiers initially had to serve in the army for life. However, following the successful war against the Ottomans in 1787–91, Catherine the Great rewarded her troops with the reduction of the service term to twenty-five years in 1793. Alexander considered proposals to reduce military service to twelve years but could not implement them in wartime.

Following exemptions of the clergy and nobility, the Russian recruitment system turned into selective conscription that was limited to underprivileged estates. Each taxpaying community (*tiaglye*) had to provide its share of the levy quota. The recruitment system initially depended on the commissars dispatched to the countryside, who were supervised by provincial governors and district *voevodas* (local military commanders). This civil-military symbiosis gradually developed into a *rekrutskie komiteti* (recruitment committee) and a *rekrutskoe prisutstvie* (recruiting board) convened at different towns (*priemnoe mesto*), including the provincial centre, in each province. The recruitment committee consisted of the provincial governor, the provincial marshal of nobility and the treasurer and head of the State Property Department (*gosudarstvennikh imushestv palata*), who provided general direction on the recruitment process. In practice, the recruitment board was in charge of recruitment and its members included a marshal (the leading noble in the *uezd*), a *voennii priemshik*, an official appointed by the War College (the predecessor of the Ministry of War) to supervise the process, a doctor to check the recruit's health and several clerks to maintain records.

After a levy was issued, each province had two months to provide recruits. Recruitment was a serious threat to local communities since a recruit had to serve for twenty-five years and rarely returned to the village. Therefore, the selection of a recruit was a very important and complex process. Under the 1808 regulations, each district (*uezd*) was divided into smaller units that contained several villages. Each unit was numbered sequentially and the number indicated the order of recruitment duty. Each village community – or *mir* – established its own set of principles in this regard. In general, the mir considered each village household that consisted of consanguinal or affinal persons living together on a single plot of land. Each household may have contained a few family units, and although each of these enjoyed some level of autonomy, they all were subordinate to the household patriarch. Thus, patriarchs could choose to spare their own offspring and pick remote relatives living in the same household for recruitment. In addition, a patriarch often denied marriages to his younger sons, whom he selected for service, to protect other married children.

In selecting potential recruits, the mir considered the size and wealth of each household in order to minimize damage to families that still had to work the land and pay the poll tax. Small households often avoided recruitment, but in return many of them had to pay for outfitting new conscripts. The largest and most prosperous households often had to bear the burden. However, they often evaded the draft by buying substitutes. Thus, a wealthy serf could pay a peasant from his own community to serve as a substitute, or hire a substitute from a neighbouring estate. However, this was a very expensive option and members of the mir sometimes combined their resources to collect the necessary sum. In addition, special regulations were enacted to regulate this practice. Those purchased had to be free men and could not be fugitives or deserters; foreigners were acceptable, and the purchase had to be registered with the authorities. Initially, the price was set at 360 rubles in 1783, but in 1793 landowners could buy them for 400 rubles.The price was increased to 500 rubles in 1809 and in some regions skyrocketed to some 2,000 rubles in 1810. The mir often used the recruit selection method as a tool of discipline or punishment. Thus, there were many cases when the mir selected 'troublemakers', who had committed crimes, were indolent or had accumulated debt.

Furthermore, selection also depended on the leadership of the mir, who often protected their supporters. Unable to escape military service, some peasants sought to flee their communities and the authorities regularly published announcements on fugitive peasants in local and national newspapers. Those arrested were immediately dispatched to the depots for military service.

Selection of recruits was made at the mir assembly (*skhodka*) attended by the estate manager, treasurer, village elders and household heads (*mirskie liudi*). The mir considered each household and recorded the number of members meeting the government's recruitment requirements. In general, the mir often completed its selection process within two weeks of the levy being issued and presented lists to the landlord, who made any necessary changes. The legal responsibility of the mir was not, however, limited only to recruit selection. The mir also had to cover costs of delivering recruits to an induction centre, and provide them with clothes and food. In 1808, new regulations established a monetary payment in place of food, while after 1816 the mir was burdened with providing funding for food and equipment for recruits.

The landlord then escorted prospective recruits to an induction centre where a recruiting board selected recruits. Because of the high percentage of evasion, or failure of the physical examination, the landlord usually took twice the number of required men. Recruits were assessed as to their fitness and if deemed acceptable, had their heads shaven and pledged allegiance to the Tsar. Naturally, wealthy households could secure favourable treatment of their members by bribing district clerks or board officials. After examination, recruits were then organized in groups commanded by a *partionnii ofitser* (squad officer) who took them to their assigned regiments. Landlords received a special receipt (*zachet, kvitantsia*) for each man they brought for recruitment and returned home with the remaining candidates. The receipt that landlords received for recruits gradually became a source of corruption. Because a higher number of receipts were issued to those who presented recruits in advance, landlords often sold these documents to other landlords, or the village communities, who could claim them in subsequent levies and help their members avoid the draft. By the 1790s, the share of receipts presented was about 5–10 per cent.

The peasant communities not only had to provide recruits, but also had to supply outfits for them and pay their travel expenses to the recruitment boards. During the examination at the recruitment board, a recruit had to satisfy three main requirements – physical fitness, age and height. The recruiting officers initially had no experience in medicine and so their assessment of a recruit's fitness was crude at best. Although medical officers (*lekari*) were added subsequently, they tended to concentrate on the external appearance of recruits and this led to the drafting of soldiers with various internal deficiencies. Furthermore, the fitness requirement was often ignored in wartime when the demand for recruits sharply increased. During the Seven Years War (1756–63), recruiting officers frequently drafted men with a few teeth missing, which posed a serious problem since they were unable to bite off their cartridges during loading. In 1806, Alexander required recruiting doctors to pay particular attention to potential internal maladies (eye disease, mental illness, alcoholism and other disorders). Of course, the main challenge for government officials was to detect men who deliberately maimed themselves to avoid service. In the late eighteenth century, this practice became so widespread that special Imperial decrees were necessary to address them; the decree of 2 September 1771 described how draftees 'injure their limbs, cut their fingers, poke out or otherwise damage their eyes, knock out their teeth and deform their ears and feet'. To curb this, Tsarina Catherine II ordered that men who seriously wounded themselves, but could still ride a horse or drive a carriage, be drafted nevertheless. During the Napoleonic Wars, self-mutilators were recruited and assigned to such duties for which they were fit, or sent to fortresses or other locations requiring enforced labour. Special rules dealt with *skoptsy*, members of a religious sect that practised castration. They were assigned to military service in their native regions, but skoptsy leaders, teachers and those who performed castrations (*skopiteli*) were sent for service to remote provinces, including Siberia and the Caucasus.

Following the drafting procedure, recruits were issued with new uniforms. Starting in October 1808, new greyish uniforms were introduced and recruits had to hand in their peasant attire. Recruits then received a financial allowance of 1½ rubles per man and provisions (*proviant*), which usually consisted of flour, grits and salt, from their donors. Each recruit was then assigned to an *artel* (soldier corporation) of eight to ten men which enabled them to form bonds to support each other in army life and campaigns. Recruits were then marched under the command of a squad officer to their appropriate regiments. Since recruits often had to travel for several days to reach their destination, squad officers used this opportunity to introduce them to the principles of marching, bivouacking and other tasks. Naturally, recruits often took advantage of any opportunities to escape. During the Napoleonic Wars special regulations were adopted to determine routes and rules of marching and billeting.

Arriving at their units, recruits were assigned to veteran soldiers (*diadka*), who guided them through the transition to military life, introducing them to weaponry, drill and commands. Soldiers initially had to serve in the army for life. However, following the successful war against the Ottomans in 1787–91, Catherine the Great rewarded her troops with a reduction of the term of service to twenty-five years in 1793. Although regulations allowed soldiers to take leave (*otpusk*), in practice officers rarely granted any. Initially, regimental commanders had the prerogative of issuing leave. This led to widespread abuse of power since commanders often granted leave in return for labour services and a special decree was issued on 15 December 1738 to prohibit this practice. Under Catherine the Great, further regulations were devised to control the granting of leave. Two Imperial decrees of 1792 and 1793 specified that the commander-in-chief had to approve leave on a case-by-case basis and complete special forms with details of the duration of leave and the destination. Four years later, Tsar Paul I implemented further regulations; the number of soldiers absent from a unit was now specified, and soldiers received no pay during leave. During the Napoleonic Wars, Alexander also restricted the granting of leave to retain the maximum number of troops available.

To minimize difficulties in introducing recruits to military life, and to provide the army with well-trained soldiers, the Ministry of War created twenty-six Reserve Recruitment Depots (*zapasnoe rekrutskoe depo*) between 1806 and 1809. Arriving at the depot, recruits were organized in units and trained for nine months, learning manoeuvring, marching, military regulations, bivouacking and target practice. The staff of each depot consisted of six companies composed of one officer, four non-commissioned officers and forty soldiers (that had at least three years' experience) who trained recruits. In addition to these troops, each division also assigned 1 staff officer, 2 drummers, 3 barbers and 3 physicians, as well as 1 officer, 1 NCO, and 10 soldiers from an invalid company (*invalidnaia rota*) for guard duties at supply and ammunition magazines. Thus, there were some 7,600 regular troops assigned to 26 depots. All depots were subordinated to the Chief Commander of Reserve Recruits, who was, in turn, directly responsible to the Minister of War. In August 1809, new regulations stipulated limited cavalry recruitment to no less than 80 but no more than 350 men at each depot. In March 1811, the Reserve Recruit Depots were renamed Recruitment Depots (*rekrutskoe depo*) and assigned to divisions, thus establishing the so-called First Line.

In late 1811, on the eve of war the following year with France, the Ministry of War initiated a new series of changes in the recruitment system. Now two lines of reserve recruitment depots were organized. The depots of the First Line were organized on the basis of army divisions and designated to train some 80,000 recruits. A so-called Second Line of ten depots was established at garrison battalions at Petrozavod, Novgorod, Tver, Moscow, Kaluga, Tula, Orel, Kursk, Kharkov and Ekaterinoslavl. It was designed to provide initial training of recruits without uniforms and weapons and then transport them to the depots of the First Line. The Recruit Depots of the First Line were soon organized into divisions and brigades.

In late 1811, the recruitment depot system was subject to further substantial changes. First, special regulations were passed on recruitment in artillery depots. Depots now trained foot and horse artillery companies.

Table 1.2 Recruitment Depot System in November 1811 (Cities in Parentheses Refer to Headquarters)

1st Division (Toropetz)	
1st Brigade (Olonetz)	Kargopol Depot (6th Division)
	Olonetsk Depot (21st Division)
2nd Brigade (Staraya Rus)	Podgoshin Depot (25th Division)
	Starodub Depot (14th Division)
	Kholmy Depot (5th Division)
3rd Brigade (Belyi)	Toropetz Depot (4th Division)
	Belyi Depot (17th Division)
	Vyazma Depot (3rd Division)
4th Brigade (Yelna)	Yelna Depot (23rd Division)
	Roslavl Depot (2nd Division)
Artillery Brigade	Pskov Depot
	Smolensk Depot
2nd Division (Romna)	
1st Brigade (Novgorod-Severskii)	Starodub Depot (7th Division)
	Novgorod Severskii Depot (24th Division)
2nd Brigade (Romna)	Konotop Depot (18th Division)
	Romna Depot (26th Division)
	Akhtyrsk Depot (12th Division)
3rd Brigade (Zmiev)	Zmiev Depot (15th Division)
	Izumsk Depot (11th Division)
4th Brigade (Elisavetgrad)	Chigrin Depot (22nd Division)
	Novomirgorod Depot (8th Division)
	Elisavetgrad Depot (10th Division)
	Oliviopol Depot (16th Division)
Artillery Brigade	Bryansk Depot
	Glukhov Depot
Separate Brigade under Military Governor of Novorossiisk (Taganrog)	Ivanovo Depot (13th Division)
	Taganrog Depot (19th Division)
	Azov Depot (20th Division)

The Pskov and Smolensk Depots were divided into 6 foot and 1 horse artillery companies each; a foot company included 2 officers, 2 *feyerveikers* (lierally 'fireworker', i.e. artillery specialist), 20 *vice-feyerveikers*, 21 convoy privates (*konvoinii riadovoi*), 2 drummers and 232 recruits, while horse companies had 3 officers, 8 *feyerveikers*, 16 *vice-feyerveikers*, 52 convoy privates, 3 trumpeters and 180 recruits. Bryansk Depot was organized into 4 foot and 3 horse companies. Its foot company had 3 officers, 6 *feyerveikers*, 18 *vice-feyerveikers*, 44 convoy privates, 2 drummers and 257 recruits; horse artillery companies were organized in a similar way to that of the Smolensk Depot. Glukhov Depot was divided into 5 foot and 2 horse companies; a foot company had 3 officers, 4 *feyerveiker*, 20 *vice-feyerveiker*, 30 convoy privates, two drummers and 242 recruits, while horse artillery companies had a similar structure to that of other depots. In late November 1811, depots were instructed to allocate between 600 and 900 recruits for cavalry training. These troops were organized into squadrons and designated as the 6th squadron for dragoon regiments, and the 11th or 12th for uhlans (lancers) and hussars. In December 1811, the First and Second Recruitment Divisions were renamed the First and Second Reserve Corps and their commanders became directly subordinated to the Minister of War.

The 1812 campaign put an enormous strain on the recruitment system and provides effective examples of the system at work. In February 1812, when the First and Second Armies of the West were moved closer to the borders, each infantry regiment had its Second (reserve) battalion detached and its grenadier company directed to newly organized combined grenadier battalions. In March 1812, reserve forces of 97 battalions and 65 squadrons were organized into 8 infantry and 4 cavalry divisions. The depots of the First Line were transformed into 10 infantry and 4 cavalry divisions and 4 reserve artillery brigades. Furthermore, by June 1812, besides three major armies in the first line of defence, there were also two reserve corps organized behind them. The First Reserve Corps (at Toropetz) was under the command of General Lieutenant Egor Müller-Zakomelsky, and the Second Reserve Corps (at Mozyr) under General Lieutenant Fedor Ertel. During operations in 1812, additional reserve forces were raised to reinforce the main Russian Army. General Dmitri Lomanov-Rostovsky supervised the training of recruits of the 82nd Levy and raised twelve new reserve regiments. In July, militias were called and additional troops were recruited from various regions. Cossacks provided 26 new cavalry regiments, while the Volga and Ural regions organized 24 new units with some 13,000 men. In Ukraine alone, the Poltava and Chernigov provinces raised 15 Cossack cavalry regiments in late summer.

The majority of soldiers in the Russian Army came from the Russian central provinces, while newly occupied or annexed territories were usually exempt from recruitment. Cossacks were divided into different *hosts* and had a prescribed quota of troops to be provided. National minorities were effectively integrated within a special recruitment system. Thus, Bashkirs and Meshcheriaks, Turkic-speaking semi-nomadic tribes inhabiting lands beyond the Volga, were organized into the Bashkir-Meshcheriak Host, which included eleven Bashkir and five Mescheriak districts. These tribes provided troops to protect the Orenburg Line from the Ural Mountains to the Caspian Sea. Bashkirs supplied some 5,000 men annually and supported the Orenburg Cossacks in border patrolling.

During the 1806–7 campaign the Bashkir Host also organized several 500-man regiments, 2 of which eventually took part in the fighting against the French. Although exceptionally brave, these troops were poorly armed, often with medieval swords and bows, and untrained in the conventional warfare of the age. The famous Russian guerrilla commander Denis Davidov recalled seeing two Bashkir regiments arriving to reinforce his troops in Poland in 1807; they were 'armed with bows and arrows, wearing caps with long ear-flaps and dressed in weird-looking caftans, riding on short, bulky mounts that lacked any elegance'. Davidov noted ironically, 'We were supposed to believe that their appearance was intended to impress Napoleon with the notion that all the peoples and nations under Russia's rule were ready to rise up against him and give him real cause to worry.'

After serving twenty-five years, soldiers retired and became *raznochintsy* (literally, 'men of various ranks'). They were subordinated to the provincial administrations and occupied a special stratum in the social structure of the Russian population. Most of them had no access to an occupation or other means of subsistence. Upon retirement, they received only a small amount of money, a passport and clothes. Some soldiers had shares of collective money (*artel'nie den'gi*) which they could use upon retirement. Although free to return to family and friends, these soldiers often had no one to turn to for support after spending decades in the army. They were now free to move throughout the Empire and provide for themselves on condition that they did not become criminals or vagrants. In certain cases, the recruitment system allowed for retired men to re-enter service. Thus, during the 1806 campaign in Poland, retired soldiers were called up for temporary service against the French. To encourage their re-enlistment, an Imperial decree of October 1806 provided special incentives: they were required to serve at least three years before they could be released, but were then awarded a special medal on a red ribbon with the inscription '*Za userdie k sluzhbe*' ('For zeal of service'). Those who served four years were promoted to non-commissioned officer rank and had their pay increased by 3 rubles a year. For six years of service, in addition to non-commissioned officer rank, soldiers were granted full pay for life and a silver medal to be worn on a sky-blue ribbon and inscribed '*v chest' zasluzhennomu soldatu*' ('To honor a worthy soldier'). The following year, a new Imperial decree laid down further conditions for re-enlistment. Troops were classified into four groups of those fit to serve in the army (1st), militia (2nd), provincial or state commands (3rd) and those to be returned to their residences. It is noteworthy that under this new decree, anyone refusing voluntarily to enter service could be compelled to enlist. Starting in 1808, the non-commissioned officers who were discharged to civil service but wished to re-enlist were to be restored in their ranks upon the orders of division commanders.

In addition to levies, the Russian recruitment system also had several other options for conscripting soldiers. Any person detained by the police without identity papers was classified as a vagabond and was turned over to the military authorities. Starting in 1802, these vagabonds could be recruited even if they were under regulation height. However, these individuals had a detrimental effect on the units, often tried to run away and caused other problems with regimental authorities. After 1805, new regulations stipulated that these persons should be sent to garrison regiments and battalions instead of replacement recruit depots (*zapasnye rekrutskie depo*). Until 1811, criminals and petty delinquents were also subject to conscription; the latter often were students expelled from their institutions or civilians involved in fights. Regimental authorities often protested against conscripting criminals because they were difficult to train and had an unfavourable influence on others. Under new rules, those who committed serious crimes were sent to work in mines, government factories or military labour companies in fortresses.

The Russian recruitment system also included the practice of 'capitulation' (*kapitulyatsiya*), whereby military authorities could accept volunteers or negotiate terms of surrender with enemy troops, who then 'volunteered' for Russian service. An Imperial decree of 18 July 1797 allowed the acceptance of volunteer recruits in Lithuania in addition to conscripts. Those wishing to enter service based on capitulation could do so if they did not come under one of the other categories of persons eligible for recruitment. For example, a serf or peasant could not use capitulation since he was already in the recruitment system. The strains of a particular campaign usually led to the creation of a number of units through the recruitment of volunteers into regiments called *verbunochnye*. The war against France in 1807 produced several examples of this and in March of that year, an Imperial decree laid down specific provisions for it. Regiments were to be recruited from all classes of free Russians and foreigners who were not subject to the poll tax and not subject to other service obligations. As an additional incentive for enlistment, military authorities were allowed to spend up to 30 rubles per person to induce them to enlist. Recruits had to be young, healthy and in all ways suitable for service. The length of service was prescribed to be not less than six years, and anyone who served fifteen years was promised a land allotment as settlement. If a man was wounded or crippled in action and was no longer fit to serve, he could be transferred to an invalid unit if he so desired and receive a pension. However, this practice also caused some difficulties with regard to clergymen who escaped the monotony of monastic life by joining the army. Seven months after the Imperial decree, special directives prohibited recruitment of any clergy without the consent of the clerical authorities. In addition, this recruitment procedure varied by regions; the capitulation length of service in Finland was set at six years, but if these soldiers committed any transgressions or deserted, their service time was annulled and they had to serve another six years.

Another interesting aspect of the recruitment system was the provision for nobility to fund and raise new regiments. Thus, during Napoleon's invasion of Russia in 1812, several wealthy landowners raised regiments from volunteers, who then served in the regular army. In September 1812, Collegiate Assessor Skarzhinsky, a wealthy landowner from Kherson, raised a 100-man squadron from his serfs, whom he provided with uniforms, weapons and horses from his own resources. Even more famous was the case of the senior procurator of the Senate's 6th Department, Count Dmitriev-Mamonov, who raised and funded, at his own expense, an entire cavalry regiment. He was granted the rank of major general and chief of his regiment. However, the regiment lacked discipline and training and soon became notorious for its unreliability. It was disbanded in 1814 and its officers and soldiers were transferred to regular cavalry regiments. The volunteers could be called up for service again if they failed to specify at the time of recruitment that they wanted to be excluded from future levies. Thus, on 15 March 1799, Sanktpeterburgskiye Vedomosti reported that a certain Ankudinov, who volunteered for service in the 1780s, had been recruited for the second time in the Old Ingermanland Regiment. Despite his wife's petitions that he volunteered on condition that he would not be included in future levies, military authorities ruled against her, arguing that their investigation had revealed that her husband stipulated no such condition when he voluntarily entered service.

Persons volunteering for service had to satisfy various requirements. Tsar Alexander initially retained regulations laid down by his predecessors. Candidates had to submit their request to the commander of the regiment they desired to enter and provide documentation regarding their birth, baptism and social class, references describing their behaviour, evidence of education (if applicable), medical certification of health and fitness for military service, and certification from the applicant's local authorities and community that they had no objection to his enlistment. Naturally, theory and practice often differed and these requirements were not completely followed in many cases. More important was the problem of widespread fraud when applicants claimed to be nobles. In 1803, Alexander required that documents attesting nobility be verified by the Office of Heraldry and the Inspection Department. Seven years later, local representatives of the nobility had to provide detailed certification for noble children, indicating all relevant documents supporting their claims. Nevertheless, the problem was not solved and it haunted the authorities for decades to come.

Foreign volunteers were treated with caution and accepted with lower ranks. In practice, this meant acceptance within the non-commissioned officer ranks as a sub-ensign (*podpraporshchik*) in the infantry, junker (*yunker*) in the cavalry and fire worker (*feierverker*) in the artillery. In 1801, two directives dealt with Austrian deserters who wished to enlist. The first decree of 9 November specified that they were not to be allowed to settle anywhere and assigned to units removed from the Austrian borders. However, one month later, another decree cancelled the first and allowed Austrian deserters 'to be settled and choose their way of life as they wished'. The 1812 campaign in Russia produced a great number of prisoners, some of whom expressed their desire to enlist in the Russian Army. Under Imperial directives, special units, the most famous of them being the Russo-German Legion, were established and employed in the regular armies.

OFFICER RECRUITMENT

The size of the officer corps fluctuated during the Napoleonic Wars. While there were 399 generals, 297 colonels, 466 lieutenant colonels and 1,654 majors in 1797, 12 years later the numbers had changed to 495 colonels, 442 lieutenant colonels and 1,176 majors. The total size of the officer corps can be estimated as some 12,000 officers in 1803, over 14,000 in 1805–7 and between 15,000 and 17,000 men in 1812.

Like many other reforms, the formation of the Russian officer corps is closely tied to the military reforms of Peter the Great, who forced the nobility into mandatory military service. Nobles had to begin military service as privates with eventual promotion to officer rank but exploited a loophole in the system by enlisting their children at the time of their birth or in infancy. By the time the children grew up, they had already attained officer's rank without any experience or training. Russian monarchs tried to prohibit this procedure and Peter the Great himself required all officers in the regiment to vote on granting new officer rank with the Tsar having final say on their decision. In 1764, new regulations prohibited enlisting any youth below the age of 15. The only exception were the children of soldiers, who could be assigned to units before turning 15, but only as clerks or musicians. Alexander also forbade accepting young noblemen under the age of 16 in the Quartermaster Section of the Imperial Retinue and the artillery.

Nevertheless, this process continued for decades through nepotism and rampant corruption in the army. Thus, future Field Marshal Peter Rumyantsev (1725–96) was enlisted in the Imperial Guard at the age of 5; future Field Marshal General Peter Volkonsky (1776–1852) was enlisted in the Life Guard Preobrazhenskii Regiment on the day of his baptism; he began active service at age 16, receiving the rank of ensign within a matter of weeks and two years later he was already an adjutant in his own regiment. Prince Peter Dolgoruky, who played such an important role in the Russian defeat in 1805, was enlisted in the Life Guard Izmailovskii Regiment at age 2½ months. He became a captain at 15, major at 16, colonel at 20 and major general at 21. Nepotism and patronage were indeed very important in finding any position or vacancy because of the abundance of young noblemen ready for service. Sergey Glinka noted that in the Guard regiments new appointments usually took place on the first day of the new year; so, at the end of December, 'the secretary [in charge of these appointments] would be pestered with questions: ''Will my son get in?'' ''Has my nephew been put on the list?'' and so on.' Another contemporary described the significance of becoming an officer: 'Everyone who has obtained his first officer rank and a sword knows that there is scarcely any pleasure on earth to compare with this reward.'

Initially, the length of service for nobles was not determined and often meant serving for life. Tsar Peter III promulgated the Charter of Liberties in 1762 abolishing mandatory military service for the nobles, but the army remained the only honourable career for young noblemen and the number of noblemen enlisting in the army continued to rise. By 1782, there were some 108,000 male nobles in Russia, and they virtually flooded the army. Since the regimental ranks were filled, new vacancies of supernumeraries (*sverkhkomplektnye*) had to be created. Eventually, the excess of supernumeraries, particularly of the Guard officers, became a major problem. Thus, by 1792, there were 6,134 non-commissioned officers and 3,502 privates – almost a 2:1 ratio – in the Life Guard Preobrazhenskii Regiment. Thus, frequently, large groups of Guard officers were appointed to regular army units.

As for foreign officers entering Russian service, they were initially accepted with their previous ranks, but as foreigners filled the Russian Army, the government realized the importance of regulating the process. Under Tsarina Elisabeth, foreign officers, upon entering Russian service, were reduced by one rank; only the sovereign could make an exception to this rule. In some cases, foreigners were refused service because of their criminal past or other activities. It is noteworthy that while French émigrés were encouraged to enter Russian service (Prince Condé had an entire such corps in Russian service), the authorities viewed with suspicion French deserters and often refused to accept them in the army.

Civil officials also supplied officers in the army, although certain restrictions were set for them. Non-noble officials could join the military only as NCOs and with Imperial consent; noble civil officials were allowed to begin military service with the rank of junker. This restriction was set to prevent the massive influx of non-noble civilians to acquire an officer's rank that also carried the status of nobility. Retired military officers or those in the civil service were accepted back to the army with a military rank corresponding to their civil rank, but seniority was determined by the date of their retirement. Military retirees had to appeal in writing to the Tsar, submit certain required documents for consideration and pledge an oath to the Tsar upon acceptance. Beginning in 1808, those who failed to join their units within four months of acceptance were discharged from the army without a right to enlist again; however, they could submit documents explaining their absence. Court-martialled officers could return to the military depending on the severity of their crimes. Those discharged for intoxication or insubordination could rejoin the army as privates or, in exceptional cases, as NCOs. In some instances, the discharged or court-martialled officer could serve in *opolchenye* (militia) forces without officially returning to military service. During the 1812 campaign, hundreds of former officers volunteered for the army and many of them had to serve in *opolchenye* forces without being formally accepted into the military. On average, they were restored to their former rank after a year of service.

After enlisting, a nobleman was usually conferred the rank of non-commissioned officer, but had to serve as a soldier for three months before actually receiving the rank. Of course, patronage and nepotism played an important role in advancement. Many senior officers ensured that their sons or relatives served in their units and received promotions in a timely or expedited fashion. Civil servants, who transferred to the military service, usually had their officer epaulettes within one to three years, depending on their previous civil rank and position. The timeline was considerably longer for non nobles, who usually had to wait between five and seven years to become officers. NCOs from the soldier ranks were in the worst position because they usually served over ten years before making officer's rank.

Despite the perennial problem of incompetent officers in the army, the Russian military education system was rather multi-faceted. The highest institutions were the Page Corps, Tsarskoe Selo Lycée, the 1st and 2nd Cadet Corps, followed by the Corps of Foreign Fellow Believers, Grodno (later Smolensk) Cadet Corps, the Imperial Military Orphan Home and the Regiment of the Nobility. Of these, the two most important institutions were the 1st and 2nd Cadet Corps. Between 1762 and 1800, the 1st Cadet Corps commissioned over 2,180 officers and in 1812 alone it furnished the army with 180 officers. Among its graduates were some of the most famous officers in the army, including General Field Marshals Peter Rumyantsev, Alexander Prozorovsky and Mikhail Kamensky, Generals Mikhail Vorontsov, Karl Toll, Peter Repnin, Ivan Weilmarn, Peter Melissino, Mikhail Kakhovsky, Admiral Ivan Kutuzov and others. The 2nd Cadet Corps was equally famous and productive. Between 1765 and 1800, it trained over 1,500 cadets and in the first quarter of the nineteenth century it supplied another 793 officers, with 184 of them graduating in 1812. The corps produced such distinguished officers as Field Marshal Mikhail Kutusov, Generals Fedor Buxhöwden, Aleksey Arakcheyev, Peter Müller-Zakomelsky, Aleksey Korsakov, Vladimir Iashvili, Alexander Seslavin and others. In the upper levels of the officer corps, out of some

500 generals participating in the 1812–15 campaigns, 45 graduated from the 2nd Cadet Corps, 35 from the 1st Cadet Corps, 22 from the Page Corps, 7 from the Corps of Fellow Believers, 4 from the Schklov Cadet Corps and 11 from the Naval Cadet Corps. However, some prominent commanders, such as Peter Bagration and Matvei Platov, received no formal military education whatsoever.

The quality of instructors and graduates, however, remained poor. Military subjects were taught briefly and erratically and many junior officers emerged untrained and illiterate. The records of service demonstrate interesting data on the graduates of military institutions. In 1812, only slightly over half of Russian officers (1,061 out of 2,074 men considered) could read and write. Yet at the same time, many were fluent in several languages, with 30.4 per cent (630 men) speaking French and 25.2 per cent (522 men) German; English (17 men) and Italian (10) were less popular languages. It is noteworthy that only 61 officers (2.9 per cent) studied the military sciences and even fewer (7, representing 0.3 per cent) were taught tactics. Many officers, especially those in the artillery, were familiar with mathematics, with 23.2 per cent competent in arithmetic, 10.6 per cent in geometry, 6.5 per cent in algebra and 3.5 per cent in trigonometry. Even if a young nobleman got through the cadet corps, he still faced the daunting problem of adapting to life in the army. Sergey Glinka, an officer and a graduate of a cadet corps, commented that 'after completing a classical education, [his fellow cadets] collapsed under the weight of their learning when they encountered ordinary officers [in the army]; in despair, they took to Bacchus' cup [i.e. drinking] and so were prematurely lost to the service'. Some of them perished imitating the feats of classical heroes on the battlefield. During the 1812 campaign, General V. Vyazemsky complained to Tsar Alexander, 'There are many schools [in Russia], but only a few of them are first-rate.'

HIGH COMMAND

Under Paul I, the overall command of military forces was in the hands of the War College. The Tsar also had effective command of the army through the War Chancellery. Such duplication of authority often confused matters and Alexander considered several proposals to reorganize the command structure. In 1802, the Ministry of Military Land Forces was formed, and the War College was turned into an executive bureau within the ministry. The Imperial War Chancellery continued to operate until 1808. Between 1803 and 1808, the Ministry was reorganized and divided into provisioning, commissariat, accounting, legal, engineering, artillery and medical departments. In 1808–10, the Ministry of Military Land Forces expanded its authority, subordinating the Imperial War Chancellery. In 1810, the Imperial State Council was established, which included the Department of Military Affairs. On 27 January 1812, the ministry was renamed the

Ministry of War. A new statute freed the ministry from numerous petty responsibilities and granted wider powers to divisional commanders. The new ministry was governed through the chancellery and the council and was divided into seven departments of artillery, engineering, inspectorate, legal, provisioning, commissariat and medical.

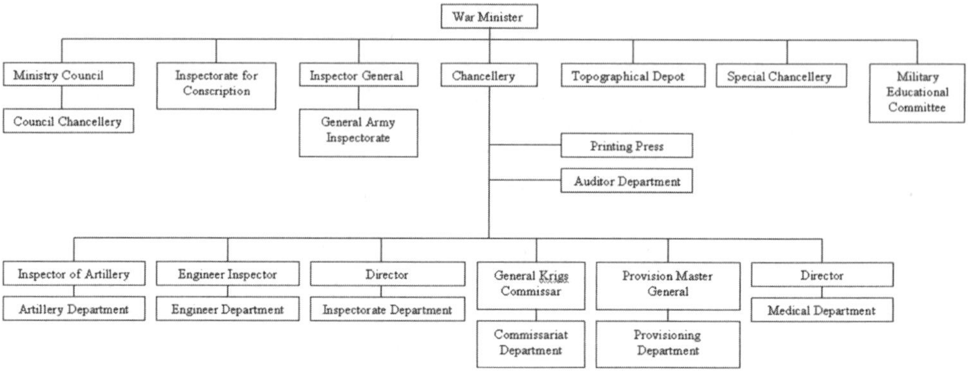

Throughout the Napoleonic Wars, the Russian Army operated without a separate General Staff and His Imperial Majesty's Suite on Quartermaster Service performed these functions. Organized in 1797, the Suite was commanded by the quartermaster-general, General Arakcheyev in 1797–99 and General Paul Sukhtelen in 1801–8. In 1804, the Suite staff comprised 5 generals, 39 staff and 62 junior officers and 45 column guides (*kolonovazhatii*), who were assigned to local headquarters. After 1807, foreign officers, including Carl von Clausewitz, Carl Pfuel and Ludwig Wolzogen, were accepted into the Suite. Under General Vorontsov's leadership, the Suite was reorganized in November 1810 and divided into archive, Suite Depot (led by General Oppermann) and chancellery of four sections: the 1st for current affairs, the 2nd for topography, the 3rd for routes and the 4th for treasury matters. The functions of the Suite were further determined during the reforms of 1810–12. Two main sections were established under the direction of the quartermaster-general: the 1st section was responsible for intelligence gathering, the 2nd directed the drafting of dispositions, the movement of troops, the selection of positions and instructions to local commanders. In 1812, the Suite staff consisted of 10 generals, and 58 staff and 99 junior officers; over the next 2 years, the number of officers serving in the Suite increased to over 130 men. In December 1815, Alexander signed a decree establishing the General Staff, which incorporated the Suite.

ARMY ORGANIZATION

Upon his accession to the throne, Tsar Paul launched a series of reforms to transform the army. His Gatchina Troops, trained in the Prussian style, became the pattern for the rest of the Imperial army. New drill regulations were introduced in December 1796, while new uniforms included the notorious Prussian pigeonwings and queues. The officer corps was purged and 7 field marshals, over 300 generals and more than 2,000 officers were expelled between 1796 and 1799. Regiments went through a major transformation as regimental commanders lost their power and regimental *chefs* (colonel-proprietors) gained virtually unlimited authority over their units; for the duration of Paul's rule, units were designated after the chefs. Ten jäger corps and three separate battalions were soon transformed into separate regiments. Under the 1796 regulations, a heavy cavalry regiment comprised five squadrons while light cavalry was organized into two battalions of five squadrons. Paul's reforms were most beneficial for the artillery. Lighter artillery pieces were introduced and artillery batteries were armed with 12pdr (medium and small) and 6pdr guns, plus ½ pud and ¼ pud unicorns. Specific regulations were adopted for barrels and carriages. The artillery was organized into 1 horse and 10 field battalions, each consisting of 5 companies. Each field artillery company included 4 medium 12pdr guns, 4 small 12pdr guns and 4 ½ pud unicorns. The horse artillery company consisted of 6 6pdr guns and 6 ¼ pud unicorns. Infantry regiments were also assigned artillery pieces. The army was deployed between fourteen military inspectorates (*inspektsia*). Two inspectors (infantry and cavalry) regularly examined troops in each inspection, while the Inspector of All Artillery supervised all of the artillery. Emphasis was placed on drilling and parade appearance, rather than on actual tactical manoeuvres. In January 1801, the army had 446,059 men: 201,280 infantrymen, 41,685 cavalrymen, 36,500 artillerymen, 96,594 garrison troops and 70,000 men in special units (i.e. Prince Condé's corps).

On Alexander's accession, the main military forces comprised the following forces: infantry – 3 Guard, 13 grenadier, 69 musketeer and 19 jäger regiments; cavalry – 4 Guard, 13 cuirassier, 11 dragoon, 8 hussar, 2 horse and 3 regular Cossack regiments; artillery and engineer service – 4 field and 1 horse artillery regiments, 1 pioneer regiment and 8 pontoon depots. The first few years of Alexander's reign saw a gradual transformation of Russian military forces. After the 1802 reforms, an infantry regiment was organized into 3 battalions of 4 companies each and the average strength of units varied between 1,500 and 1,700 men. Although the army had ad hoc divisions on campaign, the conversion to a divisional system was initiated in 1806, when the first 18 divisions were formed. The normal strength of a division was 18,000–20,000 men. By 1812, Russian forces increased to almost 700,000 men, including 362,000 infantry, 86,920 cavalry, 52,500 artillery, 75,000 garrison troops and up to 120,000 irregulars.

The infantry included heavy and light infantry and garrison troops. In 1812, the heavy infantry included 4 Guard, 14 grenadier, 96 infantry and 4 marine regiments and the Caspian Sea Marine Battalion. The garrison infantry consisted of the Life Guard Garrison Battalion, 12 garrison regiments, 20 garrison battalions and 42 battalions and 4 half-battalions of the Internal Guard. Infantry forces also included invalid companies. Each regiment included 2 to 4 battalions, each comprising 4 companies. Regimental chefs commanded the regiments and the 1st battalion was designated the chef battalion (*shefskii*) and carried the chef's name. In the chef's absence, the regimental commander or commanding officer commanded the unit. After October 1810, a regular infantry regiment consisted of two active battalions (1st and 3rd) and one replacement (2nd, *zapasnoi*) battalion; after November 1811, the 4th reserve (*rezervnii*) battalion was assigned to the recruitment depots. The grenadier companies of the 2nd battalions were often amalgamated to establish combined grenadier battalions. Light infantry regiments did not carry flags, while the line infantry units usually had six flags (two for each battalion, except for the 4th battalions). One of the flags was considered regimental and often referred to as 'white', while the others were known as 'coloured'.

Infantry regiments were organized into brigades, which in turn made up divisions, themselves formed into corps. Two regiments comprised a brigade; three brigades (1st and 2nd infantry, 3rd jäger) made a division. In a grenadier division, all three brigades contained grenadiers. Each division had field artillery consisting of one battery and two light companies. Divisions were designated by numbers and, by mid-1812, there was 1 Guard infantry division, 2 grenadier divisions and 24 infantry divisions. Later, additional divisions were established to reinforce the army, including the 28th and 29th Divisions from the Orenburg and Siberia garrisons forces. The 30th–37th Divisions were raised from the 2nd battalions of the first twenty-seven divisions and the 38th–48th Divisions from the 4th battalions of the remaining divisions.

The light infantry gradually increased in the course of the Napoleonic Wars. In 1812, it consisted of two Guard and fifty jäger regiments and the Guard *ekipazh*. In addition, during the Russian campaign, special jäger regiments and battalions were organized within the *gubernia opolchenyas*. The jäger regiments were structured in a similar way to the line infantry units. Each infantry division had one jäger brigade, usually the third.

After the 1801 reorganization, heavy cavalry comprised 5 squadrons, of which 4 were active and 1 in reserve. In 1803, the number of cuirassier regiments was set at 6, while the dragoons increased to 22. By 1805, there were 4 Guard regiments, 6 cuirassier, 30 dragoon, 8 hussar and 3 uhlan regiments, while in 1812, Russian cavalry included 6 Guard, 8 cuirassier, 36 dragoon, 11 hussar and 5 uhlan regiments. The Russian Guard cavalry consisted of 4 regiments of 5 squadrons each, 2 heavy (Chevalier Guard and Life Guard Horse) and 2 light (Hussar and Cossack).

Unit strengths varied greatly; on average, a heavy cavalry regiment consisted of 1 commanding officer, 40 officers, 70 NCOs, 17 trumpeters and 660 privates. Light cavalry regiments were divided into 2 battalions of 5 squadrons each; each regiment included 1 commanding officer, 67 officers, 120 NCOs, 21 trumpeters and 1,320 privates. One squadron from each battalion was designated as a reserve while the remaining units were on active duty. On campaign, the reserve squadron remained in depot and trained recruits as replacements. The regimental chef commanded each cavalry regiment and the 1st squadron was usually named after him.

Two or three cavalry regiments were often organized into a brigade and three brigades (two heavy and one light cavalry) were united to form a cavalry division. In 1812, divisions were further organized into cavalry corps. Cuirassier brigades had a separate designation from the general cavalry brigades. By 1812, there was 1 Guard cavalry division, 2 cuirassier divisions and 8 cavalry divisions. In March 1812, eight new cavalry divisions were formed: the 9th–12th Divisions were organized from the replacement squadrons, while the 13th–16th Divisions were raised from the cavalry recruiting depots.

After the 1812 campaign, the cavalry went through major adjustments. As a result, 2 dragoon regiments were transformed into cuirassier regiments, 1 dragoon regiment into a hussar regiment, 7 dragoon regiments into uhlans and 8 dragoon regiments into horse-jägers. In late December 1812, new cavalry divisions were formed – 1 Guard cavalry, 3 cuirassier, 4 dragoon, 2 horse jäger, 3 hussar and 3 uhlan divisions. Each division now included four regiments and each regiment consisted of six active and a replacement squadron.

Tsar Alexander continued his father's reforms of the artillery. Starting in 1802, a special commission supervised the process of modernization. In 1803, the artillery train, which was previously manned by civilians, was placed under military control. New aiming devices (*dioptre* and *quadrant*) and caissons were introduced in 1802–3. In 1803, 3pdr unicorns were distributed to jäger units. The field artillery was reorganized; regimental artillery was detached from units and formed into separate light artillery companies. In 1804, it was organized into regiments comprising 2 battalions of 4 (2 heavy and 2 light) companies each. In 1805, Inspector of All Artillery Alexey Arakcheyev launched a series of reforms to modernize the artillery. Known as 'the 1805 System', these measures introduced standardized equipment, ammunition and guns. However, following the Russian defeat at Austerlitz, further changes were made in the artillery. In 1806, artillery regiments were reorganized into brigades, attached to infantry divisions, of two heavy, one horse and two light artillery companies. New artillery regulations prescribed specific instructions for artillery deployment and fire. By 1812, the artillery consisted of the Guard and (regular) army branches. The regular artillery consisted of 27 field artillery brigades (972 guns), 10 reserve brigades (492 guns) and 4 replacement brigades (408 guns); each brigade included 1 heavy and 2 light companies of 12 guns each. Cossack forces also included two horse artillery companies with the third one being raised in 1813. Artillery companies were armed with 12pdr and 6pdr guns, ½ pud and ¼ pud unicorns. Of these, 2 guns were organized into a squad (*vzvod*) commanded by a non-commissioned officer; 2 squads formed a division and 3 divisions made 1 company led by a staff officer.

Chapter Three

The Austrian Army

David Hollins

Aside from the 1807 and Peninsular campaigns, Austrian troops served their monarch, Emperor Franz (II of the Holy Roman Empire until 1806 and I of Austria from 1804) by taking some part in nearly every campaign of the Revolutionary and Napoleonic Wars. In 1806, an Army of Observation in Bohemia posed a worrying threat to the French emperor, while in 1812, the Kaiserlich-königliche Armee (Imperial and Royal Army) would send an Auxiliary Korps of 30,000 men to Russia to form Napoleon's right wing. Its reputation for its capabilities, leadership and battlefield performance was as mixed as the nationalities which served under its flags. Victorious at Neerwinden, Würzburg, Stockach, Second Caldiero, Aspern and Leipzig, it would impress Napoleon in his hard-won victories at Marengo and Wagram before emerging triumphant in 1815.

Traditionally, the Austrian Army has been viewed as an antiquated force, which underwent a sudden transformation in 1807 to become successful against Napoleon's French by adopting his methods. In fact, the story is rather different. Austria's greatest weakness was financial and economic, as its economy was largely still agricultural, while industry and commerce had only really developed in the western lands. At its height, expenditure on the military consumed 45 per cent of state income. When the last Turkish war ended in 1791, military expenditure was reduced to 16.4 million *Gulden*, but then rose steadily to reach a nominal 87 million *Gulden* by 1801. Drastic reductions brought it down to 34.5 million by 1804 against a background of rapidly rising inflation. The 1809 war took expenditure to 253.2 million, but following effective national bankruptcy in 1811, it was reduced to 30.4 million *Einlösungsscheine* (the new paper currency, each unit being worth about 5 *Gulden*), before rising again to 150 million *Einlösungsscheine* for the Wars of Liberation (1813–14). Consequently, the Habsburg Empire lacked the capacity to deploy more than one major field army properly, so that any secondary army would be poorly equipped and supplied. It was hard to reinforce the field armies as the French threw ever more men into the front line. Similarly, in peacetime, the money was not available for training camps or maintaining a large standing force. The Austrian military could not invoke nationalism, due to its multi-ethnic composition, but had to rely on an *esprit de corps* and the increased willingness of the population to fight in the later years after experiencing the devastation inflicted by the Grande Armée. The reluctance of the eastern territories to give up old privileges and limits on the agricultural manpower taken by the military became ever more apparent as western possessions were lost to Napoleon.

Hobbled by severe financial and manpower problems, the army underwent a series of reforms, which took it from the relatively small professional army which had fought the Seven Years War (1756–63) to a mixed professional and partly popular army, which made the single largest contribution to the Wars of Liberation. Indeed, it was under Austrian command that the Allies achieved victory at the decisive battle (and largest engagement in history prior to the First World War) at Leipzig in October 1813, which ended Napoleon's ambitions. The army had performed well in the Seven Years War, coming within a whisker of crushing Frederick's Prussians, but during the late 1760s the overhaul of the army began to convert it into a uniform and modern force to serve the Habsburg state. While the artillery and staff systems continued their pre-war development, the 1769 regulations formalised and standardised the drill of all the troops. Although (like the 1791 French and other regulations) these regulations could be over-elaborate and make demands for perfection of a standard that could not be met by new recruits during wartime, they represented a standard set of regulations for a European army focused on linear tactics, but with features which would be adapted and developed later. The short wars with Prussia and Turkey later in the century, followed by the opening confrontations with France, demonstrated that a key problem was with equipment. Thus, from 1795, the Militär-Hof-Commission sat for six years (initially chaired by *Feldmarschall* Nostitz-Rieneck and, from 1798, *Feldmarshallleutnant* Unterberger) to overhaul the kit. The main results were a simpler 1798-pattern uniform, the famous crested helmet and a move to a standard musket, copied from the French 1777 pattern (although it took ten years to supply it across the whole army, which had to make do with a mix of patterns and calibres in the meantime with all the supply problems that these changes entailed).

Following the end of the French Revolutionary Wars in 1801, Archduke Charles began his reform programmes, initially confined only to army administration, but committees under *Feldmarschalleutnant* Mack and *Generalmajor* Grünne reviewed the performance and regulations of the infantry and cavalry, respectively. Mack would attempt to introduce several of the ideas developed by the committees on the eve of the War of the Third Coalition (1805), but the confused implementation affected the army's performance and following its rapid defeat, the next reform period from 1806 to 1808 saw the abandonment of some plans and the proper implementation of others. Although popular formations had been proposed or assembled in Belgium in 1793, Vienna in 1797 and Bohemia in 1800, it would be 1808 before the nationalist party at Court, led by *Erzherzog* Johann (Archduke John) and Foreign Minister Stadion, got their way and a *Landwehr* (popular militia) was raised in the western provinces of the Empire. Following a contribution of a *Korps* to Napoleon's invasion of Russia in 1812, the *Landwehr* idea was mixed with a proposal for reserve battalions, enabling the army to be expanded quickly to fight in the campaigns of 1813–14, when many of the previous reforms came to fruition.

The army was administered by the *Hofkriegsrat* (Imperial War Council), whose presidency was a politically contentious post. From 1801–6, it was part of the short-lived Ministry of War together with the General Staff. The Foreign Ministers often exercised their influence over the Emperor to ensure that he appointed some protégé of theirs. A mixed civilian/military body, the *Hofkriegsrat* was a competing centre of military planning against the Staff, giving the Foreign Minister considerable influence over that process, as well as the appointment of senior commanders. Its failure to arrange a proper system of supply greatly limited the army's operational capabilities. In 1801 its new President, Archduke Charles, reduced its staff from 202 to 150 and reorganised it into three departments: the Military Department, responsible for overall management, artillery, engineering and the Military Frontier; the Political-Administrative Department, which handled recruitment and remounts, equipment, logistics, pay and medical services; and the Justice Department, which dealt with disciplinary matters.

The army's primary role was as the sole cohesive force binding together the territories of the Habsburg monarchy, which ruled lands stretching from Antwerp on the Belgian coast to Milan in northern Italy and Lemberg (Lvov) in the modern Ukraine, with a total population in 1792 of about 24.4 million. The core of the Empire was the western Hereditary Lands: Germans (23 per cent of the overall population) dominated Austria proper, the Vorlände enclaves in southern Germany and the western half of Bohemia, including Prague. Czechs (11 per cent) dominated eastern Bohemia and Moravia, although Germans were prominent in Austrian Silesia. Carniola and eastern Styria were predominantly Slovene, while the Littoral (the coastal area around Trieste) comprised a multiplicity of local nationalities. The main eastern component of the Empire was the lands of the Hungarian Crown: Hungary proper (including the Banat to the south) had much of its population to the west and was dominated by Hungarians (14 per cent) with German enclaves, while the Banat had a large Serb (or Illyrian) population. Slovaks (5 per cent) dominated Upper Hungary. Just 28 per cent of Siebenbürgen's population was Hungarian (including the related Szeckler populations, which were mostly in the eastern Military Frontier area) as the province was dominated by Romanians (also known as Wallach) with German Saxon settlements in the southern Military

Frontier areas. The Kingdom of Croatia was mostly Croat-populated (73 per cent of the province and 3 per cent of the total) with larger Serb populations in Slavonia (the Serb population again numbered about 3 per cent of the total). To the south, the Military Frontier was largely Croat in the west with Serbs mostly in the centre and outposts of Romanians and German settlers in the Banat Frontier District. The Italian territories (Lombardy and Mantua, which were lost in 1797, and Venetia, which was held from 1797 to 1805, before all were recovered in 1814) and the Austrian Netherlands (Belgium) were mostly populated by their native peoples. Dalmatia, acquired in 1797, added a mix of Croats, Serbs and some Italians with Montenegrin, Bosnian and Turkish communities. Galicia and Lodermaria were acquired under the First Partition of Poland in 1772, the Bukovina from Turkey in 1778 and West Galicia under the Third Partition in 1795, bringing a population of about 2.76 million, with Poles to the west and Ruthenes (Ukrainians) to the east, together with large Jewish populations. Spread out across the eastern territories were 135,000 gypsies plus assorted Bulgars, Armenians and Ladins.

RECRUITMENT

The western provinces were mostly subject to conscription, although the units which were recruited in northern Italy, Belgium, Vorarlberg and the Tyrol had to rely exclusively on volunteers. Conscription had been introduced in 1781, based on regimental rolls in each *Rayon* (district), which until 1807 was divided into 16 *Werbebezirke* (sub-districts). All able-bodied men between 17 and 40 were liable, although it was mostly the 18–26-year-olds who were taken. However, there were many exemptions for the nobility, skilled trades, most townsfolk and married men, so the burden fell on the younger sons of rural peasants and the urban proletariat. The men were visited, measured and formally enrolled, although the local authorities or conscript's family could provide a fit substitute, usually from the dregs of society. Conscripts could also buy themselves out of service for 500 *Gulden*. Until 1806, the Imperial Army was permitted to maintain recruiting stations in those smaller Holy Roman Empire states which did not have their own forces, and thereafter stations were maintained on the northern borders to take German volunteers. This valuable source of volunteers produced about half the western regiments' NCOs due to the higher local education standards. In addition, all of the regiments from the main Hereditary Lands (Austria, Bohemia and Moravia) had an *Aushilfsbezirk* (supplementary recruitment district) in the newly acquired Polish possessions, each district being shared between two regiments and providing half a battalion to each. Despite the loss of the Austrian Netherlands (Belgium) in 1794, 20 years later in 1814 about 10,000 Belgians remained in Austrian service, of whom more than 1,500 were officers. Joseph II's Edict of Toleration of 1781 lifted most restrictions on Jews and by 1789, the first

Jewish *Freiherrs* (landless nobility) were created. Initially, during the 1780s, they served in the Fuhrwesen as that was partly civilian, but the large Jewish population in the acquired Polish territories led to many more Jews joining up. More than 35,000 Jews served in the army during the wars, although officially none were to be commissioned until 1815.

In the eastern lands, an annual quota was taken in agreement with the Hungarian, Siebenbürgen and Croatian national assemblies to maintain the local unit strengths. Their contribution would rise from 35,000 to 64,000 troops across the period, so about 6,000 recruits were required each year. Each local authority (*Komitat* or *Stand*) would be allocated its own quota, which it would attempt to fill by various ruses to avoid damaging the local economy. However, most were raised as volunteers (80 per cent of those enlisted in the early 1790s). These districts also had to supply much of the smaller horsestock used by the light cavalry units, although the Imperial authorities maintained ranches in the east and bought in larger western horses, especially heavy draught horses.

The number of military service exemptions was so large that by 1801 the western districts were 20,000 short of the numbers required (just 1 in 70 of the population) and only 1 in 130 of the eastern population was available. The best men tended to be taken by the cavalry and artillery, so the revelation in 1802 that 27,000 potential conscripts in the western lands were 'absent, unwissend wo' (missing, whereabouts unknown) prompted a change in the conscription service term from 25 years (effectively for life) to 10 years for the infantry, 12 for the cavalry and 14 for the artillery and technical services. Manpower requirements brought another change to 14 years in all arms on 11 June 1811, although Hungarian troops were required to serve for 25 years throughout the wars.

Volunteers from within the Empire enlisted for six to eight years, while foreigners signed a minimum 'capitulation' of six years and an extra bounty of up to 32 *Gulden* was offered for a longer term. Approximately 35 per cent of the army's manpower came from this source, particularly in the cavalry, although foreigners were limited to a maximum of one-third of any regiment. Those units which lost their recruitment grounds were initially filled out with volunteer recruits from Germany until 1806 and from disbanded *Freikorps* until new districts could be organised. The main change came in 1807 when eleven regiments' recruiting areas were moved to Galicia, at which point all, except the Moravian regiments, lost their *Aushilfsbezirk*. After defeat in 1809, eight infantry regiments were disbanded.

The Empire's financial problems meant that up to 40 per cent of the infantry were on furlough in peacetime and some infantry units had dropped to as low as twenty-five men in a company by August 1803. The ever-increasing number of troops required to engage the French led to this system being developed in 1808 into a plan for each western regiment to raise two reserve battalions. These would be made up of men who had been enlisted and then placed on furlough, or the recently released, who would be called in for training for four weeks in the first year and three in the second. Nothing was done before the war of 1809, but in September 1812, the *Hofkriegsrat* revived the idea of raising reserve *Landwehr* battalions in 1813 for the western infantry regiments. Most would raise a fourth and a few had five battalions. In Galicia, the 7 infantry regiments raised an additional 'reserve' 6-company battalion plus a depot division (2 companies), while the Moravian regiments each raised an extra reserve 4-company battalion and a small depot from their *Aushilfsbezirk*. This made the fundamental difference in 1813, in contrast to 1809, because the 3rd battalions were composed of trained troops, while the 4th/5th (*Landwehr*) battalions could be stationed in garrisons to relieve the regular troops. Together, the Galician reserves and the *Landwehr* added nearly 50,000 infantry to the army.

THE MILITARY FRONTIER

The Military Frontier (*Militärgrenze*) was divided into six districts, which were sub-divided into administrative Regiments. The first five districts made up the 'regulated' Frontier, guarding the Adriatic coast and Danube–Save river system. Its near 700,000 inhabitants lived mainly in the traditional Balkan communal homesteads (Zadruga), Croats to the west, Serbs in the centre, with a mix of German settlers and Wallach-Serbs to the east. They provided thirteen infantry regiments. Beyond, guarding the Carpathian Mountains, lay the 'unregulated' Frontier, which was subject to local laws and supplied four regiments from a population of Szeckels, Wallachs and German settlers. Farms were held by families in return for military service and every male was enrolled at birth. In the Frontier districts males were liable for service from the age of 14, but no more than one brother per family would serve at any time.

Croatian General Command

Karlstadt District: IR (Infantry Regiment) 60/GR (Grenzer Regiment) 1 Licca; IR61/GR2 Otttocac; IR62/GR3 Ogulin; IR63/GR4 Szluin.

Warasdin District: IR64/GR5 Warasdin-Kreuz; IR65/GR6 Warasdin-St Georg.

Slavonia District: IR66/GR7 Gradiska; IR67/GR8 Brod; IR68/GR9 Peterwardein

Banal District: IR69/GR10 1st Banal; IR70/GR11 2nd Banal.

Banat District: IR71/GR12 Deutsch-Banater; IR72/GR13 Wallach-Illyrisch.

Unregulated Frontier (Siebenbürgen)

IR73/GR14 1st Szeckler; IR74/GR15 2nd Szeckler; IR75/GR16 1st Wallach; IR76/GR17 2nd Wallach.

Under the 1764 regulations, each Regiment was to supply 2 battalions of 6 companies each with a third reserve of 4 companies, each company numbering 240 strong. Each Regiment also provided a Lands-Defensions-Divsion of two companies from less fit men as local defence. In addition, there was a contingent of 256 sharpshooters armed with the unusual Doppelstutz weapon with its rifled and smooth-bore barrels. There were 243 artillerymen (reduced to 50 in 1807) per regiment to service the pairs of 3pdr guns attached to each battalion. The Seressaner scouts provided 200 men to each Karlstadt and Banal Regiment with a small contingent of 50 given to the Deutsch-Banater, although these troops only served in the Balkans.

In reality, the last Turkish war and a series of famines made it impossible for the Grenzers to field more than a few composite District battalions in the War of the First Coalition (1792–97). During the Second Coalition, the western Regiments (1–11) fielded their two battalions with an additional composite battalion from the Banal District and four from the Slavonia Regiments. The eastern Districts continued to field ad hoc battalions, made up from their regiments, the Banat fielding 5, the Siebenbürgen Szeckler 6 and the Wallach 3. During the War of the Third Coalition (1805), the Grenzer copied the Line organisation to field three four-company strong battalions, before reverting to the previous structure. The Karlstadt and Banal Districts were occupied by the French from 1809 until late 1813, so their troops served in the French Army for four years. The more distinctive brown jackets were not worn on field duty until after the 1809 campaign. Flags were rarely carried in battle as the battalions were usually operating in smaller sub-units.

THE OFFICERS, GENERALCY AND LEADERSHIP

For its own internal reasons, French Revolutionary propaganda painted the Austrian Generalcy as dominated by the German Catholic aristocracy and this myth has survived. Most hereditary nobles were of the *Graf* rank (the equivalent of the French *Comte*) notwithstanding which the title represented very little in terms of wealth and power. The title 'von' did not denote hereditary nobility – for thirty years' service as an officer, exceptional service or on appointment to the Generalcy, ennoblement to *Freiherr* (landless nobility) brought the title 'von (surname)' or sometimes '(surname) Freiherr von (locality or event)'. In addition, the Order of Maria Theresa was established after the victory at Kolin in 1757 to reward conspicuous bravery and, at the lowest level, the *Ritterkreuz* (Knight's Cross) gained the holder the title of 'Ritter von (surname)'. This order was opened to the ranks in 1799 and further awards brought promotion to the *Kommandeurkreuz* (Knight Commander's Cross) and the highest accolade, the *Grosskreuz* (Grand Cross).

In reality, most Generals were not nobles, but drawn from across the whole Empire and from Germany (under the former Holy Roman Empire arrangements), while the last Alsatians and Irish in the army were joined by émigré French in the 1790s. Many, including Hohenzollern-Hechingen, Hotze and Vukassovich, made their names leading advance guards or by displaying conspicuous bravery in leading troops in difficult assaults. Several would rise from the ranks to find a General's cane in their knapsacks, notably Frimont, Mack, Smola, Prochaska and O'Reilly. The officer class was drawn mostly from the Austrian and Bohemian/Moravian lands in the west, together with the more densely populated western parts of Hungary. However, many came from the smaller Holy Roman Empire states, including the Bellegardes and Rouvroys from Saxony. All Generals had to hold the Order before promotion to the Generalcy. They and all regimental (known as *Stabs* – Staff) officers were appointed by the *Hofkriegsrat*. Officers from the Austrian Netherlands and the last of the Alsatians spoke French, while the Italians were among the best educated. However, adventurers from all across Europe, including the ubiquitous Irish, could be found among them. All, however, had to master German to receive their commission.

Junior officer billets up to *Hauptmann* (Captain) could be purchased, as the authorities took the view that the buyer would be a more enthusiastic officer. The regimental *Oberst* (Colonel) approved all junior officer appointments, as the *Inhaber* (Proprietor) had a purely ceremonial role. Most officers began their army careers as *Kadetts*, who paid a fee to hold the rank, and many would come from military families. Graduates from the *Theresienakademie* (Maria Theresa Academy) at Wiener Neustadt and the *Ingenieurschule* (Engineer School) at Gumpendorf near Vienna were designated as *Fahnen-Kadett* (until 1798, when their role of carrying the unit flag was given to senior NCOs with the rank of *Führer*) and *kk. Ordinari-Kadett* (or *Kaiser Kadett*), a maximum of six being allowed in each regiment at any time. However, most were *Privat-Kadetten* (or *ex-propriis Gemeine*), who had been selected from the more able conscripts and particularly volunteers. Infantry cadets would normally hold the position for a year and act as Vize-NCOs before being commissioned. Most cavalry *Kadetts* would learn their trade as NCOs for up to ten years before being commissioned, as they needed to demonstrate their patrol and small-unit leadership, but this allowed for faster promotion in the light cavalry, as they would gain experience of '*der kleine krieg*' (literally, 'the small war'), more quickly, especially in wartime. Leadership of both light infantry and cavalry beyond the main battlelines required both officers and NCOs to demonstrate independence and initiative. However, there were on-going problems with the officer class in the 1790s and several accounts claim a preference among the officers for banqueting over instructing their men. Many were veterans of previous wars and so getting older, while Zach's

1798 report claimed that the interests of most lay outside martial skills and that there was a prevailing view that avoiding defeat was the priority. The training camps of 1802 and 1804 revealed that many could not direct their men properly and lacked much personal initiative. However, the influx of newer, young officers to replace the losses of the Revolutionary Wars and expansion of the army, especially the commissioning of NCOs to lead the *Landwehr* battalions in 1809, created a more enthusiastic and energetic officer corps. In addition, officer education was improved: in 1808 new cadet schools were opened at Graz and Olmütz to supplement the Academies.

Within the units, the system emphasised the training of more able soldiers to be NCOs by a shadow system of Vize ranks. An able *Gemeiner* would initially be made a *Gefreiter* and be in charge of a tent *Kameradschaft* of eight men, whom he would mentor. Then, he would be promoted to *Vize-Korporal* (Acting Korporal), which required that he be able to write to the same standard as he could read and undertake all the duties of a *Korporal* (the equivalent of both Corporal and Sergeant), especially setting a good example to the men. In wartime, the Vize-NCOs would assume full rank, doubling the NCO numbers per company. The senior NCO in each company was the *Feldwebel* (Sergeant Major) and the most senior, the regimental Adjutant, would be guaranteed a commission. Conspicuous bravery brought silver and gold medals for bravery, while from 1799, the award of the Order of Maria Theresa also brought a commission. By 1814, senior NCOs were being commissioned in the field for gallantry.

THE UPPER COMMAND SYSTEM

One of the key areas in which Austria's army differed from the others was in its senior command structure. The biggest problem facing all commanders was the rapidly growing size of their army. The commanding general had to balance the task of leading the army with answering to his political masters in Vienna. After the disastrous defeat in the War of the Austrian Succession (1740–48), it was clear that no 'great brain' would be available, and so a series of reforms in the eighteenth century produced the command system, which sought to spread the workload around and thereby allow the Commander-in-Chief the time to consider the bigger strategic picture.

The 1757 regulations had created the *Grosse Feldgeneralstab* and *Kleine Generalstab*. Following changes in the 1769 overhaul, a permanent staff of about thirty officers was established under the Director: the *Generalquartiermeisterleutnant* (Deputy Chief of Staff), 3 *Obersten* (Colonel), 3 *Oberstleutnants* (Lieutenant Colonel), 8 *Major* and 14 *Hauptleute* (Captain). In peacetime, the staff would conduct surveys of future probable theatres of war and should hostilities look likely, start the campaign operational planning. This enabled capable junior officers to view the staff as a career option and established greater continuity of personnel. In wartime, the staff was expanded with junior officers, appointed by the Viennese authorities. At that stage, several senior officers would be promoted to *Oberst* and *Major* rank and the *Grosse* staff would be augmented by the *Kanzleipersonal* (Secretariat) and a group of engineers, comprising one *Oberst* or *Oberstleutnant*, 2 *Majors*, 4 *Hauptleute*, 4 *Oberleutnants* and 4 *Unterleutnants*. The *Grosse* staff was divided into three: first, the *Intrinsecum*, led by an *Oberst* and two *Majors*, who dealt with the internal administration of the headquarters, keeping the operational journal and directing operations. In effect, the whole staff was now subordinate to them; secondly, two pairs of an *Oberstleutnant* and a *Major* with the Pioneers dealt with external activities; and thirdly, the Inspection Service headed up by a Major of the Day, who dealt with the transmission of orders, enemy deserters and prisoners of war. The *Kleine Generalstab* comprised the requisite support troops in three divisions. The 1st division comprised 4 companies (50 men each) of Pioneers, 14 mounted and dismounted Boten (Guides and Wegmeister) and a Pontonsabteilung. The 2nd division comprised the *Stabstruppen* (staff infantry) and the 6 men of the *Stabsquartiermeister* section. The 3rd division comprised the *Stabsdragoner* (Staff cavalry), the five *Stabswagenmeister*, the two priests, two men of the *Auditoramt* and the seven *Generalgewaltiger* (Provosts). The infantry and cavalry units were only formed in wartime from surplus troops in the garrisons.

The regulations shifted the administrative tasks to the Adjutant-General. While the leadership of the General Staff was drawn from the peacetime staff, army commanders continued to select a few adjutants, usually colonels and majors, but often from the minor nobility, headed by the General Adjutant, who answered directly to the Commander-in-Chief. He ran two administration departments handling internal administration, ensuring collection of unit returns and other related tasks, while a third was tasked with obtaining intelligence on the enemy and organising raids. The *Flügel Adjutants* were the junior officers, who also were used as messengers.

This arrangement left the Chief of Staff to act as the chief adviser to the Commander-in-Chief, whom he had to keep informed of all operations, and undertake the planning function by developing the various options. He was expected by the regulation to have both infantry and cavalry experience, as well as knowledge of cartography, be a good fast rider and possess the gift of *coup d'oeil*.[1] The Chief had originally been responsible for intelligence gathering and spies, cartography, camps, specialist units (especially Pioneers and *Jäger*), supplies and hospitals, military justice and distributing orders. In 1757, he was given the additional responsibilities of selecting battlefields, concentrating the troops, preparing plans and formations, together with selecting the troops' line of march, while delegating the routine work to his senior staff officers. Consequently, the

Chief of Staff now became the General's chief adviser in planning and operations and a highly influential figure, who also directed the light troops to track enemy movements. The Chief of Staff could go where the Commander-in-Chief wished and lead special *korps*, the advance guard or rearguard and special missions. The Chief of Staff was responsible for the operations of the army and its internal administration, so he could allocate the jobs among the available staff officers and was consequently the most powerful man in the command structure. He would direct all the operational planning, allowing some nominal commands to be taken by Imperial princes. The importance of this position meant that the Chief of Staff was supposed to be a *Feldmarschalleutnant* (lieutenant general), but from the start of the French wars in 1792, as separate armies were created in Germany and Italy, it increasingly became a post filled by able *Obersten* (colonels) and *Generalmajors*, assisted by *Majors*, as they were trained staff.

The only other specified positions on the staff for senior officers were the technical commanders: the Director of the Artillery (who controlled the reserve guns) and the Director of Technical Troops. The basis of operational planning is intelligence gathering, so, the only other designated position was for a junior officer, who was known as the *Capitaine des Guides*. A *Hauptmann* (captain), his job was the collation of intelligence data to provide an intelligence assessment for the planners, created from the reconnaissance units' reports from the front line and long-range penetration of enemy forces. This junior officer thus had to be fully aware of army operations. However, the importance of spies meant that the 1769 regulations include two pages setting out the specific duties of a Chief of Staff in this part of his job:[2] he would deal with the most important himself and would be responsible for paying them enough to keep working. This assessment would then form the basis of the next planning phase and also of the (often written) advice to the Commander-in-Chief and reports back to Vienna. Defeat in the Second Coalition led to the formation in 1801 of the *Korps für Kundschaftszwecke* (intelligence purposes), staffed by able line officers.

The 1769 regulations were constructed on the assumption of only one army being in the field, but building on the experience of detached forces used in the Seven Years War, the Turkish War of 1788–91 required a different approach to direct the separate field armies. The *Hofkriegsrat* in Vienna would allocate the commanding officer and staff, together with the appropriate numbers of units, to each theatre. The senior officer allocated to each army would become its Chief of Staff and would then direct the allocation of units to the various columns or separate detachments (usually called *korps*). A small group of staff would then be allocated to each formation.

In 1792, the peacetime staff under *Generalmajor* Andreas von Neu, the *Direktor of the Generalquartiermeisterstab*, comprised 3 *Obersten*, 2 *Oberst-*

leutnants, 5 *Majors*, 8 *Hauptleute* and 12 *Oberleutnants*.[3] On the outbreak of war, the staff was expanded to 1 *Feldmarschalleutnant* as the *Generalquartiermeister*, 2 *Generalmajors*, 1 *Oberst*, 3 *Oberstleutnants*, 8 *Majors*, 16 *Hauptleute* and 8 *Oberleutnants*. The *Generalquartiermeisterstab* of 1792 began with a peacetime strength of 30, but expanded to 128 in 1798 and over 150 by the end of the War of the Second Coalition in 1801.

Army commanders knew they were short of staff officers and regularly pleaded for more of them. While it was quite possible to draw in suitably trained officers from the line, progress through the ranks of the staff was much slower than in the line, so attracting the best men was difficult. Staff officers were drawn from line units and many would later return to them, the intention being that they would prove themselves as leaders during their time with the staff. Appointed by Vienna, they were meant to be fit men who were able and well educated, keen to expand their knowledge and had already shown themselves to be capable of handling geometry, trigonometry and geography, as well as establishing camps, understanding tactics and planning the attack or defence of fortifications. Junior officers taken into the staff usually had two to four years' military experience and the main abilities required were technical knowledge, to be able to write clearly, ride, conduct cartography and explain the overall plan to column commanders.

The Low Countries campaign of 1792–95 brought further changes. Lacking confidence in Neu, who had assumed the post of Chief of Staff to the only operational army at this stage, the army commander, Saxe-Coburg, soon replaced him with his former General Adjutant, Karl Mack, who devised the *Instruktionspunkte für die gesamte Herren Generals* issued on 13 March 1794. The last of these nineteen points sets out the roles of the staff officers, which required a full understanding of the tasks in the previous eighteen points. The staff officers had to be able to direct the laying out of camps as well as both offensive and defensive operations at corps level, while helping the busy General in any way possible, so they needed to be instruments of action. They had to be able to conduct reconnaissance of the ground and enemy to report back clearly and concisely, to direct the movements of bodies of troops to reach key points and hasten attacks on those points, direct a pursuit after a victory and to continue to report back as the pursuit progressed. On a lower level, they had to be able to set out the sentries properly and direct raids against the enemy, while being unafraid to seek the help of the Chief of Staff when they needed it. The emphasis was laid on officers being independent from the Chief of Staff, but a lack of training made this a statement of the ideal, rather than the reality.

Nevertheless, increasingly, the Staff became a training ground for future senior commanders, as staff majors were required to lead small formations and special missions – Staff Majors Mesko and Neipperg led the capture of

Mount Cenis in April 1800. Few of the Chiefs of Staff were graduates of the military schools, but most had joined as *Kadett* officers from two main sources: the technicians from the artillery and engineers, who were often employed in directing siege warfare in the late eighteenth century – men such as Johann Prochaska (artillery), Anton Zach and Johann Chasteler (engineers) – and those who rose from the infantry, including Peter Duka, Anton Mayer, Franz Weyrother and Heinrich Schmitt. A third smaller group drawn from the infantry and cavalry initially served as Adjutants before being appointed Chief of Staff with little or no time on the General Staff – notably Karl Mack, Johann Radetzky and Max Wimpffen. While it was not an absolute rule, there was also a tendency for those who came from the technical branches or were trained at the Engineer Officer School in Vienna to take a more complex and scientific approach to planning than their infantry counterparts. There are clearly two lines of thought – the famously complex battle plans of Mack at Tourcoing and Weyrother at Austerlitz stand in contrast to the simplicity of Schmitt and Mayer's campaign plan of 1796 in Germany.

This system required that on campaign and before a battle, multiple copies of the plans were issued. They would be drawn up by the Chief of Staff and the details filled in after the last discussion with the General. At Wagram, wounded in the first French attack on 5 July 1809, Archduke Charles agreed with his senior staff that only a surprise counterattack by the wings of the army offered any chance of success. Wimpffen drew up the plan, while Charles was being attended to and the Archduke merely signed the document after adding in the important times.[4] The orders were then issued as complete copies, although all the writing produced critical delays at Austerlitz and Wagram.

In a battle or when the army had detached corps, a small number of staff would be allocated to each column commander as a smaller version of headquarters. The senior officer, usually a *Major*, would be the chief of the column staff and his principal task would be to help the commander to understand what Army headquarters intended. There are many references in army records to these columns as *Korps*, simply meaning a force larger than a division or a separate column operating away from the main army. This system gave the Austrians an important advantage over the French: the commanders of flank formations and corps could understand what was going on across the operational concepts underlying the campaign or battle planning and act to help as required without further instructions. At Marengo, Ott soon realised that the main part of the army was having difficulty crossing the Bormida and without seeking further instructions, sent his advance guard under *Generalmajor* Gottesheim to attack the French right and reduce their ability to oppose the frontal attack. However, the disadvantage was that a copy of the plan could go missing and one is known to have fallen into Napoleon's hands just prior to Rivoli in 1797.

Although the peacetime General Staff had considerable planning responsibilities, they were not involved in army administration or policy-making. The administration was conducted by the *Hofkriegsrat*, which was usually under the influence of the Foreign Ministry, and this body enjoyed more influence over the Emperor. The *Hofkriegsrat* would appoint the army Commanders-in-Chief in the name of the Emperor, but this was in reality more of a political role – the commander would be responsible to Vienna for fulfilling those overall objectives and leading and inspiring his men in battle. As today, overall campaign objectives for the Austrian Army were set by the politicians in Vienna, who often also established their own planning staff, referred to as 'advisers' just to confuse the situation. As preparations for war began, plans would be devised by this mix of the General Staff, the politicians' advisers and some of the senior field commanders. However, once in the field, within that remit, the Commander-in-Chief and his Chief of Staff would devise the operational plans. It is popularly believed that the Vienna *Hofkriegsrat* tried to direct campaigns at a great distance, but, in fact, they realised the importance of the Chief of Staff to ensure overall control of operations. Thugut, who was Foreign Minister for much of the 1790s, gathered willing senior staff officers, notably Weyrother, Zach and Chasteler, and arranged for them to be appointed as Chiefs of Staff to ensure his control of both Austrian and, in 1799, Russian forces. This potential conflict between military and political priorities caused considerable problems within the field armies – the other officers resented the situation and could not understand why some decisions were being taken that seemed to be contrary to military requirements.

Mack's 1794 instructions were extended by Archduke Charles in his 1796 *Observationspunkte*. Distance and sometimes military success combined to reduce Vienna's direct influence, so that in 1796, Archduke Charles was able to insert his own advisers, *Oberst* (Colonel) Heinrich Schmitt and *Major* Anton Mayer, to lead his staff and direct operations. The Archduke accurately described the primary duty of the staff to be working out operational plans for a lengthy period ahead and for the Chief of Staff in particular: 'he is duty bound to consider all possibilities related to operations and not view himself as merely carrying out those instructions'.[5]

In 1801, Archduke Charles began his reform programme in his new position as Minister of War and President of the *Hofkriegsrat*. One of his first moves came on 20 March 1801, when the peacetime staff was changed to include a peacetime *Generalquartiermeister* at the head of the organisation – a senior officer drawn from the ranks of the staff. The world's first peacetime Chief of Staff was *Feldmarschalleutnant* Duka. A specific department was created for war planning. However, it was already clear that many of the defeats of the 1790s arose from the burden of work laid on the

Chief of Staff and that in order to face the genius of Bonaparte, an Austrian Chief of Staff would need to focus much more on planning and operations to provide maximum assistance to the Commander. The *Generalquartermeister* was expected to be an able man, whose primary duty was to spend his time working up scenario-based ideas and plans, depending on the political circumstances as they might arise. The Archduke understood the workload problem, but he was also familiar with the issues faced by a Commander-in-Chief when the *Generalquartermeister* held so much power. He was proved correct in 1805, when the all-powerful Mack led the army in Germany to disaster. As the *Generalquartermeister*, he had been able to remove Mayer as Army Chief of Staff and effectively take over, while officially only adviser to Archduke Ferdinand d'Este.

Charles had already instituted changes in Italy, where he commanded the army in 1805, with Zach as his Chief of Staff. His *Dienstvorschrift* (service regulation) of 1 September 1805[6] again sought to expand and build on Mack's ideas and marks a clear new stage in staff development:

Army Commander-in-Chief

Political Correspondence	Operations Directorate	Service Directorate
Geheimkanzlei	Army Chief of Staff	Armee Generalkommando
	Staff Officers	Logistics Staff
	Artillery Director	General Adjutant
	Technical Director	Adjutants General
		Flügel Adjutants

As part of his overall intention to develop initiative among officers, this plan set out the roles of the individual staff officers and placed responsibility for the performance of those tasks on the individual officer rather than the senior supervisors. The individual staff officer was now far more than a 'mere executor of the issued orders'. The Chief of Staff's role was now to direct Operations, Planning and Intelligence (known in modern parlance as G2 and G3). The administration of the army, its supply and military justice (G4 and G5) were given to the Armee Generalkommando, which was a mix of the tasks previously allocated to the Staff Dienst department and the Adjutant Staff, although the General Adjutant was still directly responsible to the Commander-in-Chief. The Archduke's own views reflected what has become the modern approach – 'The Chief of Staff stands at the side of the Commander-in-Chief and is completely at his disposal. His sphere of work connects him with no specific unit. The Commander-in-Chief decides what should happen and how; his chief assistant works out these decisions, so that each subordinate understands his allocated task.' The Chief of Staff, Charles maintained, should be the commander's right-hand man and, in effect, the senior commander in the army, while the Commander-in-Chief was responsible to his political masters in Vienna.

Appointed *Generalissimus* in 1806, Charles introduced the new organisation across the army and formalised the arrangements within three directorates: Political Correspondence, Operations & Planning and Service. Each *Korps* staff was a smaller version of the Army Command system, where the *Korps* Chief of Staff was responsible for directing operations, while being aware of the overall headquarters plan and objectives. The problem – as always in Austria – was the lack of peacetime training, caused by financial problems. The peacetime staff in 1806 stood at just 61, but was expanded on the outbreak of war in 1809 to over 170. That provided enough officers to perform the junior roles, but there was a distinct lack of senior experienced men: II *Reserve Korps'* Chief of Staff was a *Hauptmann* (captain). The introduction of permanent *Korps* to the army was not in fact a dramatic change attempting to mirror Napoleon's approach, but a simple aid used by the peacetime Chief of Staff, Anton Mayer, to develop his war planning, and was just a reversal of the previous allocation system. Such was the size of the armies in 1809 that Mayer arranged the available units and staff into symmetrical *Korps* with staff allocated before naming the senior *Korps* commanders. As the war began, several of these *Korps* were adjusted in size and shape. In 1813, the same system was used, but the sub-units were known as Armee Abteilungen.

The final phase of the development of the Austrian staff began in 1811, as Radetzky, who was both peacetime Chief of Staff and a member of the *Hofkriegrat*, began his own reform programme. His proposals in *Uber die bessere Einrichtung des Generalstabs* prioritised the Chief of Staff's managerial and supervisory role. His task was now to take charge of all the staff officers and the various departments would be under their own directors. Radetzky maintained that it was essential to unite the Adjutants and Staff officers. Otherwise the army commander was just managing the two branches, which had produced damaging results: in 1800 in Italy when Zach and Radetzky himself were openly opposed to each other; in 1809 the performance of the army command suffered as Wimpffen and Grünne vied for influence over Charles. The Chief of Staff could then look at the whole army and its operations, so that he could be aware of everything happening in headquarters as the Commander-in-Chief's right-hand man. The training of staff officers, where Austria had been deficient in previous campaigns, received greater attention, with a training plan written by J.B. Schels and winter classes for the officers from 1811 onwards.[7] In this system lay the beginnings of a formal staff corps, whose members could also specialise further in operations, intelligence and logistics.

In 1813, Prince Schwarzenberg enjoyed complete independence from Vienna's politicians as all the monarchs had agreed on his appointment as Commander-in-Chief of the Allied armies. Although it was a full-time political task for the Prince to keep them happy, his position enabled him to confirm Radetzky as Allied Chief of Staff for the campaign of 1813. Within the political requirements, Metternich's policy was to defeat Napoleon, but not to destroy his army. Radetzky could agree the operational strategy, known as the Trachenberg Plan, with the Prussian Scharnhorst, the Head of Operations, the Saxon Langenau and the Russian general, Toll. While his boss dealt with the political leaders and was responsible for fulfilling their policy objectives, the staff could handle the plan's implementation. At Leipzig, they would coordinate the largest army Europe had ever seen in battle, whereas Napoleon's army was operating on internal lines and barely larger than that at Wagram.[8] The 1813 organisation was thus:

Schwarzenberg (Army Commander-in-Chief)

↕

Radetzky (Army Chief of Staff)

↓ ↓ ↓

Political Correspondence | Operations Directorate | Service Directorate

Led by their own chiefs, the Political Correspondence department performed the role of the G1 policy department; the Operations Directorate covered G2 and G3 with intelligence specialists and planners; the Service Directorate covered G4 logistics and G5 army administration. Writing in 1905, the German historian Horsetzky said: 'only Radetzky as Chief of Staff to Schwarzenberg with Langenau as Chief of the Operations Directorate, took over and directed those tasks, which are today considered to be the tasks of the Chief of Staff'.[9]

ARMY ORGANISATION: INFANTRY

The infantry regiments were composed of two types: the Hungarians in their distinctive blue trousers, drawn from the eastern territories, including Civil Croatia, Siebenbürgen and the Banat, alongside the German regiments in all-white uniforms, which came from the western and Polish territories. They were each composed of 3 battalions, the first 2 of 6 companies with a third of 4 companies as the depot. Each company in theory comprised about 16 NCOs and 200 men, although in 1807 this was reduced to a more realistic 153 men (173 in Hungarian units). In wartime, the first 2 battalions would be expanded by 2 NCOs and 20 men per company, while the third battalion would be expanded to 6 companies with men who had been on furlough (Beurlaubte) or recently recruited and a new depot division (2 companies) formed to train the next recruits. Although the additional men in each company were supposed to be recalled from Beurlaubte, the third battalion was usually left on garrison duties, so that it was usually stripped out to reinforce the first two, leaving the third battalions composed of largely recruits and inexperienced NCOs. In 1809 this was repeated, but the third battalions were put into the field, where their poor performance meant that they had to be marched off for extra training in Bohemia just before the Battle of Aspern-Essling (21–22 May). The introduction of the reserve system and ex-*Landwehr* volunteers meant that the battalions in the campaign of 1813 could be filled out with troops who had received at least some prior training, particularly the third battalions, which could now be deployed in the field.

Each regiment had a separate Grenadier division (two companies) with a company strength of 120 men, which would be kept at full capacity as much as possible by taking the best men available from the parent unit. Until 1798, each of the twelve Hungarian regiments had an additional small fourth battalion of 640 men, which performed the same roles as a German third battalion, but these were then consolidated to form the basis of four new regiments (IRs 60–62 plus IR48, which had lost its Italian recruiting ground). In wartime, the Grenadiers would be merged with other divisions to form Grenadier battalions (usually of six companies, although some were of four). Infantry Regiments 5, 6 and 77 supplied troops for the garrisons and so were mostly half-invalids.

Shortly before the War of the Third Coalition in 1805, the *Generalquartermeister Feldmarschalleutnant* Mack implemented the organisational changes which had been proposed in the committees established in 1801. Under this system, each regiment was divided into six battalions of four companies: each had its own Grenadier battalion as the senior Leib Battalion of each regiment, the next four being the 1st–4th Fusilier Battalions and the sixth being the depot battalion. The organisation was adopted in both of the armies in Germany and Italy, but the infantry reverted to its former arrangement after the defeat at Austerlitz.

Following the territorial losses after the 1809 campaign, eight regiments were disbanded, although four were re-raised in Italy after the army of the former kingdom was taken over in July 1814. IR4 Deutschmeister was probably the most famous regiment, due partly to its role as the Vienna Hausregiment (the Guard regiment in the four main Habsburg capitals), but IR51 from Siebenbürgen was probably the toughest and alongside its sister unit, IR31, the Splenyi regiment (known to the French as 'Legion Infernale') was regularly deployed on arduous rearguard assignments. It was, however, IR61, whose men won the most (forty-six) gold and silver bravery medals between 1805 and 1815, closely followed by IRs 14, 27, 32,

33, 37, 39, 49 and 53. After its performance at Wagram, IR42 was awarded the right to beat the Grenadier March on parade.

REGIMENTAL TITLES/RECRUITMENT AREA

IR1	Kaiser Franz II; 1806 Kaiser Franz	Moravia
IR2	Erzherzog Ferdinand Carl; 1806 Hiller; 1814 Tsar Alexander of Russia	Upper Hungary
IR3	Erzherzog Karl	Lower Austria
IR4	Deutschmeister; 1814 Hoch- und Deutschmeister	Lower Austria
IR5	Garrison regiment; 1808 1st and 2nd Garrison Battalions	
IR6	Garrison regiment; 1808 3rd and 4th Garrison Battalions	
IR7	C. Schröeder; 1809 Grossherzog Ferdinand of Würzburg; 1814 Grossherzog Ferdinand of Tuscany	Moravia
IR8	Huff; 1798 vakat (vacant); 1801 Erzherzog Ludwig	Moravia
IR9	Clerfayt; 1798 vakat; 1802 Czartoryski-Sangusco	Belgium; 1807 Galicia
IR10	Kheul; 1798 vakat; 1802 Margrave of Ansbach-Bayreuth; 1806 Mittrowsky; 1809 Reisky von Dubnitz	Bohemia; 1813 Moravia
IR11	M. Wallis; 1799 vakat; 1801 Erzherzog Rainer	Bohemia
IR12	Khevenhüller; 1792 Manfredini; 1809 Fürst Alois Lichtenstein	Moravia
IR13	Reisky von Dubnitz; 1809 disbanded; 1814 reformed; 1815 Wimpffen	Carniola; 1814 Venetia
IR14	Klebek; 1811 Erzherzog Rudolf	Upper Austria
IR15	d'Alton; 1793 vakat; 1797 Prinz von Oranien; 1799 vakat; 1801 von Riese; 1806 Zach	Bohemia; 1813 Moravia
IR16	Terzi; 1800 vakat; 1802 Erzherzog Rudolf; 1806 Lusignan	Styria
IR17	Hohenlohe; 1796 vakat; 1801 Prinz Reuss-Plauen	Bohemia
IR18	Stuart; 1809 d'Aspre; 1809 Fürst Reuss-Greitz	Bohemia
IR19	Alvinczy; 1810 vakat; 1813 Prinz Hessen-Homburg	Hungary
IR20	Kaunitz-Rietberg	Silesia

IR21	Gemmingen; 1807 vakat; 1808 Prinz Rohan; 1810 Albert Gyulai	Bohemia
IR22	Lacy; 1802 Prinz Sachsen-Coburg-Saalfeld; 1815 Prinz Nassau-Usingen	Moravia
IR23	Grossherzog Ferdinand; 1803 Elector of Salzburg; 1806 Grossherzog of Würzburg; 1809 disbanded; 1814 reformed; 1815 Mauroy de Merville	Lower Austria; 1807 W. Galicia; 1814 Lombardy
IR24	Preiss; 1799 vakat; 1801 C. Auersperg; 1806 vakat; 1808 Strauch	Lower Austria; 1807 Galicia
IR25	Brechainville; 1799 vakat; 1801 Spork; 1808 Zedwitz; 1809 vakat; 1810 de Vaux	Bohemia
IR26	W. Schröeder; 1800 vakat; 1803 Hohenlohe-Bartenstein; 1814 Prinz Willem of Orange; 1815 King Willem I of the Netherlands	Carinthia
IR27	Strassoldo; 1809 Chasteler de Courcelles	Styria
IR28	Wartensleben; 1799 Frelich; 1815 Kutschera	Bohemia
IR29	O. Wallis; 1799 vakat; 1803 Lindenau	Moravia
IR30	de Ligne; 1815 Nugent	Belgium; 1807 Galicia
IR31	Orosz; 1792 Beaulieu; 1794 Benjowsky	Siebenbürgen (Hungary)
IR32	S. Gyulai; 1802 N. Esterhazy	Hungary
IR33	Sztaray; 1808 vakat; 1809 Colloredo-Mansfeld	Hungary
IR34	A. Esterhazy; 1794 vakat; 1799 Kray; 1804 Davidovich; 1815 Wied-Runkel	Hungary
IR35	Brentano; 1793 Wenkheim; 1794 vakat; 1802 Duke of Modena; 1803 Erzherzog Maximillian; 1807 Erzherzog Johann; 1809 Argenteau	Bohemia
IR36	U. Kinsky; 1793 vakat; 1797 Fürstenberg; 1799 vakat; 1801 Kollowrat-Krakowsky	Bohemia
IR37	de Vins; 1798 vakat; 1803 Auffenburg; 1807 vakat; 1808 F. Auersperg; 1808 Weidenfeld; 1813 Mariassy	Banat (Hungary)

IR38	Herzog von Württemburg; 1809 disbanded; 1814 reformed; 1815 Prochaska	Belgium; 1807 W. Galicia; 1814 Lombardy
IR39	Nadasdy; 1800 vakat; 1803 Duka	Hungary
IR40	Mittrowsky; 1809 Herzog von Württemburg	Moravia
IR41	Bender; 1798 vakat; 1803 Grand Duke of Württemburg; 1805 Herzog von Sachsen-Hildenburghausen; 1806 vakat; 1808 Kottulinksy; 1815 Fürst Hohenlohe-Bartenstein	Vorlände; 1803 Vorarlberg; 1807 Galicia
IR42	Mathesen; 1792 Erbach-Schönberg	Bohemia
IR43	Thurn; 1806 Simbchen; 1809 disbanded; 1814 reformed; 1815 Paar	Carniola; 1814 Lombardy
IR44	Belgiojoso; 1797 vakat; 1801 Bellegarde	Lombardy; 1798 Vorlände; 1803 Bukovina; 1807 Galicia
IR45	Latterman; 1806 de Vaux; 1809 disbanded; 1814 reformed – vakat	Styria; 1807 Salzburg; 1814 Italy
IR46	Neugebauer; 1806 Chasteler de Courcelles; 1809 disbanded	Tyrol; 1807 Bukovina
IR47	F. Kinsky; 1805 Vogelsang	Bohemia
IR48	Caprara; 1794 Schmidtfeld; 1795 disbanded; 1798 reformed; 1799 Vukassovich; 1809 Simbchen; 1815 Radivojevich	Mantua; 1798 Hungary
IR49	Pelligrini; 1797 Kerpen	Lower Austria
IR50	Stain; 1809 disbanded	Upper Austria; 1807 W. Galicia
IR51	Splenyi	Siebenbürgen (Hungary)
IR52	Erzherzog Anton Victor; 1804 Erzherzog Franz Carl	Hungary
IR53	J. Jellacic; 1814 Hiller	Croatia-Slavonia (Hungary)
IR54	Callenberg; 1800 vakat; 1802 Morzin; 1805 Froon	Bohemia
IR55	Murray; 1803 Fürst Reuss-Greitz; 1809 disbanded	Belgium; 1807 W. Galicia

IR56	W. Colloredo-Waldsee	Moravia
IR57	J. Colloredo-Waldsee	Bohemia; 1808 Moravia
IR58	Vierset; 1794 Beaulieu	Belgium; 1807 Galicia
IR59	Jordis; 1815 Grand Duke of Baden	Upper Austria
IRs60–76 were occupied by the Grenzer regiments until 1798		
IR77	Garrison regiment (Belgium); 1795 disbanded	
IR60	1798 Formed; 1801 Ignaz Gyulai	Hungary
IR61	1798 Formed; 1802 St Julien	Banat (Hungary)
IR62	1798 Formed; 1802 F. Jellacic; 1810 Wacquant-Geozelles	Hungary
IR63	1798 Formed; 1799 Erzherzog Josef Franz; 1807 L. Baillet-Merlemont; 1811 Bourgeois; 1811 Bianchi	(Belgium); 1801 Venetia; 1804 Vorlände; 1807 Galicia
IR64	1801 Formed as the Tyrolean Feldjäger Regiment; 1808: broken up to provide Jäger battalion cadres	Tyrol; 1806 Inner Austria

ARMY ORGANISATION: GRENADIERS

Although only four or five Hungarian Grenadier battalions were fielded by the whole army, the sight of a large Hungarian, Slovak or Szeckel in his bearskin and blue trousers made such an impression on the French that many of their memoir authors declare that they engaged these battalions as some sign of their own bravery in battles like Marengo and Eckmühl – where none were actually present. Aside from 1805, all the Grenadier battalions were formed by combining the division (two companies) from each regiment into battalions. The First Coalition (1792–97) combinations were: 1/12/40, 2/32/34, 3/4/46, 7/20/56, 8/22/29, 9/30/58, 10/41/54, 11/18/21, 13/26/43, 14/50/59, 15/28/57, 16/27/45, 17/36/47, 19/37/53, 23/24/49, 25/35/42, 31/51, 33/39/52, 38/55 plus two Würzburg companies, 44/48. The Second Coalition (1798–1801) combinations were: 1/7/12, 2/31/60, 3/35/50, 4/16/23, 8/44/46, 9/30/58, 10/18/36, 11/15/47, 13/14/43, 17/27/57, 19/34/39, 20/22/29, 21/42/54, 24/28/45, 25/37/51, 26/40/59, 32/48/53, 33/52, 38/55, 41/49/56, 63.

In 1805, each regiment's Leib Battalion was composed of the previous two Grenadier companies wearing bearskins as the Alt-Grenadiere, and two were drawn from the infantry, continuing to wear their helmets and known as the Jung-Grenadiere. The 1809 combinations were: 1/29/38, 2/33/39, 3/50/58, 4/49/63, 7/18/21, 8/22/60, 9/55/56, 10/11/47, 12/20/23, 13/43, 14/45/59, 15/28/57, 16/26/27, 17/36/42, 19/52/61,

24/30/41, 25/35/54, 31/32/51, 34/37/48, 40/44/46, 53/62. In 1810, the combinations were made permanent and were based on the provinces in which the parent regiments were raised: 1/12/57, 2/19/33, 3/4/63, 7/20/56, 8/22, 9/24/44, 10/29/40, 11/25/54, 14/49/59, 15/8/47, 16/26/27, 17/18/21, 30/41/58, 31/51, 32/39, 34/37/60, 35/36/42, 48/52, 53/61/62. When four regiments were re-formed in Italy in 1815, they added 13/38 and 23/43.

In the early wars, the Grenadiers joined light infantry and cavalry, forming the solid support or even to fight in looser order. However, this proved unsuccessful and from 1796, the Grenadiers formed (often in combination with Kürassier in northern Europe) elite reserve units. They were usually in two groups – the smaller would be used during the fighting to reinforce key points, while the larger would be held back until required to decide a battle. Throughout the wars, individual battalions would be employed in storming key positions. Although the battalions would often use a company as skirmishers in the earlier wars, combat in open order was expressly forbidden for the Grenadiers under the 1807 regulations.

ARMY ORGANISATION: LIGHT INFANTRY

The large battlefields of the period meant that they would include villages and broken terrain, which created a constant need for light infantry. The Austrians had found in the Turkish wars that small units of *Jäger* could be attached to Line infantry to pick off Turkish cavalry. These were recruited in small companies as professional soldiers from mountain hunters and woodsmen, who were formed into full battalions in the Revolutionary Wars, although they often fought in smaller subunits. The twelve companies of German (1790 Dandini; 1792 Mahoney; 1799 d'Aspre) and single battalion of Belgian Jäger (Le Loup) were joined by two Tyrolean battalions. Exempt from conscription, the Tyrol provided IR46's volunteers, while the Tyrolean authorities had to maintain a militia for call-up in an emergency. From these troops, volunteers were raised, particularly for their sharpshooting skills, to form the Tyrolean Jäger in the 1790s. The remains of the three formations were massed into IR64 in 1801, but in 1808, the need for light troops led to the disbandment of the regiment. Each of its 9 2-company divisions became the rifle-armed division of the 9 new *Jäger* battalions, which each then recruited their 2 carbine-armed divisions from Bohemia, Moravia and Austria. In 1813, a 10th and 11th Battalion were formed in Inner Austria, while recruiting for a 12th began in Galicia and Moravia.

The lack of Grenzers led to the raising of several volunteer *Freikorps* units in the War of the First Coalition. From the west came French émigrés in the Bourbon and Rohan Legions (2 battalions each) with the Carneville Freikorps (3 companies); the Belgians of the Lüttich Freikorps (1 bat-

Table 3.1 The Light Battalions of the War of the Second Coalition

		Former Unit	Nationality	Recruiting Area
LB1	Strozzi	O'Donnell	Galician	Galicia
LB2	Carl Rohan	Bourbon; 1 co. each from Rohan and Erzherzog Karl Legions	French/Walloon	Venetia
LB3	Am Ende; 1800 Bach; Watlet	Grün-Laudon	Hungarian	Venetia
LB4	Bach; 1800 Am Ende	Grün-Laudon	Hungarian	Venetia
LB5	Radivojevich	Mihailovich	Serb	Serbs north of Military Frontier
LB6	Trautenberg	Gyulai	Croat	Civil Croatia/Hungary
LB7	Otto; 1800 Schmelzern	Gyulai	Croat	Civil Croatia/Hungary
LB8	vakat	(Wurmser)		Serb/Croat
LB9	Greth; 1800 Siegenfeld	Gyulai	Croat	Civil Siegenfeld Croatia/Hungary
LB10	Siegenfeld; 1800 Greth	Gyulai	Croat	Venetia
LB11	Carneville	2 cos each from Carneville, Erzherzog Karl and Anhalt-Zerbst	French/Walloon/German	Venetia
LB12	Rubenitz; 1800 Steigentesch	O'Donnell	Galician	Galicia
LB13	Munkacsy; 1801 Zechmeister	Gyulai	Croat	Civil Croatia/Hungary
LB14	Louis Rohan; 1801 Reichenstein	Bourbon; 1 co. each from Rohan and Erz. Karl	French/Walloon	Venetia
LB15	Mihailovich	Mihailovich	Serb	Civil Croatia/Slavonia/ Lower Hungary
(LB16)	Ertel	Dalmatian Light Infantry	Italian/Turkish/Dalmatian	Dalmatia
(LB17)	Buonacorsi	Italian Light Infantry	Former Piedmontese troops	

talion)[10] and Lüttich Freiwillige (2 companies) (after Belgium was lost, these units were merged and from 1796 known as the Archduke Charles Legion and based in Trier, Germany). From the east came the 5 Gyulai (Croats) and 2 Mihailovich (Serb) battalions, together with 8 companies of Croat-Slavonian Sharpshooters; from Hungary came the 2 battalions of Grün-Laudon and from the recently acquired Polish possessions (Galicia and Lodermaria) came 2 more battalions of the O'Donnell Freikorps; from Bosnian refugees from the last Turkish War, 2 battalions of Wurmser Freikorps (also known as the Red Mantles) were formed. The city of Vienna provided a single Vienna Freiwillige Jäger battalion in 1796.

In 1798, most of the survivors were regularised as fifteen Light Infantry battalions, although the 8th was never formed as the authorities decided to keep the Wurmser Freikorps as a separate unit. Two irregular battalions of Dalmatian and ex-Piedmontese Infantry were also known informally as the 16th and 17th Battalions.

Together with the Wurmser Freikorps, the Croat-Slavonian Sharpshooters were kept separate from the Light Battalions. In 1799, recruiters in Turin raised a *Jäger* battalion under Major Brentano (1800 Mariassy) and three battalions of Lower Austrian Sharpshooters were formed.

Few units were formed for the war of 1805 and only two companies of Vienna Freiwillige Jäger were attached to the field army. The *Landwehr* troops in 1809 were permitted to form *Freiwillige* battalions, which fought both as light and line infantry. The entire Vienna City Landwehr formed the 6 battalions of Wiener Freiwillige, while Bohemia provided another 6 as the Erzherzog Karl Legion (the 1st being the Waltrich Jäger) and Moravia 3 more battalions as the Moravian Freikorps. Additional volunteers formed the small Carneville Freikorps (3 companies) and were joined by the Lobkowitz Jäger (4 companies) from Prague and Vienna Sharpshooters (3 companies). Each of the five Inner Austrian Districts provided a battalion for the Inner Austrian Freikorps with an additional 6th Battalion from Trieste, although only the 2nd and two companies of the 5th Battalion were *Jäger*. A *Freikorps* battalion was also raised in Dalmatia.

The campaigns of 1813–14 brought the same urgent need for new light infantry. Two battalions of Westphalian deserters formed the Austro-German Legion, while four Italian Light Battalions were taken over as the Kingdom of Italy collapsed. Bohemian volunteers provided two battalions of German Light Infantry and two more were raised in Italy as the Italian Light Infantry. From the east came two battalions of Siebenbürgen Jäger and four battalions of Serb Freikorps (many being refugees from the rebellion in Turkish-held Serbia). Dalmatia once again mustered a battalion and a Sharpshooter battalion was raised for field service from Tyrol.

ARMY ORGANISATION: CAVALRY

The Austrian cavalry was divided into two types: *Schlachtenkavallerie* (Battle Cavalry), which were all recruited in the western empire, and *Leichte Kavallerie* (Light Cavalry). In 1792, the *Schlachtenkavellerie* was composed of 2 Karabinier (Carabinier), 9 Kürassier (Cuirassier) and 6 Dragoner (Dragoon) regiments. The *Leichte Kavallerie* comprised the remaining units: 6 regiments of Chevauleger (Light Horse) from the western empire, 8 of Husaren (Hussars) from Hungary and one of Uhlanen (Lancers) from the Polish territories. The Karabinier and Husaren regiments had eight squadrons, while the remainder had six, each with a depot squadron. The regiments were numbered in a single series, but grouped by type:

Carabinier:	CR5	Herzog Albert von Saxe-Teschen
	CR6	Kronprinz Franz; April 1792 Kaiser Franz II
Kürassier:	CR4	Hohenzollern
	CR10	Zeschwitz
	CR12	Kavanagh
	CR14	Nassau-Usingen
	CR20	Jacquemin; 1793 Mack
	CR21	Wallisch; 1794 Prinz Karl von Lothringen
	CR27	Czartoryski
	CR29	Erzherzog Franz d'Este
	CR33	Ansbach
Dragoner:	CR3	Kaiser
	CR9	Savoyen
	CR26	Erzherzog Joseph; 1795 Erzherzog Johann
	CR37	Coburg
	CR38	Württemburg
	CR39	Waldeck
Chevauleger:	CR1	Kaiser
	CR7	Kinsky
	CR13	Modena
	CR18	Karaczay
	CR19	Levenehr
	CR28	Lobkowitz
	CR31	Latour

The training requirements of the cavalry meant that the squadrons were kept at near full strength in peacetime, approximately 150 men per squadron in the heavy cavalry and 170 in the light cavalry, although the Husaren squadrons could be expanded by another 10 in wartime with Insurrection volunteers. After nearly 25 years of almost complete peace, the 8 regular and 1 irregular (Szeckler) regiments were able to field a total of 14,700 men at the start of the last Turkish war in 1788, where they were particularly effective in countering Turkish light cavalry. The Husaren continued to prove their capabilities in the more difficult Italian terrain in the French Revolutionary Wars. The unregulated Military Frontier provided one regiment, the Szeckler. In addition to infantry, the Wurmser Freikorps provided a regiment of Husaren, kitted out in eighteenth-century Grenz Cavalry uniforms and armed with lances, but alongside the infantry, this unit was disbanded in 1801.

Husaren:	CR2	Kaiser Leopold II; April 1792 Kaiser Franz II
	CR11	Erdödy
	CR16	Blankenstein
	CR17	Palatine Erzherzog Alexander; 1795 Palatine Erzherzog Joseph
	CR30	Wurmser
	CR32	vakat; 1794 Erzherzog Ferdinand d'Este
	CR34	Vecsey
	CR35	Barco; 1797 Meszaros
	Szeckler Grenz Husaren	
	Wurmser Freikorps Husaren 1795 formed; 1801 disbanded	

Under the 1798 overhaul, the cavalry units were renumbered by type. The elite Karabinier were reduced to Kürassier regiments of 6 squadrons, so the resulting 4 surplus squadrons were added to the remains of the French émigré Royal Allemand Dragoons and mercenary Anhalt-Zerbst Dragoons to form a new (KR6) regiment, taking the total to 12. The spending cuts of 1802 hit the Schlachtenkavallerie hardest – they were reduced to 8 Kürassier regiments of 8 squadrons each and 6 Dragoner.

Kürassier:	KR1	Kaiser Franz (ex-CR6)
	KR2	Erzherzog Franz d'Este (ex-CR29)
	KR3	Herzog Albert von Saxe-Teschen (ex-CR5)
	KR4	Czartoryski (ex-CR27); 1802 disbanded
	KR5	Zeschwitz (ex-CR10); 1802 disbanded
	KR6	Melas (new); 1802 becomes DR6
	KR7	Prinz Karl von Lothringen (ex-CR21)
	KR8	Hohenzollern-Hechingen (ex-CR4); 1813 Grand Duke Constantine of Russia
	KR9	Nassau-Usingen (ex-CR14); 1802 new KR5; 1806 Sommariva
	KR10	Mack (ex-CR20); 1802 new KR6; 1806 vacant; 1807 Gottesheim; end May 1809 Prinz Moritz Lichtenstein
	KR11	Ansbach (ex-CR33); 1802 disbanded
	KR12	Kavanagh (ex-CR12); 1801 Kronprinz Ferdinand; 1802 new KR4

The Dragoner and Chevauleger were merged into a single, multi-purpose type of Leichte Dragoner in 1798 and several of these units are known to have fought dismounted in the War of the Second Coalition in both Germany and Italy. The former units had all worn white jackets, aside from the 1st and 2nd Chevauleger, but in theory, the new Leichte Dragoner were all to be in green jackets. The lack of money meant that probably the white-coated units never acquired green jackets during the 1798–1801 period. In 1793, a division (two squadrons) each of Saxe and Bercheny French Hussards had deserted to Austria and in 1798 became part of the new 13th Leichte Dragoner (probably the unit responsible for the murder of French diplomats at Rastatt in 1799).

LD1 Kaiser (formerly CR1)
LD2 Kronprinz Erzherzog Ferdinand (formerly CR3); 1802 disbanded
LD3 Erzherzog Johann (formerly CR26)
LD4 Karaczay; 1801 Hohenzollern (formerly CR18)
LD5 Modena (formerly CR13); 1802 disbanded
LD6 Coburg (formerly CR37); 1802 disbanded
LD7 Waldeck (formerly CR39)
LD8 Wurttemburg (formerly CR38)
LD9 Lichtenstein (1798 raised from Staff dragoons); 1802 disbanded
LD10 Lobkowitz (formerly CR28)
LD11 Latour (formerly CR31)
LD12 Kinsky (formerly CR7)
LD13 1798 raised; 1801 Rosenberg
LD14 Levenehr (formerly CR19)
LD15 Savoyen (formerly CR9)

After 1801, the Dragoner and Chevauleger split up again into six regiments each:

DR1 Erzherzog Johann (formerly LD3)
DR2 Hohenlohe (formerly LD7)
DR3 Grand Duke of Württemburg; 1809 Knesevich (formerly LD8)
DR4 Levenehr (formerly LD14)
DR5 Savoyen (formerly LD15)
DR6 Riesch (formerly KR6)

CL1 Kaiser Franz II; 1806 Kaiser Franz (formerly LD1)
CL2 Hohenzollern (formerly LD4)
CL3 O'Reilly (formerly LD10)
CL4 Vincent (formerly LD11)
CL5 Klenau (formerly LD12)
CL6 Rosenberg (formerly LD13)

A 7th Chevauleger Regiment, wearing green jackets, was formed in Lombardy in 1814 with Graf Nostitz-Rieneck as its Inhaber.

In 1798, the Husaren were likewise reduced to six squadrons each. The surplus divisions (two squadrons) from the existing eight regular Husaren regiments were re-formed to create the 5th and 7th Husaren Regiments, while the Szeckler were regularised as HR11. The Wurmser Freikorps Husaren were disbanded in 1801. However, in the following year, a new unit, the Palatinal was raised as the regular HR12. The formation of 3 new regiments and regularisation of the Szeckler in 1798, each with strength increased to 4 divisions again, provided 12 regiments for battlefield use during the Napoleonic Wars. All Husaren units were raised from Hungary proper, except HR2, raised in Siebenbürgen (Transylvania) and HR11, which was mostly raised from the Szeckel and Romanian populations in the Grenz districts of eastern Siebenbürgen. From 1802, the *Leichte Kavallerie* retained its 6 Chevauleger regiments, 2 Uhlanen regiments plus a newly raised 3rd in 1801, and 12 Husaren regiments. In 1813, two divisions of Hungarian volunteer Velites were raised from volunteer former Insurrection cavalrymen to provide an extra fifty men for each regiment, aside from the two raised in Siebenbürgen, (HRs 2 and 11). As Austria's heavier cavalry became outnumbered, the Husaren were deployed in increasing numbers and larger formations on the battlefield – nine regiments would fight at Dresden in August 1813.

HR1	(ex-CR2) Kaiser Franz II; 1806 Kaiser Franz
HR2	(ex-CR17) Erzherzog Joseph
HR3	(ex-CR32) Erzherzog Ferdinand d'Este
HR4	(ex-CR34) Vecsey (1802) Hessen-Homburg
HR5	vakat (vacant); 1801 Ott; 1809 Radetzky; 1814 Prince Regent George of Great Britain
HR6	(ex-CR16) Blankenstein; 1814 Wilhelm Erbprinz von Württemburg
HR7	vakat (1801) Fürst Johannes Lichtenstein
HR8	(ex-CR30) Wurmser; 1799 Nauendorff; 1802 Kienmayer
HR9	(ex-CR11) Erdödy; 1806 Frimont
HR10	(ex-CR35) Meszaros; 1802 Stipicz; 1814 King Friedrich Wilhelm III of Prussia
HR11	(ex-Szeckler Grenz Husaren) Szeckler (no Inhaber)
HR12	1802 raised as Palatinal Husaren; Erzherzog Palatine Joseph

The Uhlanen (lancers) were drawn from the parts of Poland acquired in 1772 and 1795. The first Uhlanen *Pulk* was raised in 1784 with 600 men and over the following year it was expanded to three divisions and named the Uhlanen Freikorps, although initially each division was separately attached to three Chevauleger regiments. Expanded to twelve squadrons, so that each of the six Chevauleger regiments had an attached Uhlanen division in the last Turkish War, the survivors were assembled in 1791 to form the 1st Uhlanen Regiment. In 1790, Oberst O'Donell raised his Freikorps in Galicia, including two Uhlanen divisions, which were augmented by a new division in 1791 to become the Uhlanen Freikorps under Major Degelmann. In 1798, this unit was regularised as 2nd Uhlanen. The 3rd Regiment was raised in 1801 from the existing Uhlanen regiments and Dragoner and the 4th in 1813 from the other Uhlanen regiments and other light cavalry. The Uhlanen regiments had a strength of 1,576 men in the 1790s, but from 1798 adopted the Hussar organisation.

1st Uhlanen	1791 raised; Meszaros; 1797 Merveldt; 1815 Saxe-Coburg Saalfeld
2nd Uhlanen	1790 raised; Degelmann; 1798 regularised; vakat (vacant); 1800 Schwarzenberg
3rd Uhlanen	1801 raised; Erzherzog Karl
4th Uhlanen	1813 raised; Kaiser Franz

In his last-minute changes in 1805, Mack tried to reduce the squadron sizes to 131 heavy cavalry and 151 light cavalry in eight squadrons per regiment, but the result was chaos and understrength squadrons. In 1806, the heavy *Schlachtenkavllerie* regiments had 6 squadrons of 135 men, while the *Leichte Kavallerie* fielded 8 squadrons of 150 men each, partly a tacit recognition that the dominance of heavy cavalry in warfare was ebbing away. After the war of 1809, cost pressures forced a reduction in unit strengths to four heavy or six light squadrons per regiment.

Some additional cavalry units were raised throughout the wars. A few squadrons of French cavalry emigrated during the First Coalition: two squadrons each of Saxe and Bercheny Hussards, which were absorbed into the 13th Leichte Dragoner in 1798; the four squadrons of Royal Allemand Dragoons would join the new 6th Kürassier together with the mercenary Anhalt-Zerbst cavalry. French émigrés formed two squadrons of Carneville Freikorps, four squadrons of Bourbon and twelve squadrons of Rohan cavalry. German volunteers had joined French émigrés to form four squadrons of Bussy Jäger zu Pferd in 1795, which later absorbed the other émigré units to form eight squadrons in all in 1798. Aside from the Hungarian Insurrection cavalry, which provided the Neutra regiment to the main field army, the 1809 war saw the raising of the volunteer Primatial Husaren regiment and two squadrons of Carneville Freikorps cavalry. In 1813, two regiments of Westphalian Hussars deserters formed the cavalry of the Austro-German Legion.

Although the NCO and junior cavalry leadership was good, especially the Husaren under such wily *Obersten* as Simonyi and Prochaska, the real problem for the Austrian cavalry was a lack of capacity for large-scale charges. The lack of money for exercises and the significant reduction in the size of the cavalry after 1801 meant that few leaders had the requisite experience to direct these formations. Several able cavalry *Obersten*, including Ott, Schwarzenberg and Riesch were promoted to the Generalcy, but despite several being made *General der Kavallerie*, this rank only reflected their origins in the cavalry and did not assign them to the direction of cavalry formations. After the death of Karl Hadik at Marengo, only Prinz Johannes Lichtenstein and Frimont stood out as prominent cavalry leaders, Lichtenstein directing most of the big charges between Würzburg in 1796 and Aspern in 1809. The *Leichte Kavallerie* and some Dragoner units were spread out across the army formations with mixtures of light cavalry and infantry making up the advance guards and forming the outpost lines. The remaining Dragoner and the Kürassier units were massed into the army reserve, so there were no concentrated cavalry formations within the rest of the army. The Husaren would perform most of the advance guard duties, usually by divisions (two squadrons) spread across the whole front of the army.

ARMY ORGANISATION: ARTILLERY

Austria's gunners were the best trained in Europe and operated the Lichtenstein system, originally created in 1753. Designed by Feuerstein, it represents the key step-change in the historical development of gunnery, as larger calibre pieces were made light enough by a reduction in the barrel length and metal strapping of the carriages for the 6pdr to become the standard field gun and for 12pdrs to become battlefield weapons. Gribeauval made a poor effort at applying Fürst Lichtenstein's principles to existing French designs, but Napoleon himself used many captured Austrian weapons and largely copied the design in the Yr XI system.[11] The Lichtenstein system produced a series of 3, 6, 12 and 18pdr guns with 7 and 10pdr howitzers for field use, together with heavier 12, 18 and 24pdr *Verteidigung* (defence) and *Belagerung* (siege) guns, all based around a standard design principle of a longer, straighter carriage with just six wheel sizes (in two types) to carry lighter, shorter bronze barrels. The design could cope with the defence and siege weapons, the barrels of which were 50 per cent longer and some *Verteidigung* guns had heavier iron barrels. Gribeauval's fortress gun carriage design with a single rear wheel in a channel had to be significantly modified by Zimmermeister Reitner in 1762 and it was this design which was used at five key defensive fortresses. Frederick the Great's mobile batteries prompted the development of the Austrian *Kavallerie-Geschutze* (Cavalry guns, so called because, due to their speed, they needed a cavalry escort) in the 1780s in the form of a 6pdr gun and 7pdr howitzer. The ammunition wagons were standardised into two four-wheeled sizes, which used the ordinary wheels. Some old two-wheeled carts were used by the Cavalry howitzers, but the Cavalry batteries' immediate-use ammunition was carried by packhorses.

Austrian powder was regarded as the best quality and most powerful per unit in Europe. Field and siege rocket units were formed up in 1811, but only saw action at Hüningen in 1815.

In peacetime, all the artillery came under the *Direktor General*, and was organised into the *Feldartillerie* (field artillery), *Garnisonsamt* (garrison guns) and the *Feldzeugsamt* (the administration, which also included the Cavalry pieces and directed repair and maintenance, testing and powder supply). Manpower was provided by the three artillery regiments (increased to four in 1801), which mainly recruited in Bohemia and Moravia, and the Bombardier Korps, a unit that gave the Austrians a key advantage in artillery use. The Bombardiers were chosen from the best officers and men in the artillery regiments and put through intensive training for five years before the men graduated as *Feuerwerker* and *Korporals* to direct the gun crews and, particularly, provide the skilled knowledge for the howitzers. The very best men stayed an additional two years and would join the regiments as *Oberfeuerwerker* with a commission being likely within four years. Although this meant that many officers were relatively old, the gun crews were actually directed by skilled NCOs. The remaining artillerymen were trained in the regimental schools for one year. The regulations dated from 1757, but it was only necessary to update them with more direction on the deployment of batteries in 1808. The technical manual, *Die Artillerie Lehre*, was updated every year and contained both mathematical tables and technical information about powder and guns.

In the earlier part of the period, each infantry regiment was allocated a pair of 3pdrs as battalion guns (although in Germany, a single 6pdr would replace every third pair of 3pdrs). The remainder of the ordinary and all the Cavalry guns were organised in batteries and held in reserve under the direction of the *Army Feld-Artillerie-Direktor*, each ordinary battery comprising 6 guns and 2 howitzers with the Cavalry batteries having 4 6pdrs and 2 7pdr howitzers. Increasingly, the battalion guns were being massed, so in 1808, *Artillerie-Direktor* Colloredo made the logical change of organising all guns, except the light guns used by the Grenzers, into 3 types of battery: brigade (8 light guns), position (6 heavier guns and 2 howitzers) and Cavalry batteries (4 6pdrs and 2 7pdr howitzers). Some advance guard and in Italy several brigade batteries retained the 3pdr in 1809, but most brigade batteries were composed of 6pdrs, while the position batteries were a mix of 6 and 12pdr guns. Of the 742 field guns, allocated to 108 batteries, 60 per cent were 6pdrs with about 12 per cent each being 3 and 12pdrs with the rest being howitzers. The calibres were becoming increasingly heavier and in 1813 the Army of Bohemia had 11 12pdr and 2 18pdr batteries among its 52 batteries. Four gunners supervised by a *Korporal* for each pair of guns would serve an ordinary field gun or howitzer. The labour for the battalion guns was provided by infantrymen allocated from the parent unit, known as Handlangers, while until 1802 the Artillery Fusilier Battalion provided the men to move the ordinary guns in the reserve. The failure of ad hoc arrangements for the reserve guns in 1805 led to the creation of the Handlanger Korps in 1808, which supplied labour for all the ordinary guns, each of the 40 companies serving 2 or 3 batteries. Cavalry guns were fully crewed by qualified artillerymen and two Bombardiers would be in each howitzer crew. Since the mid-eighteenth century, artillery horse-team drivers had been fully militarised and became part of the Fuhrwesen in 1771, although most horses were drafted or bought in as war preparations began. The Cavalry guns were moved by the Kavallerie-Geschütz-Bespannungs-Division, which was formed in 1783 from the best drivers and horses. Although drawn from the Fuhrwesen, it was commanded by an artillery officer with an *Oberfeuerwerker* as his deputy, who dealt with the howitzers.

Often overwhelmed by the sheer numbers of French troops, many of Austria's gunners made their name skilfully handling batteries to halt French advances, including Frierenberger, Zadrazill, Schurzinger, Swrtnik, Stein and Fasching. Vega, Gillet and several others were noted siege gunners, while Rouvroy, Reisner, Kollowrat-Krakowsky and Perczel de Bonyhad made their names as Army Artillery Directors. Several more became prominent with their direction of the mobile Cavalry batteries, both to halt French advances and to launch swift attacks on them: most famous was Josef Smola, but this group includes Shuhay, Thiel, Moritz, Christ and Dietrich. Most of these men started as gunners or drummers, but went on to reach the rank of *Oberst* (colonel) and some made the Generalcy, including Smola, Dietrich, Kollowrat-Krakowsky (who transferred from the infantry as an *Oberst*) and Walper.[12]

ARMY ORGANISATION: TECHNICAL SERVICES

The Genie- und Fortifikationsamte (Engineering and Fortification Authority) directed the technical services. Its Director was supported by the all-officer Engineer staff, composed of 37 senior officers and 132 junior officers. Raised in 1747, their role was the construction and maintainance of fortresses, joining the army in wartime to deal with fortification work. They also directed a battalion each of Mineurs (miners) and Sappeurs (sappers), which would supply contingents to the field armies in wartime. The miners would deal with underground tunnelling at sieges, their officers being skilled in mathematics.

Raised in 1760 on the advice of the French siege engineer Gribeauval (who led contingents during the Seven Years War), the sappers were tasked with all the labour required at sieges and for building field fortifications, drawing only the strongest men, who would often work in a helmet and *kürass* breastplate as protection from enemy fire.

In the field, the Pioneers were low-skilled labourers, who constructed field fortifications and roads as well as clearing obstacles and handling the *Laufbrücken* (long trestle bridges, laid over long beams) for crossing smaller watercourses. They were only raised as battalions in wartime from 1758, but became a standing formation in 1806 and in 1809 fielded 9 divisions of about 400 men each, one attached to each *Korps*. The larger *Kriegsbrücken* (war bridges), mostly composed of pontoons, were built by the Pontoonier, who had been formed into a full Pontoonier-Bataillon in 1769. Established in 1764, the Tschaikisten riverboatmen of the Military Frontier were based at Titel, where the Theiss met the Danube River. Initially composed of four companies, the battalion was expanded in 1797 to six with a reserve company. The Tschaikisten manned shallow-draught riverboats, measuring 10 to 24m to guard the frontier. In wartime, they would augment the Pontooniers and assist the Pioneers with the *Laufbrücken*.

Formed in the eighteenth century to replace unreliable civilian drivers and horse teams, the *Militärfuhrwesen* (train) had several components: the Verflegungsfuhrwesen was raised in 1771 and became a formal korps in 1782, supplying the heavy transport teams and equipment for the Artillery, Pontoonier, Pioneer, Laufbrücken and the field bakeries. In all, 46 Bespannungs-Divisionen were allocated to the artillery. Secondly, the Packwesen, which supplied the pack animals and drivers for the army's supply requirements, was formed in 1784. The third was the Beschäl- und Remontierungsfuhrwesen, which was the remount service, supplying horses from across the Empire. The Fuhrwesen had retained a civilian element, called up in wartime to provide both drivers and horses for moving supplies to the field armies and magazines, but the service was fully militarised in 1808, when its officers acquired equal status with the rest of the army.

Medical services were limited in wartime and regulations required that officers were attended to first. Field hospitals (*fliegende Spitäler*) followed the army and were established in villages behind the main lines, staffed by attendants drawn from half-invalids and the less-attractive soldiers' wives. First-aid stations would be established in battle behind the centre and wings under the direction of *Stabschirurgen* (staff surgeons), who would provide the initial treatment before casualties were moved to the hospitals in empty supply wagons. Four garrison hospitals were founded in 1808 and a medical cart would accompany each regiment into battle as its own first-aid station. To prevent the loss of fit men moving casualties, a *Sanitätskorps* was raised in 1809 to bring wounded soldiers into the field hospitals and help care for them. In wartime, the army was usually operating far from the home depots, so horses that became ill or were lightly wounded in combat were treated in *Feld-Tier-Spitäler* (field veterinary hospitals) behind the army, which were run by a senior officer and a *Tierarzt* (vet) with an assistant and a chemist, supported by smiths plus supernumerary junior cavalry officers and NCOs. All of the non-specialists were drawn from retired cavalrymen or from the depot garrisons; the vets and chemists from the kk Tierspital. Raised in 1767, the *Tierarztspital* (veterinary hospital) was manned by half-invalids from the cavalry regiments.

Keeping an eye out for deserters and the borders were the Militärgrenzkordontruppen, which were reorganised in 1807.

ARMY ORGANISATION: THE *LANDWEHR* AND INSURRECTION

Known collectively as the Sedentärtruppen, these second line and largely untrained troops were poorly equipped and only fit for local defence duties. At the behest of Erzherzog Johann (Archduke John), the *Landwehr* was created on 8 June 1808 to form the home defence for the western provinces to release trained regular troops from garrison and communications guard duties. Bohemia supplied 55 battalions, Moravia and Silesia 12, Lower Austria 19 plus 6 from Vienna City, Upper Austria 15, Styria 13, Carinthia 5, Carniola 10, Salzburg 4, Trieste and the Littoral 2, and Gorizia and Gradisca 2. Half of the officers were local worthies, while the others were drafted from the line, which led to many NCOs being commissioned. Poorly equipped with a variety of old musket patterns and most not wearing anything more than peasant clothing under an *Oberrock* (greatcoat) with a peasant's broad-brimmed hat, their performance in action was poor, except for the Styrian battalions at Raab on 14 June 1809. Short of troops, Archduke Charles called twenty-three battalions to Vienna earlier that month and attached them to line regiments for further training, but after their first experience of being under fire on 5 July at Wagram, many deserted during the night.

The origins of the Insurrection went back to the seventeeth century and this feudal levy was organised in the 4 Hungarian districts (above/below the Danube and above/below the Theiss), within which were 19 infantry battalions at its largest extent in 1809, and 98 squadrons of Insurrection Husaren, based on the local *Komitate* (counties). The call-out had to be authorised by the Hungarian Diet, although in 1797, when some western units were called up, it was organised by the Komitat authorities. In 1808, the Diet agreed to a standing Insurrection of 60,000 troops, which their Habsburg Palatine (viceroy), Archduke Joseph, could call out without further reference. Its complete failure in the Battle of Raab meant the dissolution of the Insurrection a few years later. In Croatia and Slavonia, the Insurrection comprised separate organisations: the Personal, Banderial and Portal, providing fifteen battalions and a few Husaren squadrons. Siebenbürgen's Insurrection (4 infantry regiments and 1 Husaren regiment) guarded the Carpathian Mountains border passes. A small similar force was raised on the Littoral (coastline).

FLAGS

The main pattern in service at the start of the wars was the 1780 pattern introduced by Joseph II to reflect his policy of moving away from reliance on the Holy Roman Empire to focusing on Habsburg Lands. It is often known as the 1792 pattern, but that only differed in the Buchstaben (Emperor's cipher) being 'FII', appearing on either side of the complicated central shield with its many quarterings, and carrying all the coats of arms of the territories held or claimed by the Habsburgs. The Walloon infantry regiments' Ordinärfahnen added some local symbols, including the red cross of Burgundy behind the Doppeladler and the arms of St Omer beneath it. Each infantry regiment carried two flags per battalion: the 1st or Leib Battalion carried the white Leibfahne and one yellow Ordinärfahne, while the others used two Ordinärfahnen. As an object of near religious significance with the Madonna and Child on the obverse, the Leibfahne was always carried by each regiment's 1st Battalion.[13] The Grenadier battalions only ever took a single spare Ordinärfahne from one of the regimental depots when marching out for war, except in 1805.[14]

The 1804 pattern flag was issued under an Imperial Patent of 11 August 1804 as a restatement of the title of Holy Roman Emperor at the time of the creation of the Austrian Empire, but the production order was not issued until 28 March 1805. It appears only two were ever made. As the new organisation was implemented, an Imperial decree of 22 June 1805 reduced the flags to one per battalion, the Grenadier (or Leib) Battalion carrying the white Leibfahne and the others carrying one Ordinärfahne each.

In 1806, when the army reverted to its former organisation, so did the flags, i.e. the Leibfahne plus one Ordinärfahne for the 1st (Leib) Battalion, two Ordinärs for the others. The 1806 pattern, introduced under an Imperial decree of 6 December 1806, reflected the Emperor's new primary Austrian title and was used until 1816. The provincial shields were moved individually to the outer edge of the eagles' wings and the Buchstaben were abandoned. However, in 1808, the number of flags was reduced to one per battalion, the Leibfahne then being the only flag of the 1st Battalion. The cavalry carried Standarten, which were smaller versions of the Fahnen, with each division having a standard.

Many of the surplus 1806 flags were issued to the *Landwehr* battalions. However, the Styrian battalions carried variations on a local saint (obverse) and the Styrian panther (reverse) in green and white, as was the edging. The Wiener Freiwillige were presented with 1806 pattern Ordinärfahnen, while three battalions of the Erzherzog Karl Legion carried flags dating from the 1800 Legion: The 1st's flag displayed the arms of Bohemia on the obverse and Moravia on the reverse against a white background with red flames at the edges; the 2nd's was a five-barred flag in yellow over blue with a black Doppeladler on each side;[15] apparently the 4th Battalion carried a rather crude red flag with some local symbols on a central shield.

Insurrection flags displayed a mix of national and local coats of arms. The multi-coloured Ehrenbände ribbons were only worn on the flag on ceremonial occasions.

TRAINING AND TACTICS

All regulations were issued in German, so all officers and NCOs had to be literate in the language. However, they would then explain the instructions to their men in their native tongue. In both the 1784 consolidation and 1807 overhaul, the regulations were grouped in a series of steps – the men and NCOs had to know the *Dienst* (service) and *Abrichtungs* (basic drill to company level) regulations, while junior officers had to be familiar with the Exercier (manoeuvre) regulations. From 1806, they received further instruction from a series of booklets, the *Beiträge zum practischen Unterricht im Felde* (*Contributions to practical education in the field*), which added to officer education by supplementing the basic regulations. Senior commanders had the 1784 regulations setting out their duties, but it was only Archduke Charles' *Grundsätze der höheren Kriegskunst* in 1806 (probably written mostly by Mayer) that sought to lay out a strategic philosophy. The space allocated to the experiences of the last Turkish and the French Revolutionary Wars reflected the army's need for a dual capability to face either foe.

Across the period, there was increased use of massed formations in battle, but the cost of the drill camps required to practise this kept such training to a minimum. At the *Ubungslager* (drill camp) held at Minkendorf in 1803, just 21 battalions of infantry, 3 Kürassier and 2 Husaren regiments took part, while the spring 1805 exercises in Italy required that line infantry played the role of the Grenzers, who had not yet arrived from their domestic agricultural duties. During the 1806–9 period, it was impossible to finance any camps, where the direction of large combinations of troops could be practised, and from 1801 the army was not fighting frequently enough for its leadership to gain practical experience against their battle-hardened French opponents. Between 1801 and 1813, much of the army only experienced seven months of campaigning.

Austria's Generals understood the French approach of 'total war', but knowing that Austria could not emulate it, adopted a generally cautious approach. This was consistent with the late eighteenth-century strategic cordon, designed to defend the Empire's long frontiers. While the Belgian campaign of the War of the First Coalition had featured several sieges, that aspect was soon abandoned. Tactically, the army used the standard linear approach and would fight in two *Treffen* (battlelines), with the second usually formed in columns until the armies engaged, and a smaller third *Treffen* as the reserve. The infantry would form in long lines, three ranks deep with light cavalry usually on the flanks. The Reserve artillery and especially the Cavalry batteries would move to key points as the battle developed. From the time of the 1769 regulations, the third rank had, however, also been formed into separate, large *Züge* (platoons), which were then used for various tasks, including extending the regimental line, forming flank guards and *Feldmarschall* Saxe-Coburg's especially effective tactic of forming small hit squads to deal with French skirmishers. This was necessary due to the chronic shortage of Grenzers, so Mack's 1794 regulations for the army in Belgium continued to emphasise the use of these third-rank troops as skirmishers. The line infantry were quite capable of skirmishing, even breaking down whole regiments into open order (notably IR7 at Tournai in May 1794), although it became necessary for the senior command to remind junior commanders that at most only a third should be used in open order to take or hold villages and broken ground, a task usually performed by the light infantry. The noted French light infantry leader Duhesme recognised their effectiveness in Belgium:

> These advance guards, well handled, only disputed their ground long enough to make us waste time and men. They brought us from one position to another till they reached that which they really meant to defend. There they let us use up and scatter our last battalions whose ardour generally shattered itself against their entrenchments. Then fresh troops issued from them in the most perfect order; they, in their turn, threw out skirmishers upon our flanks, and thus they charged at advantage troops dispersed and fatigued, corps in disorder and unable to rally most of their men.

Cavalry in the earlier period formed in three ranks and tended to charge in small formations as the division of two squadrons was the basic tactical unit. The last Turkish War (1788–91) had produced an emphasis on mounted firepower, so all the cavalry were armed with carbines as well as swords (or curved sabres for the Husaren and Uhlanen). It was only when fighting the Turks that the Kürassier were issued with backplates and tailed helmets for additional rear protection. Fighting the French required a tactical shift to larger formations and the reduced use of firing weaponry (the Kürassier abandoned most of theirs in 1798). They maintained a complete superiority over the French in most battles of the Revolutionary Wars, securing the flanks and allowing the infantry to maintain a steady volley fire in line, while mounting charges to decide battles like Würzburg in September 1796. However, fighting in the terrain of northern Italy with its small fields separated by trees and ditches made it hard to make this superiority count. The likelihood of fighting in such terrain was one reason for the significant reduction in the *Schlachtenkavallerie* in 1801, in favour of the *Leichte*. The move to two ranks began in 1796, but was only set out in the provisional 1804 regulations, confirmed in 1806.

Well-established tactics dictated that a commander open a battle by pounding key sectors in the enemy line with the heavier batteries and then deploying the mobile guns at the important points. The French had a range advantage as they used bigger charges, their effective range (distance to first graze of a round shot fired at zero elevation) of 700 paces (500m) being about 200 paces more than the Austrians' 500 paces (350m), but once the Austrians closed the range to their advantage, their fire was more accurate than the French. The battalion guns would operate ahead of the main infantry lines in small ad hoc batteries and only withdraw when enemy troops came too close. The Cavalry guns, with their increased speed, were now the primary weapon, rather than the supporting weapon of the mid-eighteenth century, as they could operate with a small light cavalry escort. At Neerwinden in 1793, Smola took his Cavalry battery forward from the lines with a small Hussar escort and engaged Miranda's column for more than 3 hours before the infantry even arrived. Then he added several heavy calibre weapons and battalion guns to break it apart and prepare the way for the decisive Austrian cavalry charge, which threw the French back in disorder, before directing batteries in support of the infantry attacks. When Dumouriez renewed his attack, Smola once again took what remained of his battery forward together with 2 12pdrs and 2 6pdrs to within 300 paces of the French line and poured canister into it. A few days later, he directed a decisive battery attack at Löwen.

At Famars, Duka and Rouvroy placed a Cavalry battery on the front of each of four columns (advancing over difficult ground) and smashed through the French position. Throughout the 1790s, in battles involving about 30,000 men per side, the Austrians were regularly deploying 17–18 gun batteries, notably at Würzburg and Marengo, holding parts of the line or on the advance. Cavalry batteries were standard parts of advance and rearguards – Freirenberger's battery halted a French advance at Austerlitz to extricate Bagration and two batteries wrecked Beaumont's cavalry at the end.

The *Observationspunkte* issued by Archduke Charles in 1796 to his senior commanders in the campaign in Germany shows a fundamental shift. The long lines of infantry were now broken up into separate brigades to improve control. Infantry and cavalry would usually form in two ranks instead of three. Reflecting an emphasis on decisive attacks, the role of light troops was downgraded: 'Regular well-drilled and steady infantry cannot be impeded by skirmishers. All the shooting and skirmishing decides nothing'. In contrast, there was increased emphasis on moving troops in column rather than in line, prior to close contact, where the troops would again form lines. Charles was also recognising the new realities of war – training should not only be aimed at improving the physical condition of the troops, but also their teamwork and initiative, thereby increasing the troops' innate courage and capabilities. Artillery was to be massed in batteries, although this would only be formalised across the army in 1808.

The 1806–7 regulations are often considered to be a major overhaul of the way the infantry fought, but in fact they represented little change with a continued emphasis on linear tactics, while columns were used more for manoeuvre. Nevertheless, they changed the view of the soldier as a machine – directed by his superiors, in the 1769 regulations – to a humane approach, designed to invoke an *esprit de corps* and devotion to duty among the men. Corporal punishment was abolished (although desertion remained a capital offence), but was reinstated when Markgrafneusiedl village was set alight just before the Battle of Wagram. Many of the elaborate drills were discontinued, but the emphasis remained on linear formations to bring the maximum number of muskets to bear on the enemy. Two additional sections in the 1807 *Exercier-Reglement* cover Masses and skirmishing. A Mass was simply a column of march (with the sub-units spaced a unit frontage from each other so they could each form to the flanks) which was then closed up to half-distance between each sub-unit or fully closed up. As armies became larger, the density per unit of frontage increased and so more men had to be packed in together, while the loss of cavalry superiority after 1801 meant infantry formations had to be deeper and more solid to defend against outflanking. Although more vulnerable to artillery fire than squares, they could be formed much more quickly and then moved. The regulations provided for Battalion Masses formed on a company frontage (with each company three ranks deep) and a smaller version, the division Mass (two companies on a half-company frontage), as well as regulating how they would fire volleys to meet cavalry attacks. At Aspern, the battalions set off in open columns of march, closing to half-distance as the French became visible and then closed up as the skirmishers engaged. Several Battalion Masses were broken up by French artillery fire and the most effective formation was found to be a division Mass formed on a company frontage, so that the depth was six ranks, which was known from a century earlier to be firm enough to hold off cavalry. The Masses were formed up *en echequier* (chessboard style) with artillery in the gaps, a formation that broke the French cavalry charges. Thereafter Battalion Masses were usually only used in the early stages of battles for deployment marches.

The section of the *Reglement* dealing with skirmishers is one of the few regulation texts from the period. It was designed as a training manual for skirmishers drawn from the third rank of each company (where the more intelligent *Gemeine* (privates) could be found) and also, based on the cavalry practices confirmed in their 1807 regulations, sought to lay out a basic guide for the formations operating with larger support sub-units behind the skirmish screen.

Little changed in the last wars as the division Mass remained the main tactical formation in battle and Schwarzenberg's August 1813 'Instructions' confirmed the old practice of the second *Treffen* and reserve remaining in column (closed up to Battalion Masses in battle) throughout the action. The maximum number of skirmishers remained one-third per battalion, although the units tended to use volunteers rather than just the third rank, and would when necessary use them to reinforce the *Jäger* and other light troops in the outer screen and for advance guard duties.

In 1809, the Treaty of Schönbrunn limited the Austrian Army to 150,000 men, but despite the 1811 state bankruptcy, the reserve system helped to keep 260,000 troops on the rolls, although the army was hard-pressed to equip and supply the 30,000 troops of the Auxiliary Korps, which joined Napoleon's disastrous 1812 invasion of Russia. Nevertheless, with the lifting of many conscription exemptions and taking of under-age men, the Austrian Army managed to assemble 479,000 combatants by August 1813. As Austrian troops arrived in Paris in 1815 as part of the Allied occupation, this multi-national army had achieved its primary purpose: after twenty-three years of war and upheaval, the Habsburg Empire still existed.

NOTES

1. 1769 regulations, p. 19.
2. The 1769 *Generalreglement* was combined with other regulations and consolidated in the 1786 *Generalreglement*, where the reference is at: Book 1, Part 2, Chap. VIII, p. 145f.
3. *Kriegsgeschichtliche Abteilung des k.u.k. Kriegsarchivs: Kriege gegen die französische Revolution* (Vienna, Seidel, 1905), Vol. 1, p. 2 (based on the 1792 *Militär Almanac*, p. 9).
4. M. Rauchensteiner, *Kaiser Franz und Erzherzog Carl* (Vienna, Verlag für Geschichte und Politik, 1972), p. 108.
5. The Archduke's *Denkschrift* was published in *Osterreichische Militärische Zeitschrift* (Vienna, Streffleur, 1860), III, 229–33.
6. The 1805 *Vorschrift* is reproduced in O. Regele, *Generalstabschefs aus vier Jahrhunderten* (Vienna, Herold, 1966), p. 55.
7. J.B. Schels, 'Memoire fur Offiziere, die sich zum Dienst des GQM Stabs bilden wollen', in *Ost. Militarische Zeitschrift 1811* (Vienna), Vol. 4, p. 77ff.; G. Rothenberg, *Napoleon's Great Adversaries* (London, Batsford, 1982; reprt 1995), p. 173.
8. *Kriegsgeschichtliche Abteilung des k.u.k. Kriegsarchivs: Befreiungskriege 1813* (5 vols, Vienna, Staatsdruckerei, 1911–13), Vol. V, *Leipzig*.
9. A. Horsetzky, *Kriegsgeschichtliche Ubersicht der wichtigsten Feldzüge in Europa seit 1792* (Vienna, Seidel, 1888), p. 31f.
10. The Lüttich (Liege) Freikorps flag is a white cross with each quadrant divided diagonally into two, apparently red over blue. The flags of IR32 Esterhazy have a blue background in place of the usual yellow on their 1792 Ordinärfahnen. The 1806 pattern IR17 Ordinärfahne does not have white flames pointing outwards, suggesting just red and black inward-pointing flames.
11. The only good survey of the whole subject is A. Dawson, P. Dawson and S. Summerfield, *Napoleonic Artillery* (Marlborough, Crowood Press, 2007).
12. See A. Dolleczek, *Geschichte der österreichischen Artillerie* (Graz, Akademische Drück und Verlag, repr. 1970), pp. 696–708.
13. Pierre Charrie, the authority on French flags, also researched Austrian flags carried in Russia in 1812. IRs 2, 9, 19, 30, 32, 33, 34, 41 and 58 were still carrying the 1792 pattern.
14. Dr F. Kaindl, *Von den gemalten zu den gewebten Feldzeichen* (Wien, Schriften des Heeres-geschichtlichesmuseum, 1969), Vol. 4, pp. 39–49).
15. G. Amon von Treuenfest, in *Österreichische Militärische Zeitschrift 1883*, Vol. III, p. 259.

Chapter Four

The Prussian Army

Oliver Schmidt

As a result of its bitter defeat in the War of the Fourth Coalition of 1806–7, Prussia lost half its territory and a series of military reforms were undertaken to improve leadership and modernise tactics. Great emphasis was laid on the training of officers and other ranks to prepare them for all the circumstances they might encounter on campaign. As a result of the decision to recruit only Prussian subjects and by improving the treatment of soldiers, the public image of the common soldier was radically enhanced. This was one of the pre-conditions for the introduction of general conscription in Prussia in 1813 and 1814 for the duration of the war. This chapter will focus on the most important aspects of the administration and organisation of the Prussian Army during the period from 1803–15.

ARMY ADMINISTRATION AND ORGANISATION

The Adjutant General

The king had at his personal disposition adjutants general, holding the rank of colonel or general, and several wing adjutants, whom he employed for special tasks, and occasionally also for diplomatic missions. A Wing Adjutant (*Flügel-Adjutant*) was always a staff officer. By virtue of seniority the senior Adjutant General (*General-Adjutant*) served at the head of army administration, reported directly to the king and represented the latter when conducting business with military authorities. All orders, reports, proposals, requests and other related matters passed through his hands. By 1809, however, his role had been superseded by the head of the War Department.

The Supreme War Council (to 1809)

The Supreme War Council (*Ober-Kriegs-Kollegium*) served as the central body for the administration of the army. On 21 November 1796, it was reorganised into four independent departments, the positions of president and vice-president of the Supreme War Council becoming effectively honourary titles. The first department (*Erstes Departement*) was in charge of infantry, cavalry and artillery in general, including their mobilisation, as well as of stocks, provisions and quarters for the army. The responsibilities of the second department (*Zweites Departement*) concerned uniforms, weapons, equipment and financial affairs. The third department (*Drittes Departement*) dealt with invalided soldiers. The fourth department, the department of engineers (*Ingenieur-Department*), performed a fairly independent role but also encompassed engineering and thus was responsible for the construction and maintenance of fortresses, as well as of equipment and siege work. Several departments stood subordinate to the Supreme War Council: the General Legal Department (*General-Auditoriat*), the General War Cash Office (*General-Kriegskasse*) and the Military Registry (*Geheime Kriegs-Kanzlei,* literally the (king's) personal war registry). In order to arrange for the provision of food for the army, upon mobilisation a field subsistence department (*Feld-Verpflegungs-Departement*) was created.

The head of the first department of the Supreme War Council served simultaneously as head of the Military Department (*Militär-Departement*) of the General Board of Finance and Administration (*General-Direktorium der Finanzen und Administration*), which was basically responsible for financial transactions relating to the military. However, its tasks also involved organising the provision of supplies for the troops on marches or during the annual reviews and resolving disputes between military and civilian authorities which could not be sorted out at the local level. On 10 May 1808, the artillery branch of the first department was transfered to the fourth department, which took the name, Artillery and Engineer Department (*Artillerie- und Ingenieur-Departement*). Shortly thereafter, on 15 July, the Higher War Council was initially re-organised into two main departments, the first of which (*Erste Hauptabteilung*) managed everything relating to the organisation and command of the army, while the second (*Zweite Hauptabteilung*) was responsible for all financial affairs.

The Ministry of War (from 1809)

By an order of 25 December 1808, the Higher War Council was renamed the War Department (*Kriegs-Departement*), its first and second main departments designated as the General War Department (*Allgemeines Kriegs-Departement*) and the Military Economy Department (*Militär-Ökonomie-Department*), respectively. This new organisational structure was put into practice from 1 March 1809, but from this time the War Department was already often referred to as the Ministry of War (*Kriegs-Ministerium*). The War Department was divided into three subdivisions. If nobody else was appointed as Secretary of War (*Kriegs-Minister*), the head of this department was to fulfill that role, and was a member of the Privy Council (*Staatsrat*). Its first subdivision (*Erste Division*) was responsible for everything relating to army personnel, especially officers. The head of this subdivision was at the same time head of the whole War Department.

The Military Registry stood subordinate to this subdivision. Its second subdivision (*Zweite Division*) was concerned with recruitment, training, education and army organisation, as well as manoeuvres, tactics and strategy. For the latter purpose, a staff officer of the General Staff was attached to it. The third subdivision (*Dritte Division*) was in charge of artillery, engineers and fortresses. A staff officer of artillery and one of engineers were attached to this subdivision. The Department of Military Economy was divided in four subdivisions. Its first subdivision (*Erste Division*) was responsible for financial affairs. The General War Cash Office was subordinate to this subdivision, which also dealt with the quartering of troops and the army orphanage in Potsdam. Its second subdivision (*Zweite Division*) was responsible for organising the provision of food for the troops. The third subdivision (*Dritte Division*) dealt with everything relating to clothing the army. Its fourth subdivision (*Vierte Division*) managed the affairs of invalid soldiers. Alongside these two main departments stood the War Commissary (*Kriegs-Kommissariat*), led by the General War Superintendent (*General-Kriegs-Kommissarius* or *General-Kriegs-Kommissair*). He had one superintendent (*Kriegs-Kommissair*) as an assistant, and one superintendent each was attached to the six brigades of which the army consisted. In peace time, the War Commissary was to prepare all the stocks and equipment required to mobilise the army, as well as to supervise the supplies of the army generally. During periods of hostility, the War Commissary was responsible for all provisions for the army and administered the Field Cash Office (*Feld-Kasse*), from which expenses for mobilised troops were paid. Troops that were not mobilised continued to be paid from the General War Cash Office.

The Ministry of War (from 1814)

On 28 August 1814, the Ministry of War was reorganised again, into five departments, designated by numbers only. The first department essentially encompassed the tasks of the former second and third subdivisions of the War Department, and was divided into sections for the army (specifically, infantry and cavalry), the artillery and the engineers, respectively. The second department consisted of the General Staff, responsible for preparing the army for future operations. The third department was the former first subdivision of the War Department. The fourth department consisted of the former Department of Military Economy, except its fourth subdivision. The fifth department was formed from the former War Commissary. The additional Department for Invalids (*Departement für die Invaliden*) was formed from the former fourth subdivision of the Department of Military Economy.

THE GENERAL STAFF

The Prussian General Quartermaster Staff (*General-Quartiermeister-Stab*) was reorganised by an order of the king dated 26 November 1803. It was divided into three departments, one department (*Brigade*) for the eastern part of the state (the area on the right bank of the River Vistula), another for the western part (west of the River Elbe), with a third department covering the southern part, in effect the remainder of the kingdom. The General Quartermaster (*General-Quartiermeister*) managed the General Quartermaster Staff, while a Lieutenant General Quartermaster (*General-Quartiermeister-Lieutenant*) stood at the head of each department. This division into three departments ceased after 1807. Its tasks in peace time were to develop operational plans for the next conflict, to study defensive or offensive positions in potential theatres of operation, suitable sites for army encampments on Prussian territory and to produce detailed maps useful for future operations. After 1808, activity focused on exploring possible theatres of war and the study of recent campaigns. On 29 January 1810, the king directed that officers of the General Staff should serve for some time with different branches of the army in order to widen their practical knowledge. On mobilisation, officers of the General Staff were distributed amongst the staffs of the various generals in command.

THE GENERAL INSPECTIONS

From 1763 regimental cantons were grouped together in General Inspections (*General-Inspektion*) of cavalry and infantry, with each General Inspection under the direction of a General Inspector (*General-Inspekteur*). On 4 November 1796, his task was defined as collecting the reports sent in from regiments and forwarding them to the Higher War Council, organising the mobilisation of regiments, supervising the instruction of officer candidates, maintaining military hospitals and schools for soldiers' children, sorting out local problems with civilian authorities and supervising the administration of the light battalions stationed within the boundaries of their respective inspections. The field artillery and the lancer corps formed state-wide inspections of their own. All inspections ceased to exist in the course of 1806 and 1807. On 16 February 1810, Major-General von Yorck was made General Inspector of all light troops (rifles, fusilier battalions and hussars) in order to prepare them for field duties. This position was abolished on 13 April 1812 as it was no longer necessary.

ARMY BRIGADES

On 9 and 16 September 1808, the army was reorganised into six divisions that were named after the provinces in which they were located. However, probably owing to the restrictions imposed on the strength of the army by the Convention of Paris, the king preferred to apply to these six divisions the designation *Brigade* (Brigade). The brigades were renamed *divisions* as late as 5 September 1818. The officer in charge of a *Brigade* was known as a general of brigade (*Brigade-General*), with two brigadiers (*Brigadiers*) under him at the head of the infantry and cavalry, respectively. The artillery had a state-wide general of brigade of its own. The main task of a brigadier was defined on 24 December 1808 as ensuring that the units in his brigade remained ready for field duties at all times, by means of organising combined manoeuvres. He supervised the brigadiers and assumed their role if the position fell vacant. If problems arose between the regiments, the general of brigade was to solve them, as well as any disputes between the army and civilian authorities concerning recruitment.

An order of 3 August 1808 laid down that in peace time the task of the brigadier was to ensure the units' tactical readiness for war. He also had to supervise discipline, jurisdiction and other internal regimental matters without, however, interfering directly. Regarding the preparation of light units for field duties, each February a special brigadier was appointed to every army brigade. The regimental commanders of the three artillery regiments acted as brigadiers, while a special brigadier oversaw all nine horse artillery companies. On campaign, the general of brigade was to lead the brigade, including the two brigadiers commanding the units of their respective arms. The six brigades were mobilised this way for the spring campaign of 1813, by which time extra reserve artillery and reserve cavalry were attached to every army corps. As the army expanded that year, more brigades were added and the original six ceased to exist. An order of 6 March 1813 changed the designation of general of brigade to brigade chief (*Brigade-Chef*) and of brigadier to brigade commander (*Brigade-Kommandeur*).

An order from the king dated 27 July 1813 declared that the *Landwehr* (literally country defence – a rough equivalent to militia) regiments who were part of the field army should not fall under the command of the brigade commander, but rather directly under that of the brigade chief. If two *Landwehr* regiments were assigned to one brigade, a particular brigade commander for these two regiments was to be appointed, although this practice ceased during the autumn campaign. On 20 September 1814, a brigade chief specifically for the Guards was appointed, and on 21 February 1815, all Guard infantry and cavalry units as well as the two grenadier regiments were grouped together in Guards and grenadier brigades, respectively.

THE GOVERNORS

After 1808, a governor (*Gouverneur*) resided in the capitals of five provinces, though not all these positions were always occupied. By 1812, there was a governor-general (*General-Gouverneur*) assigned to several provinces: one for East and West Prussia, one for Pomerania and Brandenburg and one for Upper and Lower Silesia. Sometimes the king honoured a commander of a town or fortress with the title of governor, but these posts should not be confused with those of provincial governors. On 24 December

1808, a governor's tasks were defined as overseeing fortresses and supervising both the units of their assigned brigades as well as those that did not form part of a brigade (e.g. artillery, pioneers and invalid soldiers). He was also in charge of distribution of the units within the province, inactive officers and settling the more severe problems arising between military and civilian authorities. Units quartered in the capitals or fortresses were always considered as falling under the direct command of the governor of the province, although generals of brigade and brigadiers, having first notified the governor, were free to issue them with orders concerning their training. Between 15 March 1813 and 3 June 1814 general governments were temporarily replaced with the military districts. On 21 June 1815, they were finally dissolved, having already lost most of their responsibilities to the military governors on 3 June 1814.

MILITARY DISTRICTS

On 15 March 1813, the king ordered Prussian territory to be divided into four military districts (*Militär-Gouvernement*), one each for Silesia, for the area between the rivers Elbe and Oder, for the lands lying between the Oder and the Vistula, and for territory east of the Vistula. At the head of each district was a military governor (*Militär-Gouverneur*) in charge of all military affairs, including supplies and command over static troops, as well as a civilian governor (*Zivil-Gouverneur*), one of whose main tasks was to organise food and transport for the army. Both were to co-operate very closely and were jointly responsible for the formation of the *Landwehr*. On 9 April 1813, a fifth military district was created for the former Prussian possessions on the left bank of the River Elbe, which had been lost in July 1807 by the terms of the Treaty of Tilsit. On 19 November 1813, the king decided to create two military districts instead: one for the area between the rivers Elbe and Weser and one for the area between the rivers Weser and Rhine. On 3 June 1814, the military districts on the right bank of the River Elbe were dissolved, though those on the left bank remained unaffected.

THE GENERAL COMMANDS

On 18 June 1814, three commanders for the troops and fortresses in Silesia, in Kurmark, Neumark and Pomerania, and in East and West Prussia, respectively, were nominated, receiving the title general in command (*Kommandierender General*). Their responsibilities were defined on 28 August 1814 as supervising the training and preparing for operations the troops and fortresses under their command. Their area of authority was known as a general command (*General-Kommando*). On 3 October 1815, four more general commands were created, one each for Posen, (the new Prussian parts of) Saxony, Westphalia and the Rhineland.

REGIMENTAL NAMES

Since the eighteenth century, with few exceptions, every infantry and cavalry regiment had a regimental *chef* (*Regiments-Chef*), or proprietor, an honorary position which by that virtue did not furnish him the privilege of commanding his regiment in person. The equivalent in the British Army would be akin to 'colonel-in-chief'; i.e. the relationship between a member of the Royal family, in the capacity of holding an honorary colonelcy, and his or her regiment, such the 'the Princess of Wales's Royal Regiment'. If there were two *chefs* of the same name, they received the prefix '*Jung*' (young) and '*Alt*' (old) according to their seniority, e.g. in 1806: Infanterie-Regiment Alt-Larisch and Infanterie-Regiment Jung-Larisch. If the regimental *chef* died or was pensioned and was not replaced immediately, until the appointment of a new *chef* the regiment retained the name of the old one with the French prefix '*vacant*' or sometimes the Latin prefix '*vacat*'. Usually this was abbreviated as '*vac.*', e.g. in 1806: Infanterie-Regiment vac. Borcke.

Unofficially, regiments were numbered within their category of unit, according to the real or assumed date of their creation. The order of regiments was fixed by the king in 1788, though this seniority number (*Stamm-Nummer*) was not part of the regiment's name, even though it has been used by scholars for easy reference ever since. The fusilier brigades had a general as well as a regimental commander, bearing the title of brigadier (*Brigadier*), though they were named after the provinces in which they were cantoned rather than after an individual. Single battalions, primarily those of the grenadiers or fusiliers, were usually referred to by the name of their commander, e.g. Grenadier-Bataillon Fabecky, commanded by Major v. Fabecky of the Infanterie-Regiment Dierike.

As late as 1 October 1806, the king ordered that when compiling orders of battle regiments should always be designated by their number of seniority, grenadier battalions by the combined numbers of their two parent regiments, and for batteries the number of the artillery regiment to which they belonged. It appears, however, that this was instituted only with respect to the main army of 1806. On 7 November 1808, regiments received a designation according to the province from which they were mainly recruited, in order to avoid the frequent changes of names resulting from an out-going regimental *chef*. While seniority numbers were used in the army lists, this was not considered part of the regimental name and was not used in reports. Lancer regiments were initially identified by numbers, but these were replaced with provincial designations on 31 May 1809.

On 14 November 1808 the king allowed those regiments that still retained a regimental *chef* to continue to bear his name, e.g. Pommersches Husaren-Regiment v. Blücher. On 29 December 1809, however, this was to be discontinued, except for those regiments whose *chef* was a member of the Royal family, such as the Brandenburgisches Dragoner-Regiment Prinz Wilhelm. On 1 July 1813, the king ordered that henceforth the Guards should hold seniority over all other regiments. Since 1808, the Foot Guards had had the seniority number 8, and the Garde du Corps the number 3 amongst the cuirassiers. These numbers now being free, the infantry regiments with the seniority numbers 9 to 12 moved up by one, receiving the numbers 8 to 11, while the Brandenburg Cuirassier regiment changed its seniority number from 4 to 3. This, however, had no bearing on the names of these five regiments since, as explained earlier, their seniority number was not part of their regimental name. The new cavalry and infantry regiments that were formed in March 1815 (including the renamed reserve regiments) received no provincial designations before 5 November 1816, after the final decision respecting the placement of their garrison was reached. At the same time, seniority numbers at last became part of the regiments' names.

INFANTRY

Line Infantry until 1807

Following an order of 28 February 1799, from 1 June of the same year each infantry regiment consisted of two field battalions of five musketeer companies each, plus two grenadier companies. The grenadier companies of two regiments each were combined into a grenadier battalion, which was to act independently on a permanent basis both in peace time and during hostilities. Every infantry regiment, except the Guards, contained a third musketeer battalion (3. *Musketier-Bataillon*) of four companies, which acted as the regimental depot and therefore upon mobilisation did not march into the field with the army, but instead trained reinforcements. For those old soldiers who had become unfit for service, there was one invalid company (*Invaliden-Kompanie*) per regiment. Including the Guards, there were sixty infantry regiments. The formation of the 60th, Infanterie-Regiment Chlebowsky, had been ordered on 23 November 1802. Its third battalion was immediately created in order to train 400 men per year for the first 2 battalions, but by the outbreak of the war of 1806, only 2 provisional companies had been formed. By order of 31 October 1806, these two companies and their 3rd battalion were combined into a field battalion (*Feld-Bataillon*).

On 5 July 1806, the king ordered that in future every infantry regiment should consist of 3 field battalions of 4 companies each, plus 2 grenadier companies and 1 depot company (*Depot-Kompanie*). By order of 1 December 1807, the designation of this company was to be changed to garrison company (*Garnison-Kompanie*), though owing to mobilisation for the 1806 campaign, the execution of this order was postponed. At the end of the war in July 1807, due to the capitulations of fortresses and of units in the field, only nine complete regiments still existed (nos 2, 8, 11, 14, 16, 42, 52, 58, 60, the latter of only one battalion), and of fourteen regiments (nos 4, 7, 17, 30, 31, 33, 38, 46, 47, 50, 51, 53, 54, 55) only their 3rd battalion had survived. Of one regiment (no. 15), only a detachment remained. The complete grenadier battalion Jung-Braun (formed from the grenadiers of regiments 31 and 46) also remained, but was incorporated on 22 October 1807 into the grenadier battalion Wangenheim (8/42).

For manoeuvering, companies, which were always formed in 3 ranks, were split into 2 platoons each, so that a musketeer battalion consisted of 10 platoons while grenadier battalions consisted of 8 platoons each. On 1 October 1806, Lieutenant-General von Rüchel altered this system of organisation for the corps under his command, ordering that his regiments should consist of 3 battalions deploying in 2 ranks instead of 3. The 1st and 3rd battalions were to consist of 3 companies subdivided into 6 platoons, with 1 piece of artillery each, the 2nd battalion of 4 companies of a total of 8 platoons with 2 guns. He sought, however, to combine the regimental guns of a brigade into a single brigade battery.

PROVISIONAL AND RESERVE BATTALIONS, 1806–7

On 25 October 1806, the king ordered that from the provinces that had not yet been occupied by the French cadres had to be sent to Königsberg in order to form provisional battalions from them, each of four companies. On 14 January 1807 as well as their designation being changed from provisional battalion (*Provisorisches Bataillon*) to reserve battalion (*Reserve-Bataillon*) they were named after the province from which the cadres hailed and received a number, e.g. 1. Neumärkisches Reserve-Bataillon. Altogether, 6 West Prussian, 6 East Prussian, 3 Pomeranian, 3 Neumark and 1 Silesian reserve battalion were formed. The twelve West and East Prussian reserve battalions were disbanded after the end of the war.

FUSILIER BRIGADES UNTIL 1807

Light infantry regiments were named fusilier brigades (*Füsilier-Brigade*), each consisting of three battalions of four companies each. Their number had been fixed at eight on 18 February 1800. The designation of brigade instead of regiment was chosen because these units were purely administrative entities. On campaign, the battalions contained therein were employed independently, and on mobilisation every fusilier battalion established a depot of its own. At the end of the war, out of the original 24 battalions, only 8 complete units, detachments from a further 3 battalions and 14 fusilier depots still existed.

NEW FORMATIONS DURING THE CAMPAIGN OF 1806–7

After the catastrophe of 1806, in the regions and fortresses still occupied by Prussian forces many provisional units were formed from dispersed soldiers, recruits and volunteers. Some of these units had already been dissolved during the war in consequence of the capitulation of fortresses, but formations noteworthy for the fact that they had survived include the following: in the West Prussian fortress of Graudenz, the fusilier battalion v. Danielewitz was formed during the siege from men from dissolved fusilier battalions who had escaped and taken refuge there; in Pomerania, the Pomeranian provisional grenadier battalion (Pommersches Provisorisches Grenadier-Bataillon), better known after its commander as grenadier battalion v. Waldenfels (who took command on 18 February 1807 and was killed on 14 June), and the Pomeranian provisional fusilier battalion (Pommersches Provisorisches Füsilier-Bataillon) or fusileer battalion v. Möller, were formed at the fortress of Kolberg. Both consisted of four companies.

In the Silesian fortresses, a 4th battalion of infantry regiment Grawert (no. 47) and a 4th and 5th battalion for infantry regiment Alvensleben (no. 33) were formed. There were three reserve battalions, named after their commanders: v. Falkenstein, v. Dresler and v. Glan, the latter battalion usually referred to as national battalion v. Glan (National-Bataillon v. Glan), as well as grenadier battalion v. Losthin. In addition, in Silesia at the end of the war there remained twelve companies of light infantry, grouped in six divisions. Of these companies, 2 were designated as sharpshooters (*Schützen*), 8 as rifles (*Jäger*), 1 as fusiliers (*Füsilier*) and 1 as grenadier rifles (*Grenadier-Jäger*, owing to their being furnished with grenadier caps).

THE RE-ORGANISATION OF 1807–8

An order of 20 November 1807 laid down a new system of organisation for infantry, which was to become effective as of 1 January 1808. Each of the still extant line infantry regiments was to consist of 2 musketeer and 1 light battalion (*Leichtes Bataillon*, formerly a fusilier battalion, and was renamed from 1 December 1809 as *Füsilier-Bataillon*) of 4 companies each, plus 2 companies of grenadiers and 1 depot company (renamed garrison company on 1 December 1807). Some of the isolated battalions were merged, while others remained unaltered. On 21 November 1807, from three battalions a new regiment was created under the name Pomeranian (from 7 September 1808 the 2nd Brandenburg) infantry regiment. On 27 November 1807, from the garrison that had defended the fortress of Kolberg, two regiments were formed, which on 7 September 1808 received ordinary provincial designations, but on 14 September 1808 were instead renamed the Kolberg infantry and Life infantry regiments (Leib-Infanterie-Regiment), respectively. Due to the limitations imposed on the size of the army by the Convention of Paris, on 21 November 1808 the 2nd Brandenburg regiment was dissolved. On the same day the king ordered that all infantry units in Silesia should be consolidated into only two regiments. As a result, at the beginning of 1809 there were twelve infantry regiments, including the Guards. On 26 November 1808 the king decided that the Life infantry regiment should have a complete battalion of grenadiers (known as the Life Grenadier battalion) to compensate for the Guards, which had no extra grenadier companies.

COMBINED REGIMENTS OF 1812

For the 1812 campaign the king ordered that from the two regiments composing every brigade, two musketeer and one fusilier battalion were to be selected by lot in order to form a provisional regiment that was to take the field, with each such regiment identified simply by number. The purpose of this unusual system of organisation was to give parts of every regiment the opportunity of gaining some campaign experience. Only in the Brandenburg brigade was the complete Life infantry regiment (without its grenadiers) selected, as the king preferred the Guard infantry to remain with him.

RESERVE REGIMENTS OF 1813

In order to facilitate the training of new recruits, on 25 June 1811, for every battalion (except the Guards and the Rifles) a drill depot (*Exerzier-Depot*) was formed and combined into regimental drill depots, with drill depots formed for the cavalry and artillery as well. On 26 September 1812 the king ordered that as of 1 November the two regimental drill depots of a brigade should be combined into a brigade depot, with the exception of the East and West Prussian and the Brandenburg brigades, for the time being. This reform proved short-lived, for on 12 January 1813 these brigade depots were dissolved, the regimental depots re-established and all regimental depots brought to battalion strength, with an appropriate title, *Depot-Bataillon*. On 3 March 1813, these depot battalions were renamed as the 3rd battalion (*Drittes Bataillon*) of their regiment. On 1 February 1813 every line battalion of the army was to form a reserve battalion (*Reserve-Bataillon*), providing NCOs and experienced men for its cadre, the men being drawn from recruits. These reserve battalions were numbered, for example, the 4th Reserve battalion of the Life infantry regiment. Some battalions that had already been formed were integrated into this system.

Including the 3rd battalions, nine reserve battalions were formed in West Prussia, four of them having been named the 1st to 4th East Prussian militia battalions (Ostpreußisches Miliz-Bataillon) before 1 February 1813. In East Prussia, seven battalions were formed: the 1st to 4th East Prussian Musketeer Reserve battalion (Ostpreußisches Musketier-Reserve-Bataillon), and the 1st to 3rd Lithuanian Fusilier Reserve battalion (Litauisches Füsilier-Reserve-Bataillon), all of which retained their respective names until 1 July 1813. In Pomerania, 10 reserve battalions were raised, including 2 3rd battalions, while another 8 were initially named the 1st to 8th Militia battalions. In Silesia five 3rd battalions and twenty reserve battalions were created. In total, up to the armistice of June 1813, fifty-one reserve and 3rd battalions were formed, though on 28 May seven of these had been dissolved in order to bring the other battalions up to full strength. On 19 June two were used to replace the battalions converted to form the 2nd Guard infantry regiment. On 1 July 1813, out of the remaining forty-two battalions, a 12th Line infantry regiment and the 1st to 12th Reserve infantry regiments (Reserve-Infanterie-Regiment) were formed. The 1st, 3rd and 5th Reserve regiments consisted of four battalions, which were later dissolved.

THE REORGANISATIONS OF 1814–15

On 14 and 19 October 1814 the six grenadier battalions were formed into two independent grenadier regiments. The Russian and the Austrian emperors became the *chefs* of these two regiments, which bore their names: Kaiser Alexander Grenadier-Regiment and Kaiser Franz Grenadier-Regiment. On 25 March 1815, the infantry was raised to thirty-two regiments, using existing formations. The 1st to 12th Reserve regiments were renamed the 13th to 24th infantry regiments. The Lützow infantry regiment received the number 25 and the Elbe infantry regiment the number 26. The 27th was formed from the reserve battalion of the Elbe infantry regiment, and the Reiche and Hellwig infantry battalions. The infantry of the formerly independent state of Berg became the 28th and 29th regiments, the infantry of the German Legion the 30th and 31st regiments. The 32nd infantry regiment was initially to be created from former Royal Saxon infantry. After a rebellion of Saxon troops at Liège, the intended composition of the 32nd was ordered to be changed on 5 June 1815, and three *Landwehr* battalions to be used instead. This formation was complete as late as 25 November 1815.

RIFLEMEN

The Rifle regiment (*Feldjäger-Regiment*, meaning literally field huntsmen regiment) consisted of three battalions of four companies each. Equipped with rifles, its rank and file were composed of huntsmen, their sons or the sons of rangers, who after discharge received the right to be employed in the royal forests – a privilege the men of the sharpshooter battalions raised in 1808 and 1815 did not enjoy. During the 1806 campaign, rifle companies were distributed individually amongst the various army corps. After the disastrous defeats in October, nine companies in Pomerania and East Prussia and a small detachment in the Silesian fortress of Kosel were reformed from dispersed riflemen who had rejoined the army. Only two of the original companies of rifles reached the fortresses of Kolberg and Graudenz and thus remained intact at the end of the war.

On 14 and 16 November 1808, a new rifle battalion of four companies was formed from the rifles, named the East Prussian Rifle battalions (Ostpreußisches Jäger-Bataillon). On 21 November, two more independent battalions of four companies each were formed, one for the Guard from former riflemen, a second known as the Silesian Sharpshooter battalion (Schlesisches Schützen-Bataillon) from the best light infantrymen from the units in Silesia. On 16 March 1812 a depot for the East Prussian Rifle battalion, which had been mobilised for the campaign, was created. On 12 January 1813, the other two battalions also received a depot each; all these depots were dissolved after the 1814 campaign. On 19 May 1814, the number of rifle battalions was augmented by the Guard Sharpshooter battalion (Garde-Schützen-Bataillon).

On 18 April 1815, the rifle company of the former German Legion was taken into Prussian service. It took part in the 1815 campaign in the 5th Brigade with the designation of field rifle company (*Feldjäger-Kompanie*). On 9 August 1815, it was augmented with Saxon riflemen and called the Field Rifle Battalion of II Army Corps (Feldjäger-Bataillon des II. Armeekorps). On 29 August, it was renamed the 3rd (changed on 24 November to the 2nd) Rifle Battalion (Jäger-Bataillon), and received a provincial designation as late as 5 November 1816. In addition, on 3 October 1815, the Rhenish Sharpshooter Battalion (Rheinisches Schützen-Bataillon) was created.

NORMAL INFANTRY

On 14 May 1811, the formation of the Normal-Infanterie-Bataillon was ordered for the purpose of standardising the drill and service of all infantry units. 'Normal' has to be understood here in the sense of setting the norm, with officers and men detached from all line regiments for one year, after which they were to return to their regiments to be replaced by others. On 19 June 1813 the battalion was incorporated into the newly formed 2nd Foot Guard regiment.

GUARD INFANTRY

The infantry of the Royal Guard consisted of four battalions, which were named the Grenadier Guard Battalion (Grenadier-Garde-Bataillon, designated no. 6) and the Regiment of Guards (Regiment Garde, of three battalions, designated no. 15). The most prestigious of this latter unit was the 1st Guard Battalion (1. Bataillon Garde). To underline this contrast, sometimes only the 2nd and 3rd battalions were referred to as the Regiment of Guards (Regiment Garde). The guard units did not have depot battalions or invalid companies. Since the ordinary ranks in the Guard battalions were known as grenadiers, in order to differentiate them the men of their grenadier companies were called wing grenadiers (*Flügel-Grenadiere*). While it was ordered on 16 May 1799 that on campaign these four companies were to remain with their respective battalions, in peace time they formed a combined Guard Grenadier battalion (Garde-Grenadier-Bataillon, also known as the Grenadier-Bataillon der Garde, Flügel-Grenadier-Bataillon or, after its successive battalion commanders, Grenadier-Bataillon v. Forstner, and, from 28 May 1806, Grenadier-Bataillon v. Schwichow).

Only one small detachment of the Guard survived the capitulations of 1806, and on 4 November it was ordered to form the nucleus of a new depot of the Guard. Reinforced by dispersed Guardsmen and convalescents who had rejoined the army, as well as new recruits, it was reorganised into two companies on 24 January 1807. Slowly increasing in strength by the return of other Guardsmen, from 26 April 1807 the unit was designated a battalion, and on 27 June 1807 expanded from two into four companies. On 12 November 1808, the Foot Guard regiment (Garde-Regiment zu Fuß or, alternatively, Regiment Garde zu Fuß) was reformed into two battalions, to be augmented by a third, the Guard Fusilier Battalion (Garde-Füsilier-Bataillon), in 1809. On 21 November 1808, the organisationally independent Guard Rifle Battalion (Garde-Jäger-Bataillon) was created.

On 19 June 1813, the 2nd Foot Guard Regiment (2. Garde-Regiment zu Fuß) was created from the normal infantry battalion and one battalion each of the Life and Kolberg regiments. The old Foot Guard regiment added the number 1 to its name. On 19 May 1814, a Guard Sharpshooter Battalion (Garde-Schützen-Bataillon) was ordered to be formed from natives of the principality of Neuchâtel, which had been returned to Prussia by France.

In the summer of 1812, a depot for the Guard infantry was formed, followed by a second the following year. Both were dissolved on 22 August 1814, together with the depot of the Guard Rifle Battalion.

A secret article in the Convention of Paris of 8 September 1808 had limited the total strength of the Prussian Army to 42,000 men. The number of regiments was restricted, as well, with only the composition of the Royal Guard to be freely determined. In order to comply with this, French authorities were informed that the Life regiments named in 1808 constituted parts of the Royal Guard, though in reality neither they, nor the two grenadier regiments formed in October 1814, enjoyed the privileges of that formation.

CAVALRY

Cuirassiers and Dragoons (until 1807)

The 14 cuirassier regiments all consisted of 5 squadrons each, 2 of them (nos 10 and 13) enjoying Guard status. Two other regiments carried the distinctive names Life Regiment (Leib-Regiment, no. 3) and Life Carabiniers (Leib-Karabiniers, no. 11), without having any particular status or bearing the names of their respective regimental *chefs*. Only the regiments numbered 4 and 13 still existed at the end of the war, together with some parts of regiments nos 3, 5, 6, 8 and 11 (nos 5, 6 and 11 including their depots) and the depots of regiments nos 2, 7, 9, 10 and 12.

There were fourteen dragoon regiments, the formation of the last having been ordered on 24 January 1803. They had 5 squadrons each, with the exception of the dragoon regiments Königin (no. 5) and Auer (no. 6), which since the time of King Friedrich Wilhelm (Frederick William) I consisted of 10 squadrons, grouped into 2 battalions. On 5 March 1806, Queen Louise was made *chef* of dragoon regiment no. 5, which was henceforth called the Queen's Dragoon Regiment (Dragoner-Regiment Königin, or Königin Dragoner-Regiment). When the queen died on 19 July 1810, this regiment continued to bear this name, and indeed bore it until it was dissolved after the First World War. At the conclusion of the 1807 campaign, the regiments numbered 5, 6, 7, 8 and 13 remained intact, as well as some parts of regiments numbered 1, 3 and 4, together with all three of their depots. In addition, the depots of regiments nos 2, 9, 10, 11 and 12 still remained.

Based on an order of 6 May 1799, during the 1806 campaign a squadron of staff dragoons (*Stabs-Dragoner*) was created for the Main Army headquarters, the personnel of the squadron supplied by detachments from the dragoon regiments and other cavalry regiments and used for protecting the field cash office and transports, but also for carrying despatches. The unit was, however, dissolved during the course of the campaign.

Hussars (until 1807)

The 10 hussar regiments consisted of 10 squadrons each, grouped into 2 battalions of 5 squadrons. Included amongst the hussar regiments as regiment no. 9 was the lancer corps. Regiment no. 11 had been created in 1792, with a strength of only one battalion of five squadrons. As of 25 September 1795 it had no *chef*, so from its canton bore the name Ansbach Hussar Battalion (Ansbachsches Husaren-Bataillon), though this was changed to hussar battalion v. Bila (Husaren-Bataillon v. Bila) when v. Bila, its commander from 1792, became regimental *chef* on 15 April 1806. In addition, there were two small independent hussar detachments, one in Berlin and one in Magdeburg, each with its own uniform, and the soldiers of these acted as orderlies carrying despatches. The hussar detachment in Berlin (Husaren-Kommando zu Berlin) was dissolved on 21 August 1808, the detachment in Magdeburg having already been broken up with the capitulation of that fortress on 11 November 1806. At the end of the 1807 campaign, regiments nos 4 and 5 still existed in their entirety. Of regiments nos 1, 2, 6, 7, 10 and 11, some parts still remained, including their depots. Regiment no. 8, whose chief was Major-General v. Blücher, was forced to capitulate at Ratkau on 7 November 1806, but most of the men escaped and rejoined the army, reforming 5½ squadrons plus the depot, although the king considered the regiment as dissolved. Of regiment no. 3, only the depot survived.

Lancers (until 1807)

An order of 14 October 1799, which became effective on 1 June 1800, reorganised the lancer corps (Korps Towarczys, the denomination Towarczy being a corruption of the Polish word '*towarzysz*', which means comrade), dividing it into a lancer regiment (Regiment Towarczys) of ten squadrons and a lancer battalion (Bataillon Towarczys) of five squadrons. The corps was ranked amongst the hussars and bore the seniority number 9. Its troopers were drawn from the local Polish-speaking petty nobility in the province of New East Prussia, with all receiving the rank of carabinier. Upset by the high rate of desertion amongst Polish noblemen in the lancer corps, on 22 March 1807 the king ordered that they should lose the privilege of joining the lancers, and be regarded as equal to all the other recruits of the districts in which they lived. The fifth squadron of the lancer battalion consisted partly of tartars (Tartaren, a designation for Muslims), who had a Muslim chaplain (*Kaplan*) attached. However, for lack of recruitable Muslims, on 27 March 1806 this squadron lost its peculiar status. The lancers did not have a depot until, upon army mobilisation in 1805, a provisional depot was formed, and on 6 February 1807 the king ordered that the lancer regiment and battalion should maintain depots like the hussars.

PROVISIONAL FORMATIONS OF 1806–7

As in the infantry, the cavalry possessed many provisional formations in the field as well as in the fortresses. Only the more important ones shall be mentioned here.

By orders of 23 December 1806, eight provisional regiments were formed in East Prussia from regimental depots and complete cavalry regiments, as well as from dispersed soldiers who had rejoined the army. The first organisation was altered on 28 December, and on 12 January 1807 the king ordered these eight provisional regiments reformed by leaving out the regimental depots. Thus 1 provisional cuirassier regiment, 2 provisional dragoon regiments and 3 provisional hussar regiments were formed, each regiment (Brigade) consisting of four squadrons. By 20 December 1806, from the depots in Silesia, twenty squadrons in four battalions (named after their commanders, v. Görtz, v. Rumpf, v. Reisewitz and v. Wostrowsky) had been created. In February 1807, after the failed relief of the fortress of Schweidnitz, these squadrons had to take refuge in Austria and were dissolved. From dispersed soldiers, volunteers and the men remaining in the depots, ten new squadrons were formed up to June 1807, amongst these a squadron designated Horse Grenadiers (Grenadiers à Cheval; they were dragoons wearing grenadier caps until May 1807).

THE REORGANISATION OF 1807–8

On 16 October 1807, the lancer corps was reorganised into a single lancer regiment (Ulanen-Regiment) of 8 squadrons, the hussar regiment no. 5 was reduced to 8 squadrons and all other cavalry regiments (including the Queen's Dragoons) were reduced to 4 squadrons. An exception was the Garde du Corps, for which the order to be reduced to four squadrons was issued as late as 15 March 1808. Dragoon regiment no. 6 was split into a cuirassier and a dragoon regiment. Smaller detachments were also merged, so that in September 1808 the cavalry stood at 4 cuirassier regiments (including the Garde du Corps), 6 dragoon regiments, 6 hussar regiments (including the former regiment no. 5 of 8 squadrons, which had been awarded the name Life Hussar Regiment on 7 September 1808) and a lancer regiment.

On 5 December 1808, the Upper and the Lower Silesian Hussar Regiments were merged into a single hussar regiment, the 1st Silesian, and the ten individual squadrons of cavalry in Silesia that remained from the campaigns of 1806–7 were combined into the 2nd Silesian Hussar Regiment. On 23 November 1808, the lancer regiment and, on 20 December 1808, the Life Hussar Regiment were both split up into two independent regiments of four squadrons each. In May 1809, trying unsuccessfully to incite an uprising in northern Germany, Major von Schill deserted with the regiment under his command, the 2nd Brandenburg Hussar Regiment, which the king declared disbanded on 18 May 1809. On the same day a third lancer regiment was created to replace it.

COMBINED REGIMENTS IN 1812 AND FORMATIONS IN 1813

As in the infantry, for the 1812 campaign combined cavalry regiments were formed: 1 lancer, 2 dragoon and 3 hussar regiments, each from 2 squadrons selected by lot from 2 different regiments, the cuirassiers remaining unaffected. By an order of 26 March 1812, the two squadrons that were not mobilised formed cavalry depots for their regiments, whereas the drill depots of the cavalry that had been created on 25 June 1811 were dissolved. The number of regular cavalry regiments was not increased in 1813, but some changes to their organisation were undertaken. On 12 January the king declared that every regiment should form a depot squadron, and on 1 February orders specified that some of those regiments that had squadrons serving with the Prussian auxiliary corps were to form a combined regiment with a common depot squadron, while others should remain at a strength of two squadrons, with only half a depot squadron. Not until the armistice in June were the last regiments that had been split up for the 1812 campaign reunited.

NATIONAL CAVALRY

On 14 February 1813, representatives from the province of East Prussia volunteered to raise and equip a regiment of volunteers at their own expense to be known as the East Prussian National Cavalry Regiment (Ostpreußisches National-Kavallerie-Regiment). On 27 March, moreover, representatives of the provinces of Pomerania and Silesia were authorised to raise like regiments. These were named the Pomeranian Light National Cavalry (Pommersches Leichtes National-Kavallerie-Regiment) of 3 squadrons, and the Silesian National Hussar Regiment (Schlesisches National-Husaren-Regiment) of 4 squadrons, out of which only 2 were ever mobilised due to problems of recruitment and a shortage of equipment. On 28 October, the Elbe National Hussar Regiment (Elb-National-Husaren-Regiment) was also created, eventually reaching a strength of four field and one depot squadron.

THE REORGANISATION OF 1815

On 7 March 1815, the king ordered the creation of the 4th Cuirassiers, the 7th and 8th Dragoons, the 7th to 9th Hussars and the 4th and 5th Lancers, each initially of three squadrons. For this purpose, the existing cavalry regiments were to provide a squadron each. Many cavalry regiments were not able to create a fourth field squadron before the beginning of the Waterloo campaign. On 25 March 1815, the Elbe National Hussar Regiment was renamed the 10th Hussar Regiment, the Berg Hussar Regiment became the 11th Hussars and the cavalry that was to be absorbed from the Kingdom of Saxony was to become the 12th Hussar Regiment. The Lützow Cavalry Regiment was renamed the 6th Lancers, the Hellwig Cavalry became the 7th Lancers and, due to insufficient numbers, the two regiments of the German Legion had to be combined to form the 8th Lancers.

NORMAL CAVALRY

On 27 March 1811, like its counterpart in the infantry, the king ordered the creation of a normal cavalry squadron (*Normal-Eskadron*), consisting of a normal dragoon company (for cuirassiers and dragoons) and a normal hussar company (for hussars and lancers). In April 1812 these units were ordered to be augmented to squadron strength as of 1 June, and renamed Normal Guard Dragoon Squadron and Normal Guard Hussar Squadron.

GUARD CAVALRY

The cuirassier regiments Garde du Corps (no. 13) and Gensd'armes (no. 10) comprised the two Guard cavalry units, both of which shared the same particular organisation, their squadrons being subdivided into two companies each. The Gensd'armes were dissolved when its field squadrons capitulated in 1806, but the Garde du Corps was to retain its division into companies until 1888. On 29 March 1809, selected men of the 2nd Silesian Hussar Regiment were chosen to form a Life Lancer Squadron (Leib-Ulanen-Eskadron), which on 16 February 1810 was attached to the Garde du Corps and on 6 March 1810 was renamed the Guard Lancer Squadron (Garde-Ulanen-Eskadron). On 23 February 1813, the Guard Light Cavalry Regiment (Leichtes Garde-Kavallerie-Regiment) was created from the Guard Lancer Squadron, the two Guard Normal Squadrons and a newly formed Guard Cossack Squadron (Garde-Kosaken-Eskadron, ordinary Prussian cavalrymen dressed in Cossack-style uniforms and armed with lances). In 1813–14, both the Garde du Corps and the Guard Light Cavalry Regiment had a squadron of volunteer riflemen attached, which were named the Guard Volunteer Cossack Squadron (Garde-Volontair-Kosaken-Eskadron; they were also dressed in Cossack-style uniforms) for the former, and a Guard Volunteer Squadron (Garde-Volontär-Jäger-Eskadron, split in two in April 1813) for the latter. On 21 February 1815 the Guard Light Cavalry Regiment was dissolved and its squadrons combined with squadrons of the three old National cavalry regiments and a squadron of the Queen's Dragoons (no. 1) to create a Guard Dragoon, a Guard Hussar and a Guard Lancer regiment.

The pre-1806 Hussar Regiment no. 2 had been designated by King Friedrich Wilhelm I his Life Hussar Corps in 1739, and continued to use the title *Life* unofficially over the following decades. From the 1790s it was again officially known as the Life Hussar Regiment, together with the name of its *chef* (since 19 October 1805 the Leib-Husaren-Regiment v. Rudorff). As a result of an order of 2 February 1797, its officers thereafter ranked ahead of all others of equivalent rank in other hussar regiments. Apart from this, the unit did not enjoy any other privileges and was not considered part of the Guard. Similarly, the new Life Hussars of 1808 did not enjoy the privileges of the Guard.

THE HORSE FIELD HUNTSMEN CORPS

The Horse Field Huntsmen Corps (Feldjäger-Korps zu Pferde, or Reitendes Feldjäger-Korps) had been created in 1740. It was recruited from sons of rangers who after their service received the right to be employed in the royal forests. They were attached individually to staffs or sometimes units, and employed as guides (*Kolonnen-Jäger*) or, for the most part, as couriers (*Kurier-Jäger*). This corps existed throughout the Napoleonic Wars.

ARTILLERY

Before 1808, the artillery consisted of field artillery (including a pontooneer corps) and fortress artillery. In 1808, this distinction ended, and every Prussian artilleryman was trained to handle all types of guns, as well as howitzers and mortars.

Foot and Horse Artillery (until 1807)

In 1806, the foot artillery consisted of four regiments of two battalions each. An independent ninth battalion had been formed on 1 January 1796, but on 20 August 1805 its remaining three companies were transferred to the new horse artillery regiment, two of its companies having already been converted into horse artillery in 1799. On mobilisation, every company was employed to man one or two field batteries or artillery train formations. For the 1806 campaign, 6pdr batteries nos 1, 2, 3, 4, 5 and 8, 12pdr batteries nos 1, 2, 4, 5, 7, 8, 16, 17, 19, 22, 23, 24, 26, 27, 29, 30, 31, 32, 33, 34, 35, 36, 37, 38 and 39, as well as 7pdr howitzer battery nos 1 and 4 were mobilised, together with different artillery train formations. The batteries were usually referred to only by the name of their commander, a practice continued to a lesser extent in the campaigns of 1812–15. At the end of the war, only 6pdr batteries nos 1 and 8 and 12pdr batteries nos 31, 34, 37 and 39 still existed, all of them of the 4th Artillery Regiment, which was the only one of the four artillery regiments that was not dissolved.

The Horse Artillery Regiment had been created by an order of 20 August 1805 by converting the three companies of the 9th (Foot) Artillery Battalion into horse artillery companies and uniting them with the other seven horse artillery companies already in existence. On mobilisation, each company was used to man two field batteries. Horse batteries nos 1 to 20 were mobilised for the 1806 campaign, out of which batteries nos 7, 8, 9, 10 and 13 remained extant at the end of the campaign.

REGIMENTAL ARTILLERY

Every infantry company had some artillerymen attached who on mobilisation manned the regimental guns. On campaign, the fusilier battalions were to receive 1 3pdr gun, the other infantry battalions including the grenadiers 2 6pdr guns and the 3rd battalions, if also mobilised, 2 3pdr guns. However, in 1806, nearly all of the 3pdr regimental guns were not taken into the field. The Rifle Regiment did not have regimental artillery. On 1 October 1806, General Lieutenant v. Rüchel announced for the corps under his command that he might order them to form a battery from the regimental guns in each brigade. On 23 November 1806, the Prussian king ordered the army in East Prussia to unite the battalion guns into batteries of four to eight guns. After 1807, regimental artillery was abolished, though during the 1812 campaign the East Prussian Rifle Battalion made use of a captured 3pdr gun. In early 1813, this weapon was handed over to the newly formed 3pdr foot battery no. 1.

FORTRESS ARTILLERY

An order of 30 October 1800, which was to become effective on 1 June 1801, fixed the number of companies for manning fortress guns at fifteen, one fortress artillery company (*Festungs-Artillerie-Kompanie*) for each fortress, with the companies in the larger fortresses being of higher strength. An additional four fortresses contained only a small detachment (*Kommando*) of fortress artillery each. Only six of these companies and detachments still existed when the Fortress Artillery Corps was merged with the field artillery in 1809, the others having been dissolved with the capitulations of the fortresses to which they had been assigned.

THE REORGANISATION OF 1808

During the campaign of 1806–7, several provisional artillery units were created, some of which were not dissolved at the end of the war. On 24 November 1808 the king ordered that all extant artillery units were to be consolidated into 3 new artillery regiments, each regiment (*Artillerie-Brigade*, the designation *Artillerie-Regiment* being reintroduced as late as 1850) to consist of 3 horse and 12 foot companies. Each artillery regiment was commanded by a brigadier (*Brigadier*), the head of the whole artillery being Prince August von Preußen (the younger brother of Prince Louis Ferdinand von Preußen, who died in combat at Saalfeld on 10 October 1806) in the position of brigade general of artillery (*Brigadegeneral der Artillerie*). In addition, there was a brigadier for the horse artillery, responsible for supervising its tactical training, whereas in disciplinary matters the horse companies remained subordinate to the brigadier of the artillery brigade to which they belonged.

In 1809, one company of every artillery regiment was designated an artisan company (*Handwerks-Kompanie*), these being used for the construction and repair of the artillery and related equipment. On 20 June 1811, an independent musket manufacturing company (Gewehr-Handwerks-Kompanie) was formed from qualified soldiers and attached to the musket manufactuary in the Silesian town of Neiße.

Upon mobilisation, the personnel of the companies was used to form artillery batteries as well as laboratory trains, ammunition supply trains and artisan trains. A laboratory train (*Laboratorien-Kolonne*) and an artisan train (*Handwerks-Kolonne*) both followed the army, the former for producing ammunition, the latter for repairing damaged artillery equipment. An ammunition supply train (*Park-Kolonne*) consisted of spare caissons (ammunition wagons) and limbers with their ammunition, as well as ammunition carriages for infantry and cavalry. Some of the companies were not mobilised but used for manning fortress guns. The numbering of batteries and train columns essentially followed the order of their actual mobilisation, but naturally there were exceptions due to delays in communication and the fact that batteries were mobilised in fortresses all over the country. A 6pdr foot battery and a horse battery were to be composed of 6 6pdr guns and 2 7pdr howitzers each, a 12pdr foot battery of 6 12pdr guns and 2 10pdr howitzers. A 7pdr howitzer battery consisted of 8 7pdr howitzers.

THE MOBILISATION OF 1812 AND PROVISIONAL COMPANIES

Following an order of 12 March 1812, for the Prussian Auxiliary Corps the horse batteries nos 1 to 3, the 6pdr foot batteries nos 1 to 4, a half-12pdr battery (halbe 12pfündige Fuß-Batterie, bearing no number), the ammunition supply trains nos 1 to 5 and the bridging trains nos 1 and 2 were mobilised, mostly from the Prussian Artillery Regiment, as it was closer to the area of operations.

On 12 January 1813 the king ordered the creation of provisional artillery companies to be manned by recruits drawn from various cantons: 13 of them in the Prussian Artillery Regiment, 14 in the Brandenburg Artillery Regiment and 17 in the Silesian Artillery Regiment. These companies were identified by number (e.g. 1. provisorische Kompanie der Preußischen Artillerie-Brigade), though the number 13 in the Brandenburg Artillery Regiment remained vacant until June 1815, so that the numbering of its provisional companies extended to 15. When in 1814 the 1st company of the Prussian Artillery Regiment was transfered to the Guard, it was replaced by the 4th company, and the latter in its turn was replaced by the 1st provisional company of this brigade. Likewise, in 1814, the 1st horse and foot companies of the Brandenburg Artillery Regiment were replaced by its 5th and 6th provisional companies, respectively. Originally, a provisional artillery company (*provisorische Artillerie-Kompanie*) was to be stationed in fortresses, but field batteries were formed from several of them instead. The batteries and artillery trains mobilised in the 1813–15 campaigns from men who did not belong to a regular or provisional company were nevertheless assigned to one of the three artillery regiments indicated above.

MOBILISATIONS FOR THE 1813 AND 1814 CAMPAIGNS

In January or February 1813, half a 10pdr howitzer battery was formed under First Lieutenant Baumgarten. It was also called 10pdr howitzer battery no. 1 (10pfündige Haubitz-Batterie no. 1). On 1 February 1813, the formation of horse batteries nos 4 to 10, 6pdr foot batteries nos 4 to 13 and 16 (nos 14 and 15 remaining vacant for the moment, and the former 6pdr foot battery no. 4 receiving the number 6 instead), and half a 12pdr battery to augment the already existing half-battery to 12pdr foot battery no. 3 (nos 1 and 2 remaining vacant for the moment) was ordered. In addition, 3pdr foot battery no. 1 was created, which was to remain the only battery of this calibre. On 8 February 1813, 6pdr batteries nos 14, 15, 17 and 18, 12pdr foot battery no. 1 (of eight guns, without any howitzers) and howitzer battery no. 1 were ordered to be formed. In early 1813, First Lieutenant v. Liebermann formed from four captured guns a 6pdr battery, which was usually referred to as half battery Liebermann (Halb-Batterie Liebermann, bearing no number).

On 29 April 1813, the formation of a further twelve batteries was ordered, of which however only ten were initially created: horse battery no. 12, 6pdr batteries nos 20 to 27 (no. 19 remaining vacant for the moment) and 12pdr foot battery no. 2. With the exception of 6pdr foot battery no. 24 and 12pdr foot battery no. 2, these units were destined to be assigned to the *Landwehr*. Still, they constituted ordinary artillery units and did not wear *Landwehr* uniforms. The remaining two batteries, 6pdr foot batteries nos 28 and 29, were formed during the armistice of 1813. During that hiatus, half-battery Liebermann was augmented to become 6pdr foot battery no. 19, and half-battery Baumgarten was dissolved, its four howitzers divided between 12pdr foot batteries nos 1 and 4, augmenting the former to ten guns. In addition, 12pdr foot batteries nos 4 to 6 were formed. Shortly after the end of the armistice, 12pdr foot battery no. 7 and 6pdr foot batteries nos 30 to 33 were created, nos 30 and 33 being half-batteries. On 10 December 1813, 6pdr foot half-battery no. 30 was transformed into horse half-battery no. 13. New 6pdr foot batteries nos 30 and 34 were formed in early 1814, the former for use with the *Landwehr*. On 8 May 1814, the battery of Lützow's Freikorps was absorbed into the regular artillery as horse battery no. 14.

MOBILISATIONS FOR THE 1815 CAMPAIGN

The plan for the 1815 campaign envisaged the following allocation of artillery to each of the 6 army corps: 3 horse batteries, 5 6pdr foot batteries, 3 12pdr foot batteries, 1 7pdr howitzer battery, 6 ammunition supply trains, 1 laboratory train and 1 artisan train. In April 1815, 6pdr foot batteries nos 27 and 32 were transformed into horse batteries nos 16 and 17, and 6pdr foot half-battery no. 33 was used to augment horse half-battery no. 13 to full strength. Numbers 27, 32 and 33 remained vacant, as well as 28, 29, 31 – the three 6pdr foot batteries bearing the latter numbers being transformed into 12pdr foot batteries nos 15, 13 and 14, respectively. In May 1815, 6pdr foot batteries nos 35 to 37 were mobilised, the latter from the former Berg foot battery. On 15 April 1815, the horse batteries of the former German Legion were incorporated into the Prussian service as horse batteries nos 18 and 19. The ammunition supply train of the former German Legion was also integrated as number 19 (Train-Kolonne no. 19). Horse batteries nos 15 (for the Guard Corps) and 20 were mobilised in May 1815, the latter by augmenting the former Berg horse half-battery. On 1 April 1815, the 3pdr battery was transformed into howitzer battery no. 2, and in May howitzer batteries nos 3 to 6 were mobilised, together with 12pdr foot batteries nos 8 to 12 and 16 to 19. As the batteries of the Guard artillery were to receive the first (i.e. the lowest) numbers in each type of battery, in September 1815 horse batteries nos 1 and 2 were renumbered nos 21 and 22, respectively (nos 4 and 15 remaining vacant), and 6pdr foot battery no. 1 received the number 38 instead (no. 4 remaining vacant as well).

GUARD ARTILLERY

Before 1808 no Guard artillery existed. On 7 December 1808, a horse artillery company was selected to become the Guard Horse Artillery Company (reitende Garde-Artillery-Kompanie) and seven days later the king also created a Guard Foot Artillery Company (Fuß-Garde-Artillerie-Kompanie). These two Guard companies became the first horse and the first foot companies of the Brandenburg Artillery Regiment. In early 1813, these companies were used to form a Guard 6pdr foot and a 6pdr horse battery, which were named Reitende (Garde-)Batterie Nr. 4 and 6pfündige (Garde-)Fuß-Batterie Nr. 4. That both Guard batteries received the number 4 was coincidental, horse batteries nos 1 to 3 and 6pdr foot batteries nos 1 to 3 having already been formed from the Prussian Artillery Regiment. In early 1813, 6pdr foot battery no. 4 which had taken part in the 1812 campaign was assigned the number 6 instead. By order of 22 December 1813, a Guard Artillery Corps of its own was formed. For this purpose, the two Guard companies were separated from the Brandenburg Artillery Regiment. On 12 April 1814, moreover, the 1st company of the Prussian Artillery Regiment (which had formed 12pdr foot battery no. 1) was transferred to the Guard. In May 1815, horse battery no. 15 was formed for the Guard, raising the number of Guard batteries to four. Also in 1815, ammunition supply train no. 37 was mobilised for the Guard. As late as September of that year, Guard batteries were to receive the first numbers of their type of battery, so that Guard horse batteries no. 4 and 15 were designated 1 and 2 respectively, while 6pdr Guard foot battery no. 4 was renumbered to 1.

PIONEERS

Until 1806, the Pontooneer Corps (Pontonnier-Korps), which was technically part of the artillery corps, consisted of three companies. Only one company still existed at the end of the campaign. The Miner Corps (Mineur-Korps), of four companies, performed pioneer work in fortresses and in the field. Two of these companies remained operational when the war of 1806–7 ended. The Engineer Corps (Ingenieur-Korps) comprised only officers. By orders of 4 November 1809 and 12 February 1810, the United Engineer and Pioneer Corps (Vereinigtes Ingenieur- und Pionier-Korps) was created from existing pontooneers, miners and engineer officers, consisting of three brigades (the Prussian, Brandenburg and Silesian, respectively), each of several engineer officers and one company of pioneers. In 1812, an augmenting company (Augmentations-Kompanie) of pioneers was formed for the Silesian brigade. In March of the same year, three field pioneer companies were mobilised for the Prussian Auxiliary Corps that marched into Russia.

On 4 March 1813, the king ordered the formation of another four field pioneer companies, as well as three new fortress pioneer companies. By the beginning of 1814 the number of fortress pioneer companies had been raised to eight. From 2 August 1813, the seven field pioneer companies were no longer to be known by their provincial designation, but instead by number. After the county of Mansfeld had been reoccupied in late 1813, on 25 December the Mansfeld Pioneer Battalion (Mansfelder Pionier-Bataillon) of four companies was raised from local miners, at the cost of the province, to be employed in fortresses, though its companies joined the field army in 1815. On 20 April of that year two more field pioneer companies were formed.

VOLUNTEER RIFLEMEN

In order to provide young men of the educated classes with the chance to join the army without having to serve alongside ordinary soldiers who mostly came from the lower classes, on 3 February 1813 the king declared the creation of detachments of volunteer riflemen (*Freiwillige Jäger-Detachements*). These were attached as separate companies and squadrons to infantry battalions and cavalry regiments. Aspiring volunteers had to equip themselves at their own expense, but were allowed to select the regiment they wanted to join. The designation of volunteer rifleman (*Freiwilliger Jäger*) was also given to volunteers who joined the cavalry, even though only a few of the mounted detachments actually carried rifles. When Prussian forces re-occupied the provinces west of the River Elbe that had ceased to exist by the terms of the Treaty of Tilsit in 1807, detachments of volunteer riflemen were created there as well. Owing to the absence of line regiments from these areas, such formations were attached to *Landwehr* regiments or deployed as independent units. On 30 April 1814, a month after the end of hostilities, the volunteer rifle detachments were dissolved, though on 7 April 1815 the king ordered the creation of new ones for the Waterloo campaign.

PROVINCIAL RESERVE INFANTRY

In order to increase the number of units available to serve as fortress garrisons and for coastal defence, on 17 August 1805 the king ordered the formation of 26 provincial reserve regiments, known by the name of the province in which they were raised. Every provincial reserve regiment (Land-Reserve-Brigade) was to consist of three battalions of four companies each, though the battalion from Anspach (Ansbach) and Bayreuth was not raised at this time. The rank and file, to be led by retired officers returned to service, were drawn from those who had served for twenty years in the army, from invalids fit for garrison duty and from other men not needed for the field army, including young recruits. On 9 December 1805, the Supreme War Council was directed to raise these new formations in the coming year. With the purpose of relieving the burden from the Supreme War Council, the creation of these battalions was to be organised by provincial authorities, who were subordinate to the General Board of Finance and Administration. The latter, however, proved obstinate and raised objections, thus delaying execution, so that by the outbreak of the 1806 campaign in the autumn of that year none of these provincial reserve battalions had been raised.

LANDWEHR, 1813–15

On 17 March 1813, the king ordered the *Landwehr* to be formed. Early plans had intended the *Landwehr* to be used only within the country's boundaries, but by 1813 this had been changed, and some *Landwehr* units even reached Paris in 1814 and again in 1815 after Waterloo. Recruited from men who had not been selected for the regular army, *Landwehr* units consisted of infantry and cavalry, but no artillery, raised and equipped by civilian provincial authorities instead of the Ministry of War. Nevertheless, after their formation they were deployed and treated exactly like regular army units. Whenever possible, men composing a particular battalion or squadron were to hail from the same town or district. A total of 4 battalions and 1 cavalry regiment were to form a brigade, with 2 or 3 of these brigades to form a division. On 29 July 1813, however, *Landwehr* brigades and divisions were dissolved, the infantry being formed into regiments of four battalions and the cavalry regiments becoming independent. *Landwehr* regiments were usually known by their province as well as a number, but often simply referred to by the name of their commander or their home town or district. On 19 November 1813, the number of field battalions per regiment was ordered to be reduced to three, with the fourth becoming a reserve battalion for training reinforcements; needless to say, this directive could not be immediately carried out. At the end of the year, in the re-occupied provinces west of the River Elbe, additional *Landwehr* regiments were raised.

On 27 August 1814, *Landwehr* regiments were grouped together in mixed divisions of purely *Landwehr* infantry and cavalry, but for the 1815 campaign they were again assigned to brigades of the regular field army rather than consolidated in entire *Landwehr* divisions. On 3 September 1814, a law introduced general conscription without exemption. Henceforth, the *Landwehr* was to be composed of two contingents: the first contingent (*Aufgebot*), which was to reinforce the field army, was composed of young men who had not served in the regular army, and were aged between 26 and 32 years. The second contingent, being destined for garrison duties, was composed of all other able men up to the age of 39. However, for the

1815 campaign, only part of this second contingent was raised, in consequence of an order of 15 May.

FREE CORPS

Free corps (*Freikorps*) were units raised by individuals with the permission of the king, but at their own expense, though often financed by collections and sometimes provided with supplies, especially weapons, from the army, which supplied food and pay once a corps actually came into existence. Here only the more important free corps are listed:

Schill's Free Corps

Second Lieutenant von Schill was given permission on 13 January 1807 to raise a free corps. By 7 February it had grown to 3 squadrons of dragoons, 2 squadrons of hussars and 2 battalions of infantry (1 of 4 companies and the other of a single company), as well as 1 company of rifles. It also contained a small detachment of artillery consisting of 1 1pdr and 4 3pdr guns. Over subsequent months the infantry was increased to 2 battalions of 4 companies each and a third battalion of 2-company strength. By an order of 18 October 1807 the cavalry was reformed into 4 squadrons and renamed on 1 July 1808 the hussar battalion v. Schill, becoming the 2nd Brandenburg Hussar Regiment in September 1808. On 27 November 1807, the infantry was reorganised into a single battalion of 4 companies, called the light battalion v. Schill, which in 1808 was assigned to the Life Infantry Regiment. The artillery contingent to Schill's corps was disbanded in October 1807.

Krockow's Free Corps

On 27 December 1806 Captain count von Krockow was permitted to raise a free corps of riflemen (*Frei-Jägerkorps*) consisting of 1 squadron of mounted troops and 1 battalion of 5 companies, including 2 3pdr guns. This corps took part in the defence of Danzig, and was dissolved on 27 July 1807.

Marwitz's Free Corps

Captain von der Marwitz received permission to raise a free corps on 20 March 1807, up to a maximum strength of ten squadrons of dragoons and four companies of infantry. On 17 June this was reduced to the strength it actually reached of two companies and four squadrons. The corps was dissolved on 20 September.

Lützow's Free Corps

On 18 February 1813 Major von Lützow was authorised to create a free corps, mainly composed of foreigners (*Ausländer*, which in this context means non-Prussian subjects), which rose to a strength of 3 battalions of 4 companies each, 4 squadrons of cavalry (hussars and lancers), as well as some artillery. The 3rd company of the 3rd battalion was formed exclusively from volunteers of Tyrolean birth, and was dissolved on 18 June 1814. The corps also contained 1 horse and 3 (for a short time, 4) foot detachments of volunteer rifles. On 19 January 1814 the corps was ordered to be split into separate infantry and cavalry regiments, though this was not carried into effect until after hostilities ended in April 1814.

Schill's Free Corps

Hoping to profit from his name, in March 1813, Major von Schill, brother of the popular hero of 1806–7 and 1809, was ordered to raise a free corps in northern Germany, which amounted to two squadrons. On 4 August 1813, his unit was to be joined to Hellwig's Free Corps, but the Crown Prince Bernadotte of Sweden, to whose army the corps belonged, countermanded this order, so that the corps did not join Hellwig's cavalry until 12 May 1814, after the conflict had ended, as a result of a new order from the king.

Hellwig's Free Corps

Major von Hellwig of the 2nd Silesian Hussar Regiment was given permission on 29 April 1813 to form a raiding corps (*Streif-Korps*) of two squadrons and some volunteer riflemen from his regiment. Later he was allowed to raise two further squadrons (one of them comprising volunteer riflemen) and a battalion of three companies, most of whose men were deserters or prisoners from the Confederation of the Rhine. At the end of the 1814 campaign the two original hussar squadrons returned to their regiment and the volunteer riflemen were disbanded. Once augmented by Schill's cavalry, Hellwig's three squadrons became known as Hellwig's Cavalry Regiment (Hellwigsches Kavallerie-Regiment). The infantry battalion also bore his name (Hellwigsches Jäger Bataillon).

FOREIGN BATTALIONS

On 10 March 1813, Captain von Reiche received permission to raise a foreign rifle battalion bearing his name (Ausländisches Jäger-Bataillon von Reiche) from former Prussian subjects living on the left bank of the Elbe. It reached a strength of five companies plus a detachment of volunteer riflemen. On 12 March 1813, Lieutenant Colonel von Reuß was permitted to raise one or more battalions of foreign troops, also bearing his name (Ausländer-Bataillon von Reuß). Many of his men consisted of prisoners of war from the Confederation of the Rhine. By the time of the armistice, a second foreign battalion had been raised, and on 5 July 1813 the king ordered the creation of a third battalion, to form the Elbe Infantry Regiment (Elb-Infantry-Regiment), the men to be raised from areas west of that river. A fourth battalion, designated the reserve battalion of the regiment, was formed on 21 November.

FOREIGN UNITS TAKEN OVER IN PRUSSIAN SERVICE

The Thuringian Battalion

On 13 April 1813, Prussian troops captured a battalion of Saxons from the minor Saxon duchies – part of the forces of the Confederation of the Rhine. When the battalion volunteered to fight for the Allies, it was taken into Prussian service under the name 1st Thuringian Battalion (1. Thüringer Bataillon, though a second battalion was never formed). On 23 November, the unit was ordered to be dissolved, the officers and men being allowed to return home or to remain in Prussian service. Nevertheless, the unit continued operational until finally disbanded on 8 May 1814.

The German Legion

This legion, consisting of infantry, cavalry and artillery, had been formed in Russia in August 1812 from German prisoners of war, hence its original name, the Russo-German Legion (Russisch-Deutsche Legion). On 1 September 1814, Prussia assumed responsibility for supplying the Legion, by then known simply as the German Legion (Deutsche Legion). On 18 April 1815 it was absorbed into the Prussian Army.

Berg Troops

In late 1813, the Grand Duchy of Berg was occupied and provisionally administered for the Allies under Prussian military authority, known as the General-Gouvernement Berg. A hussar regiment, infantry, artillery, volunteer riflemen and *Landwehr* were raised. As agreed at the Congress of Vienna, Prussia annexed Berg, together with its troops.

Saxon Forces

In addition to Berg, the Congress of Vienna also decided that Prussia would receive a substantial part of the Kingdom of Saxony. This naturally affected the Saxon Army, which was split up, with the rank and file distributed beween the two states according to their place of birth, while the officers could choose whether to join the Prussian Army or to remain in Saxon service. When, however, the disbandment of the infantry was due to take place on 2 May 1815 (the formal cession of Saxon territory to Prussia would occur on 22 May), some formations mutinied. The revolt was quickly put down, but as a consequence all Saxon units were dissolved and their personnel distributed across the Prussian Army, except for the cavalry, which formed the new 12th Hussars.

Chapter Five

The British Army

Gregory Fremont-Barnes

As an island nation, Britain naturally devoted a far greater proportion of its resources to the Royal Navy, the responsibilities of which extended beyond the defence of the nation to wider strategic interests, than to the army. When war with France began in 1793, the army, which numbered a mere 45,000 men, had not fought in a major conflict in the decade since the end of the War of American Independence (1775–83), from which it emerged with a respectable battlefield record but a bruised sense of inadequacy as a result of the disasters at Saratoga and Yorktown.

The army's main responsibilities lay in the colonies and in the maintenance of order in restless Ireland. A massive two-thirds of the nation's troops were serving abroad at the outbreak of war with Revolutionary France, leaving a tiny disposable force available for amphibious operations on the European continent. Even had the bulk of the army remained at home, it would still have paled in comparison with its continental counterparts, which numbered in the hundreds of thousands. Thus, the main burden of the war on land for the first two coalitions (1792–97, 1798–1802) stood squarely on the shoulders of Austria and Russia, with Prussia, Spain and a host of smaller powers in support. This would remain so until 1808, when, with the rising in Spain against French occupation, an expeditionary force sent to Portugal under Lieutenant General Sir Arthur Wellesley (better known as the Duke of Wellington) would begin the gradual build-up of British forces in the Iberian Peninsula. Under Wellington the army would ultimately oust the French from Portugal and Spain and invade France itself even before Britain's allies crossed the Rhine in January 1814.

With world-wide responsibilities but with the Navy the senior service, the army possessed an insatiable appetite, as can be seen from the table below, which provides the strength of the rank and file from private up to and including corporal. Total strength – to include sergeants and officers – can be determined by adding one-eighth to each figure:

Year	Cavalry	Infantry	Total
1804	16,729	119,751	136,480
1806	23,396	142,177	165,573
1809	27,391	183,223	210,614
1813	28,931	201,538	230,469

Recruitment came largely from the lowest classes – those who sought an alternative to prison, adventure or, most commonly, release from poverty, as Moyle Sherer observed:

> Wander where he will, a regiment is ever, to a single man, the best of homes ... For him, who by the want of fortune or other controlling circumstances, is debarred the exquisite happiness of reposing his aching heart on that blessed resting-place, the bosom of a wife – for such a man there is no life, save one of travel or military occupation, which can excite feelings of interest or consolation. The hazard of losing life, which a soldier is often called on to encounter, gives to his existence, as often as it is preserved, a value it would, otherwise, soon cease to possess ... if it is painful at a certain age, to think that, when you fall, no widow, no child, will drop a tear over your grave – it is, on the other hand, a comfort to know, that none are dependent upon your existence; that none will be left unprotected and in misery at your death.[1]

The record of the British Army during the war with Revolutionary France was mixed. Like his other eighteenth-century predecessors, especially his father, William Pitt (Prime Minister, 1783–1801, 1804–6) dispatched numerous minor expeditions – such as to Flanders in 1793–95 and to North Holland in 1799 – in order to divert French attention from the main theatre of war, but none of these made much of an impact on the greater strategic aims sought by Allied nations such as Austria, Prussia and Russia, who contributed far more substantial numbers of troops. The British Army also had a poor record of co-operation with the Navy, on which it obviously depended for its transport and supply, and unlike the continental armies lacked a permanent system for organising regiments into formations higher than brigades, though a divisional system was later employed during the Peninsular War and in the Waterloo campaign.

Certainly the army enjoyed a number of successes in the West Indies in the 1790s, but this was by no means universal, with setbacks particularly notable on St Domingue (now Haiti). But far greater enemies awaited the army there: yellow fever, malaria and other tropical diseases ravaged the forces sent to that theatre, possibly accounting for as many as 100,000 deaths or invalid discharges. The most significant success enjoyed by the army during the 1790s was Sir Ralph Abercromby's expedition to Egypt in 1801, but by then the French Army had been isolated for over two years and no longer posed a serious threat to the strategic interests of the Second Coalition (apart from the Ottoman Empire, of course) – and certainly no longer to British interests in India, as had been the case when Napoleon first arrived in 1798.

By the time the Napoleonic Wars began in 1803, the Commander-in-Chief, the Duke of York – an ineffective field commander but a superb administrator – had instituted a number of important reforms, while Sir John Moore had introduced light infantry and new training methods for the infantry as a whole. The government had by then begun to realise the folly of an understrength army and had raised its capacity to over 200,000 men, though many of these were still required for home defence and colonial policing; thus, the forces sent to Hanover and Naples in 1805 were again merely diversionary (and not terribly effective at that) and extremely small compared to the massive armies fielded by Austria and Russia in the main theatre of campaign. Having said this, from 1808 onward the army's role in Portugal and Spain would grow year by year, so that in the comparatively short space of four years it would become a first-rate fighting force second to none in Europe. The crucial – some would say decisive – role played by British troops at Waterloo, albeit as part of a larger Anglo-Allied and Prussian effort, was proof of the enormous progress made by the army in the preceding decade.

HIGHER ORGANISATION

At the outset of the Napoleonic Wars the army possessed no larger unit than a brigade, consisting of two or more infantry battalions, all under the command of a 'brigadier', which constituted an appointment rather than a rank, since he might in fact not be a brigadier general but rather the senior battalion commander, in which case his battalion was led by the second in command. The staff of a brigade comprised only a handful of individuals, above all the brigadier's aide-de-camp and his brigade major. If more than one brigade served together, the senior brigadier held command. No higher structure was implemented until 1807, during the expedition against Copenhagen, when Sir John Moore structured his army based on 4 divisions of 2 infantry brigades and 1 cavalry brigade. The division became the standard higher formation when Sir Arthur Wellesley was given independent command in the summer of 1809, and maintained this system for the remainder of the war. Naturally, army organisation varied according to circumstances, but each division comprised 2, 3 or 4 infantry brigades and their commissariat. Initially, with artillery available only in short supply, no permanent allocations were made, although companies tended to be assigned to specific divisions.

If divisions appeared more or less uniform on paper with respect to their structure, their constituent parts tended to vary qualitatively, though Wellington sought to alleviate this disparity by intermingling stronger and weaker units, as well as green and veteran troops, so that quality remained fairly uniform across divisions, while at the same time less reliable units benefited from the presence of those with greater field experience. This was particularly necessary during the Waterloo campaign, where the duke commanded regiments most of which either contained new recruits and therefore lacked Iberian experience, or which had not served in Spain and

Portugal at all – many of the veteran battalions being then in America and Canada. This left Wellington with forces of mixed quality as compared to the first-rate army he had led only the year before. From 1809 Portuguese units were integrated into the army at brigade level, but when this proved unsatisfactory the Portuguese were consolidated into their own brigades, with these integrated at the divisional level.[2] The army never adopted the corps system like the French and other continental powers, though it is fair to say that Wellington's divisions – albeit only about 6,000 men strong – shared much in common with these higher formations insofar as they could operate independently, possessing as they did their own staff, artillery, commissariat and reconnaissance capability.

INFANTRY

Though the infantry of the 1790s were not of impressive material, by the time of the Peninsular War (1808–14) great improvements had been made in training and morale. Under Wellington's command the infantry became one of the finest in Europe: extremely reliable, dogged and stalwart in battle, and capable of issuing a disciplined fire which the French found themselves utterly incapable of matching.

Regular infantry regiments were numbered up to 104 by 1815, though there had been more in the 1790s, mostly of short-lived units. In addition to these were three regiments of Foot Guards. Most regiments held titles as well as a number, indicating an affiliation with a county or territory from which most of the ranks were recruited, though in many cases these designations did not reflect the true geographical origins of the men at all. From 1805 onward, however, regulations allowed men from the militia to join the regular army, thus raising the local composition of recruits who normally enlisted in their county formation. Regiments from the Highlands and Ireland were drawn from those places for the most part, the former in particular characterised by distinct uniforms including a kilt and feather bonnet. Scottish regiments had proud martial traditions, and most had distinguished themselves in battle.

Theoretically, the basic unit of organisation was the regiment, usually consisting of two battalions, but because these rarely served together in the field, it was the battalion that actually functioned as the basic administrative unit. Thus, the two operated independently, with the second battalion frequently serving in a completely different theatre, often on another continent. One battalion of a regiment might, for instance, be stationed or on operations as far away as Gibraltar or India. Sometimes one battalion remained at home, where it served for recruitment purposes and sent out drafts to keep up the strength of its sister battalion on campaign.

In 1808, at the start of the army's campaigning in the Iberian Peninsula, there were 103 regiments of the line, 61 of which consisted of the usual 2 battalions. A further 37 regiments possessed 1 battalion, 1 had 4 and

2 regiments had 3 each. There were also 2 rifle regiments: the 60th (Royal Americans), which had 7 battalions, and the 95th Rifles, which had 3. Units designated as 'Fuzileers' (fusiliers) were actually no different from the ordinary line regiments except in minor variations in uniform (but particularly in headdress, for they wore fur caps instead of leather shakoes) and the fact that they were descended from regiments that had once carried a fusil – a lighter form of musket.

The Foot Guards, together with the Household Cavalry, made up the elite of the army. In the case of the infantry, their normal established strength was much larger than ordinary regiments of the line, and their conduct and performance in battle was also generally higher. The 1st Foot Guards had 3 battalions, and the other 2 Foot Guards regiments had 2 battalions each. Guardsmen were better paid, and their officers held double rank, which meant that, for instance, a lieutenant in the Foot Guards was the equivalent to a captain in a line regiment.

Officers could rise through the ranks through the normal course of seniority or through distinguished battlefield performance, but the quickest route to promotion was through the purchase of a commission, by which an officer paid for a rank sold to him by another, more senior, officer. On the mere transfer of funds came a promotion in rank, irrespective of other considerations. Wellington generally favoured this system; indeed, in the decades after the Napoleonic Wars when he served as Commander-in-Chief at Horse Guards, he maintained the system with a staunch conservatism. On the other hand, during his years on active service he condemned the fact that he had little power to promote officers of genuine ability, so entrenched had the purchase system become. In fury he wrote:

> It would be desirable, certainly, that the only claim to promotion should be military merit; but this is a degree of perfection to which the disposal of military patronage has never been, and cannot be, I believe, brought in any military establishment. The Commander-in-Chief must have friends, officers on the staff attached to him, etc., who will press him to promote their friends and relations, all doubtless very meritorious, and no man will at times resist these applications; but ... I, who command the largest British army that has been employed against the enemy for many years, and who have upon my hands certainly the most extensive and difficult concern that was ever imposed on any British officer, have not the power of making even a corporal!!![3]

This, of course, meant that the higher ranks were beyond the reach of any but the most affluent members of society, a fact that preserved the social exclusivity of the officer corps and accounted for the very high proportion of aristocrats and landed gentry in senior command, particularly in the Household regiments, where commissions were more expensive than those in the line. Although the purchase of commissions continued until abolition occurred under Cardwell's reforms in the 1870s, many of Wellington's contemporaries decried the system for its failure to reward those worthy by dint of merit. J.F. Neville, who served in the Peninsula, observed that in the opening years of that conflict, in addition to the injustices of competent men going unnoticed, the system enabled the downright inept and, as he saw it, the socially unqualified to occupy all levels of command:

> It would be fulsome flattery to give the name of 'AN ARMY' to an unwieldy concourse of men, necessarily ill-disciplined, from the fatal circumstance of their being ill-officered ... the most barefaced profligacy prevailed throughout every military department. Whatever was connected with the army-establishment was, more or less, a dirty job, and a public robbery. Commissions were thrown away on persons unworthy of bearing them, or incapable of performing the duties which the letter and spirit of them religiously enjoined. *Boys at school*, smarting under the wholesome application of *birch*, were field-officers in the British army, and regularly received their daily pay, as a *just* remuneration for the important services which they were rendering to the State! The brother or relative of a *petty prostitute*, was complimented with the command of a regiment, while the son of a low, but opulent *mechanic*, by the means of a bribe, saw himself at the head of a troop of horse, which he had neither the courage nor the abilities to lead ...[4]

Each battalion consisted of 10 companies, 8 of which were 'centre' companies (so named from the position they held in line formation); the other 2 were 'flank' companies. The company positioned on the right flank consisted of grenadiers, in theory the biggest men of the battalion, while the left-flank company was made up of light infantry – usually the smallest and quickest men. In the light infantry and the rifle regiments all the companies were identical, with no grenadiers. A full-service line regiment theoretically consisted of about 1,000 rank and file, or about 10 companies of 100 men each. With officers, non-commissioned officers and drummers, this would bring the total up to about 1,100 men. However, this figure was rarely attained on campaign, though numbers in one battalion could be bolstered by drawing men from the second battalion. Indeed, it was not unusual for regiments to fall below 750 effectives (men actually present and fit for action) at the start of a campaign and reach an average of about 550 in the midst of operations. By the summer of 1812, for instance, only 1 line battalion numbered over 900 men and 12 battalions mustered fewer than 400 men each. If a battalion fell too far below operationally effective strength, it might be temporarily amalgamated with another under strength unit to form a provisional battalion until the two components could be brought back up to strength with reinforcements sent out from their respective recruiting depots back home.

The basic firearm of the infantry was the Brown Bess musket, a smooth-bore flintlock weapon. This fired a spherical lead ball about an ounce in weight. Its range and accuracy left a great deal to be desired and dictated the shoulder-to-shoulder formations and close-order tactics of the day. Unless faced with a large mass of men, a musket-armed soldier was extremely unlikely to hit his target unless exceedingly proficient.

Similarly, unit cohesion could not be maintained except by tightly packing the ranks, so battles almost invariably consisted of large opposing blocks of infantry blazing away at one another at extremely close ranges – with sometimes devastating results. In theory, while a musket ball could strike a man at 200yd, actual effective range was under 100yd, as Colonel George Hanger noted at the time:

> A soldier's musket, if not exceedingly ill bored and very crooked, as many are, will strike the figure of a man at 80 yards; it may even at a hundred; but a soldier *must be very unfortunate indeed* who shall be wounded by a *common musket* at 150 yards, provided his antagonist aims at him; and, as to firing at a man at 200 yards with a common musket, you may just as well fire at the moon and have the same hope of hitting your object. I do maintain, and will prove, whenever called on, that no man was ever killed, at two hundred yards, by a common soldier's musket, by the person who aimed at him.[5]

Infantry also carried socket bayonets, except for officers, each of whom armed himself with a pistol and a sword. Each soldier carried sixty rounds of ammunition and could fire one round in approximately 30 seconds – perhaps twice as quickly as his French counterpart. British infantry did not drive back attacking columns with firepower alone, however; the psychological effect of employing the bayonet – even if contact was not actually made – against a shaken enemy in the wake of a series of devastating volleys was often enough to repel a French attack, especially if the defending infantry had emerged from the reverse slope of a hill, a tactic that Wellington frequently employed both in the Peninsula and at Waterloo. The first example of the superiority of the line over the column was demonstrated at the Battle of Maida in 1806, during an expedition to Calabria, with the practice refined in Spain and Portugal, as brilliantly described by one French officer thus:

> ... the French infantry ... charges the infantry of the enemy with shouldered arms. This manoeuvre is executed ... deployed or in close columns of divisions it has often succeeded against the Austrians and other troops, who begin firing at too great a distance; but it has always failed against the English, who only open their fire within a short

> distance. When the English infantry is near the enemy ... it generally executes its movements in close columns of divisions, but it always deploys to fight ...
>
> In order to defend a height, the English infantry does not crown the crest, as practised by the infantry of other armies; it is placed about fifty yards behind the crest, a position in which it is not seen if the ascent be at all steep; it has almost always some skirmishers along the slope, which must be climbed in order to attack it. The musketry and the retreat of the skirmishers inform it of the enemy's arrival; at the moment that they appear it gives them a discharge of musketry, the effect of which must be terrible at so short a distance, and charges them immediately. If it succeeds in overthrowing them, which is very probable, it is satisfied with following with its skirmishers, does not pass the crest, and resumes its position ... It can easily be imagined that a body which charges another, and which is itself charged, after having received a fire which has carried destruction and disorder into its ranks, must necessarily be overthrown.
>
> I now give an instance of a fact, which ... offers at once an example of the force of military discipline, of the influence of officers and non-commissioned officers, and of the excellence of the manoeuvres employed by the English against the French ... [at Talavera in 1809] the troops were deployed on both sides. The French charged with shouldered arms, according to their custom. Being arrived at a short distance, and the English line remaining immobile, the soldiers hesitated to advance. The officers and non-commissioned officers cried to the soldiers: 'Forward – march – do not fire!' – some of them even exclaimed 'They surrender!' They then continued their forward movement, and were very near the English line, when it opened a fire of two ranks, which carried destruction into the French line, stopped its progress, and produced some disorder. While the officers cried to the soldiers, 'Forward, do not fire!' and the fire had commenced notwithstanding their efforts, the English, leaving off firing, charged with the bayonet. Every circumstance was favourable to them – good order – the impulse given – the determination to fight with the bayonet: among the French, on the contrary, no longer an impulse – the surprise occasioned by the unexpected resolution of the enemy – disorder – they had no alternative but flight.[6]

Light infantry regiments were more adept in the use of the musket than were ordinary line regiments, partly as a result of lessons painfully learned during the War of American Independence. Skirmishing, scouting, flank cover and screening had often been more crucial in the broken ground and forests of North America than they were in the open fields of Flanders and the Rhineland. Light infantry regiments were found to be all the more necessary when ordinary line regiments found themselves confronted by the annoying fire of the French *tirailleurs*, who normally screened friendly units moving inexorably forward in column. The British had lost some of these skills by the 1790s, but through the limited efforts of officers such as Sir David Dundas, who reformed methods of infantry manoeuvre, and above all Sir John Moore light infantry eventually came into its own and could match their opposite numbers in the field, utilising skills of an entirely different ilk to the virtual automatons of the line regiments, who generally fired by half-companies; rather, the light infantryman exhibited intelligence and self-reliance, since he had to employ his initiative and make the best use of natural cover, as a contemporary training manual explained:

> Vigilance, activity, and intelligence, are particularly requisite ... The intelligence chiefly required in a light infantry man is that he should know how to take advantage of every circumstance of good ground which can enable him to harass and annoy an enemy, without exposing himself ... In some situations they must conceal themselves by stopping, in others they must kneel, or lie flat ... Against regular infantry they must hover round these continually ... In such a situation light infantry can be opposed not otherwise than by men acting in the same manner with themselves ... *To fire seldom and always with effect* should be their chief study ... Noise and smoke is not sufficient to stop the advance of soldiers accustomed to war ... a considerable proportion of their force should at all times be kept in reserve. The men who are scattered in front ought to be supported by small parties a little way in the rear; and these again should depend upon, and communicate with stronger bodies, further removed from the point of attack ... In advancing the reserves must not be too eager to press forward ... In retiring, the skirmishers must keep a good countenance, and avoid hurry. They must endeavour to gall the enemy from every favourable situation, and make him pay dearly for the ground he acquires ...[7]

The conversion of line regiments to light ones took place in 1794, but so rapidly did this latter type of the infantry expand in the Iberian Peninsula that several such regiments – initially formed into the Light Brigade – later grew to divisional strength and came to be regarded as an elite formation of Wellington's army. While light infantry uniforms looked very similar to those of the line, the soldiers' muskets were slightly shorter (and consequently lighter) and sometimes had backsights to aid in aiming.

Rifle-armed detachments and sometimes whole units had existed for some time on the continent, particularly in the German states, where the utility of the weapon, first appreciated by hunters and estate managers, was eventually grasped by the more forward-thinking continental tacticians of the era of the Seven Years War (1756–63). The rifle, though slower to load than the musket and requiring more training, proved significantly more accurate, and an adept rifleman, taking advantage of available cover on the battlefield, could sometimes pick off mounted officers and gunners with impunity. The 95th Foot, which would attain great fame in the Napoleonic Wars, was formed in 1800 and equipped with the Baker rifle, which could be fired from a prone position (unlike a musket) and whose grooved rifling on the inside of the barrel offered superb accuracy. Whereas a musket-armed soldier would be lucky to hit an individual at 100yd, a rifleman could do so easily even at twice that distance. With this advantage riflemen could oppose French skirmishers, whose inferior weapons could not reply in kind. The 95th wore distinctive dark-green uniforms to aid in camouflage and to render them visibly distinct from the line regiments.

All line infantry and light battalions carried two flags, known as the Colours, which held a status akin to that of holy relics, used to symbolise the attachment of the men to their regiment, and through it to the sovereign and nation. Each battalion possessed a King's Colour, in the form of a large Union Flag, and a Regimental Colour, distinguished by the shade of the regimental facings, with a small Union in the upper corner nearest the pole, with a large St George's Cross embroidered on it for regiments with white or black facings so that the flag could not be mistaken for one of surrender in the case of the former, or be obscured amidst the smoke of battle in the case of the latter. Both bore the regiment's number and name, any badges associated with that regiment and its battle honours, though most were not granted these last until after the Napoleonic Wars. As the Colours possessed a somewhat mystical status, they naturally became the focus of attention in battle, partly as an identifier for members of the regiment keen to maintain unit cohesion, but also by the enemy, who sought to capture them. The Colours and the Colour party frequently came under fire, making the task of escorting them an extremely hazardous one, as William Lawrence of the 40th Foot recalled of action on the afternoon of Waterloo:

> I was ordered to the colours. This, although I was used to warfare as much as any, was a job I did not at all like; but still I went as boldly to work as I could. There had been before me that day fourteen sergeants already killed and wounded while in charge of those colours, with officers in proportion, and the staff and colours were almost cut to pieces. This job will never be blotted from my memory: although I am now an old man, I remember it as if it had been yesterday. I had not been there more than a quarter of an hour when a cannon-shot came and took the captain's head clean off ...[8]

CAVALRY

One of the most notable features of the British cavalry of this era was its numerical strength. Unlike the continental powers, Britain possessed a very small mounted corps, for in colonial warfare the terrain and climate often did not suit this arm, in amphibious operations the conveyance of cavalry was particularly problematic and until the middle of the Peninsular War the mounted arm was not required in larger numbers. Once the army grew in order to face the sizable French forces that Napoleon deployed in the Peninsula, the need for substantial numbers of cavalry naturally arose. In May 1809 there were only just over 3,000 cavalry in Portugal; there were about the same number at the Battle of Talavera in 1810 and fewer than 2,000 at Fuentes de Oñoro in the following year. While the overall strength of the cavalry rose over time, its relative proportion within the army remained about the same – around 10 per cent.

British cavalry at the start of the wars were divided into three types: the Household regiments; the dragoons, of which the senior version were the Dragoon Guards, which with the ordinary dragoon regiments were designated as 'heavy', as were the regiments in the Household Brigade; and the light dragoons, the difference being that the heavy dragoons were intended for use on the battlefield to execute the charge, whereas light cavalry, while also able to fight in pitched battles, could also perform duties like scouting, skirmishing and protecting baggage trains and lines of communications. In 1806, the army converted some light dragoon regiments into hussars, on the pattern of their continental equivalents that had proven themselves so effective in the eighteenth century. Like the infantry, the basic cavalry unit was the regiment, two or more of which formed a brigade, two or more of which composed a division. A regiment was itself subdivided into squadrons, and then of troops, with the number of troops varying depending on the official establishment at the time. Official strength was over 600 officers and men, though on campaign this often could not be met, and regiments frequently fell below 500.

When the Revolutionary Wars began, the heavy cavalry were armed with a rather unbalanced sabre which proved as inadequate for cutting as for thrusting. According to the 1796 manual that set out the principles of cavalry manoeuvre and the use of weapons, troopers were advised to employ the cut or slash in preference to the thrust used by most continental heavy cavalry. In 1796 the heavy cavalry were issued with a new pattern sabre, a heavy, unwieldy, blunt-pointed weapon that was retained through to Waterloo. If it made contact with its target in a downward stroke it caused dreadful injury, though it was less likely to kill an adversary than a thrust delivered by a French cavalryman.

British cavalry also carried firearms – various types of muskets and carbines – though these were even less effective than their infantry counterparts. Cumbersome and adding unnecessary additional weight to already heavily equipped troops, such weapons seldom benefited the heavy regiments, which rarely performed picket duty or fought as skirmishers as did their compatriots in the light regiments. All officers and troopers also carried a pistol or a pair of pistols, though with such a short range these weapons were practically useless except when nearly within arm's length of an opponent.

The cavalry generally performed well in action insofar as they charged the enemy with great dash and enthusiasm; though herein lay their chief defect – lack of control. Having defeated, for instance, enemy infantry, instead of reforming and returning to friendly lines, troopers would gallop on through the enemy's position until the horses were blown and their own formation's cohesion broken. Finding the cavalry now vulnerable, the enemy counter-charged with their mounted reserve, drove back the attackers and thus reversed the initial success, not least because no reserve had been maintained to counter such an eventuality. With troopers seldom trained to rally, it is scarcely surprising their officers could not exercise proper command and control, leading Wellington ascerbically to comment:

> It is occasioned entirely by the trick our officers of cavalry have acquired of galloping at every thing, and their galloping back as fast as they gallop on the enemy. They never consider their situation, and never think of manoeuvring before an enemy – so little that one would think they cannot manoeuvre, excepting on Wimbledon Common; and when they use their arm as it ought to be used, viz., offensively, they never keep nor provide for a reserve. All cavalry should charge in two lines, of which one should be in reserve; if obliged to charge in one line, part of the line, at least one-third, should be ordered beforehand to pull up, and form in second line, as soon as the charge should be given, and the enemy has been broken and has retired.[9]

ARTILLERY

Field artillery fell into two categories: 'foot' and 'horse', indicating the speed with which a battery was conveyed. As the Royal Artillery was a very small enterprise within the army as a whole, and especially in comparison with its continental counterparts, no British field commander could ever assemble massed batteries in the manner of the French or the Russians. This was a consequence of limited resources and a shortage of trained personnel; the artillery, being a technical arm, required considerably more advanced training for its officers and gunners and hence the sale of commissions was not permitted, as it was in the infantry and cavalry. Other factors accounted for limitations on the size of the artillery. Whereas militia and yeomanry units could provide ready trained men for the infantry and the cavalry, no such equivalent existed with respect to artillery, since virtually no formation possessed ordnance. Even for those fit and keen to learn gunnery, places at the instructional college at Woolwich were limited, and thus however many guns the Royal Artillery might procure from government arsenals, there was never a large enough corps of trained officers and men to make use of them all.

In practical terms this all meant that an army in the field possessed relatively few, albeit well-served, guns. In April 1809 Wellington had only about 1,000 artillerists and support staff and 30 pieces of ordnance – nothing like the number fielded by the French in Spain even when accounting for the small size of Wellington's army at that time. As the army expanded during the Peninsular War, so too did the number of guns that accompanied it; yet proportionally, the artillery continued to remain small and, although of reasonably good quality, it was unable to play a decisive role in battle.

The army never fielded large numbers of guns, in contrast to those of its continental allies, which therefore denied Wellington the ability to mass his guns in order to batter a particular point in the enemy's front in preparation for an assault. Nevertheless, the artillery was well officered and crewed and pains were taken to deploy the guns carefully and select the most suitable targets for the tactical situation in question, as prescribed by the basic manual of the day:

> ... guns must be positioned as to produce a cross-fire upon the position of the enemy, and upon all the ground which he must pass over in an attack ... [it may] be united to produce a decided effect against any particular points ... the *débouchés* of the enemy, the heads of their columns, and the weakest points in the front ... the cross-fire of the guns must become *direct*, before it can impede the advance of the troops; and must annoy the enemy's positions nearest to the point attacked, when it is no longer safe to continue the fire upon that point itself. The shot from artillery should always take an enemy in the direction of its greatest dimension; it should therefore take a line obliquely or in flank; but a column in front.[10]

Like all other armies, the Royal Artillery used smooth-bore cannon (properly referred to as guns or field pieces) and howitzers, the latter employed to fire shells over obstacles with a high trajectory and therefore had to be in line of sight of the target lest they hit friendly troops. Guns usually consisted of 9-pounders, 6-pounders, or 3-pounders, named for the weight of the projectile, of which gunners could employ several types: round shot, a solid iron sphere and by far the most common form of ammunition; canister, a thin metal tin containing musket shot that broke open on leaving the barrel, creating the effect of a shotgun; and shell, a hollow sphere containing gunpowder and a fuse that exploded after a timed delay. 'Shrapnel' or 'spherical case' was a form of this ammunition, fired from a howitzer and timed (if the gunner calculated the correct range and elevation) to shower the target with musket balls from above. This form of ordnance was unique to the British Army.

The horse artillery differed from the foot artillery by virtue of its rapidity of movement, as its purpose was to support the cavalry in action or to limber up (that is, to hitch each gun to a wheeled, horse-drawn vehicle known as a limber), move and unlimber quickly in order to assist the infantry. Speed was facilitated by providing mounts for all the gunners or by seating them on the limbers and battery vehicles, whereas the men of the foot artillery, apart from the officers, had to proceed on foot. The guns themselves were always conveyed by teams of horses, but they could be manhandled short distances without them in extreme cases. The horse artillery, being more mobile, naturally employed lighter guns, mostly 6-pounders, though eventually they adopted 9-pounders like their counterparts in the foot artillery.

In addition to shrapnel, the Royal Artillery possessed another innovative weapon peculiar to the British Army: rockets. The Mounted Rocket Corps, associated with the Royal Horse Artillery, fired small tripod-mounted projectiles with an explosive head, invented by Sir William Congreve and first used in action in 1804. Wellington was sceptical of their efficacy, though rockets were employed in the attack on Copenhagen in 1807, in the Peninsula, at New Orleans in 1815 and at Waterloo in the same year. The rockets' main disadvantage was obvious for even a lay observer to see: their flight was exceedingly erratic, it was impossible to predict where they would land and their explosive effect was minimal. Yet despite all these shortcomings, rockets seriously affected enemy morale, causing otherwise-steady troops to become disordered and sometimes flee. Finally, siege guns were also employed, especially in Spain, where Wellington relied on 18- and 24-pounders to reduce the fortresses of Ciudad Rodrigo and Badajoz in January and April 1812, respectively.

THE COMMISSARIAT

The Commissariat functioned to supply soldiers with their daily ration, a responsibility that of course ultimately rested with the government to furnish. The British service contrasted strongly with that of the French, the latter of whom sought wherever possible to 'live off the land' or to requisition, usually by forcible means, supplies, whereas the acquisition of food without proper compensation to the supplier constituted plundering and carried a severe penalty. All purchases were made either in cash or with a ticket which amounted to a promissory note for future payment. For the most part the army met its obligations and the local peasantry did not suffer from false promises or unpaid bills, but it must be stressed that Iberian agriculture provided little in the way of a surplus, so British forces relied heavily on sustenance furnished from other sources.

The daily ration to ordinary ranks consisted of hard biscuit, not unlike its counterpart in the Navy, and thus required either softening by being soaked in water or broken to bits by pounding. A typical daily ration for a soldier consisted of 1½lb of flour or bread (or 1lb of biscuit), 1lb of beef or ½lb of pork, ¼ pint of peas, 1oz of butter or cheese and 1oz of rice. Horses on home service received 14lb of hay, 10lb of oats and 4lb of straw per day. Infestation by weevils or maggots was not uncommon and the men largely pooled their food together and cooked it in a common pot, with boiling the most common method. If they happened to be billeted at an inn or a private home, the owner might prepare their meals.

Notwithstanding the fact that most British forces operated on friendly soil during the Napoleonic Wars (i.e. in Spain and Portugal), the Commissariat faced a daunting task in meeting the supply needs of even the moderately sized army that Wellington led. A division of 7,000 men, for instance, required for its daily needs 10,500lb of bread, 7,000lb of meat and 7,000 pints of wine. Alcohol was supplied in large quantities, with a quart of beer for each man constituting the standard issue and more available for private purchase. Even still, the men often subsisted on half rations where the Commissariat could not supply the need, or even endured short periods of no rations of any kind. Wellington often complained about the Commissariat's apparent inefficiencies, characterising one of its officers thus:

> He appears to me but little calculated to do the business I require from him. I want him to assist me in obtaining a knowledge of the mode in which the connection between the troops and the several civil departments is regulated; to know how all that business is now going on here; and to see how we can make the matter work better than it does under the existing regulations. He thinks of nothing but new regulations and establishments ... but it is not his business to propose them, nor mine to carry them into execution ... You will hardly believe that we were obliged to pick up the French shot in our camp to make up ammunition for Arentschild's guns, his reserves having been left behind at Saragoça, and there being no Portuguese means of transport to carry on the ammunition ... I have reported the state of things to the British Government, and they will do as they please.[11]

The Commissariat fell under the jurisdiction of the Treasury, and thus its staff were civilians, free from military discipline and standards. Commissaries received no formal training and could be grossly inefficient, often supplementing their meagre incomes through corrupt practices. Treasury officials could appoint friends and family members through patronage, and qualifications were not imposed until 1810, which even then only required a commissary to have reached the age of 16 and spent a year as a clerk. The Commissary Department assigned assistant-commissaries, deputies and clerks to every infantry brigade and cavalry regiment, the whole superintended by the Commissary-General and his own assistant and deputies, who did not necessarily bring much more experience to the job than those beneath them. But even the most efficient and conscientious commissaries found their task daunting, not least owing to excessive administration in the form of red tape and regulations.

Military transport originally had been the responsibility of the Corps of Royal Waggoners, established in 1794, but this institution proved a dreadful failure, so the Treasury returned to the eighteenth-century institution of civilian drivers and wagons hired as required. This was only marginally superior to the former system, for it required employing thousands of Portuguese peasants conveying goods in springless ox carts over primitive roads. This worked side-by-side with the Royal Waggon Train, founded in 1799, which reached a strength of 1,900 by 1814. This functioned under military control, with teams supplied by the government and vehicles of various descriptions run by the army.

MEDICAL SERVICES

Ignorance of medical science rendered the medical services rudimentary at best and woefully inadequate at worst. The failure of doctors to understand the necessity of practising basic hygiene meant that wounded soldiers enjoyed little prospect of survival if wounded, for death from infection often followed any surgical procedure owing to the use of unsterilised instruments or unclean hands.

Army medical services came under the superintendence of the Medical Board, which consisted of the Surgeon General, the Physician General and the Inspector General of Hospitals, all of whom were civilians with their own practices, and thus did not always devote sufficient time to the needs of the service. Each of these men controlled his own department, with provision of medical supplies the responsibility of the Apothecary General and non-medical supplies for hospitals the task of the Purveyor General. Fitness for the former post was not an issue, for it had remained a hereditary office for six decades by the time of the Peninsular War.

In most cases the medical services did not direct matters as a whole, obliging officers within individual regiments largely to manage their own affairs. Each battalion had a surgeon with the equivalent rank of a captain and two assistant-surgeons, holding the equivalent rank of lieutenant, who received their appointment directly by the battalion's or regiment's colonel, for there was no over-arching medical corps – indeed none would be founded until 1898. With chronic shortages of (necessarily inadequately trained) staff surgeons and with apothecaries often standing in their stead, the medical services amounted to a lamentable institution by even late nineteenth-century standards, notwithstanding the conscientious efforts of most personnel who laboured under immense disadvantages, including the total absence of any form of organised evacuation of, or procedure for treating, the wounded. Typically, buglers and drummer boys acted as stretcher-bearers, but with no established system in place for such fundamental tasks, the wounded often lay for hours, overnight or even days on the battlefield before receiving attention. Surgeons not only had to purchase their instruments out of their own funds, but received no trained assistance in the form of orderlies or attendants unless they took it upon themselves to explain basic first aid to whoever had been assigned to them.

During action, a battalion surgeon might erect a makeshift 'aid post' somewhere in the rear, but he had no means of following the unit if it moved elsewhere and possessed limited means of conveying the wounded, with most being expected to move themselves further to the rear, usually without any help, for fit men from the parent unit were not to be detached for this task lest they weaken the fighting capability of the formation. If they could not move themselves, the wounded had no choice but to remain *in situ* until someone came to their assistance. Even if they received some form of first aid and survived their ordeal, the wounded, removed from the field by blanket, had little to look forward to in the form of the 'hospital' to which they would be conveyed by cart, which without springs caused untold agony to the occupants and left many to die from the bleeding caused by jolting. Buildings termed 'hospitals' amounted to little more than a locally requisitioned structure where patients were fortunate to occupy a bed, but might share space on the floor in unventilated corridors with virtually nothing in the way of sanitation. Damaged limbs required amputation, for contemporary doctors knew no better method of preventing the onset of gangrene, whereas wounds to the abdomen were probed and the ball or shrapnel removed with forceps.

George Napier described how, having been hit in the arm with a grapeshot at Ciudad Rodrigo in January 1812, he underwent the standard medical procedure for such a wound:

> ... I must confess that I did not bear the amputation of my arm as well as I ought to have done, for I made noise enough when the knife cut through my skin and flesh. It is no joke I assure you, but still it was a shame to say a word, as it is of no use ... Staff Surgeon Guthrie cut it off. However, for want of light, and from the number of amputations he had already performed, and other circumstances, his instruments were blunted, so it was a long time before the thing was finished, at least twenty minutes, and the pain was great. I then thanked him for his kindness, having sworn at him like a trooper while he was at it, to his great amusement ...[12]

Surgery consisted of primitive means – bone saws and knives – with amputation conducted without the benefit of anaesthetic, many patients dying either from excessive blood loss or simple shock. Although the importance of maintaining hygienic conditions was not understood, significant improvements came into use with the appointment in 1811 of Dr James McGrigor as Inspector General of Hospitals in the Peninsula. There he created portable pre-fabricated hospitals which followed the army, so obviating the need for evacuating the wounded by springless Portuguese carts.

Until the First World War disease continued to take a much greater toll on soldiers' lives than wounds or the infections that often followed, with or without surgery. Something on the order of 80,000 men died or were incapacitated by disease contracted in the West Indies in the 1790s, caused by the fact that doctors had no understanding of the causes of such diseases or how to combat epidemics as occurred during the Walcheren campaign of 1809 in Holland, where over 4,000 men died from a malarial disease dubbed 'Walcheren fever'. With total ignorance of such endemic diseases, doctors could offer no effective cure. It is therefore unsurprising that Wellington should beg the authorities back home not to send him any more regiments that had recently served on Walcheren, for he feared the spread of disease in an army about 30 per cent of whose personnel already suffered from one form of illness or another at any given time.

ROYAL ENGINEERS

The Corps of Royal Engineers were responsible for all engineering tasks. As with the artillery, the engineers came under the authority of the Board of Ordnance. All engineers were officers and never reached the numbers required, especially for work in the Peninsula, where when the war ended Wellington still had only just over 200, of whom most were not even field officers. As engineering was a technical arm, like the artillery, commissions were only furnished to men with proper training, which was acquired from the Engineers' specialised school at Woolwich, with promotion dependent upon seniority as opposed to purchase. Engineers undertook excessive amounts of work, though unlike their colleagues in other branches of the army, they received higher pay while serving overseas. They focused their attention on major engineering tasks such as surveying, bridge-laying or siege work, with less complex matters such as temporary field works left to the infantry. Most of the work fell on junior engineers, who suffered heavy casualties in the field, for they constantly found themselves exposed to enemy fire, especially during siege operations, with the mortality rate of one in four reached in the Peninsula. Officers from line regiments who temporarily assumed engineering responsibilities – the only means of making up for such horrendous losses – were known as 'assistant engineers', though this is not to suggest that they were totally ignorant of engineering matters, as some had transferred into the infantry from the Engineers or had served in the East India forces in that capacity.

In contrast to the quality of the engineer officers was the nearly total absence of support available to them, for while they performed prodigious feats – most notably the construction of the Lines of Torres Vedras – and succeeded in various epic sieges (some excessively costly, most notably at Badajoz in 1812), they relied almost exclusively on untrained manual labour and infantrymen with no skills in engineering. There were 'other ranks' in the form of the Royal Military Artificers and Labourers (from 1798 called the Royal Military Artificers), consisting of twelve companies each under a sub-lieutenant – a former NCO, as well as a staff sergeant supplied by the Royal Artillery. Such men were not qualified engineers, but instead builders, carpenters and others trained in some sort of trade who could keep fortresses to the required standard of defence. By no means could Wellington call upon the whole of their complement, for while 8 served in Britain, 2 were stationed in Gibraltar, 1 in Canada and 1 in the West Indies. Most remained in these garrisons for the whole of the Napoleonic Wars and hence were of no practical use in the field, supplying only minor contingents for instance to the Peninsula where they appeared in such small numbers as to have virtually no effect on operations. At Ciudad Rodrigo, for example, Wellington had only eighteen artificers, and only eight at Burgos.

With the enormous losses suffered at Badajoz the army reformed this branch entirely, so that in the same month a new corps was created, the Royal Military Artificers, also known as Sappers and Miners, who became the Royal Sappers and Miners in 1813, with a strength of 2,800 men, their companies under officers of the Royal Engineers. The rank and file received training in their various skills at Chatham so that in 1813 there were 300 with the army in the Peninsula, furnishing good service at the siege of San Sebastian and at Bergen-op-Zoom, in Holland.

A separate engineering establishment, formed in 1798, was accountable directly to Horse Guards rather than to the Board of Ordnance and known as the Royal Staff Corps. It began as a headquarters and four companies but reached battalion size in 1809, though it never operated as an intact unit, its companies being detached for duty where needed. The rank and file also received training as infantry, and thus supervised the groups of ordinary infantry who on occasion performed manual labour. Officers of the Staff Corps performed duties that mirrored those of the Royal Engineers and Quartermaster-General's department, since they performed engineering and surveying work. At the outset the engineers had no transport of any kind, relying entirely on what vehicles, drivers and teams that the artillery could sacrifice. By the time the Napoleonic Wars ended each division contained a Sapper and Miner company, its own transport and entrenching tools for 500 infantry. During the Waterloo campaign Wellington had 800 Sappers and Miners, 41 Royal Engineer officers,

160 wagons and over 1,000 horses, as well as 550 drivers, some of these from the Royal Artillery and the others local Belgian civilians.

HEADQUARTERS STAFF

Unlike continental armies, the British Army possessed a very small staff organisation, with the actual headquarters consisting of but a handful of officers, all completely bereft of training, notwithstanding the existence of the Senior Department of the Royal Military College at Sandhurst, which trained so few staff officers that the headquarters might not contain any on campaign. Specifically, apart from generals (known as 'general officers'), garrison commanders and those in command of overseas bases, there were only ten full-time staff officers in the entire army, all of whom served as the Permanent Assistants of the Quartermaster-General's Department. The remaining staff officers arrived only when detached from regimental duty, normally from units already operating in the theatre in which the army was then serving.

Staff officers served in one of two departments: those of the Adjutant-General and the Quartermaster-General, the latter of which was responsible for marches, quartering of troops and their conveyance. The Adjutant-General's office was responsible for equipment and discipline, as well as prisoners of war. There was no staff officer specifically allocated for the collection and analysis of intelligence. Wellington displayed a preference for the Quartermaster-General's department, owing to his liking of George Murray, its head, over that of William Stewart, who led the Adjutant-General's Department. Both departments came under Wellington's direct supervision. Intelligence in theory came under the authority of the Adjutant-General's Department, but in Spain and Portugal the Quartermaster's Department came to overshadow it and eventually assumed most of the important staff functions. The heads of these departments were aided by assistants and deputy assistants – officers detached from their regiments for this purpose.

Apart from these two main departments, headquarters of the main field army often included the commanders of the Royal Engineers and the Royal Artillery, the Commissary-General and his staff, the Deputy Paymaster-General, the officer in charge of the medical services for that campaign, the Judge-Advocate, and any liaison officers sent by Allied powers. A personal staff, known as his 'household', accompanied each general, plus at least one ADC for a major-general, two for a lieutenant-general and at least three for the senior commander in theatre. Generals were free to make appointments at their own discretion, opening the practice to nepotism on a wide scale, with relatives or friends' sons, irrespective of their qualifications, finding themselves in the field often with little to recommend them but fortunate connection. Still, not much was required of them beyond keeping up communication between the general and the units under his

Dragoon trooper and
pper. Although trained to
ght both mounted and on
ot, during the Napoleonic
Wars they seldom
lismounted during action.
(*Fremont-Barnes collection*)

nch Dragoons in action
Nancis. Wearing the
tinctive bearskin cap
tead of the crested
met associated with
linary troopers, this elite
adron charges Russian
antry during the
npaign of 1814.
mont-Barnes collection)

(*Left*) French lancer, 1812. Use of this specialised weapon required more training than the curved sword associated with other light cavalry regiments. It performed deadly execution when infantry found themselves unable to keep their powder dry in heavy rain. (*Fremont-Barnes collection*)

(*Right*) French carabinier, like their cousins the cuirassiers, a type of heavy cavalry, though in the former's case sporting a breast but no back plate. (*Fremont-Barnes collection*)

French cuirassiers charge over the breastworks of the Great Redoubt at the Battle of Borodino, 7 September 1812. (*Fremont-Barnes collection*)

ısh lancers of the Imperial Guard reaching the Spanish guns at the summit of the pass at ıosierra – the Napoleonic equivalent of the charge of the Light Brigade at Balaclava in 1854. *nont-Barnes collection)*

ıch cuirassiers awaiting the order to attack at the Battle of Wagram, 5 July 1809. *nont-Barnes collection)*

(*Left*) Michel Ney, arguably Napoleon's greatest marshal, seen here during the retreat from Mosco when he earned the nickname 'bravest of the brave' for his extraordinary leadership while commanding the rearguard. (*Fremont-Barnes collection*)

(*Right*) Marshal Joachim Murat, who led Napoleon's cavalry in numerous battles – most notably a Eylau in 1807 – with the dash and recklessness so characteristic of the age. (*Fremont-Barnes collection*)

Grenadiers of the Imperial Guard relaxing in their quarters. (*Fremont-Barnes collection*)

ench line infantry at Vitebsk fending off Cossacks during the campaign of 1812.
·emont-Barnes collection)

arshal Ney leading French grenadiers during the disastrous retreat from Moscow in late 1812.
·emont-Barnes collection)

Cossacks, irregular light cavalry who performed superbly as skirmishers, scouts and raiders, but whose lack of discipline rendered them virtually useless against formed troops. (*Mikaberidze collection*)

General Bagration's infantry ferociously defend the *flêches* at Borodino, 7 September 1812, which the French eventually took after suffering appalling losses. (*Mikaberidze collection*)

eneral Kutusov, field commander of Russian forces during the campaign of 1805. He tried to avoid ı encounter at Austerlitz, but was unable to do so owing to Tsar Alexander's presence as supreme ›mmander. He replaced Barclay de Tolly as commander in the 1812 campaign, pursuing Napoleon lentlessly during the retreat from Moscow. *(Mikaberidze collection)*

Austrian cuirassier (left) and dragoon, 1812.
(Fremont-Barnes collection)

Austrian gunner (left and centre) and artillery officer (right). (*Fremont-Barnes collection*)

Hungarian grenadier (left) an Tyrolean chasseur, 1812. Hungarian – as opposed to German – infantry were distinguished in the Austrian Army by their distinctive cornflower blue trousers. Chasseurs, or *shützen* in German, were generally recruited from gamekeepers or hunters, noted for their marksmanship.
(*Fremont-Barnes collection*)

Line infantryman (left) and Chasseur à Cheval, 1812.
(*Fremont-Barnes collection*)

russian foot artilleryman (left) and horse artillery officer, 1812.
(*Fremont-Barnes collection*)

Prussian Royal Guard, 1812: cuirassier (left) and infantryman, the former having disencumbered himself of his armour, pistol and cartridge box. (*Fremont-Barnes collection*)

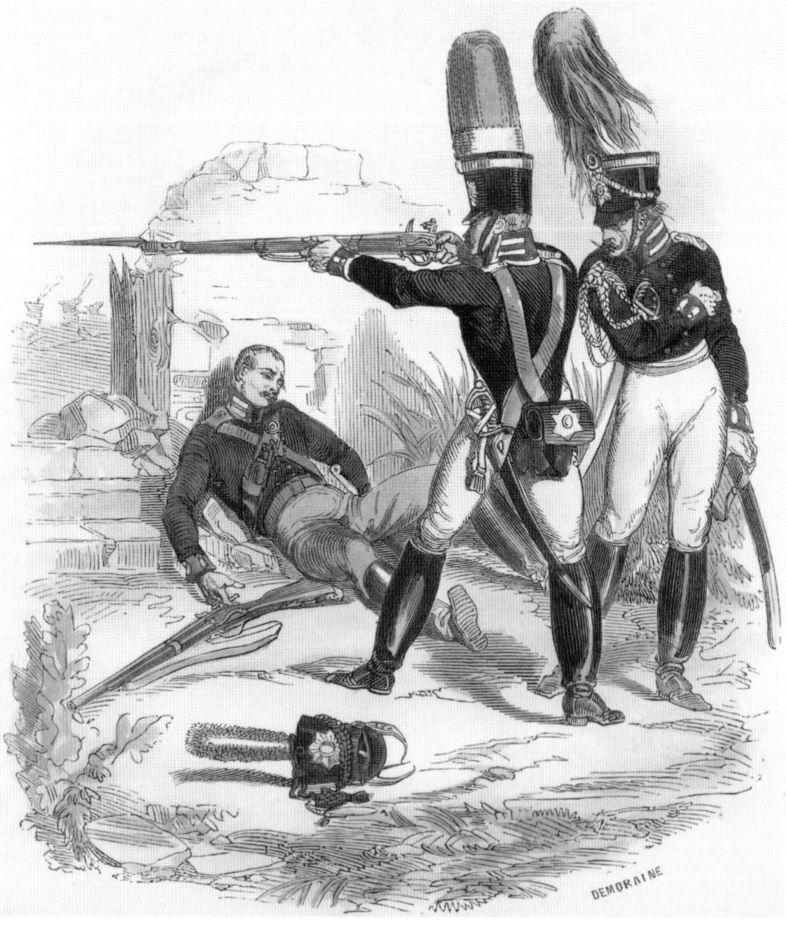

Prussian Royal Guard, 1812: chasseur (left), fusilier (centre) and fusilier officer (right). (*Fremont-Barnes collection*)

Lancers of the Prussian Royal Guard, 1812: trooper (mounted) and senior officer. (*Fremont-Barnes collection*)

Prussian infantry of the line: colour-bearer (left), private (centre) and officer (right).
(*Fremont-Barnes collection*)

British infantry at the Battle of Talavera. (*Fremont-Barnes collection*)

British infantry and gunners repulsing a French sortie during the siege of Ciudad Rodrigo, January 1812. (*Fremont-Barnes collection*)

tish heavy dragoons charging French infantry and guns at the Battle of Salamanca. *emont-Barnes collection)*

ellington and his staff at the Battle of Waterloo, 18 June 1815. *(Fremont-Barnes collection)*

Napoleon addresses Bavarian troops at Abensberg, 20 April 1809. Most German troops were eager to serve under Napoleon's command and responded well to his style of personalised leadership. (*Gill collection*)

Saxon Cuirassiers charge Austrian infantry at Dresden, 27 August 1813. While some units faltered and many were less capable than in previous wars, regiments like the Saxon heavy cavalry continued to perform well even in 1813. (*Gill collection*)

e infantry from Saxony (left and centre) and rttemburg (right), 1812. *(Fremont-Barnes collection)*

Bavarian Royal Guard, 1812: grenadier (left) and officer of artillery. *(Fremont-Barnes collection)*

Gendarmerie d'Elite, part of the heavy cavalry of the Royal Italian Guard. *(Schneid collection)*

Italian Guard Carabiniers. *(Schneid collection)*

Italian troops of General Pino's 15th Division, part of Eugène's IV Corps, advancing into Russia, 1812. *(Schneid collection)*

command; thus, an officer swift and fearless on horseback could generally perform his task, though it was an exceedingly dangerous one, for he was necessarily mounted and operated singly, which meant his position was exposed and his role known to the enemy, who regularly shot at him as he sought to locate, in the midst of action, the commanding officer of units – and often those in the front line. At Waterloo, 2 of Wellington's 8 ADCs were killed, while all 3 of Picton's were wounded on the same day. In addition to ADCs, each general had a Military Secretary, responsible for handling his superior's correspondence. Lord Fitzroy Somerset, later to become Commander-in-Chief in the Crimea as Lord Raglan, served in this post during most of Wellington's time in the Peninsula and would lose his arm at Waterloo. Divisions and brigades maintained their own staff officers, responsible for the transmission of orders and for performing daily routine duties relevant to the division or brigade.

INTELLIGENCE

The army possessed no officer specifically tasked with the vital function of gathering and examining intelligence. Reports came in from light cavalry assigned as scouts or sent on outpost duty – often operating ahead of the army in the advance guard – together with 'observing officers' who rode in the wake of the main force to determine enemy strength and movements, occasionally travelling great distances behind enemy lines. Such reports often came directly under Wellington's eye or less often under officers on his staff. Sometimes 'observing officers' drew rudimentary maps of terrain to supplement the very poor maps then in existence. In the early part of the campaign in Spain, Sir John Moore had very little knowledge of the roads, such as there were, and not until well into Wellington's campaigns were reliable maps produced by various officers, who also collated information gleaned from captured French despatches – often the product of guerrilla operations. Naturally, enemy communications were normally written in code, but Major George Scovell, of the Quartermaster-General's Department, proved himself invaluable in breaking their ciphers, providing Wellington at times with knowledge of French plans before the enemy had even executed them. Spanish guerrillas also reported intelligence directly to British officers, together with individuals working within a network of informants and 'correspondents' maintained by Wellington, such as civilian British nationals living in Spain. French deserters also at times supplied information.

THE KING'S GERMAN LEGION

Space precludes mention of the various foreign corps attached to, or serving alongside, British forces, but no study can be complete without reference to the King's German Legion. When in 1803 the French occupied the north German state of Hanover – a patrimony of King George III and therefore owing loyalty to the British Crown – the 15,000-man Hanoverian army was disbanded in July by a convention that allowed its soldiers to serve where they liked, so long as they did not fight France unless they had been formally exchanged as prisoners of war. The British government refused to recognise this convention, which enabled the king to establish a new corps of Hanoverian troops into what later became known as 'The King's German Legion' (KGL). The formation grew rapidly with a variety of units created for all three major arms, which included Germans from across central Europe whose territories had been absorbed by the Confederation of the Rhine or who simply wanted to oppose the French and found a convenient method of doing so by entering British service. Within 2 years of its formation the King's German Legion consisted of 4 line and 2 light battalions, a dragoon and light dragoon regiment and 5 batteries of artillery.

When the Legion accompanied a British expedition to the Elbe and Weser rivers in November 1805, large numbers of recruits flocked to join their fellow Germans, enabling the Legion, once back in Britain in January 1806, to expand to ten line battalions and five cavalry regiments, making the KGL a virtual Hanoverian army in exile. Thereafter, however, with French control fully exerted over Germany, very few Hanoverians joined the Colours, especially after the French satellite kingdom of Westphalia absorbed Hanover in 1807. The national make-up of the Legion thereafter became somewhat diluted by the addition of foreigners of various nationalities, but officers remained almost entirely Hanoverian and the quality of leadership continued to be outstanding throughout the period, with many British observers noting the fine quality of all KGL units, including their impressive standard of musketry, marching and discipline.

By the time the Legion was deployed in Portugal in 1808 it had become an integrated part of the British Army – not simply an allied contingent like the Portuguese – operated according to British orders and standard army procedure, and was organised, armed and clothed like its British counterpart. In the course of the Peninsular War the KGL reached such a high standard that its regiments came to be regarded as some of the best in the army as a whole. The light cavalry in particular functioned especially well in 'outpost' duties, but earned particular accolades for its conduct at Garcia Hernandez when the cavalry performed the extremely unusual feat of breaking infantry in square. In the summer of 1812 the Legion numbered just over 14,000 men, but between its formation and its dissolution at the end of the Napoleonic Wars about 28,000 men served in its ranks. Its record of service was diverse, with action seen in the Mediterranean and Sicily in 1808–11, in the expedition to Walcheren in 1809, in Italy in 1814 and in north Germany in 1813–14. After Napoleon's first abdication in April 1814, all personnel not drawn from Hanover were discharged, with the remaining men intended to form the nucleus of a reformed Hanoverian army. This did not take place until after the Waterloo campaign, however, as a result of which the KGL served in the campaign of 1815 at a much-reduced strength, their units substantially weaker than their British counterparts owing to the loss of non-Hanoverians released the year before. As such, a typical KGL battalion numbered only about 420 men, though even at this size they performed extremely well at Quatre Bras and Waterloo. More notably, in the latter engagement, approximately 400 KGL light infantry held the fortified farm at La Haye Sainte until the evening and only relinquished the place after they had expended all their ammunition and could no longer hold out with bayonets alone. The fact that only forty-two escaped bears testament to their utter dependability and doggedness in combat.

NOTES

1. M. Sherer, *Recollections of the Peninsula* (London, 1823; published by the author), pp. 261–2.
2. They did not form part of the British Army and are therefore dealt with in the chapter on Portuguese forces.
3. Quoted in Sir Herbert Maxwell, *The Life of Wellington* (London, 1899), pp. 122–3.
4. J.F. Neville, *Leisure Moments in the Camp and Guard-Room* (York, 1812; published privately by 'A Veteran British Officer'), pp. 98–9.
5. G. Hangar, *To All Sportsmen* (London, 1814), p. 205.
6. Marquis de Chambray, 'Reflections on the Infantry of Our Days', in *Philosophie de la Guerre*, translation in the *United Services Journal* (1834), vol. ii, pp. 505–7.
7. *A Manual for Volunteer Corps of Infantry* (London, 1803), pp. 30–3.
8. W. Lawrence, *The Autobiography of Sergeant William Lawrence*, ed. G.N. Bankes (London, 1886), p. 210.
9. Wellington to Hill, 18 June 1812, *The Despatches of Field Marshal the Duke of Wellington during his Various Campaigns*, compiled by Lt-Col Gurwood, 12 vols (London, 1834–38), vol. ix, p. 240.
10. R.W. Adye, *The Bombardier and Pocket Gunner* (2nd rev. edn, London, 1802), p. 26.
11. Wellington to Beresford, 11 May 1811, *Despatches*, vol. vii, p. 531.
12. George Napier, *Passages in the Early Life of Gen. Sir George Napier*, ed. by his son, Gen William Napier (London, 1884), p. 219.

Chapter Six

The Armies of the Confederation of the Rhine

John H. Gill

Germany constituted a major source of manpower for Napoleon, partly in the form of unique units such as the 'Westphalian Regiment', but mostly through the Confederation of the Rhine, or Rheinbund, an institution founded by treaty in July 1806 that grew to include all of the German states between the Rhine and the Elbe. Required by the treaty to supply soldiers to fight alongside French forces, the 39 member states committed themselves to place a total of some 121,000 men at Napoleon's disposal. They usually met this commitment, and the larger states often provided more. The result was a bewildering array of German contingents marching across Europe from Madrid to Moscow (and sometimes to both) from 1806 to 1813. Differing widely in size, dress and military competence, these troops can present the modern observer with an impossible tangle of titles, uniforms and home countries. Sometimes even their French commanders and allies found them difficult to understand, and their regiments often appear on contemporary situation reports with misleading French translations of German unit designations or odd approximations of officers' names. As a result, many later commentators have tended to treat them as an undifferentiated group, classing them simply as 'non-French' and assuming thereby that their presence in an order of battle chart represented a diminution of the combat potential of the formations to which they were attached. Yet nuance is important in assessing the multitudinous Rheinbund contingents as their loyalty and value on the battlefield varied by country, by campaign, and over time. A brief essay cannot do justice to the complexity of the Confederation and the thousands of men who marched, fought and died as French allies during this period, but it is hoped that the following will serve as an introduction to the intricacies of an institution that supplied some of the largest (and smallest) allied armies to fight under Napoleon's eagles from the height of the Empire to its catastrophic collapse in Germany in 1813.[1]

FROM EMPIRE TO CONFEDERATION

The Rheinbund was a mechanism for exerting French influence in the region between the Rhine and the Elbe. When Napoleon came to power, this area, often called the 'Third Germany' as it was neither Prussian nor Austrian, consisted of a congeries of secular and ecclesiastical territories ranging in extent from moderately sized duchies to microstates and individual abbeys. All of these fell within the broad embrace of the Holy Roman Empire (*das heilige römische Reich deutscher Nationen* or, for purposes of this essay, simply the *Reich*) under its Habsburg emperor, Franz II. Long an arena of confrontation among its powerful neighbours, Prussia, Austria, and France (with Russia taking a lively interest), these parts of what we now consider 'Germany' were potentially a prize asset, offering important commercial, political and military resources. Under the aegis of the *Reich*, these states and other political entities had contributed troops and funds (though seldom as many or as much as stipulated by the *Reich* constitution) to fight against France during the Revolutionary Wars (1792–1802). The area also served as a key recruiting ground for the Austrian and Prussian armies; indeed, the King of Prussia's dominions included significant properties west of the Elbe. A convoluted sequence of events fundamentally altered this jigsaw puzzle landscape during the last decade of the eighteenth century and the first five years of the nineteenth, as French power expanded across the Rhine and the courts of Austria and Prussia concerned themselves with other issues (principally the partitions of Poland).

In the wake of Austerlitz and the Treaty of Pressburg (December 1805), Napoleon's interests and those of the middle German monarchs converged. The French emperor, seeking to consolidate his dominance of central and southern Germany, established an alternative institution, the Confederation of the Rhine, in July 1806 and announced that he would no longer recognise the old *Reich* or its Diet. All too aware of the shift in power towards France and hoping to expand their own realms, sixteen German princes signed the founding treaty and formally withdrew from the *Reich* on 1 August. Franz (better known to the Anglophone world as Francis) II, who had declared himself 'Franz I of Austria' in 1804 in anticipation of the *Reich*'s demise so as to retain an imperial title, renounced all claims to the crown five days later. The Holy Roman Empire of the German Nations thus dissolved after a thousand years of existence at the heart of Europe. Napoleon and the Rheinbund took its place.

The Rheinbund served Napoleon's interest in several ways. In the first place, it provided France with a buffer zone on its western frontiers, an area where French dominance would prevail and adversaries would have difficulty penetrating. Secondly, it deprived the Empire's enemies of the region's military and economic resources, while conversely granting France relatively unfettered access to German manpower and wealth.

Napoleon would find this useful in everything from providing endowments for his imperial nobility to prosecuting his economic war with Britain. It is likely he also saw the elder German ruling houses as a source of legitimacy for his own new dynasty, seeking to ally his relatives to some of Europe's oldest noble families by carefully selected marriages (such as arranging the wedding of his stepson, Eugène de Beauharnais, to Princess Augusta Amelia of Bavaria's ancient Wittelsbach family). Most significant of these benefits for Napoleon's purposes were the military forces that resulted from the new alliance. These amounted to more than 65,000 men from the original member states, and subsequent additions would almost double the total by the autumn of 1808 when the final state, the Duchy of Oldenburg, joined. France, of course, was also a member of the alliance and Napoleon, as the Confederation's 'Protector', obliged France to provide 200,000 soldiers for the 'common defence'.

At the same time, Napoleon was neither the only beneficiary from the alliance nor the only actor in the system. Most of the German states almost certainly would have preferred to remain neutral, but this was impossible for small to middle powers wedged between Austria, Prussia and France. Joining the Rheinbund was therefore the only viable option as French power expanded. At the same time, however, these states, though certainly not wholly independent, had their own interests and could often evade or mitigate French demands, especially those that did not come from Napoleon personally.[2] Self-preservation and fear of French reprisals were therefore key motivations for the German princes, but they also had reasons of their own to join and they endeavoured to exploit the situation to their own advantage. First of all, most of the member monarchs acquired vast new territories and commensurate, or exaggerated, new titles as they signed their copies of the alliance treaty. The electors of Bavaria, Württemberg and Saxony were all elevated to kingships, while the rulers of Hesse-Darmstadt and Baden became grand dukes, to cite only a few of the more prominent. Moreover, while committing many of their soldiers to Napoleon and subordinating their foreign policies to those of France, they largely retained internal sovereignty. This was by no means always the case, and some states found themselves pressured into accepting the French civil code or other intrusions. At one end of the spectrum, the Grand Duchy of Berg, intended as a 'model state', came to be ruled by France. At the other end of the spectrum, however, many of the older, established rulers seized on the opportunities presented by the Confederation to institute substantial programmes of reform and centralisation for their own benefit, especially increasing the power to the reigning monarch vis-à-vis domestic estates, the privileges of which had been protected by the old *Reich*. Among these reforms were often dramatic military changes in everything from the position of the soldier in society to recruitment, conscription, officer promotions, training, organisation, tactics and uniforms.

Even hairstyles altered as officers discarded eighteenth-century wigs and soldiers cut off their queues. It is not possible to cover all of these factors for every army here, but several general observations are useful before discussing the contingents and their campaign participation.

First, it is worth reiterating that the various German armies were in need of considerable reform as they emerged from the *Reich* experience. The inefficiency and lassitude associated with the old system were not suited to the type of warfare Napoleon practised. That is not to say that all of the *Reich* troops were incompetent or lacked courage in combat. As a general rule, however, contingents under the old system were slow to assemble, usually had little to no training (for men or horses), were often missing basic items of equipment and seldom had any opportunity to develop unit spirit and cohesion. The composition of the Fugger Cuirassier Regiment, a typical south German case, illustrates some of these problems: with a nominal war strength of 608 men, the regiment drew on 60 separate political entities with contingents ranging in size from the Bishop of Augsburg's 96 troopers to the Abbot of Mönchsroth, who was required to send 2 mounted and equipped cuirassiers.[3] Officers were often selected only for their political connections or were old and unfit for active campaigning, while soldiers could be vagabonds, inveterate gamblers, drunkards and other petty criminals that had been 'sentenced' to military service in lieu of other penalty.[4] The challenges such troops posed to their leaders and the impression they would evoke in society may be imagined. 'Being "taken into the ranks as a soldier" was considered a punishment, like a prison', lamented a Bavarian officer.[5] Beyond issues of composition, training and organisation, Napoleon's expectations left soldiers of the *Reich* breathless. In particular, the speed and duration of marches and the rapid succession of engagements were beyond their experience. Writing to then-Elector Max I Joseph of Bavaria in December 1805, for instance, a Bavarian general expressed his astonishment that his little command had covered 80–90km in three days. Likewise, Napoleon, signing a treaty of alliance with then-Elector Friedrich of Württemberg in October 1805, expected that duchy's troops to be on the march within two days, yet the entire war was finished in three months, less time than it might have taken for a district contingent to assemble under the old system. Others would soon experience a similar sense of shock at the new pace of operations.

Secondly, while part of the impulse for reform came from the French, who wanted reliable allies in the field, much of the drive was generated internally. Professional soldiers in the German forces endeavoured to emulate the skills and accomplishments of the French Army and strove to meet the expectations of the premier commander of the age. Even before the creation of the Rheinbund, for instance, Bavaria, Württemberg, Baden and others had recognised the gap between themselves and their contemporaries, especially their French foes, and had initiated limited reforms on their

Table 6.1 The Rheinbund: Members and Contingents

State	Date Joined Alliance	Population (on joining)	Treaty Contingent
Arenberg (D)	12 July 1806	65,000	379
Baden (GD)	"	924,300	8,000
Bavaria (K)	"	3,500,000	30,000
Berg (GD)	"	931,000	5,000
Frankfurt (GD)	"	299,800	968
Hesse-Darmstadt (GD)	"	541,000	4,000
Hohenzollern-Hechingen (P)	"	14,000	93
Hohenzollern-Sigmaringen (P)	"	39,000	197
Isenburg (P)	"	34,000	291
Von der Leyen (P)	"	5,000	29
Liechtenstein (P)	"	4,500	40
Nassau-Usingen (D) and Nassau-Weilburg (P)	"	272,000	840
Salm-Kyrburg (P)	"	39,500	215
Salm-Salm (P)	"	34,000	108
Württemberg (K)	"	1,211,000	12,000
Würzburg (GD)	"	311,000	2,000
Saxony (K)	11 December 1806	2,276,000	20,000
Saxony-Gotha (D)	15 December 1806	187,000	1,100
Saxony-Hildburghausen (D)	"	33,000	200
Saxony-Koburg (D)	"	61,000	400
Saxony-Meiningen (D)	"	48,000	300
Saxony-Weimar (D)	"	111,000	800
Anhalt-Bernburg (D)	18 April 1807	35,190	240
Anhalt-Dessau (D)	"	54,000	350
Anhalt-Köthen (D)	"	28,840	210
Lippe-Detmold (P)	"	70,540	500
Schaumburg-Lippe (P)	"	20,100	150
Reuss-Ebersdorf (P)	"	7,800	90
Reuss-Greiz (P)	"	21,800	90
Reuss-Lobenstein (P)	"	7,500	90
Reuss-Schleiz (P)	"	16,500	90
Schwarzburg-Rudolstadt (P)	"	58,000	325
Schwarzburg-Sondershausen (P)	"	56,000	325
Waldeck (P)	"	50,000	400
Westphalia (K)	11 November 1807	2,612,000	25,000
Mecklenburg-Strelitz (D)	10 February 1808	70,000	400
Mecklenburg-Schwerin (D)	22 March 1808	328,630	1,900
Oldenburg (D)	14 September 1808	159,500	800

K = Kingdom, GD = Grand Duchy, D = Duchy, P = Principality

own. German monarchs also understood that they gained credibility and a degree of leeway with Napoleon if their armies performed well in reviews and in combat; ineptitude, on the other hand, would invite imperial intervention and could further curtail their internal autonomy. In many cases, the larger states had an advantage, being able to write and retain their own drill manuals and hold to their own organisational structures. Smaller states, or those that appeared torpid or incompetent, on the other hand, would be forced to accept French drill and French tactical organisations.

Thirdly, coming from the loose framework of the old *Reich* and motivated in large part by a desire to assert their own independence, the Rheinbund monarchs and their subjects, soldiers included, exhibited little pan-German nationalism. Instead, they were largely particularist, focused on their own states, their own parochial interests and often at odds with their Rheinbund neighbours. When rebellion broke out in Bavaria's Vorarlberg region in 1809, for example, Württemberg's King Friedrich resented having to send his troops to fight insurgents in his fellow king's lands. At the same time, authorities in Baden feared that the domineering Friedrich would use the opportunity to occupy parts of their territory under the guise of military necessity and would then present a case to Napoleon for retaining the occupied areas after the war. Furthermore, most officers and men had no special affection for Austria or Prussia, the two large German powers that had repeatedly exploited, abused or neglected the 'Third Germany' for decades or longer. There were certainly prominent exceptions to this generalisation. Bavaria's young Crown Prince Ludwig was a passionate pan-Germanist and vociferously anti-French, for example, and northern states like the Mecklenburg duchies inclined decidedly towards Prussia. On the whole, however, although there was a sense of belonging to a larger German cultural world, this vague sentiment did not translate into an automatic reluctance or refusal by Rheinbund troops to fight for Napoleon if their sovereigns so ordered. Of course, at a practical level, systems of reward and punishment, both German and French, reinforced loyalty to one's sovereign and thus dutiful obedience within the Rheinbund, but many, perhaps most, men also found themselves caught up in the excitement of serving under the great French emperor. 'As if touched by an electrical charge, the entire army was suddenly filled with joy and hope', recalled a Bavarian artillery corporal when Napoleon arrived at Abensberg on 20 April 1809. Fighting 'under the eyes of the emperor' was professionally fulfilling as well as exciting. Even a somewhat sceptical and cynical Saxon hussar officer, watching Napoleon from close range at Wagram, remarked 'Only now, in this eternally memorable hour, could I say that I have seen a battle!'[6] This enthusiasm would fade after the Russian disaster as the composition of armies changed and Napoleon's situation deteriorated, but it was not feigned and remained surprisingly strong even under the most trying circumstances.

Fourthly, the Rheinbund was not static. Although most of its non-military aspects quickly atrophied or never matured, significant political and territorial changes influenced the scope and nature of military capabilities. The increase in size experienced by almost every member of the alliance, for example, not only served as an incentive for the various rulers, but also provided them with larger population and economic bases upon which to draw for their military forces. Bavaria's acquisition of the Tyrol, or the addition of Hanover to Westphalia, are two examples. Furthermore, as most of the states were now unitary (that is, their lands were geographically connected, not fragmented across the face of Germany, Belgium and western France), they were somewhat easier to administer and offered a greater possibility of creating armies that were more cohesive and national than had ever been feasible under the *Reich*. Composite creations like the Fugger Cuirassiers would be the exception rather than the norm under Napoleon. Border adjustments and exchanges of territory were not uncommon in the Confederation to promote state cohesion or satisfy a particular ruler's desires, but Napoleon also instituted major changes based on his own judgment. Concluding in 1809, for instance, that Bavarian misrule was the principal cause of the vicious Tyrolian uprising, he removed the lower half of the region from Bavaria and placed it under the Kingdom of Italy, compensating Bavaria with several Danubian districts won from Austria during the war that year. Finally, Napoleon sometimes changed the Confederation in arbitrary ways to address what he perceived as the interests of France and his dynasty. The most dramatic example of this came in 1810 when he extended direct French rule across the North Sea coastline in a vain effort to enhance the economic blockade of Britain. This sweeping measure erased his brother Louis' Kingdom of Holland, eliminated the autonomy of the Hanseatic cities, redrew the borders of several north German Rheinbund states and eradicated the Duchy of Oldenburg. As the reigning duke was an uncle of Tsar Alexander, the expungement of his realm became one of the growing number of irritants that paved the road to war in 1812.

THE RHEINBUND AT WAR: THE STATES AND THEIR ARMIES

1805: Prelude to Confederation

Even before the creation of the Confederation, three German sovereigns signed bilateral treaties of alliance with France in the wake of Austria's invasion of Bavaria in September 1805. Bavaria, having promised 20,000 men, organised 6 brigades, each consisting of 2 infantry regiments, a light battalion, a cavalry regiment and a half-battery of 6 guns. Attached to Marshal Jean Baptiste Bernadotte's I Corps, 5 of the Bavarian brigades entered Austria, 3 diverting to the Tyrol, while the other 2 accompanied the army into Moravia. Here, under *General-Leutnant* Carl Philip Freiherr von Wrede, they fought a series of small engagements near Iglau from

2–6 December as the war was being decided at Austerlitz. Württemberg hastily assembled a force of 9 infantry battalions, a cavalry regiment and 16 guns, in all approximately 6,500 men. Departing Stuttgart in early October, the division reached Linz on 13 November and remained there on garrison duty until early January, its only contact with the enemy being a few small skirmishes. A brigade of 2,300 Badeners in 5 weak battalions barely even entered Austrian territory, remaining at Braunau on line of communications duty.

Bavaria: From Devotion to Disaster

Bavaria provided the largest Rheinbund contingent and, through the size of the contingent and the proven competence of its troops, was able to retain its own drill and organisational structure throughout the period of the alliance. Additionally, the monarchy's size and its strategic position as a buffer between Austria and France meant that it did not have to send troops to Spain. In all other cases, however, Bavaria was a major contributor, and in 1809 it went well beyond its formal treaty commitment.

The Bavarian Army, as we have seen, was already modernising as the *Reich* was fading into history, and this process accelerated as officers serving alongside the French in 1805 experienced firsthand the speed and relentless operational tempo expected of Napoleon's troops. By the autumn of that year, the army consisted of 13 line infantry regiments (each of 2 field battalions), 6 light infantry battalions (a seventh was formed in 1807), 2 dragoon regiments, 4 chevaulegers regiments and 3 artillery battalions. Each infantry battalion had four companies of fusiliers and one of grenadiers, but the grenadiers, unlike the Austrian and Prussian arrangements, remained with their home battalions and were not detached to form separate grenadier battalions. Depot troops were established on the basis of 1 company per battalion (thus 2 per regiment) in the infantry and 2 depot squadrons per cavalry regiment. These depot troops would be especially important in 1809 when many saw active combat service in response to the threat of Tyrolean insurgents. Furthermore, one of the cavalry depot squadrons often accompanied division and corps staffs on campaign to provide couriers, orderlies, scouts and guides. In terms of drill, a team of experienced officers had drafted new training regulations for the infantry during 1804–5; these borrowed from the French, but retained a distinctly Bavarian stamp. The use of light infantry received particular attention, and twenty especially clever and agile men in each company were designated as *Schützen* to perform light infantry functions. Bavarian regimental commanders would rely on these men in the coming campaigns and the number per company would rise to thirty-six in 1809, with an entire company of *Schützen* assigned to each battalion two years later. Tremendous changes were introduced in the artillery as well, with the revival of light artillery, the creation of permanent batteries and the formation of a train battalion. The net result of the reforms was significant enhancement of the army's capabilities.

This impression of the need to adapt was only heightened in 1806 as two Bavarian divisions joined the Grande Armée for the war against Prussia. Placed under Napoleon's brother Jerome, the 1st and 2nd Bavarian Divisions, along with the Württemberg contingent, conducted a series of generally successful sieges of Prussian fortresses in Silesia from November 1806 to the end of the war in July 1807. From February to May, however, the 2nd Division (under Wrede) marched east to join the French V Corps north of Warsaw. Reinforced to 13,300 men, the division won a tidy victory at Pultusk on 14 May, but the war was rapidly drawing to a close and there were no further actions. Wrede, however, did have his men re-enact Frederick the Great's triumph at Leuthen as a training exercise before the two divisions returned to Bavaria in November.

Other Bavarians also had a role in the war. Detached from the main contingent in November 1806, the 1st Chevaulegers performed well at Eylau and Heilsberg. Additionally, a brigade of 3 battalions, a chevauleger regiment and a battery (3,200 men) left Bavaria in June 1807 for the Baltic coast. It participated in the invasion of Swedish Pomerania, but saw little real combat before marching home in December.

The Bavarians had had few chances to prove themselves under Napoleon's eye from 1805 to 1807, but 1809 provided ample opportunity. The army's three divisions, combined into VII Corps under Marshal François Lefebvre, played a key role in containing and repelling the Austrian invasion in April, displaying great tactical proficiency in both withdrawal and attack in the wooded hills south of Regensburg. Outpost duty was a weakness, but the Bavarians made excellent use of the *Schützen* assigned to each battalion. Following these opening battles, most of VII Corps' tasks were associated with line of communications protection at Linz (June–July) and suppression of the rebellion in the Tyrol. Wrede's 2nd Division, however, conducted an extraordinary march to Vienna (close to 200km in four days) in time to participate in the Battle of Wagram, and fought well at Znaim.

Where there was glory to be won in fighting the Austrians, combat in the Tyrol brought only the misery and mutual atrocities of a vicious insurgency. In order to quell the rebellion three large-scale offensives were required, and success only came when Bavarian thrusts from the north were matched with French and Italian advances from the east and south. The tension associated with this campaign led to considerable Franco-Bavarian friction, culminating in Napoleon's relief of Lefebvre. The threat from the Tyrol and Austrian incursions from Bohemia also brought a significant expansion of Bavaria's armed forces as twelve new reserve battalions were formed, ad hoc units were created from depot troops,

Table 6.2 The Rheinbund: Theatres of War

Contingent	*Austria 1805*	Prussia 1806–7	Austria 1809	Spain 1808–13	Russia 1812	Germany 1813
Arenberg (27th Chasseurs)	–	x	–	x	–	–
Baden	x	x	x	x	x	x
Bavaria	x	x	x	–	x	x
Berg	–	x	x	x	x	x
Frankfurt	–	x	x	x	x	x
Hesse-Darmstadt	–	x	x	x	x	x
1st Nassau	–	x*	x	x	–	–
2nd Nassau and cavalry	–	x*	–	x	–	–
Württemberg	x	x	x	–	x	x
Würzburg	–	x	x	x	x	x
Saxony	–	x	x	–	x	x
Saxon Duchies (4th Rheinbund)	–	x	x	x	x	x
Anhalt/Lippe (5th Rheinbund)	–	x	x	x	x	x
Reuss/Schwarzburg/ Waldeck (6th)	–	x	x	x	x	x
Bataillon des Princes	–	–	–	x	–	–
Westphalia	–	–	x	x	x	x
Mecklenburg-Strelitz	–	–	x	–	x	–
Mecklenburg-Schwerin	–	–	x	–	x	–
Oldenburg	–	–	x	–	–	–

This table indicates theatres where significant portions of contingents were present, not necessarily participation in combat action.
The 1805 war with Austria shown in *italics* as the Rheinbund had not yet been formed.
*Not yet organised as 1st and 2nd Regiments.

national guards were called into service and volunteer formations were raised. Fortunately, Bavaria had a comprehensive, if not always effective, militia system upon which to draw, but the effort strained the monarchy's ability to provide equipment and qualified leaders. These new units were disbanded, deactivated or absorbed into existing regiments as the war ended, but the experience proved valuable when the army expanded to take the field against Napoleon in 1813.

With no units in Spain, the period 1810–11 was one of relative peace for Bavaria. In terms of military changes, a *Schützen* company was added to each infantry battalion to improve light infantry capabilities, and the two white-coated dragoon regiments were transformed into green-clad chevaulegers.[7] The dragoons and chevaulegers had always been used interchangeably in any case, so other than uniform colour, this conversion had no substantive effect.

Bavarians comprised VI Corps of the Grande Armée in 1812. It was a splendid army and in the best of spirits – well trained, well led, experienced and fully equipped. Under General, later Marshal, Laurent Gouvion St Cyr, VI Corps guarded the army's strategic left flank, fighting well at the two Battles of Polotsk in August and October of that year. The corps, however, had begun to dwindle and morale had begun to fade even before reaching Polotsk, and the long months there saw the Bavarian contingent rapidly diminish from disease and want. Despite considerable courage and skill in combat, therefore, the 'corps' numbered less than 4,000 men in early December when it reached 'the whirling human river' that had been the Grande Armée.[8] The Bavarians, too, soon disintegrated and by the 13th, Wrede, the senior remaining general, found himself in command of sixty-eight men – all that remained of the once-proud army.

The six Bavarian light cavalry regiments were detached from the corps in July and fought the campaign with the main army through Borodino to Moscow and back. They performed well, but suffered heavily, with the last organised unit finally dissolving in early November.

The 13th Infantry, attached to Marshal Jacques Etienne Macdonald's X Corps on the army's far left, was more fortunate. 'The regiment is in the best condition', wrote the new colonel when he arrived from Polotsk to assume command, 'what a contrast with the regiments I have just left'.[9] Retiring in good order, the regiment became part of the Danzig garrison, where it remained until December 1813.

The last year of the Rheinbund found Bavarian detachments dispersed all over Poland and eastern Germany. In addition to the 13th Infantry in Danzig, Wrede managed to assemble a wobbly division of some 6,500 in Poland and was bitterly angry when forced to detach two-thirds of them to garrison the fortress of Thorn on the Vistula. While the remainder made a wretched retreat to Bavaria, the Thorn garrison conducted itself well but was forced to surrender on 15 April. As these men were making their way home during the late spring and early summer, Bavaria was putting a new contingent into the field as 29th Division of Marshal Nicholas Oudinot's XII Corps. In contrast to its previous contributions, however, the division sent to Saxony in 1813 was poorly trained and poorly motivated. 'The skirmishers cannot skirmish, the cavalry cannot ride', complained their commander.[10] Officers were either inexperienced youths or cynical veterans who had become lackadaisical through 'exhaustion or sullenness'.[11] With only 7,500–8,000 men, the division was half the size Napoleon had demanded, and it was painfully obvious to the senior officers that their kingdom was withholding support for what leaders in Munich already perceived as a potentially doomed enterprise. The division's strength steadily eroded, until it was left with only 2,300 men under arms in early

September after the catastrophic defeat at Dennewitz. The feeble division was still in the field on 22 October when the officers confirmed that Bavaria had joined the Allies through the Treaty of Ried, signed on 8 October. Indeed, a combined Austro-Bavarian force under Wrede was already marching towards Napoleon's line of retreat. The remnants of the division thus turned homeward, but news took longer to reach the 13th Infantry in Danzig. That regiment had served with great honour, conducting itself well and resisting all efforts of the Allies to induce desertion. When it finally departed the fortress on 12 December it had earned the respect of its allies and its enemies.

Württemberg: The King's Army

Württemberg's King Friedrich was a corpulent but stern, energetic and ambitious monarch who placed a high value on his army and on personal loyalty to himself as sovereign. Like his neighbour in Bavaria, he made military service a duty and honour for his subjects, paid close attention to the national origin of his officers, promoted individuals based on merit and greatly increased the size of his realm's army through conscription. Another similarity with Bavaria was the gradual creation of an extensive militia system for national defence over and above the regular troops and the Royal Guard. New drill regulations introduced in February 1809 changed tactical instruction from a Prussian model to one inspired by, but not imposed by, France. Similarly, Württemberg seems to have retained a two-rank line unlike almost all of its Rheinbund counterparts. Another unique feature of Friedrich's policy was his maintenance of an army – line troops and guard – considerably in excess of his Rheinbund commitment.

As with the other Rheinbund monarchs in 1806, Friedrich was taken aback when a 24 September letter from Napoleon's chief of staff requested the Württemberg contingent depart for the theatre of war on 3 October. The army, with its infantry organised in individual battalions (i.e., not in regiments) and still tangled in reforms, was hardly on a war footing. It scrambled to prepare, and by 13 October, Friedrich could address his men in a farewell speech: 'Soldiers! You are designated to fight with and alongside the army that has heaped victory upon victory over the past twelve years under the greatest and grandest commander of our time ... This glorious mission will spur your courage, your bravery'. Though such addresses were routinely occasions for bombast, the king's words echoed the feelings of many officers and men in the Württemberg contingent (and in most others) during this war and for the next six years. Almost the entire army deployed on 14 October: 9 infantry battalions, 3 4-squadron cavalry regiments, and 3 batteries with 18 guns. The troops, however, had little opportunity to demonstrate their skills under Napoleon's eye. The emperor assigned Général de Division (GD) Dominique Vandamme as the contingent's overall commander and placed it under Jerome's IX Corps in

Silesia along with the Bavarians. The Württembergers performed well in numerous sieges and in the difficult 'lieutenant's war' of outposts, reconnaissances and ambushes on the army's southern flank, but thereby missed the grand battles.[12] Unfortunately, frictions developed between the Württembergers and Vandamme that would grow steadily worse over time.

The irritations left from the previous war spilled over into 1809 when Napoleon once again placed Vandamme in command of the Württemberg contingent. By now the army had expanded and changed its organisation. With the growth of the country in the wake of the victories over Austria and Prussia in the preceding several years, Württemberg had a larger population upon which to draw and Friedrich made a suitably larger army a high priority. A larger army based simply on individual battalions, however, would be both costly to administer and clumsy to command. As the kingdom went to war in 1809, therefore, its blue-clad line infantry was organised into 7 regiments known by their *Inhaber* or proprietors, each consisting of 2 4-company battalions plus a depot company. One (Neubronn) carried the title 'Fusilier Regiment' as an honorific, but was no different from the others. Although the 1st Company of the 1st Battalion in each regiment was designated a grenadier company, it did not have the same degree of special status associated with that title in other armies. Württemberg also had two *Jäger* and two light infantry battalions that both wore dark green and differed from one another only in their titles and small uniform details. These were named after their commanders and remained separate, but were routinely brigaded together. Friedrich had also raised a fourth light cavalry regiment to have two each of chevaulegers and *Jäger-zu-Pferd*. Like the light infantry, the only differences between the two types were in their designations and uniforms. The Royal Guard included a grenadier battalion and two cavalry squadrons.[13]

To meet his treaty commitment in 1809, Friedrich provided 5 infantry regiments, all 4 light battalions, his 4 line cavalry regiments, 2 horse batteries and a foot battery to Napoleon's new 'Army of Germany'. Though again under Vandamme, the Württembergers put in sterling service, especially during the April fighting in Bavaria and in the engagement at Linz on 17 May, where they bore the brunt of the fighting. The Light Brigade with the two *Jäger* and two light infantry battalions proved itself truly an elite formation, and the light cavalry was very good. The horse artillery was also excellent, but the large (ten-gun) foot battery generated many complaints owing to its heavy and cumbersome pieces.

At the same time, the challenge of rebellion posed a threat to the kingdom as the Tyrol and the Vorarlberg, former Austrian territories granted to Bavaria in 1805, rose in revolt. Friedrich relied upon his Guard and upon the two line regiments in the kingdom to defend his realm initially, but soon organised the depot companies into ad hoc battalions, assembled a depot cavalry squadron, created several temporary volunteer units, increased the Guard infantry with a *Jäger* company, built the Guard cavalry into a four-squadron regiment, formed a third horse battery and called up part of the militia (known as *Land-Batallione*). These sufficed to defeat the rebels and formed the basis for a new infantry regiment and a new dragoon regiment established in Württemberg near the end of the war. As these troops directly contributed to Napoleon's rear security, Württemberg, like Bavaria and Baden, thus greatly exceeded the stipulations of the Confederation treaty (mobilising as many as 28,600 men). The rapid expansion imposed a requirement for a large number of new officers, and many of the positions were filled by former Prussian officers despite Friedrich's wish to make his army more national.

The year 1811 brought changes in unit designation as the regiments lost their names and acquired numbers, 1st to 8th for the infantry and 1st to 5th for the cavalry. Guard units were exempt from this shift and units affiliated with members of the royal family were permitted to retain their titles in addition to the numbers. As a result, when Napoleon called for a regiment and two guns to reinforce the Danzig garrison that year, the troops that arrived in the fortress were titled the 7th Infantry, rather than Infantry Regiment Koseritz.

Württemberg contributed 4 infantry regiments, the 4 Light/*Jäger* battalions, 4 cavalry regiments and 24 guns to the Russian campaign as 25th Division of III Corps; the troops in Danzig also counted as part of the contingent. The rigours of the campaign quickly ground the division into dust. 'O! How desolate and sad are our formerly so lively marches', wrote a lieutenant on 14 June, 'No cheery song resounds, no happy laugh echoes in the ranks'.[14] By mid-August, the brigades had already been reformed as battalions, the battalions as companies. The retreat from Moscow destroyed the main contingent, and the 7th Infantry joined the army at the Berezina only to succumb to the same dreadful fate. A few dozen artillerymen left behind in Danzig surrendered with that fortress in late 1813.

Friedrich rapidly rebuilt his army after the Russian catastrophe, combining the two *Jäger* battalions and the two light battalions into new regiments, numbered 9th and 10th respectively (but consisting of only one battalion each). This period also brought a switch from the previous helmets to shakoes as headgear for the infantry and artillery. A new Württemberg contingent consisting of two infantry brigades (38th Division, IV Corps) and a cavalry brigade thus joined the Grande Armée in April 1813 and was heavily engaged at Bautzen during the spring campaign. A third infantry brigade joined 4th Corps during the armistice and a second cavalry brigade arrived to be assigned to VI Corps. The latter earned King Friedrich's wrath when it deserted to the Allies during the Battle of Leipzig without his royal permission; the brigade commander was cashiered and the two regiments (2nd and 4th) were disbanded, their men being distributed to other units. Meanwhile, privations and combat had so reduced the main contingent that its strength had dropped from 6,400 in mid-August to less than 1,000 combatants by mid-October.[15] The sad ruins of the division loyally stood by their alliance until released later in the month. Like the other Rheinbund contingents, they would soon be in action against the French.

Baden: Bravery and Zeal

Baden's experience as a French ally started poorly, at least in Napoleon's opinion. Although the new grand duchy had initiated major military reforms starting in 1803, these were based on a Frederickian Prussian model that was no longer applicable to European warfare. Moreover, the army was increasing rapidly in size as the state's territories expanded, growing fourfold from 1,976 in 1803 to more than 8,000 by the summer of 1807. Administration and training could not keep pace. The result was a painfully slow mobilisation in 1805 and an uninspiring performance in siege duty at Danzig in 1807. The contingent never reached its full strength during the latter war, its infantry component only numbering some 2,800 men with regiments that barely had the strength of battalions.

These unsatisfactory debut performances led to direct and comprehensive French intervention in everything from conscription and rank insignia to organisation and training during 1808. These measures, pursued with energy, produced an entirely new army by January 1809 with French drill and the French battalion structure of 6 140-man companies (including a grenadier and voltigeur company in each battalion). The Badeners switched to French rank insignia, but maintained their own uniforms, including the distinctive *Raupenhelm* similar to their Bavarian neighbours. They also continued to carry their own muskets, though these were slightly different in calibre from French models. In this new configuration, a brigade of three full regiments, an outstanding *Jäger* battalion, a light dragoon regiment and twelve guns participated in the 1809 war with Austria as part of the 1st Division of IV Corps. The contingent demonstrated tremendous march endurance and performed superbly at Ebelsberg, Wagram and Znaim. It also took part in the Hungarian campaign on detachment to Viceroy Eugène's Army of Italy, while the 3rd Infantry, the Light Dragoons and the foot battery fought at Aspern. Additionally, troops left behind in the grand duchy (Guard Grenadiers, Hussars, a provisional *Jäger* battalion) formed a small brigade to combat Vorarlberg rebels near Lake Constance in conjunction with the Württembergers.

In the meantime, the 4th Infantry Regiment and a foot artillery battery had departed for Spain in August 1808, exchanging its muskets for French models along the way.[16] The contingent joined the so-called 'German division' and fought honourably in Spain for the next five years, including the Battles of Talavera, Vitoria and the Bidassoa, until peacefully disarmed at Bayonne in December 1813 after the grand duchy had turned against Napoleon.

A fine Baden brigade (1st, 2nd and 3rd Infantry, *Jäger* Battalion, Hussar Regiment and a battery of eight guns), most of the men veterans, fought in Russia with IX Corps, playing a key role at the Berezina, where the Baden Hussars and Hessian Chevaulegers sacrificed themselves in successful but costly charges.[17] The brigade, numbering more than 7,600 that summer, was reduced to 425 effectives when it collected itself in Prussia on 30 December. While the field force was in Russia, Baden organised depot battalions (four fusilier companies) for each regiment. A replacement column of more than 1,100 created from these depots halted in Glogau on its way East and participated in the defence of the fortress through the spring of 1813.

A new Baden brigade (titled the 1st) and the Light Dragoons took part in the spring and autumn campaigns of 1813 in 39th Division, first in Marshal Michel Ney's III Corps (spring) and then, reinforced by the troops from Glogau, as part of Macdonald's XI Corps (autumn). A 2nd Baden Brigade was assembled during the summer and joined the Leipzig garrison, where both brigades were engulfed in the titanic battle on 19 October. With the exception of the Light Dragoons and a few guns, the entire contingent went into captivity as their grand duke joined Napoleon's enemies. Despite controversy over the end of the contingent at Leipzig, most French remembered the Badeners as troops who 'conducted themselves in every circumstance with as much bravery as zeal and loyalty'.[18]

Hesse-Darmstadt: Rivals in Courage

The history of the Hesse-Darmstadt contingent illustrates Napoleon's judicious treatment of his Rheinbund allies. Where the Badeners had displayed manifold deficiencies in their early campaigns, Napoleon had a good opinion of the Hessians despite some initial disappointments. He therefore interfered very little in their internal matters, allowing them, in particular, to retain their unique unit structure. The Hessian infantry was organised into three 'brigades', each of a two-battalion regiment of musketeers (line infantry) and a battalion of fusiliers for light infantry duties.[19] The fusiliers were uniformed in green, the musketeers in dark blue, and all wore a large bicorne for headgear until 1809. Each battalion consisted of four companies; there were no grenadiers or voltigeurs, but the fusiliers often acted independently in the performance of their light infantry functions.

In 1806, its first campaign under Napoleon, the grand duchy despatched its troops as soon as they were even close to being ready. As a result, the Leib-Garde Fusiliers and the 1st Leib Fusiliers arrived in time to fight at Jena as part of VII Corps, where they were unfortunately charged by

French hussars who took them for Prussian light infantry owing to their large bicornes and green uniforms. The rest of the contingent slowly joined the army, until all three 'brigades', the regiment of Chevaulegers, and a half-battery were in the field. This made a total of some 4,000 men, almost the entire armed force of the grand duchy. Having performed well in sieges at Graudenz and Stralsund, the Hessians returned home with considerable French praise.

Like Baden, Hesse-Darmstadt was soon required to supply a contingent for Spain. This consisted of the Gross- und Erbprinz Brigade and a half-battery of horse guns for a total of approximately 1,775 men, who arrived in Bayonne in October 1808. Like the Badeners, they were assigned to the 'German Division' and received French muskets during their passage to the Pyrenees. In addition, the 3 battalions were amalgamated into 2, organised along French lines with 6 companies each, making a curious sight as their green and blue uniforms were mixed on parade. They also received French instructors to teach them French tactical drill. All of this change, compounded by friction with the Hessian regiment's difficult commander, initially caused dissatisfaction with French generals and even came to Napoleon's attention. As the troops learned their new manoeuvres and a new regimental colonel arrived, however, the regiment (as it was now called) soon restored the excellent reputation the Hessian troops generally enjoyed among their French allies. The Hessians remained in Spain until April 1812 when almost the entire contingent was captured after stalwart resistance in the siege of Badajoz. Most men went off to internment in Britain, but a number enlisted with their opponents to avoid the rigours of imprisonment. Some 245 detached troops were collected up and sent back to their homeland in time to participate in the 1813 campaign.

Although the grand duke had almost 2,000 men serving in Spain, he contributed more than 4,800 to the 1809 war against Austria, well above his treaty commitment. This brigade of six battalions, the Chevaulegers Regiment and six guns gave excellent service as part of the 2nd Division in IV Corps. The Hessians were not only heavily engaged at Aspern and Wagram, they made significant contributions at Pressburg and in Hungary, and fought at Znaim as well. In all cases, they earned praise from their French commanders. 'I must make particular mention of the Hessian troops, who rival Your Majesty's in courage', Marshal Louis Davout wrote to Napoleon after watching the Hessians in action at Pressburg.[20]

Returning home in early 1810, some of the Hessian infantrymen were already wearing the new shakoes that would replace their old-fashioned bicornes as they embarked on the Russian campaign. The units sent to Russia were the same that had fought in Austria, but the two fusilier battalions were now combined into a provisional light infantry regiment. Moreover, the brigade quickly found itself split up, with elements detached all over the theatre of operations from Moscow to the border performing rear area duties. The Leib-Garde and Leib regiments made the retreat from Moscow as part of the Imperial Guard, fought at Krasnyi and joined the provisional light infantry regiment for a final terrible battle at the Berezina. The ravages of the campaign left the entire brigade with only 327 infantry and artillery under arms when Marshal Joachim Murat reviewed them in mid-December, but they took great pride in having saved all 6 of their guns. Thanks to returned convalescents and other detached personnel, the Hessians were able to form a provisional battalion of 604 men that remained with the Imperial Guard while the sad remainder of the contingent returned to Darmstadt in mid-January.

The Hessians fielded a new brigade in April 1813, formed by combining fresh conscripts from the homeland with the provisional battalion left over from Russia and two replacement battalions intended to reinforce the original contingent across the Niemen. This new brigade joined 39th Division and fought in the major battles of the spring campaign, but suffered badly from desertion, a problem previously rare in Hessian units. The Hessians (the brigade with XI Corps, the weak Chevaulegers with XII) participated in the major actions during the autumn campaign, most of the contingent surrendering after being trapped in Leipzig during the ill-fated retreat. The cavalry and artillery escaped to march home as their sovereign changed sides, but one battalion (2nd of the new Light Regiment) remained in French service, forming part of the garrison at Torgau until 25 November when the French commandant released it on confirming the change in political circumstances.

Saxony: Old Army in New Wars

Saxony entered the Rheinbund in the midst of war. Forced into an alliance with Prussia when that kingdom went to war with France in the autumn of 1806, the Saxons found themselves at Jena, involved in a type of warfare for which they were not prepared. The Saxon Army that year was a relic from the Seven Years War, its tactics out of date, its officers antique, its troops still wearing queues and old-fashioned uniforms, its artillery poorly organised and lacking a permanent train establishment, its muskets clumsy, its companies still being run as private commercial enterprises by their commanders. Above all, the army's mindset was antiquated, expectations were based on old norms and neither officers nor men were prepared for the remorseless pace of Napoleonic campaigning. Nonetheless, the French emperor entertained a high opinion of Saxon soldiery and moved to bring them into the alliance almost as soon as the firing had stopped at Jena. Courteous treatment of the captured Saxon officers, the promise of a kingship and other benefits quickly convinced Elector Friedrich August that his best course lay with France, and Saxony duly signed a treaty joining the Confederation in December 1806.

Although the treaty set Saxony's military contribution at 20,000 men, assembling such a number while the war was still in progress was clearly unrealistic, so Napoleon allowed the Saxons to field only 6,000 for the ongoing conflict. The bulk of these, twelve infantry battalions, were committed to siege duties at Kolberg, Danzig and Breslau. However, four cavalry squadrons fought alongside their new allies at Friedland, garnering praise from the French for their performance.

Large and strategically placed, Saxony was not asked to contribute to the Iberian struggle. Its army, therefore, had almost two years to prepare before it was next called to arms on Napoleon's behalf. To the great frustration of many younger officers, however, nothing substantial was done to improve organisation, training or mobilisation procedures. The army was thus in some embarrassment when Napoleon invited the king to prepare his troops for war with Austria in early 1809. Designated the Army of Germany's IX Corps, the troops showed much good will and responded well to the solicitations of their commander, Marshal Bernadotte, but their organisation and administration were creaky, they were slow on the march and they had no idea how to skirmish (at least as the French understood such things). The artillery was especially weak. The foot batteries were deficient in almost every respect and there was no horse artillery whatsoever. Moreover, the army's overall structure was too large (being preserved for patronage purposes), so there were simply not enough men to fill all the battalions. Bernadotte attempted to correct some of these problems during May and June along the Danube. In the first place, he sought to build a light infantry capability. Each Saxon infantry battalion had a number of designated *Schützen* supposedly able to perform light infantry functions, and it had long been Saxon practice to combine these into ad hoc units for specific purposes. Bernadotte took this much further, establishing two new *Schützen* battalions under exceptional young officers. He also endeavoured to create some light artillery, but the resulting four-gun battery proved no more mobile than the foot batteries. The marshal also reduced each regiment to battalion size and sent home all of the excess, often over-aged, cadres. On the other hand, basic Saxon drill remained the same and Bernadotte did not alter the traditional Saxon practice of combining the grenadier companies of each line battalion into separate grenadier battalions. In this structure, the corps took part in the Battle of Wagram on 5 and 6 July. The battle was a debacle for the Saxons. Despite great courage, casualties were very heavy and much of the infantry collapsed in disorder on the first evening during an abortive attack on Wagram, and again on the second day after enduring a whirlwind of artillery and musket fire in the centre of Napoleon's battle line. The fact that they wore white uniforms like the Austrian enemy made matters worse as Saxon units were several times fired upon by their French allies and by fellow Saxons. Especially on 6 July, all of this took place under the direct observation of Napoleon and dozens of French officers, leaving the Saxon Army associated with confusion, disorder and retreat in many French minds. What was left of the corps was pulled out of the line to rally, and, three days later, Napoleon disbanded it, relieved Bernadotte and appointed Général de Division Jean Louis Reynier to command what was now simply called the 'Saxon Contingent'.

The Wagram calamity, coming on top of the shocks of 1806 and 1807, spurred the Saxon king and his military administration into action. The result was a set of truly sweeping reforms designed by a committee of energetic younger generals and introduced during 1810. The basic organisational structure remained in place: 2 battalions per infantry regiment, 5 companies per battalion, 1 of which was a grenadier company that would operate separately. However, 4 line regiments were disbanded so the remaining 8 could be manned fully, while the 2 *Schützen* battalions and the Guard Grenadiers were converted to full 2-battalion regiments. A company sized '*Schützen* Corps' was also created. Additionally, regimental artillery was revived with four guns per regiment. These organisational changes came along with the introduction of new tactical regulations drafted by Saxon officers. Heavily influenced by the French model and recent combat experience, the new drill emphasised skirmishing and small, tactical columns, but acceptance of these radical changes only occurred gradually. Reform for the cavalry was less dramatic, but the Karabinier Regiment was disbanded, all regiments were brought to a full four squadrons (the Hussar Regiment with eight was an exception), and the Prinz Clemens Chevaulegers were converted to lancers in late 1811. The artillery underwent significant change, acquiring a simplified, modern system of guns and howitzers, its first set of tactical regulations and a permanent train battalion. At the higher levels of organisation, permanent divisions and brigades were established for the first time, improving unit cohesion and training, as well as command and control. Administratively, the most important reforms were a complete revamping of arrangements for inspecting the army and the abolition of the practice of company 'ownership' by senior staff officers and commanders. At the same time, the officer corps was purged of the superannuated and the inept to make way for a fresh generation of leaders. Finally, the army completely revised its uniforms, giving it a totally new external appearance to complement the internal alterations. Basic colours remained the same, with white for the line infantry (dark green for the new light infantry), dark green for the artillery, red for the light horse, and white or straw yellow for the heavies, but everything else was modernised. Uniform cut was changed, wigs and queues were discarded and bicornes were exchanged for shakoes in all cases except the heavy cavalry, who were issued with helmets. In short, the transformation was fundamental, and the army that took the field in 1812 was vastly different from its predecessors. If some aspects of the old seem to have lingered, especially in tactics, the reformed army was well trained, well equipped and well led when it departed for the Russian border in the spring of 1812.

Unfortunately for the Saxons, they would see their fine army, like those of their Rheinbund allies, vanish in the maelstrom of the Russian campaign. The contingent's 2 divisions (23,000) constituted VII Corps under Reynier and operated on the Grande Armée's far right flank in conjunction with the Austrian Auxiliary Corps. Although thereby spared some of the horrors of the central front, privations were common, there were several costly engagements and the weather was just as cold. Losses, if not as stupefying as with the Grande Armée, were still frightful, and Reynier had only some 6,000 survivors when he departed Warsaw in early February 1813. As with the other Confederation contingents, parts of the Saxon contribution served outside their 'home' corps. Most notably, the Guard and Zastrow Cuirassiers participated in the capture of the Great Redoubt at Borodino under GM Johann von Thielmann (who would command Prussian III Corps in the Waterloo campaign). Additionally, the Albrecht Chevaulegers were attached to III Cavalry Corps, while the Prinz Johann Chevaulegers and two infantry regiments joined IX Corps. All of these units and their associated artillery disappeared in the vast misery of the retreat.

The year 1813 was one of confusion, uncertainty, and woe for Saxony. King Friedrich August was caught between Napoleon and the Allies, with some officers transparently leaning towards defection, his army in ruins and his land plundered and exhausted by both sides. One of the few intact infantry regiments (Prinz Maximilian, it had been on garrison duty in the north) was surrounded and destroyed by a large Allied raiding detachment in northern Germany in early April, 400 of the men immediately agreeing to join the Allies' Russo-German Legion. The king fled west with some remaining cavalry, while the bulk of the army waited in a state of 'armed neutrality' at Torgau under Thielmann. Napoleon's victory at Lützen on 2 May brought Saxony back into active participation in the Rheinbund, and a reconstituted VII Corps, once again under Reynier, joined the Grande Armée just prior to Bautzen. Additionally, a Guard Grenadier battalion served with the French Guard and the two heavy regiments were again attached to the cavalry reserve. Thielmann defected to the Allies. The heavy cavalry performed brilliantly at Dresden, but the Saxons of VII Corps suffered terribly in the autumn fighting, and an entire battalion deserted to the enemy. By the time the contingent reached Leipzig on 17 October, it had been reduced from 14,300 in 2 divisions to a single division of 5,000. Of these, approximately 4,000 defected to the Allies en masse during the fighting on 18 October, taking 19 of their guns with them.[21] Not far away, the two cuirassier regiments continued to serve with the French until released by their monarch after the battle. Saxon infantry at Modlin and artillery detachments at Danzig, Dresden and Glogau were among the last to leave the alliance, the latter not until January 1814.

Westphalia: New Country, New Army

The large Westphalian contingent had an extraordinarily complex history shaped by powerful and often contradictory influences: Napoleon's desire to build Westphalia as a model state, while simultaneously trying to exploit it economically and militarily; French dominance of the court and the imposition of French language and governmental practices on a German populace; and difficult relations between Napoleon and Jerome, the younger brother he installed as king. Most of all, Westphalia was an artificial kingdom, cobbled together from many components. This set of circumstances did not doom it from the start, but did imply that the state would only take root if ruled with a judicious mixture of sympathy and firmness. Jerome, however, while well-meaning and intelligent, was too feckless and indolent even to learn German, let alone supply the leadership necessary to construct a solid state with a solid army. Furthermore, he too often surrounded himself with incompetent, inexperienced cronies who could neither guide him nor make up for his lapses.

Westphalia was supposed to supply 25,000 men, but Napoleon recognised that this would be impossible in the first years of the kingdom. He thus reduced the demand for men to 12,500 and instead required Westphalia to bear the cost of supporting 12,500 French troops. Many in Westphalia's government saw this situation as odious and sought to raise the new kingdom's army to a sufficient size as quickly as possible to eliminate the burden. The result was fairly impressive in numbers of troops brought into service through volunteer recruiting and conscription. Furthermore, many of the soldiers had at least some experience in the Prussian Army or in the forces of now-eradicated German principalities. Indeed, the Westphalian Army was an arena of considerable opportunity for many unemployed officers and soldiers who could count on quick promotion and reliable pay by taking Jerome's oath. Some French sergeants and many French officers, as well as some Polish lancers, were incorporated to increase the cadre of experienced leaders (and to provide a degree of loyalty should the Westphalian experiment falter). While useful, this measure also generated resentment, as did the overwhelmingly French character of the army: drill, organisation and uniform style were all French. Even the language of command in some Guard units was French. This was by no means fatal to the enterprise, and it seems highly likely the associated disgruntlement could have been managed with careful leadership and a deft hand. Such subtlety, however, was all too seldom apparent. Nonetheless, the army had enormous potential and made great progress in a short time despite these many challenges. By early 1809, the line troops consisted of 6 infantry regiments (2 6-company field battalions and a 4-company depot battalion each on the French pattern), a light infantry battalion, a chevaulegers regiment and a cuirassier regiment. There was also a substantial Royal Guard including a Garde-Grenadier Battalion, a Garde-Jäger Battalion, a Garde-Chevaulegers Regiment, a Garde du Corps company, and an affiliated battalion of Jäger-Carabinier recruited from foresters and huntsmen. The army was, however, still very much 'under construction' when it was called upon to face its first test of combat in 1809.

A division composed of three line regiments, the light infantry battalion, and two artillery batteries departed Westphalia in early 1809 with a strength of more than 7,500 men, crossed the Pyrenees into Catalonia in May and immediately joined the Berg and Würzburg contingents in the trenches around Gerona.[22] Thrown into a poorly prepared assault against an outer fort in July, the Germans suffered heavily. 'We were received with every conceivable means of destruction' recalled a lieutenant of the 2nd Westphalian Line, 'grenades, showers of burning pitch and oil, huge, plunging blocks of stone, and exploding sacks of powder'.[23] This sort of desperate combat combined with the privations and rampant sickness of the long siege wrecked the Westphalian division. By December when Gerona surrendered, the entire division numbered only some 1,500 men under arms, and by the spring of 1811 it was reduced to a small battalion. The 300 survivors finally headed home in March 1813.

The 1st Chevaulegers Regiment also spent its service life in Spain. Departing Westphalia in September 1808 with 3 squadrons (550 men), it fought all over western and central Spain (where it received lances in 1812), but was reduced to a squadron in 1813 and transferred to Suchet where it was disarmed with the Nassau light horse in December.

The Westphalian Army also weathered a crisis at home in 1809 as one of the Guard's colonels led an abortive rebellion timed to coincide with the Austrian invasion of Bavaria. The army, however, remained loyal to its young king, and Jerome showed considerable mettle in addressing his officers. This revolt quickly dissipated, but the army's showing against other rebels that spring and summer ranged from mediocre to miserable, and an amateurish campaign in Saxony was characterised by chaotic ineptitude. 'We were like a herd of cattle, driven about', wrote a lieutenant. Jerome seemed more interested in the luxuries of his travelling court than in the war, and his subordinates had no idea how to run an army in the field. 'You make war like a satrap!' fumed Napoleon.[24]

Things had improved by 1812 when some 16,600 Westphalians marched for Russia as the Grande Armée's VIII Corps under Vandamme.[25] In the intervening years, the army had been increased to 8 line regiments, 3 light battalions, 2 cuirassier regiments (Napoleon viewed these as an extravagance) and 2 hussar regiments. Each line regiment now included an artillery company, and each was supposed to add a third battalion, but only 2nd and 7th were able to do so before heading East. The Westphalians had had little battle experience as an army, but training, equipment and discipline were good when they marched for the Niemen River. 'One could rightly expect something great from them' recorded a lieutenant in the 5th Line.[26] Leadership problems at the top overshadowed quality at the lower levels. Jerome and Vandamme, who had bickered during the 1807 campaign in Silesia, soon fell out. The king relieved Vandamme, but the general's replacement, GD Andoche Junot, was a very poor substitute. Jerome himself quit the army soon afterwards. The bulk of VIII Corps participated in the march on Moscow, the Battle of Borodino (where the Westphalian cuirassiers played a key role in the capture of the Great Redoubt) and the dreadful retreat.

The new year found bits and pieces of the Westphalian Army scattered across Germany and Poland, while authorities in the kingdom attempted to raise new troops and hold the monarchy together under pressure from Allied raiders and popular unrest. Indeed, the kingdom was still forming new units during 1812 and early 1813. A Fusilier-Garde Regiment was thus established in the queen's name during 1812 (with the same structure as the line regiments), while a 4th Light Battalion was created from the troops who had returned from Spain in March 1813. From these and reformed units, a mixed division came into existence in April. This formation, however, was broken up immediately after Lützen and its constituent elements were distributed among II, XI and XII Corps. Tiny remnants fought at Leipzig, but the two Westphalian hussar regiments, sent to serve as light cavalry for II Corps, deserted or allowed themselves to be captured during August and September. Other Westphalians served in garrisons. The 1st Infantry had marched on the army's left in 1812 and was thus still intact when it became part of the Danzig garrison; the combined infantry remnants of VIII Corps were designated the 4th and 5th Regiments and assigned to Küstrin after the Russian catastrophe (surrendering in March 1814); and new formations went to Dresden. Some units, especially Guard, remained in Westphalia, including an ephemeral Guard Hussar Regiment, but their ability to protect the kingdom was minimal. Though some remained loyal, many troops threw away their weapons at the sight of Allied raiders, and Westphalia's capital fell to a bold Russian general for a time. Jerome regained the city, but the imminent end was evident, and he departed on 26 October, never to return. The Kingdom of Westphalia had ceased to exist.

The Grand Duchy of Berg: Army of a 'Model State'

Berg had many similarities with Westphalia: its infantrymen wore white uniforms, they practised French drill in French-style organisations and the grand duchy was, to a degree, also an artificial creation, stitched together from a collection of former Prussian, Bavarian, Nassau and other lands.

Napoleon initially allotted Berg to Marshal Murat and hoped to transform it into a model state for the Confederation, a task for which Murat was particularly ill-suited. Although Murat disdained the grand duchy as too small for his personal grandeur and spent little time focused on its administration, he did concern himself with the organisation and uniforms of some of his new realm's troops.

The 1st Berg Infantry was established in December 1806, using the former Bavarian 11th Infantry as a foundation. The regiment was structured in two battalions according to the French model, instructed using French drill and dressed in a modest but serviceable French-style uniform of white with blue distinctions. From May 1807 to the autumn of 1808, it served in Prussia and northern Germany, first with the besieging forces at Danzig, Graudenz and Stralsund, later as part of the garrison in Swedish Pomerania. In the meantime, orders had been issued to form two additional infantry regiments and a regiment of chevaulegers on a French four-squadron establishment, including a personal bodyguard (Garde du Corps) as its 1st Company. Murat used this opportunity to indulge his passion for splendid, or extravagant, military dress by dictating that the troopers be clothed in pale yellow with rose distinctions; it seems, however, that the men actually wore white (for dress) or grey (for field service).[27] Both infantry and cavalry soon marched for Spain, and from this point forward, it is easier to treat the foot and mounted elements of the Berg contingent separately as their meandering histories seldom intersect.

The Berg infantry was quickly reorganised to conform to the French 1808 model of 6 companies per battalion: 1 grenadier, 1 voltigeur and 4 of fusiliers. In this configuration, a brigade consisting of the first two regiments (each of two battalions) and an artillery company crossed the Rhine in December 1808 to join the siege of Gerona in 1809. Stopping in Paris en route, the men learned that Murat had become King of Naples and Napoleon had become the regent of Berg on behalf of his 4-year-old nephew Napoleon-Louis, the new grand duke. This change in political circumstances had a practical effect for the troops as they had to exchange their old shako plates and cartridge box insignia with the 'J' monogram for new ones bearing an 'N'. Like the Würzburg troops with whom they were brigaded, the siege left the Berg regiments in ruins. Reduced to a regiment and then to a lone battalion (1810), the remains of the contingent returned to the grand duchy in the autumn of 1811.

In February 1808 two squadrons of Berg cavalry, titled the 'Chevaulegers of the Grand Duke of Berg', went to Spain with Murat during his brief sojourn in Iberia. Of the 300 men, only two-thirds were actually mounted and these served first as Murat's Guard, later with the Imperial Guard until January 1809. By that time, about half had re-crossed the Pyrenees to join Murat's Royal Guard in his new dispensation as King of Naples; most of the others were incorporated into the Chasseurs-à-Cheval or

Grenadiers-à-Cheval of the French Imperial Guard. A few returned to reconstruct the regiment. With a new name, 'Chasseurs-à-Cheval of the Grand Duchy of Berg', and a new, dark-green uniform, the regiment was able to assemble all of its constituent elements in southern Germany in June 1809; it was assigned to Napoleon's rear area security forces during the war with Austria that year, but saw no action. In 1810, the regiment underwent another change in title as it received lances and became the Lanciers de Berg. In this guise, it returned to Iberia in June 1810, serving with distinction in central Spain as part of the Imperial Guard. Early in 1812, a large portion of the regiment was sent back to Berg as Napoleon prepared for war with Russia; the remainder stayed in Spain until March 1813.

As for the infantry, while the first two regiments were suffering in Catalonia, the 3rd Regiment achieved formation in early 1809 and took part in rear area security operations during the war with Austria as part of King Jerome's X Corps. In November, it was sent to the west coast of France for garrison duty. Cadres of its 1st Battalion returned to Germany in July 1811, but the 2nd Battalion stayed in France until March 1812; from June 1812, it spent a short time on the Spanish border and in Catalonia before returning over the Pyrenees in February 1813.

The various elements of the Berg contingent were assigned to IX Corps for the invasion of Russia. A second regiment of lancers had been established in 1811, and this fine unit joined the Baden Hussars, Hessian Chevaulegers and Saxon Albrecht Chevaulegers as the corps' cavalry division. The 1st and 2nd Infantry Regiments and the 1st Battalion of the 3rd were rebuilt, and a new 4th Regiment was formed. Impressive as that seemed, these infantry units never reached full strength (average battalion strength was approximately 530 men on 31 August), and the men in the ranks were almost entirely brand new 'conscripts who had never fired a shot nor seen the enemy'.[28] All seven infantry battalions, the lancer regiment and the two Berg artillery batteries vanished in the Russian snows. 'I cannot tell you in words what the army has suffered', wrote a lieutenant on 21 December, 'I have lost everything, everything: horses, clothes, equipment, health, all is lost'.[29]

Several hundred wretched survivors, combined with depot troops and II/3rd Infantry returned from Spain and formed a new 1st Infantry in 1813. Apparently fearing the men would desert if placed in proximity of Prussian troops, Napoleon assigned the regiment to garrison duty in Cherbourg. Here it was disarmed and held in prisoner of war status until repatriated in 1814.

The lancers were also re-established using cadres returned from Spain as a base. Unlike the infantry, however, Napoleon had great faith in the horsemen and an initial squadron that reached the army in April was assigned to the Imperial Guard. The lancers maintained their excellent reputation during the spring campaign and, reinforced from Berg, attained a strength of three squadrons by the end of the summer armistice. The regiment, brigaded with the Dutch Lancers of the Guard, performed superbly during the autumn campaign, but was cut off in Leipzig on 19 October. Only a few elements and individuals escaped. A new company joined the army during the retreat and participated in the Battle of Hanau on 30–31 October, probably the last Rheinbund troops to fight in a major engagement in Germany on Napoleon's side. Some of these men ended up in the Mainz garrison until its capitulation in April 1814, but the rest were disarmed in December – 'a fine reward for such long and loyal service!' wrote one.[30] Those officers whose home districts lay on the left bank of the Rhine were parcelled out to French regiments, and it is possible that some of the troopers ended up with the 27th Chasseurs, formed like the lancers of men from both banks of the Rhine. The others remained prisoners until 1814.

Nassau and the Microstates: A Corps d'Élite

The two Nassau princes present a peculiar case as their combined contingent not only included subjects from their lands, but also contributions from other princes. These took two forms. Isenburg and the two Hohenzollern principalities elected to provide their own men, but to have them incorporated into the Nassau battalions with no special status or uniform distinctions. Arenberg, Salm-Salm, Salm-Kyrburg, Liechtenstein and the Prince von der Leyen (also known as Hohengeroldseck), on the other hand, preferred to pay subsidies and allow Nassau to recruit and equip the requisite number of soldiers. This spared local rulers the awkwardness of introducing conscription and other unpopular measures. In the peculiar case of Liechtenstein, the payment system allowed that principality to maintain an independent existence even though its sovereign was a senior Austrian general. These arrangements were still being negotiated when the Nassau contingent was called to war in the autumn of 1806.

On their own, the two Nassau principalities formed four infantry battalions and a squadron of *Reitende Jäger* (chasseurs-à-cheval). Mobilisation was slow, but the 3rd Battalion reached VII Corps in time to participate in the Battle of Jena alongside the two Hessian battalions. This proved to be the only major action for the Nassauers, and the remainder of 1806 was spent on garrison duty, escorting prisoners or other rear area tasks. During 1807, however, the contingent participated in the siege of Kolberg and distinguished itself at the siege of Stralsund. In the meantime, the *Reitende Jäger* were doubled to make two squadrons, and the 1st joined the Berlin garrison in May 1807.

The Nassau troops became best known for their role in Spain. During the summer of 1808, the 4 battalions, each of 5 companies, had been formed into 2 regiments, with the 1st and 4th Battalions comprising the 1st Infantry and the 2nd Infantry composed of the 2nd and 3rd Battalions. When Napoleon called on Nassau to provide a contingent for Spain, authorities selected the 2nd Regiment (or 1st Rheinbund) and brought its battalions up to six companies each by drawing on the 1st Infantry.[31] Arriving in Bayonne on 11 October 1808, the Nassau 2nd Infantry joined the Baden and Hessian regiments in the 'German Division', and quickly established a fine reputation for discipline and appearance as well as battlefield performance. The Nassauers remained in central and northern Spain, fighting with distinction from Talavera to Vitoria and back into France where, on instructions from his sovereign, its colonel led the regiment across the lines to defect to the British on 11 December 1813.

In addition to an infantry regiment, Napoleon had wanted Nassau to contribute a battery to Spain, but the little monarchies had no guns, so the 2nd Squadron of *Reitende Jäger* was sent in place of the artillery. The squadron, arriving in Bayonne in November 1808, soon earned warm accolades from its French commanders for skill and endurance during innumerable engagements in central and northern Spain. 'They are in effect, a corps d'élite', wrote one French general, 'or, more exactly, a small band of heroes'.[32] The 1st Squadron joined its compatriots in Bayonne in July 1813 and both were transferred to Catalonia in October. Here they were disarmed at the end of the year along with other Rheinbund troops.[33]

The odyssey of the 1st Infantry (or 2nd Rheinbund) was more complex. The regiment was attached to General Rouyer's division of troops from small German states in April 1809 as war with Austria loomed. Gradually filled out with the small contingents from Isenburg and the Hohenzollern states, the men manned important garrisons, including Vienna, but saw no real action. Nonetheless, their professionalism and appearance made a good impression on their French allies. As the war with Austria concluded, the regiment rejoined Rouyer and marched off to Catalonia, where the division arrived in March 1810. When the rest of Rouyer's battalions departed in January 1811 after a cruel and costly ten months across the Pyrenees, however, the Nassauers remained behind. The Nassau regiment had also suffered heavily, but it soon rebuilt itself with replacements and convalescents. Having become one of the most reliable units in the Barcelona garrison, it still numbered 1,748 men 'present under arms' when it was disarmed in December 1813 in the wake of the defection by its sister regiment and events in Germany. Marshal Louis Gabriel Suchet, however, under whose orders the regiment was then serving, took this step with great reluctance. 'I am sorry to lose you', he announced in an order of the day on 21 December. 'I am reporting to the government how much I value you, and I am requesting that, as soon as circumstances permit, I should be allowed to return to you the weapons you have borne with honour'.[34]

Würzburg: A Habsburg in the Rheinbund

Another contingent that spent most of its service in Catalonia was the Würzburg Infantry Regiment (or 3rd Rheinbund).[35] Würzburg's Grand Duke Ferdinand was a Habsburg prince, but he was a reliable Confederation member and the troops of his small contingent served loyally throughout the Napoleonic period. At the foundation of the Rheinbund, Würzburg had a two-battalion infantry regiment, a company of chevaulegers and an artillery company. The infantry and cavalry (joined by an additional company) participated in garrison duty and sieges (Danzig, Graudenz, Stralsund) during the 1806–7 war, returning in December 1807. A year later, the grand duchy was 'invited' to send its infantry regiment to Spain. Now restructured along French lines, with French drill and French rank insignia, the regiment marched out on 14 December 1808 and spent the next five years in the gruelling Iberian conflict. Taking heavy casualties during the siege of Gerona in 1809, the regiment was reduced to a battalion in 1811 and numbered only 280 effective combatants when it was disarmed along with the Nassauers in December 1813.[36]

Meanwhile, the grand duchy had raised three new battalions for the invasion of Russia. These were numbered 2nd to 4th as the troops in Spain were considered the 1st Battalion. Along with a new regimental artillery company, the regiment joined GD Pierre Durutte's French 32nd Division of Reynier's VII Corps in the autumn, while the chevaulegers, now transformed into a French-style squadron, rode off to garrison the Baltic coast. The infantry suffered heavily in fighting on Napoleon's southern flank during November, and, leaving the 4th Battalion behind in Modlin, the remnants marched back West to rebuild. The chevaulegers, joined by a third company and the reinforced 2nd and 3rd Battalions, fought in the spring and autumn campaigns of 1813, while a new 5th Battalion was sent to strengthen the garrison of Torgau.[37] The autumn of 1813 thus saw the grand duchy with 5 battalions and a light horse squadron in action: 1 battalion in Spain, 2 in the field with Durutte's division in Germany and 2 in fortress garrisons. Badly depleted during the autumn fighting, the field battalions were destroyed at Leipzig (only forty men returned initially), while the battalions in Modlin and Torgau suffered from disease and privation of every sort before gaining release (1 December and 24 November respectively). The squadron, which 'had always distinguished itself before the enemy', also rode back to Würzburg in November.[38]

Thuringians and More: the 4th, 5th and 6th Rheinbund Regiments

As in the times of the Holy Roman Empire, Napoleon created composite units to draw on the manpower of the smaller Confederation states. The resulting formations presented a colourful and confusing tableau as men from numerous small states, each wearing its own uniform, were assembled on the parade field. Unlike the *Reich*, however, Napoleonic

France insisted on uniformity in drill, rank insignia and, in most cases, in organisation. Moreover, there was little scope for evasion or delay when summonses came from the French emperor. The units under consideration here were constructed from the contingents of the myriad small states in Thuringia combined with those of 3 principalities in north-central Germany: the 5 so-called 'Saxon Duchies', the 3 Anhalt duchies, the lands of the senior and junior princes of Reuss, the 2 Schwarzburg principalities, Lippe-Detmold, Schaumburg-Lippe and Waldeck.

These contingents were supposed to participate in the 1806–7 war, but the only troops formed in time for even minimal skirmishing were those of the Saxon Duchies, who took part in the siege of Kolberg and subsequent garrison duties (March–December 1807).[39] Battalions from Anhalt, Schwarzburg and Reuss only departed for Prussia in July (after the peace had been signed) and had returned by September; the troops of Waldeck and the two Lippe principalities took too long to raise and did not leave their home states.[40]

If they missed the war against Prussia and Russia, Schwarzburg, Lippe, Reuss and Waldeck contributed to the Bataillon des Princes (or Bataillon Princière) formed for Spain in Metz during December 1808. Equipped with French muskets, trained according to French drill and wearing French rank insignia, this odd battalion crossed the Pyrenees into Catalonia on 12 April 1809 with some 812 men. Consumed by exhausting picket, garrison and anti-guerrilla duties, however, it numbered only 184 men fit for service by June 1810 when its remaining troops were absorbed into the appropriate contingents of the 5th and 6th Rheinbund Regiments.[41]

Back in Germany, war with Austria was on the horizon in 1809, and Napoleon assembled a division of troops from the small German states under GD Marie François Rouyer to include in his Army of Germany. In addition to the 1st Nassau, this division included the new 4th, 5th and 6th Rheinbund Regiments. The first of these combined the 5 Saxon Duchies organised in 2 line battalions with the standard structure of 4 musketeer companies, 1 grenadier company and 1 voltigeur company each; it also included a Light Battalion all of fusiliers. The 5th Regiment had a battalion of Anhalt troops (1st) and 1 composed of the 2 Lippe contingents (2nd), while the 6th contained a 4-company battalion of Schwarzburg troops (1st) and a 2nd Battalion made up of 2 companies each from Reuss and Waldeck.[42] The division spent most of the war on garrison duty in Passau, but it was also involved in the second offensive into the Tyrol in August. This proved very costly for the 4th Regiment, which fought courageously but lost almost 1,000 men on 4 August when ambushed by Tyrolean rebels in a narrow gorge south of Innsbruck. The division left the 'land of murderers' after this abortive offensive and temporarily garrisoned Vienna until being withdrawn in December for duty in Spain.[43]

Assignment to Spain led to dramatic desertion, even among the battalions of the highly regarded 4th Regiment, but the division still counted 4,700 men in its ranks (including 1st Nassau) when it entered Catalonia in March 1810. The grinding Spanish insurgency, however, rapidly destroyed the division. Leaving 1st Nassau in Barcelona, the other three regiments could barely muster 500 dispirited men under arms when they crossed back into France in January 1811.

Reformed and rebuilt, the three regiments were employed in garrison duties in the new French departments on the North Sea coast (formerly Holland and the Hanseatic territories) and in northern Germany during the spring and summer of 1812. They marched for Russia in September as part of the 34th Division (or 'Division Princière'), arriving in Vilna in early December only in time to be devoured by the tide of combat, hunger, cold and misery that swept over them in the space of a few horrendous days. The 4th Rheinbund went from some 2,500 men on 1 September to perhaps 50 under arms by 12 December; the fates of the others were only slightly less shocking. The pathetic remnants of the three regiments ended up in Danzig, forming, for a time, part of a battalion comprising men from twenty-three different German states and wryly entitled the 'Europa Battalion' by its members.[44] The remaining Germans finally departed for their various homelands in December 1813.

Napoleon, in the meantime, had demanded new contingents to replace those lost in Russia, but the first Duchal Saxon battalion to be formed was still en route to the army when it surrendered to roving Prussian hussars in April and volunteered for Prussian service. New contingents were raised from all the states during the summer armistice. A new three-battalion regiment from the Saxon Duchies was assigned to the Magdeburg garrison, but the first two battalions were destroyed at Hagelberg on 27 August while on detachment. The remnants returned to Magdeburg to rejoin the Light Battalion along with new contingents from Lippe, Reuss and Schwarzburg. Desertion was soon rife (up to 50 per cent), and the French commandant released all the German troops of his garrison on 12 November 1813. Two Waldeck companies destined for Magdeburg did not even arrive: they disintegrated while en route to the fortress.[45]

Unlike the other states, Anhalt was directed to raise a 2-squadron regiment of chasseurs-à-cheval totalling 530 officers and men to help meet Napoleon's desperate need for light cavalry. One of the most ephemeral of the Rheinbund units, the regiment reached Dresden on 20 August, but was caught up in the disaster at Kulm on the 30th and destroyed.[46]

Frankfurt: Service in Spain and Russia

Frankfurt, under the rule of the Confederation's 'Prince Primate', Carl von Dalberg, initially provided one battalion of troops. Assigned to garrison duties in Germany during 1806–7, the battalion's organisation resembled the then-prevailing French structure: seven companies of musketeers and one company each of grenadiers and voltigeurs. Committed to the German division in Spain in 1808, it was drilled under French regulations, equipped with French muskets and reorganised into the new French model, retaining its elites but fielding only four centre companies. The battalion remained in Spain until December 1813 when it defected to the Allies along with the 2nd Nassau.

Across the Pyrenees and the Rhine, a second battalion was assembled to garrison Erfurt (then under French administration) during the 1809 war with Austria. In the aftermath of that conflict, Napoleon expanded Frankfurt's lands and increased its contingent to 2,800. As preparations for the invasion of Russia began, therefore, the emperor required a full regiment from Frankfurt in addition to the battalion already in Spain. The regiment, composed of new 2nd and 3rd Battalions (the troops in Spain were considered the 1st Battalion), was assigned to the 'Division Princière' and destroyed in early December 1812. The remnants joined the Danzig garrison until released in December 1813. In 1813 two new battalions were raised (re-using the numbers 2 and 3), but quality was poor and desertion high. The 2nd Battalion fought at Lützen in May, and both were sent to the Glogau garrison during the armistice along with a replacement detachment. A second replacement detachment ended up in Torgau. These two groups of Frankfurt troops, much reduced by sickness and desertion, returned in January 1814 and November 1813 respectively.

North German Princes: Oldenburg, Mecklenburg-Schwerin, Mecklenburg-Strelitz

The last monarchs to join the Rheinbund were also the most reluctant. The Duke of Oldenburg had family ties to the tsar, while the two Mecklenburg duchies were politically aligned with Russia and had close familial and cultural affinities with Prussia.

In its brief existence as a member of the Confederation, Oldenburg's contingent was organised into a six-company battalion with the 1st Company as grenadiers and the 6th as *Schützen*. Troop quality was low, motivation was poor and most of the officers had previously served Prussia, Hanover or other Napoleonic enemies. The one moment when it might have entered into combat came in August 1809, when the Duke of Brunswick led his 'Black Corps' north to take ship for England. Oldenburg's ruler, however, sympathised with Brunswick and had his men withdraw out of the way. The following year, Napoleon unseated the duke and incorporated his lands into France. Most of the men of the former duchy who marched into Russia in 1812, did so, therefore, as members of the 'French' 129e de Ligne.

Mecklenburg-Schwerin was supposed to supply the 7th Rheinbund Regiment with two battalions established on the French pattern and using

French drill. It was also to include an artillery company. All of these organisations existed on paper, but the troops were poorly trained and motivated, recruitment was insufficient and equipment deficient. Anti-French sentiment was strong. Sent to block the raiding force of renegade Prussian Major Ferdinand von Schill in May 1809, the Schwerin troops came apart after a brief exchange of fire. Troops deserted in droves, including from the Strelitz Battalion which had not even seen the enemy. The Strelitz contingent was organised into 4 100-man companies (also using French drill), but troop quality was very low and leadership weak. The local French commander bitterly complained that the sergeants and soldiers of both duchies were 'mostly Prussian deserters who had already fought against France'.[47]

Both Mecklenburg contingents were destroyed in Russia. The two battalions of 7th Rheinbund (Schwerin), 1,700 strong, marched initially with I Corps, later performed garrison duty in various depots under IX Corps and endured a final agony under what was left of III Corps. The first two companies of the Strelitz Battalion went to Moscow with 127e de Ligne (I Corps), while the other two performed security missions around Vilna. Perhaps the latter task spared the battalion somewhat as it suffered 'only' 67 per cent losses when all of its soldiers and stragglers finally returned home.[48] This was the last action for both under the Rheinbund. The two dukes split from the alliance in March 1813, becoming the first Confederation members to join the Allies.

Arenberg (or Aremberg): A Unique Unit

The Duchy of Arenberg was an unusual case in a panorama of unusual cases.[49] The wealthy duke, Prosper Ludwig, had lands in Belgian as well as German territory, the latter obligating him to a 379-man Rheinbund contingent. In addition to his Rheinbund responsibilities, Napoleon asked Prosper Ludwig to raise a regiment of light horse from Belgian volunteers with officers from the nobility. The Belgian Chevaulegers (Chevau-légers Belges or Duc d'Arenberg) was the result, with the duke himself serving as its very active commander. To meet his Rheinbund obligations, he was granted authorisation to include the contingent from his German properties in the regiment at his own expense. The result was a partial success. Officials in his German territories declined to commit their own men, so they hired displaced Prussians and Austrians to construct a contingent of 122 that accompanied the regiment as its 5th Squadron when it marched to join the Grande Armée in Prussia in 1807. Arenberg proved incapable or unwilling to supply any more troops itself, so the rest of its commitment was met by paying to support the appropriate number of soldiers in the 2nd Nassau Regiment (although payments seem to have been late and insufficient). Uniformed exactly like other chevaulegers with the exception of wearing the Arenberg cockade (red on yellow), 'the contingent' (as it was known) remained with the regiment on the fringes of the 1807 campaign in Germany and Poland, went to Denmark with Bernadotte and marched to Spain in the autumn of 1808. By that time, the Belgian Chevau-legers had been incorporated in the French Army as the 27th Chasseurs-à-Cheval (May 1808). Though now a French unit, the 27th retained its Rheinbund troopers until November 1810, when the contingent, reduced to fifty-two men and a handful of officers, was absorbed into the rest of the regiment. Thus ended what was probably a unique arrangement during Napoleon's reign: troops in foreign pay serving in a French regiment.

OBSERVATIONS

Each of Napoleon's German allies is a study in itself, with unique features in its military history that have important linkages to political and social trends specific to its own development. Considering the great panoply of campaigns, combats, marches and miseries in which the Rheinbund troops participated from 1806 to 1813, however, several general points are worth highlighting.

First, the level of troop commitments to the Rheinbund was high relative to the sizes of the different armies, but not necessarily to the size of the states. That is, with few exceptions, each Rheinbund member placed almost its entire serving military force in the field when summoned by Napoleon. Other than depots, small palace guards and domestic constabularies, few troops were left at home. On the other hand, although conscription (a new institution in most states) was widely detested, Napoleon's demands were not extraordinary when each mobilisation is considered separately. Certainly many of the states produced just as many soldiers (often substantially more) in response to Allied demands in 1813–14. What made the French requirements more burdensome (beyond the hatred of conscription) was the rapid succession of requests to rebuild forces, especially in 1813 when Napoleon's fortunes were plummeting and anti-French sentiment was on the rise. It is also useful to recall that requirements included not only men, but also hundreds of horses and large quantities of clothing, arms and equipment.

Secondly, though their experiences under the defunct *Reich* did not prepare them for Napoleon's style of warfare, over time, the German states adapted and many excelled. Some of the major states had begun reform programmes before the Confederation came into existence, but these steps generally proved halting, fragmented and inadequate. The arrival of Napoleon provided the impetus to accelerate existing reforms and initiate modernisation where it had not yet begun, both allowing and forcing armies to adapt quickly, while granting the Confederation sovereigns the internal authority to override domestic resistance. The early forays onto the Napoleonic battlefield in 1805 and 1806–7 were thus hesitant and often disappointing, both to the French and to their new allies. By 1809, however, most of the armies had improved dramatically, and the war against Austria became a 'year of emergence' for the Rheinbund troops as they moved from line of communications duties into the front lines of the greatest battles of the age directly under the eye of the emperor. At the same time, thousands of German troops now found themselves in Spain, a frightful experience that sapped much of the enthusiasm for the French alliance. Though some officers and men initially marched for the Pyrenees with professional hopes of glory and advancement, any such ardour quickly vanished in the realities of the grinding Iberian insurgency. Despite the war in Spain, many men seem to have regarded the coming war with Russia as another opportunity to display their professional skills as part of a truly grand army under Napoleon's personal command. There were exceptions (such as the Mecklenburg troops), but the armies were generally good to excellent in quality as they crossed the Niemen that fateful June. The disaster in Russia, however, had fatal repercussions for the Rheinbund. Not only did it undermine faith in Napoleon as a military leader and fuel underlying anti-French sentiment among Germans from the Oder to the Rhine, it also meant that the trained veterans of the Rheinbund armies were gone. The new contingents that took the field in 1813 were thus young conscripts with little training or experience, led either by over-aged depot officers or exhausted, combat-stressed veterans whose energy and enthusiasm had been shattered by the Russian catastrophe. The wonder is not that some of these troops defected or deserted, but that the majority remained in their ranks and often demonstrated amazing endurance under privation and astonishing courage in battle.

Thirdly, leadership, both French and German, was all-important. The Westphalian Army, for example, whose performance had been so flawed in 1809, marched into Russia with a far more competent framework of officers and sergeants from the division level down. It is not the army's fault that their king was an inept commander or that Junot was mentally unstable. Given the results obtained with other leaders commanding other contingents, there is every reason to conclude that the Westphalians would have made more significant contributions in 1812 under different commanders. Leaders such as Prince Emil of Hesse and Margrave Wilhelm of Baden earned the respect of their French allies as well as their own men, while ambitious men such as Wrede and Thielmann, though difficult subordinates, could motivate and organise their troops to accomplish extraordinary things. In many cases, however, the French side of the leadership equation was lacking. The French often had legitimate cause to complain about their Rheinbund allies, but in far too many instances, French arrogance or neglect exacerbated situations that might have been resolved to the benefit of the alliance with a bit more tact and genuine concern. All too often, the German allies experienced what the Bavarian division commander in 1813 lamented as 'the presumption and rudeness, the injustice and the disdain for foreigners' he encountered among French officers. Such attitudes soured relations and made the bonds of alliance easier to break as Napoleon's star began to fade.[50]

Finally, the history of the Rheinbund highlights the importance of nuance in reviewing the German role in Napoleon's wars. Some contingents or individual units were clearly inferior to the French in skill and motivation, but others 'rivalled their allies in courage' as Davout said of the Hessians at Pressburg in 1809. In the eyes of most contemporaries, few could match the French in impetuous elan, but many of the Rheinbund contingents could march as far and as fast or exhibit the same degree of battlefield skill and flexibility as their French comrades in arms. Of course, as noted above, Rheinbund proficiency must also be viewed in the context of time: the Badeners of 1809 had improved over 1806, the Bavarians of 1813 had declined precipitously since 1809 and the Saxon army of 1812 was vastly superior to its predecessors. In sum, then, the Rheinbund was a military success for Napoleon. Though his exactions and the overweening behaviour of many of his officers damaged relations over time, though the alliance failed or faltered in many other areas, it fulfilled the military and political purposes he had envisaged, serving as a buffer on France's western border and providing him with thousands of soldiers, while denying these assets to his enemies. Furthermore, the contingents large and small that marched under his banners for more than seven years evolved over the era of the alliance into valuable components of his armies. If a few were frail, most were reliable, some were superb and all would remember the role they had played in determining the fate of Europe during the years of the Napoleonic Empire.

NOTES

1. In addition to the sources cited below, this chapter relies on Jean Angelelli and Alain Pigeard, *La Conféderation du Rhin* (Paris, Quator, 2002); Scott Bowden, *Napoleon's Grande Armée of 1813* (Chicago, Emperor's Press, 1990); Camille Sauzey, *Les Allemands sous les Aigles Françaises* (six vols, Paris, Ternana, 1987–8); Digby Smith (Otto von Pivka), *Armies of 1812* (Staplehurst, Spellmount, 2002); Peter H. Wilson, *The Holy Roman Empire* (London, Macmillan, 1999); and the following works by the present author: *With Eagles to Glory* (London, Greenhill, 1992); history of the Bavarian army in the Rheinbund in *A Soldier for Napoleon* (London, Greenhill, 1998) (with Cynthia Joy Hausmann); and 'Vermin, Scorpions, and Mosquitoes: The Rheinbund in the Peninsula', in Ian Fletcher (ed.), *The Peninsular War* (Staplehurst, Spellmount, 1998).
2. Ferdinand von Funck, *In Russland und in Sachsen 1812–1815* (Dresden, Heinrich, 1930), p. 248.
3. Thomas Zech, 'Das Fürstenbergische Kontingent des schwäbischen Kreises 1732–1806' (Vöhrenbach, 2000), www.thz-historia.de.
4. Fr von der Wengen, 'Das Fürstlich Fürstenbergische Kontingent im Kriege von 1792–1796', *Zeitschrift der Gesellschaft für Beförderung der Geschichts-, Altertums- und Volkskunde*, Band 7 (1888).
5. Eduard Freiherr von Völderndorff und Waradein, *Kriegsgeschichte von Bayern unter König Maximilian Joseph I* (München, 1826), vol. I, p. 8.

6. [Czettritz und Neuhaus], 'Erinnerungen eines Kavallerie-Offiziers', *Zeitschrift für Kunst, Wissenschaft und Geschichte des Krieges*, vol. VII (1839), p. 56.
7. In a curious aberration, approximately sixty-six Bavarian train personnel did go to Spain with the French 3rd Train Battalion in 1808; a fortunate twenty-seven of them survived to return home in 1814 (Rudolf von Xylander, *Geschichte des 1. Feld-Artillerie-Regiments* (Berlin, Mittler, 1909), vol. II, pp. 118–20).
8. Ludwig von Seiboltsdorf, 'Das K. Bayr. Armeekorps in Russland im Jahre 1812', Bayerisches Kriegsarchiv/HS723.
9. Report to king in Max Leyh, *Die Feldzüge des Königlich Bayerischen Heeres unter Max I. Joseph von 1805 bis 1815* (Munich, Schick, 1935), p. 254.
10. Raglovich to Wrede, 31 March 1813, in Franz Schubert and Hans Vara, *Geschichte des K. B. 13. Infanterie-Regiments* (Munich, Lindauer, 1906), vol. I, p. 355.
11. Divisional reports to the king, 12 May, 28 May and 17 June 1813, Bayerisches Kriegsarchiv/B495a.
12. Detached under Lasalle, the Leib-Chevaulegers fought at Heilsberg.
13. Jäger Battalion König, the Leib-Chevaulegers, Jäger-zu-Pferd König and the 1st Horse Artillery Battery were considered part of the king's household (*Maison du Roi*) with special uniform distinctions.
14. Heinz Kraft, *Die Württemberger in den Napoleonischen Kriegen* (Stuttgart, Kohlhammer, 1953), p. 201.
15. 'Nachricht über die Begebenheiten des Königl. Würtembergschen Truppen-Corps an den Schlacht-Tagen von Leipzig im Feldzuge 1813', *Miliair-Wochenblatt* (1837).
16. The regiment sent to Spain was initially composed of I/4th and II/3rd Infantry. It was renamed 4th Infantry on 25 February 1809. Simultaneously, I/3rd and II/4th Infantry back in Baden became 3rd Infantry.
17. The 2nd Infantry initially marched with I Corps and only joined the brigade later in the campaign.
18. GD Piré, letter to the editor, *Spectateur Militaire*, vol. VII, (1829), p. 604.
19. The titles of these 'brigades', the functional equivalent of regiments in most armies, caused considerable confusion for the French, so the entries in French records are often inexact.
20. Davout to Napoleon, 3 June 1809, in *Correspondance de Maréchal Davout*, ed. Charles de Mazade (Paris, Plon, 1885).
21. Johannes Anton Larrass, 'Zur Beurteilung der Überführung Königlich Sächischer Truppen zu den Verbündeten bei Leipzig am 18. Oktober 1813', *Beiheft zum Militär-Wochenblatt* (1912).
22. The Bataillon des Princes was also present.
23. Franz Morgenstern, *Kriegserinnerungen* (Wolfenbuettel, 1912), p. 21.
24. Lieutenant Wolf in Moritz von Kaisenberg, *König Jerome Napoleon* (Leipzig, Schmidt und Günther, 1899), p. 122. Napoleon to Jerome, 17 July 1809, in Léon Lecestre, *Lettres Inédites de Napoléon Ier* (Paris, Plon, 1897), vol. I, p. 327.
25. Not including the 1st and 8th Regiments; these were detached with MacDonald's X Corps (1st) and in Königsberg (8th). Similarly, 4th Infantry joined the shattered corps with Wrede in early December.
26. Friedrich Giesse, *Kassel-Moskau-Küstrin 1812–1813* (Leipzig, Dyk, 1912), pp. 17–18. There are similar comments by others, but not all would have agreed: [Johann Gottleib Haars], *Ein Braunschweiger im Russischen Feldzuge von 1812* (Braunschweig, Scholz, 1897), p. 2.
27. The early uniforms of the regiment are obscure owing to lack of information and a host of projected uniforms that probably were never actually introduced. See J. Thomas, *Un Régiment Rhénan sous Napoléon Premier* (Liége, Vaillant-Carmanie, 1928).
28. François Réné Pouget, *Souvenirs de Guerre* (Paris, Plon, 1895), p. 210.
29. Lieutenant S.M. Sotta to his brother, in Thomas, *Un Régiment Rhénan sous Napoléon Premier*, p. 62.

30. Lieutenant Hermann, 'Die bergische Kavallerie', in P. Zimmermann, *Erinnerungen aus den Feldzügen der bergischen Truppen in Spanien und Russland* (2nd edn, Düsseldorf, Stahl, 1842), pp. 163–7.
31. The numeration of the first three Rheinbund regiments is not entirely clear. The numbers given here represent the results of the author's research, but others designate the Würzburg Regiment as the 1st Rheinbund, and assigned the numbers '2' and '3' to the two Nassau regiments. The chapter uses national designations to minimise confusion.
32. Paul Thiebault, *Memoirs* (Felling, Worley, 1994), vol. II, pp. 245–74.
33. Peter Wacker, 'Die Hzgl. Nassauischen Reitenden Jäger 1804–14', *Depesche*, Nr. 15.
34. Alfred von Roessler, *Geschichte des Königlich Preussischen 1. Nassauischen Infanterie-Regiment Nr. 87* (Berlin, Mittler, 1882), pp. 98–9.
35. Max Ruith, *Das K. Bayer. 12. Infanterie-Regiment* (Ulm, Ebner, 1902); Joseph Schuster, *Das Grossherzoglich Würzburgische Infanterie-Regiment in Spanien 1808–1813* (Munich, Zipperer, 1909); Hermann Helmes, 'Die Würzburger Truppen vor Hundert Jahren', *Archiv des historischen Vereins von Unterfranken und Aschaffenburg* (1913); Walter Kopp, *Würzburger Wehr* (Würzburg, 1979).
36. Würzburg contributed a 2-company sapper division in 1809 as well as a detachment of 25 train personnel who served with Junot's reserve corps in Germany that year and accompanied the corps to Spain; a episode from which only 8 returned.
37. Some sources mention 6th and 7th Battalions as well; a possible explanation could be that the latter two were temporary designations of replacement units that were absorbed into existing battalions.
38. Hermann Helmes, 'Die Würzburger Chevaulegers', *Darstellungen aus der Bayerischen Kriegs- und Heeresgeschichte*, vol. 11 (1902).
39. The Sachsen-Koburg contingent did not participate as the duchy was under temporary French administration in the wake of the duke's death. The Sachsen-Weimar battalion, which had fought against the French at Auerstädt, lost heavily from desertion.
40. Contingent structures were as follows: Anhalt – 5-company battalion; Schwarzburg – 4-company battalion (2 companies each); Reuss – 3-company battalion.
41. Schwarzburg-Sondershausen (1st Company), Schwarzburg-Rudolstadt (2nd), Lippe-Detmold (3rd), Schaumburg-Lippe (4th), Reuss (5th), Waldeck (6th). D. Fiebig, 'Das Bataillon des Princes', *Zeitschrift für Heeres- und Uniformkunde* (January 1934).
42. The 5th and 6th Regiments did not form grenadier or voltigeur companies until 1812.
43. Gill, *Eagles*, p. 403.
44. Johann Matthias Meinhard, *Geschichte des Reussischen Militairs* (Gera, Blachmann und Bornschein, 1842), p. 408.
45. W. Wiegmann, *Franzosenzeit und Befreiungskriege* (Stadthagen, Heine, 1915); Freiherr von Dalwigk zu Lichtenfels, *Geschichte der waldeckischen und kurhessischen Stammtruppen des Infanterie-Regiments v. Wittich Nr. 83* (Oldenburg, Littmann, 1909), pp. 109–11.
46. Egbert von Frankenberg und Ludwigsdorf, *Zur Geschichte der Truppen welche den Namen 'Anhalt' getragen haben* (Dessau, Oesterwitz, 1895).
47. Liébert to Berthier, 30 May 1809, in Albert du Casse, *Mémoires et Correspondance du Roi Jérome et de la Reine Catherine* (Paris, Dentu, 1861–8), vol. IV, pp. 103–8.
48. Klaus-Ulrich Keubke, *Tagebuch des Feldzuges in Russland im Jahre 1812* (Rostock, Temmen, 1998), pp. 46–51.
49. E.-L. Bucquoy, *La Cavalerie Légère* (Paris, Grancher, 1980), pp. 174–88; Guy van Eeckhoudt, *Les Chevau-Légers Belges du duc d'Arenberg* (Paris, Le Livre Chex Vous, 2002); Pigeard, *La Conféderation du Rhin*, pp. 41–50.
50. Raglovich to Max Joseph, 17 June 1813, BKA/495a; also letters to Max Joseph on 12 May and 9 September 1813.

Chapter Seven

The Spanish Army

Charles Esdaile

Traumatic in the extreme, the Spanish Army's experience of the Revolutionary and Napoleonic Wars deeply affected its outlook and had a lasting impact on the history of Spain. Yet by the time Napoleon was overthrown in 1814, it actually had much to be proud of, having been in continuous action against the Emperor's forces for longer than any other European army, not excluding that of Britain. What made this record still more remarkable was that it was achieved in the face of massive difficulties, whether these were the hostility of the civilian populace to the war, the existence of a guerrilla movement that constantly sapped its strength, a mood of growing anti-militarism among the political leadership of Patriot Spain, a greatly superior enemy who generally enjoyed the advantage of interior lines, the constant disruption engendered by military defeat or terrain that on the whole favoured its opponents. To have kept in the field at all, in fact, was a considerable achievement, and it is therefore distressing to note that until comparatively recently much of the anglophone historiography of the Peninsular War was very much inclined to regard Spain's soldiers with contempt, or even to ignore them altogether. A war-winning weapon the Spanish Army of the Napoleonic Wars most certainly was not, and yet it has on the whole deserved better than the scorn that has been heaped upon it.

It is conventional to begin discussions of the Spanish Army with an introduction to the armed forces of Bourbon Spain. This, however, is not very helpful. Whether the army of Charles IV (reigned 1788–1808) was good or bad (and it was in fact much better than has generally been accepted) is neither here nor there, for the simple reason that it never got the chance to fight the French as a coherent force. When Napoleon decided to intervene in Spain at the beginning of 1808, large parts of the army were stationed in Denmark and Portugal (whither they had been sent to assist the French forces as auxiliaries) or caught in the French zone of occupation in Spain, whilst most of the rest were deployed around the periphery of the country or even on its outlying islands, especially the Balearics. On top of this, those areas of Spain that rose in revolt against Napoleon were gripped by a revolution that, as will be shown, greatly disrupted the army and broke down established patterns of authority – Spain, indeed, was left without a central government. What all this meant for the army was that it never really had a chance to show its prowess under fair conditions in that it went into battle in scattered fractions that were very often adulterated by the forces of the revolution under the command of generals who frequently had only limited authority over the troops they commanded. Even had it been able to mobilise properly and, say, seek to defend the line of the Pyrenees against a French invasion, it is probable that the army would still have been beaten, but, notwithstanding the single lucky victory of Bailén, in the conditions of 1808 it had no chance whatsoever.

Yet the fact that this was so does not in itself say anything about its quality. In the period prior to 1808, enlightened thinkers had been prone to lampoon the army as a force that was fit to do little more than mount guard on the royal palace. The army, wrote one such critic, was characterised by 'a corps of generals sufficient to command all the armies of the world ... [and] a multitude of regiments short of men though hardened veterans in the art of curling their hair, whitening their uniforms with flour, marching like dancers in a quadrille, wasting powder in salvos in the meadows, and serving to oppress their fellow citizens'.[1] Such views, however, were unfair. In 1789 the army was a conventional late-eighteenth-century force, the only distinguishing feature of which was an exceptionally strong royal guard. Recruited by a mixture of voluntary enlistment and a limited system of conscription that was generally imposed only in wartime and affected only the urban and rural poor, it consisted of a typical array of conventionally organised infantry and cavalry regiments. A number of the infantry regiments were foreign – Irish, Italian, Swiss and Walloon – and there were separate corps of artillery and engineers, both of which enjoyed considerable administrative independence. Officers, meanwhile, came primarily from the nobility, though promotion from the ranks was possible and quite widespread: if such men rarely advanced beyond the rank of captain, by 1800 perhaps one-quarter of the officer corps consisted of ex-rankers (recent Spanish works, however, have suggested that opportunities for such advancement were becoming more limited). With favour at court very important in securing advancement, promotion was in general highly inequitable, and so the army suffered from having a minority of very well-connected officers who were promoted rapidly and often rose far beyond their capacity and a majority of perpetual captains and lieutenants who were both ageing and embittered. Hardly conducive to professional solidarity, this situation was to have serious results in 1808. As for other defects, Spain being desperately short of horses, there were too few cavalry, whilst the army was entirely dependent on the population for its transport: horses, oxen, mules and wagons all had to be hired at the start of each campaign, these resources thereafter being left in the charge of civilian teamsters who were prone to abscond at the first opportunity. Staff work, moreover, was generally very poor: there was no general staff as such, the personal suites of Spanish commanders rather being appointed on an entirely ad hoc basis. Above all, however, in the reign of Charles III (1759–88), the army had been run down in favour of the navy, the latter being of far greater importance in a situation where a permanent alliance with France ensured that Spain's only major foreign opponent would be Britain.[2]

The result of all this was that the war against France of 1793–95 was a difficult experience. The Spaniards fought well and even inflicted many defeats on the French, but they were unable either to recruit the number of men that they needed to fight the French with any chance of success or to finance the conflict adequately, and so were eventually forced to make peace.[3] Under the influence of the royal favourite, Manuel de Godoy, the period from 1795 to 1808 was therefore marked – contrary to the usual version of events – by a serious attempt at military reform. Thanks to the opposition of vested interests in the army and a variety of other problems, this had little effect, however: the royal guard was cut in half, the number of light infantry greatly increased and the army given some horse artillery, but otherwise all remained much as before. Indeed, in some ways matters had got still worse: desperate to build a party for himself within the upper echelons of the army, Godoy – a perennial outsider who was regarded with a mixture of fear and jealousy – had appointed many new generals with the result that by 1808 there were roughly 3½ such officers for every 1 of the 118 regiments of infantry, cavalry and artillery that, counting the provincial militia, made up the Spanish Army.[4]

Mention of Spain's generals is sure to conjure up a very negative image in the mind of the British reader with historians such as Napier and Oman having poured scorn upon them at every opportunity. In so far as the pre-war army is concerned, however, the picture is more mixed. Even the most confirmed hispanophile would have difficulty in suggesting that the forces of Charles IV were headed by military geniuses, whilst it is also clear that some of the officers who had reached the rank of brigadier or above really were men of little worth who had advanced on no other grounds than favour (perhaps the worst example is the Conde de Belveder, the singularly inept commander of the Army of Extremadura at the Battle of Gamonal: aged only 32, he seems to have owed his rise to nothing other than the fact that his father, the Marqués de Castelar, was a senior commander in the royal guard). Yet there were certainly members of the *generalato* who were at the very least competent professionals, and it is probable that in other circumstances they would have performed no worse than their counterparts in, say, the Austrian Army. Defeat would still most assuredly have come their way, but they would thus have escaped the scorn that has generally been heaped upon them. As we shall see, however, they never had a fair chance to display such talents as they possessed, whilst matters were made worse by the fact that several of the best commanders that Spain possessed either died in the uprising or chose to go over to the French (amongst this last category, perhaps the most lamentable loss was that of Tomás de Morla, an erstwhile head of the Spanish artillery who was a genuinely scientific soldier with a strong interest in military reform).[5]

Let us say, though, that the generals who actually led Spain into battle in 1808 were somewhat less than outstanding. Yet, for all the army's deficiencies, a serious analysis of the Spanish forces' performance in 1808 suggests that at least some of Spain's soldiers were capable of putting up a good fight. When Gerona repelled an enemy assault in the first days of the war, it was its regular garrison that really deserved the credit. Equally, at the Battle of Bailén on 19 July 1808 the fact that the French forces were scandalously mishandled by their commanders should not blind us to the fact that the Spanish troops who blocked the road to Madrid – almost in their entirety men of the old army – for a full day stood firm against repeated attacks in the blazing heat of an Andalusian summer and did not cede an inch of ground despite the fact that their positions were everywhere completely overlooked by those of their opponents; particularly impressive, meanwhile, was the Spanish artillery whose twelve-pounder guns were served to devastating effect and repeatedly overmastered their counterparts. And, even in the midst of defeat, Spanish troops performed well. At the Battle of Medina de Río Seco on 14 July 1808, for example, the Second Division of General Blake's Army of Galicia launched a courageous uphill counterattack that initially overran the French guns facing it and was only repelled when enemy reinforcements fell on it from both flanks. And at the Battle of Espinosa de los Monteros (10–11 November 1808) the so-called División del Norte – the troops commanded by the Marqués de la Romana who had been rescued from Denmark by the Royal Navy – proved absolutely rock-like in the face of every French attack, and was only forced to retreat when the raw Asturian levies posted to its left were routed on the second day of the action.[6]

However, to reiterate a point made earlier, it was not the Bourbon Army that actually fought the Peninsular War. The British Army that attacked on the Somme on 1 July 1916 was not the British Army that fought at Mons in August 1914 any more than the French Army that triumphed in 1793 was not the French Army that witnessed the French Revolution in 1789. In the same way the Spanish Army that fought at Talavera in July 1809 was not the Spanish Army that fought at Bailén in July 1808, and yet historians such as Napier and Oman consistently ignored this fact and wrote as if the scathing accounts of the former force that were to be found in such abundance in British memoirs were valid for the period prior to the uprising as well. In short, in traditional discussions of the Spanish Army in the Peninsular War far too little account has been taken of the impact of the uprising against Napoleon, or, still more so, the atmosphere in which the war was fought, and these factors will now be examined.[7]

One of the most dramatic events of the Napoleonic Wars – the Spanish uprising of 1808 – has been given great prominence by historians. That said, however, as a phenomenon it has very rarely been properly understood. According to the traditional version of events, Napoleon's decision to impose tight control on Spain and overthrow the Spanish Bourbons provoked a massive wave of anger that led the populace to turn as one on the invaders and launch a veritable crusade against them. Already strong on account of xenophobia and – less clearly – devotion to the Catholic Church, hatred of the French was further fuelled by the brutal response of the occupying forces and the imposition of a classic programme of Napoleonic reform, and the result was a war that found no equal anywhere else in Europe; a war, indeed, in which the heroism of the combatants was only equalled by the savagery with which they turned on the invaders. Amongst some historians there was a realisation that this image did not quite correspond to the reality and that there was a real need to assimilate such problems as desertion, riot and mutiny, all of them phenomena that were very frequent, but an answer to this problem was found in such factors as the provincialism that characterised the Spanish populace, the innate suspicion of the ruling classes as a caste that was at best effete and, at worst, downright treasonable and an instinctive belief that conventional means of warfare were not those best suited to defeating the French in Spain. To put this into more concrete terms, what this meant was that Spanish soldiers would fight heroically in defence of their own provinces but show great reluctance to fight outside them, exact a dreadful vengeance upon any general whom they believed to be suspect, as a result either of having been defeated or of behaving in a manner that was deemed to show a want of zeal, and show a strong tendency to gravitate towards alternative forms of waging war – in effect, the formation of guerrilla bands – that seemed to offer a better chance of defeating the enemy. These tendencies, it was agreed, were by no means always positive, but they were on balance seen as vices that were inherent in the virtues that had produced the uprising in the first place, and so there was seemingly little desire to delve into them any further. As for other problems, such as the all too evident collapse of enlistment in most of unoccupied Spain in the wake of the Battle of Bailén or the repeated defeat of the Spanish armies at the hands of the French, these, too, soon acquired plausible explanations, whether it was the general over-confidence produced by the victory of Bailén or the inability of the Patriot forces to develop a military organisation capable of meeting the French in open battle. In any case, what mattered was not such defects, but rather the simple fact that the Spaniards fought, kept fighting and refused pointblank to countenance defeat, let alone a political accommodation with the enemy.[8]

For many years this line of argument ruled unchallenged, but over the past twenty years a number of scholars, including both Britons and Spaniards, have developed a much more realistic appreciation of what occurred in Spain in 1808. In brief, the uprising is seen by them not so much as an expression of nationalist fury but as a huge explosion of anger and frustration in respect of which Napoleon's actions acted as little more than a catalyst. Although this is not the place to retell an argument that has repeatedly been set out in detail elsewhere, to understand the situation – a situation essential to an appreciation of the Spanish struggle as a whole – it is necessary to discuss briefly the social and political context that has achieved such prominence. The most crucial point to make here is that even before Napoleon ordered his forces to seize control, Spain was a deeply radicalised society. On the one hand long years of war with Britain had combined with natural disaster and serious structural difficulties in the Spanish economy to cause abject misery amongst large sections of the populace, whilst on the other that self-same populace had been deluded by a faction of churchmen and aristocrats eager to turn back the enlightened reforms of Charles III and Charles IV into believing that all its woes were the work of Manuel de Godoy. Nor was this an end to Godoy's misfortunes in this respect, for the anti-reformist conspirators had seized upon the exceptionally foolish and naïve heir to the throne, Prince Ferdinand, as a useful figurehead whom they could manipulate at will, and had sought to build up his credit by representing him as a saviour figure who would bring peace and prosperity.[9]

Whether Ferdinand could ever have done any such thing is highly debatable, but that is not the point: by 1808 there was a widespread conviction that the crown prince had only to succeed to the throne for Spain to be transformed into a land flowing with milk and honey: hence the wild excitement that prevailed throughout Spain when a hastily organised military coup toppled Charles IV and Godoy and placed Ferdinand on the throne in response to the latter's belated attempt to organise resistance to the French forces that were by then bearing down on Madrid. Amidst these millennial dreams, France's intervention came as a rude shock, whilst deeper seated fears also began work upon the popular mind. On the one hand the arrival of large numbers of French troops from December 1807 onwards in Catalonia and the Castiles tended to drive up bread prices and in this way spark off fears that Spain was about to experience a repeat of a terrible subsistence crisis that had assailed the country a few years earlier, and on the other the absence of the entire royal family at the infamous conference of Bayonne gave rise to an ever-growing sense of insecurity: without a king the whole of Spanish society was felt to have been placed at the mercy of the elements. And what, too, was to be made of the fact that the French not only refused to recognise Ferdinand VII, but also rescued Godoy from the captivity into which he had been flung in the wake of his overthrow? Did this not suggest that the French armies had come to Spain with the express purpose of saving the royal favourite from the retribution with which he was threatened?[10]

With rumours flying around that Spain had been betrayed by not just Godoy but a much wider circle of officials and landowners who were as eager as he was to escape the anger of the crowd, the final straw came with the so-called Dos de Mayo. An episode that has been much mythologised, this affair was certainly not the heroic patriotic uprising of legend, but rather a strange mixture of riot and mass panic. As yet only the vaguest reports had been received in Madrid as to what was happening in Bayonne and so it was assumed that there was all to play for – that Ferdinand still had every chance of persuading Napoleon to recognise him as King of Spain. Anxious to put pressure on the Emperor, and at the same time secure the approbation of the new king, a group of courtiers appear to have attempted to organise a show of popular support for Ferdinand outside the royal palace. Unfortunately, however, the plan backfired in that a French officer was attacked in the general excitement, the result being that the French commander in Madrid, Marshal Murat, sent a squadron of troops to clear the streets around the palace. Fatally enough, these opened fire, and the volleys that in consequence echoed across the city produced precisely the sort of result that might have been expected. Convinced that they were about to be massacred wholesale, the populace rushed into the streets armed with whatever weapons that came to hand, set upon such unfortunate Frenchmen as were to be found in the streets (in reality, a very small number, the bulk of Murat's forces being cantoned in the countryside around the capital) and made ready to defend themselves. This, of course, was something that they had to do soon enough: within a matter of hours, large numbers of French troops were pouring into the city and driving all before them. Here and there the fighting was quite brisk, but there was not much that civilians armed with little more than sticks and stones could do against even soldiers as raw and poorly trained as those of the first Armée d'Espagne. Notwithstanding a desperate last stand at the complex of buildings housing the Spanish army's artillery park, where, exceptionally, a handful of regular troops had joined the rioters, everything was over within a matter of hours (barring, that is, the execution during the following night of 113 men who had been seized at various points during the fighting).[11]

If the Dos de Mayo was not what it seemed, and certainly not what it was later portrayed as being, it yet played a massive role in the events that followed. What had happened in Madrid had actually been the fruit of a tragic misunderstanding, but as the news spread across Spain so the story grew that the French had launched a deliberate attack upon the inhabitants of the capital, and even that they had intended to slaughter them to the last man, woman and child. This, of course, was nonsense, but the point is that the story was believed, and that in consequence the populace was everywhere flung into a panic. In this situation, the natural response was to turn to authority for protection, but what was authority doing? Prompted by instructions from no less a person than the captive Ferdinand VII that nothing should be done that might endanger either his personal safety or his chances of securing the approbation of Napoleon, the Captains General – the senior commanders who stood at the head of each of the military regions into which the country was divided – the military governors, the provincial councils of administration and the town councils were all preaching a diet of submission to the French and claiming that Napoleon was a loyal friend who would confirm Ferdinand as King of Spain in short order. Indeed, even as French soldiers were shooting down the inhabitants of Madrid on all sides, the commander of the garrison and other officers and officials had toured the streets begging the populace to retire to their homes and promising them that all would be well. At the best of times such behaviour would have been incongruous, but in the circumstances of 1808 it appeared downright treasonable, and all the more so as, especially in the army, almost all the constituted authorities were nominees of Manuel de Godoy, Ferdinand VII not having occupied the throne long enough to replace them with his own men. To put it mildly, this was disastrous, for it appeared that, to secure their interests, the partisans of the pre-1808 order were prepared to sit by whilst the common people were massacred in cold blood, and even that they had deliberately arranged to have them so massacred.[12]

The result, of course, was a swelling wave of discontent that here and there perhaps culminated in the idea that the people must provide for their own defence and may even in a few cities have produced spontaneous uprisings when in the fourth week of May the news finally broke that Napoleon was dethroning the Spanish Bourbons in favour of a member of his own family. According to the traditional view, this is what occurred all over the country, but in reality this is far from the truth. Thus, in most cities the risings were not spontaneous at all. Driven by the realisation that the decision of the legitimate authorities to side with the French had placed them in a uniquely vulnerable situation, a variety of disaffected individuals and interest groups had seized upon the cause of rebellion as a means of securing an assortment of private objectives that had nothing to do with the question of who ruled Spain. As this last sentence implies, this move in the direction of conspiracy rested upon a wide range of different motives. Scattered around Spain there were first of all many adherents of the aristocratic and clerical *fronde* that had toppled Charles IV and Godoy in the first place, this essentially being a group that wanted to turn back the reforms of Spanish enlightened absolutism and restore the privileges, power and prestige of the Church and nobility and saw the way forward as the establishment of a regency headed by a figure who favoured their cause. Next on the list were a small number of genuine revolutionaries, most of them university teachers and other men of letters, who believed that the time had come to move Spain not backwards but forwards into a new age in which the power of the privileged corporations would be broken and the many obstacles to Spain's economic development swept away. Thirdly, there were the subaltern officers of the army, 'eternal' lieutenants and captains who had little hope of obtaining promotion and had seen their never very high salaries eroded by years of burgeoning inflation. And fourthly came a group of men harbouring a variety of personal grievances or simply driven by personal ambition: failed businessmen, officials who had been thrown out of their posts by Godoy, churchmen who had been passed over for promotion or local notables resentful of the way in which rival families had acquired a more prominent position in local society than they had. Disparate though and in many instances fundamentally opposed to one another they were, in the wake of the Dos de Mayo for all these elements an uprising in favour of Ferdinand VII suddenly became an obvious way forward, and thus was born the movement that was in effect to plunge Spain into revolution.[13]

Before going any further, an important point to note here was that there was never a single conspiracy. Instead, the idea of revolt took hold in many parts of Spain simultaneously and was elaborated by small conspiratorial cells working on an entirely local basis and in blissful ignorance of similar developments that were taking place only 50 or 100 miles away. In each case, the idea seems to have been that the rest of the country would simply rally to the standard which they themselves had raised, and that somehow the leadership would be able to impose whatever political solution it favoured on all their fellow Spaniards. If this was vague enough, meanwhile, even less attention was paid to what might come in the wake of an uprising. With French troops as yet in occupation of very little in the way of Spanish territory, however, it seems likely that the conspirators believed that a simultaneous movement of all the provinces of Spain would cause such alarm in Paris that the invading forces would simply be withdrawn post-haste.[14] In any case for the moment the first priority was arranging the details of how Seville, Zaragoza or Valencia or wherever it was were to be secured for the cause of revolution. Everywhere the pattern was more or less the same. Paid agitators were recruited to whip up the already radicalised crowds and bands of men organised to act as 'shock troops', and then at a given moment – usually the arrival of news that the Bourbons were to be overthrown, which in most cities came about 24 May, although in some places matters were postponed until the feast day of Saint Ferdinand, which happened to fall on 30 May and was an obvious moment for acts of devotion in favour of the new monarch – the revolutionary movement was set in motion.[15]

What followed was highly instructive. Broadly speaking, the existing structures of authority were everywhere swept away, and new organs of government created in their place. In most places these consisted of juntas composed of a variety of local notables (of whom more will be said below), although in both Aragón and Old Castile the solution adopted was the formation of petty military dictatorships headed respectively by a junior officer of the royal bodyguard named José Palafox and the Captain General, Gregorio García de la Cuesta.[16] Paradoxically, however, these bodies were generally anything but revolutionary in their composition. As the crowds surged onto the streets at the call to arms, so a nightmare prospect was revealed of anarchy and even wholesale murder: oppressed by years of suffering and convinced that 'traitors' were trying to cheat them of their due, the populace were out for blood and in a number of places immediately put to death a variety of individuals who were associated in some way with the regime of Godoy or happened to be particularly unpopular in the locality. With the whole structure of society under threat, the senior representatives of the Church (which had, as an institution, hitherto played almost no part in events) and the army rushed to join the insurrection, as did many representatives of property, including large numbers of men who had held positions of influence and authority in local government prior to May 1808. Their objective, of course, was to ensure that power remained in the hands of the established elites and in this they were remarkably successful. In Asturias the presence of a strong nucleus of advanced political opinion at the University of Oviedo, and, more importantly, its participation in the preparation of the uprising, ensured that the provincial junta drew some of its membership from men who were at least semi-detached from the old order, whilst here and there lip service was paid to the idea of appointing representatives of the crowd, but there was no revolutionary transformation.[17]

Power, then, was very much in the hands of the old elites, and, with very few exceptions, these were determined to maintain matters very much as they had been in the days before the uprising. To put it mildly, however, this led to massive tension, for the people had everywhere taken to the streets in large part out of a desire to change their lives for the better. What this meant was, of course, never consciously formulated, but amongst the targets of popular anger were the high rents paid by small tenant farmers, taxation, conscription, the tithe and feudal dues, whilst the hundreds of thousands of landless labourers and poor peasants also wanted access to the great estates that characterised the regions of Spain in which they tended to live. Coupled with all this, meanwhile, was a violent zeal for revenge that in the first days of the rising found its most dramatic expression in a strong desire to root out spies and traitors. At the heart of the uprising, in short, was a startling contradiction that could not but have a severe impact on the Spanish war effort, which must now be analysed.

As we have seen, war with France was not something that was clearly envisaged in May 1808, but even so the conspirators were well aware that to secure their objectives in respect of Napoleon they were going to need access to an adequate military force. The vast majority of the army having joined the insurrection, in several regions of Spain – Extremadura, Andalucía, Galicia, Valencia, the Balearics and the Canaries – there were strong forces of regular troops, but elsewhere – Asturias, Aragón, the Castiles – there was hardly a single soldier, whilst even where there were reasonable garrisons it was clear that more men would be needed. Aside from anything else, many units were badly under strength (out of an establishment strength of 182,000 rank and file, only 130,000 were on the books in 1808, and a number even of these last were probably 'ghost soldiers' who existed only on paper).[18] To make up the want, calls were immediately issued for volunteers, and for the first few days there was a reasonable response. In view of what was to come, and, indeed, what has already been said, this calls for some comment, but in practice there is no difficulty in explaining what took place. So far as the crowd had any view of the political situation at all, it may be presumed, first, that it did not regard war with France as being very likely, and, secondly, that such vision of possible hostilities that it did have was limited to the idea of defending the towns and cities that it inhabited against French assault. Military service could therefore safely be assumed to be a phenomenon that would be local in character, and, in addition, both extremely short-lived and limited to such duties as mounting guard, the propaganda of the juntas being absolutely insistent that Napoleon was terrified by developments in Spain.[19] On top of this, meanwhile, there is the issue of the time of year at which the rising took place. For landless labourers employed on great estates, in particular, the months between the spring sowing and the harvest were invariably periods of unemployment for there were few tasks that needed to be undertaken in the fields and olive groves of the great estates on which they were employed. In these circumstances, the chance of a few days' pay for doing very little was a most welcome windfall, and there were beyond doubt many such men who were only too glad to enlist. And, last but not least, one must remember that for the rest of the lower classes, too, life was currently a bitter struggle, the very generous rates of pay offered by most of the juntas therefore seeming most attractive. As Sir Brent Spencer observed of Seville, for example, 'The pay allowed these new levies ... is perhaps imprudently large. I understand they have daily ... four *reales*, which is more than double what the old regular troops receive.'[20]

In the first days of the rising, then, many men were willing to sign up for military service, whilst their numbers were swelled by others who were in effect compelled to serve by their masters, landlords or other social superiors (apprentices and servants were particularly vulnerable here, but the structure of Spanish society was such that, especially in the countryside, this sort of pressure could be applied to many other groups). How many volunteers, genuine or otherwise, came forward it is impossible to say, but the number probably ran into many thousands. In his important new social history of the Peninsular War, Fraser provides a few figures from different parts of the country – perhaps 350–400 in Morón de la Frontera, 705 men in a single day in Alicante and 300 in Igualada – whilst early actions such as Cabezón and Alcolea, both of which took place in the first week of June, saw considerable bodies of volunteers take the field (perhaps 4,500 in the first instance and 10,000 in the second).[21] So far, so good, but within a few days it had become clear that the juntas faced a growing problem. In the first place, the initial flow of volunteers appears very quickly to have dried up, and, in the second, left in many cases without either food or employment and increasingly concerned that the few days' engagement they had envisaged looked like becoming a much longer term business, considerable numbers of the men who had enlisted began to drift away. Still worse, the leaders of the insurrection and those who had rushed to join them were rapidly discovering that, far from abandoning Spain in panic, the French were putting up a fight and organising punitive columns that were soon bearing down upon many of the leading centres of insurrection. In short, what was needed was conscription, whilst this also offered the advantage of physically clearing the ever more restive crowds from the streets.[22]

From the beginning of June onwards, then, junta after junta began to impose conscription, the only exception being Catalonia where, for historical reasons connected with the suppression of that province's historic rights by the Bourbons following the War of the Spanish Succession, the authorities opted rather to persevere with voluntary enlistment. This approach met with disastrous results: of the 40,000 men that they hoped to raise, it is probable that only about half this number came forward – to be precise, the plan was to raise 40 volunteer battalions of 1,000 men, but only 28 were ever assembled and these had a combined initial strength of 20,072.[23] Generally speaking, the system adopted was based on the army's existing regulations for conscription with the highly significant amendment that all the many exemptions from military service that had hitherto existed were now abolished, including, above all, that of the nobility. On paper it might seem that this change, which, in historical terms, was certainly extremely significant, can be attributed to the need of the insurgent leaders to confront Napoleon with a total war, but in practice the motivation of the provincial juntas was rather different. For the most part dedicated, as has been seen, to defending the political and social status quo, the new authorities yet found themselves confronted with an angry and mutinous crowd which was inclined to riot on the slightest pretext, and was here and there even showing signs of a strong desire to pursue its own agenda. Knowing that conscription would be extremely unpopular, they therefore sought to sweeten the pill by sweeping aside an obvious objection to its imposition whilst yet secretly reserving the right to ensure, as the bitter American Civil War saying put it, that it would be 'a rich man's war, but a poor man's fight'. At the same time, in a further effort to persuade the populace to accept its lot and energise it for the coming struggle, the juntas and their associates embarked on a vigorous campaign of propaganda that was in part specifically designed to persuade the inhabitants that they had a real interest in the struggle (instead of the French simply being denounced as atheistic and sacrilegious, for example, much was made of the likely fate of Spain's young men as cannon fodder for the French armies should Napoleon win).[24]

In September 1808 the Patriot cause, which had hitherto been devoid of any central authority, acquired a new national government in the form of the so-called Junta Suprema Central, at which point the piecemeal efforts of the provinces were subsumed into a single policy designed to produce recruits not just for regional armies as had been the case hitherto, but for the Spanish Army as a whole. Thus, it was decreed that the regulations of 1801 (as generally amended since 1808) should now be applied throughout the entire country – something that Catalonia ignored for some considerable time – and, further, that these should be used to produce the quite unrealistic figure of 550,000 men. Yet the actual implementation of this policy was left in the hands of the provincial and municipal juntas and the town councils, and thus it was that, notwithstanding much exhortation on the part of the Junta Suprema Central, the administration of conscription never escaped from the hands of local elites who approached the problem on the basis of not social justice, but rather the preservation of their own interests and, alongside them, those of their friends. As had already been the case ever since June 1808, then, military service was only obligatory for those who lacked the political, economic and social influence necessary to avoid it. With the connivance and, on occasion, active participation of the local authorities, ballots were fixed and lists of potential conscripts interfered with, whilst on all sides local notables of all sorts scrambled to get themselves or their sons exempted from the selection on more or less fraudulent medical grounds or a variety of other pretexts. Also very useful, meanwhile, was the existence of a large number of privileged units in which the prosperous could, at least in theory, serve out the war in safety at the cost of paying for their own arms, uniforms and equipment. Typical of these 'troops of show' were the various volunteer regiments that acquired the role of providing one provincial junta or another with an honour guard; and, in addition, certain town militias such as the enormous force formed to protect the island-city of Cádiz (a place that was, until 1810 at least, not only a long way from the fighting, but also virtually invulnerable to attack from the land). And, finally, yet another bolt-hole was provided by the property owning paramilitary force known as the Milicia Honrada which was set up by the Junta Central in the autumn of 1808 to help maintain order.[25]

Amongst the populace neither the war nor conscription was ever likely to enjoy much popularity, but, with the latter administered in this fashion, the result was fury. From the very beginning, then, the Spanish war effort was confronted with a major problem. In order to avoid being pressed into the army, thousands of young men went into hiding or fled their home districts, whilst still others faked injury or illness, engaged in acts of self-mutilation or contracted hasty marriages, married men being in practice exempt from being called up. On top of this, there were also numerous acts of collective resistance – a favourite target was the public ballots held to select the recruits that had to be sent by each town and village. And, of course, the natural response of those men actually unfortunate enough to be conscripted into the army – many of whom were marched away tied together and kept under guard like prisoners[26] – was to desert at the earliest possible opportunity.

The issue of desertion will be returned to at a later point. For the time being we will rather look at the context in which this continual resistance occurred. From one end of Patriot Spain to the other the countryside was rocked by tax strikes, land seizures, riots, petty insurrections and acts of intimidation. In some cases these were certainly the work in the first instance of disaffected members of the elite, but in others they had a genuinely popular origin. Thus, it was not just conscription that was working on the crowd, but also the political, social and economic policies being pursued by the juntas. Far from being revolutionary bodies, they for the most part continued to insist on the payment of tithes and feudal dues, whilst in some instances the local elites tightened the screw still further by abolishing measures that had been taken in the reign of King Charles III to protect vulnerable tenant farmers and attempting to force down the wages earned by agricultural labourers. Desperate to maintain order, they in addition added insult to injury by introducing a variety of police measures which in one way or another made many inroads into ordinary life. Meanwhile, corruption flourished with many juntas establishing an evil reputation for peculation and nepotism.[27]

The juntas, then, were sitting on a powderkeg. By no means unaware of this, they responded in a fashion that could not but undermine the Spanish war effort. Most of their policies could not be abandoned without damaging their various sectional interests, but conscription was a different matter. Slackening off on this front might damage the struggle against France, but in much of Spain until well into the war this was something that often felt a long way away. Not surprisingly, then, the authorities frequently turned a blind eye to fraud and draft evasion or sought to meet their quotas by shipping off the halt and the lame – in other words elements of society that would not be missed in their home communities. Faced by such behaviour, the Junta Central made desperate efforts to force the local elites to do their duty, but the commissioners that it dispatched for this purpose met with a solid wall of resistance that invariably had them throwing up their hands in despair.[28] Conscription did not cease to function altogether, but the flow of recruits was never sufficient, whilst the total of 550,000 recruits was never met. The full figures for enlistment are unknown, but in the period June–October 1808 – the only one for which a reasonable estimate may be made – the total may have come to around 100,000; around the middle of 1809, meanwhile, the province of Granada – an area that had remained in Patriot hands throughout and in 1808 had a population of around 700,000 – was estimated in the year of fighting that had just passed to have sent some 30,000 men to the war.[29]

Let us accept, however, that in the first days of the war the insurgent authorities had all the men that they could handle in the first instance. The next job was obviously to fashion the crowds of recruits into a force capable of fighting the French, but in the circumstances of 1808 this was easier said than done. Not the least of the difficulties was the military's very limited influence in Patriot Spain. For a variety of reasons, the army was deeply unpopular with most classes of society. Whilst the populace hated soldiers on principle, the civilian elites were jealous of the privileged status the officer corps had enjoyed prior to 1808 and the manner in which the military governors and Captains General had come to assume important roles in local government and the administration of justice. Even when generals rallied to the uprising's result, then, this did not necessarily save them from being overthrown or even murdered, whilst those that maintained their positions found that they had no option but to bend the knee before the juntas. At the same time, the military estate itself split: denied promotion, many of the humbler subaltern officers collaborated enthusiastically with the insurgents, and made no attempt to rally round their superiors even when the latter were demonstrably loyal to the rebellion.[30]

All this had a disastrous effect on the army in that there was a serious breakdown of command and control. Rather than the new recruits being systematically fed into skeleton units based on formations drawn from the old army, there was a widespread tendency to form new regiments under the leadership of improvised officers who were frequently lacking in talent, training and experience. Whilst there may be an element of caricature here, the German commissary, Augustus Schaumann, provides us with a sharp pen-picture of what this could mean:

> The ... Spanish officers are mostly ignorant and ill-mannered. It is impossible to find a gentleman amongst them. The few of them who have attended a military school ... are very conceited and very

deficient in the knowledge of their art. They are chiefly concerned with their uniforms ... their enormously large hats [and] their long Toledo swords, which they carry under their arms, and with loafing about public walks and cafés, smoking cigars and eating and drinking and sleeping a great deal ... As the majority of Spanish officers hail from the lower orders, and feel themselves drawn to common and ordinary associates, they have no notion of inspiring respect among their subordinates. One frequently sees officers hobnobbing quite familiarly with their men, drinking out of the same glass or smoking the same cigar by turns.[31]

To return to the organisation of the Patriot army, in those parts of Spain where there was scarcely anything in the way of a regular garrison there was little option but to go down the road of forming many new regiments, but elsewhere the root of this development was the determination of the civilian notables to gain access to the privileges of the officer corps, and, still more so, of the juntas to exercise their new powers of patronage to the full. At all events the results were catastrophic, for Patriot Spain was in consequence saddled with an army that was at the least very difficult to sustain. In all some 214 new infantry regiments were created in the course of 1808, yet only 52 of these appear ever to have had more than 1 battalion. This, of course, meant that the number of regimental headquarters with all their attendant senior officers, adjutants, chaplains, drum-majors, surgeons and other non-combatants was wildly excessive: at best, there should have been no more than 107 and possibly as few as 71. Still worse, denied the depots that might have kept them up to strength and all too often limited to single battalions only, many regiments dwindled away to nothing, leaving their officers to gravitate to cities far from the fighting whilst continuing to draw their pay.[32]

Again, however, such long-term issues need not concern us as yet. Much more pressing was the issue of how the soldiers of the uprising measured up to those of Napoleonic France. For obvious reasons, the vast majority of Spain's new forces were composed of infantry: it was simply quicker and cheaper to turn out foot soldiers than it was to train fresh cavalrymen or to equip new batteries of artillery.[33] Meanwhile, until the arrival of substantial British aid – aid that, it has to be said, did not always reach the front line – arms, equipment and uniforms had all to be improvised from what was available locally.[34] By 1809 such sinews of war had become more abundant, but there remained chronic problems of discipline and training, of which there will be more discussion below. In consequence, the Spanish Army had little chance. Thus, the single lucky victory obtained at Bailén was followed by a series of terrible defeats – good examples are Gamonal, Tudela, Somosierra, Cardedeu, Molins de Rey, Uclés, Valls, Medellín, María, Belchite, Almonacid de Toledo, Alba de Tormes and Ocaña – for the

Spanish levies could barely manoeuvre or change formation on the battlefield, whilst their lack of artillery and, more especially, cavalry support placed them at a still greater disadvantage. Often in action for the first time, they were also desperately prone to the sort of panics seen at Talavera and, more particularly, Belchite, where the explosion of an ammunition wagon caused an entire army to take to its heels. Nor was there ever any chance of remedying these problems. One way forward would have been to avoid battle and adopt a defensive strategy: spread around the periphery of the country (as they were from December 1808), the Spanish armies were sheltered by massive chains of mountains, such as the Sierra Morena, whilst time would also have been gained to drill them into some semblance of order. However, this was not an option: the provisional government that ruled Spain from 1808 to 1810 needed military victories, whilst generals that jibbed at taking the field were liable to be replaced and on occasion even murdered. Yet going over to the attack was not easy either, for the Spanish field armies were necessarily operating on exterior lines whilst their starting positions were often hundreds of miles apart from one another. In consequence, it was easy for the French to defeat them in detail, whilst the disadvantages under which the generals were labouring were frequently increased by the meddling of their political superiors and the hesitation engendered by the deep dilemmas that they faced (damned if they did not fight, they knew that they would be defeated if they did). Finally, since the chief theatre of operations could not but be the open plains of the *meseta*, defeat was invariably accompanied by enormous casualties and the loss of large numbers of guns and other impedimenta. At the same time, as military service was, for all the reasons that have been discussed, deeply unpopular, the army impossible to supply in an adequate manner and joining the guerrillas a constant temptation, desertion was enormous: according to one recent study, one-third of the men conscripted in Catalonia in the course of the war disappeared in this fashion.[35]

In consequence, with each defeat the generals had to start virtually from scratch, only for their efforts almost immediately to be lost in some fresh catastrophe. Hence the fact that in July 1809 British observers could describe the Army of Extremadura – a force that had in theory been in existence for over a year, but had in that time in effect been destroyed twice over – as little more than an armed mob. Here the words of Wellington and his soldiers may be allowed to speak for themselves, those of the British commander being particularly damning:

> In the battle at Talavera, in which the Spanish army, with very trifling exceptions, was not engaged, whole corps threw away their arms and ran off in my presence when they were neither attacked nor threatened with an attack, but frightened . . . I believe, by their own fire

> ... When these dastardly soldiers run away, they plunder everything they meet ... I have found, upon enquiry and from experience, the instances of the misbehaviour of the Spanish troops to be so numerous, and those of their good behaviour so few, that I must conclude that they are troops by no means to be depended upon.[36]

Much the same feeling, meanwhile, was expressed by William Lawrence, who was in 1809 a private soldier in the 40th Foot. 'Sir Arthur Wellesley took the opportunity of reviewing the Spanish troops as they passed. They looked a fine enough set of men, but they were fit for scarcely anything except to fall into disorder and confusion.... either from not having been properly disciplined, or else because they had not good officers to command them.'[37]

In fairness it ought to be observed that the Spaniards often actually fought with great courage, particularly in the defence of besieged cities and fortresses and in situations where the French could not bring their massive tactical superiority to bear. Several good examples may be mentioned here, but the best are probably Zaragoza (Saragossa) and Gerona, both of which put up a ferocious fight in the sieges to which they were subjected in 1809, and, in the former case, quite exceptionally for the period continued to hold out house by house even when the French had not just breached the walls but got right inside the city. Indeed, even at Talavera (27–28 July 1809) most of the Spanish soldiers who were actually engaged showed far more vigour and determination than an irritated British Army ever gave them credit for.[38] But gallantry was not enough: by the beginning of 1810 Spain's soldiers had lost so much ground to the French and suffered such heavy casualties that they had literally run out of resources. There were too few men and too few guns, whilst morale had slumped to an all-time low. When Joseph Bonaparte and Marshal Soult between them decided to launch a massive offensive against Andalucía – the very heartland of the Patriot cause – in January 1810, the Spanish line collapsed in a matter of hours, leaving the invaders to advance in blitzkrieg fashion to the sea.[39]

Patriot Spain did not collapse in 1810: aside from anything else, the government – now not the Junta Central but a new council of regency – found a secure refuge in the impregnable island-city of Cádiz. However, it was now a very different war. From 1810 to 1812, all that the army could do was to seek to hang on to such enclaves of territory as the Patriot cause still possessed whilst at the same time harassing the French with raids and skirmishes. In this manner the struggle against Napoleon was sustained, but the military were never able to regain even such strength as they had possessed in 1808, with the result that the liberation of Spain in 1812–13 saw only a limited degree of Spanish participation. Indeed, even the organisational genius of Wellington, who became commander-in-chief of the Spanish Army in January 1813, proved insufficient to the task of rebuilding the army, and it was not until the autumn of that year, by which time the French had almost been cleared from the Peninsula, that substantial bodies of troops were once again available for service.[40] Yet this is not to say that the Spanish Army remained the mass of raw recruits that it had so often been in the period 1808–10. Desertion continued, but the absence of the great defeats consequent upon attempting to take on the French on their own terms in unfavourable terrain meant that opportunities for getting away were probably reduced: no longer did every Spanish army periodically scatter across the countryside in panic-stricken flight (there were exceptions such as the disastrous battles of the River Gebora and Castalla in March 1811 and July 1812, however). By the same token, meanwhile, casualties were also less severe and thus it was that Spanish soldiers began for the first time to enjoy the advantages of long service. By all accounts, tactical standards were still not high, but the French suddenly found that Spanish armies were no longer crumbling with scarcely a shot being fired. Of this the first evidence was probably encountered at the Battle of Albuera (16 May 1811) where four battalions of Spanish infantry – all of them veterans who had held together for the best part of two years – held off two French divisions and thereby saved Sir William Beresford from complete disaster. Yet this newfound resolution was to become a recurrent theme: Sagunto was a distinctly hard-fought battle, the loss of which was the result of some very poor generalship on the part of the Spanish commander, Joaquín Blake. Even at the dreadful rout on the Gebora (19 February 1811) the Spanish infantry showed more resourcefulness than had hitherto been the norm: deserted by their own cavalry and caught by surprise in a hopeless position, some regiments nonetheless attempted to save themselves by forming a gigantic hollow square and endeavouring to withdraw in good order. By the end of the war, indeed, Spanish soldiers were regularly fighting well, whilst at both Vitoria (21 June 1813) and San Marcial (31 August 1813) they particularly distinguished themselves. Nor is this last fact surprising, for many of the troops who fought alongside Wellington in 1813, such as those of the division of General Longa, were veterans of the bitter guerrilla war that is so much a feature of the Spanish conflict. At all events British observers were quite impressed. Here and there one still comes across critical voices, but on the whole the tone is quite different from that of 1809. To quote one British officer, 'Lord Wellington has collected a very powerful Spanish army, all well armed, clothed and equipped, and I very much doubt whether they have had so good and powerful a body acting conjointly for this last century.'[41]

At various points in this chapter mention has been made of the guerrillas. In many British accounts, in particular, it is implied that the popular resistance represented by these irregulars and the regular resistance represented by the army were somehow separate from one another. This, however, is not the case. The guerrilla war that the French faced in

Spain is a complex phenomenon which is not easily reduced to a single paragraph, but quite a number of forces that are often described as having been guerrilla bands – examples include the men commanded by Julián Sánchez and Pedro Villacampa – in reality turn out to have been regular units that either became trapped behind enemy lines or were deliberately sent 'into the blue' to wreak havoc on the enemy. There was a more popular guerrilla movement as well – in other words, one raised directly from the civilian population – but here, too, there was often some military input: Juan Díaz Porlier, for example, was originally an officer in an infantry regiment who was cut off at the Battle of Gamonal and took refuge in the neighbouring Cantabrian mountains with a few other survivors. Nor in many instances did it always retain its civilian character: driven by ambition, the desire to secure recognition as regular combatants and, in one or two instances, genuine vision, many of the men who had emerged as the commanders of irregular bands increasingly strove to militarise their unruly followers, clothing them in improvised uniforms and forming them into regular style units. As this generally brought them more success, they gathered more and more men around them and in this fashion eventually took the field at the head of entire divisions which sooner or later took their place in the order of battle of the regular army: one thinks here of the troops commanded by Juan Martín Díez or Francisco Espoz y Mina. Such commanders, meanwhile, did not just acquire their men from volunteers: on the contrary, impressment was widely used, whilst another useful source of recruits was enemy prisoners who had been encouraged to enlist at the point of a gun: by 1812, indeed, in the Basque provinces entire guerrilla bands – by now battalions of infantry – were to be found who had been recruited in this fashion.[42]

In large part, then, the popular conception of the Spanish guerrillas is a myth. Beyond the bands of Villacampa, Espoz y Mina and the rest, there were, indeed, many bands of armed men, some of them tiny but others running into the dozens or even hundreds, and these men certainly pounced on any French foragers and dispatch riders that they encountered. However, the influence of these irredeemably civilian elements has been greatly exaggerated. Whilst they certainly spread fear in the hearts of the invaders – unlike the commanders of the guerrilla movement proper, they rarely took prisoners and were also much inclined to use torture – the fact was that, recruited in the main from the ranks of deserters and the absolutely desperate, they were in the end brigands, who were as likely to turn on Spanish villagers as they were to attack French soldiers, and had in the end to be rounded up after 1814 by the Spaniards themselves. Nor, in reality, were they ever more than a minor menace: happy enough to pick on soft targets, it usually only took a few determined men to chase them off. Yet the very idea that ordinary Spanish citizens were taking up arms against the enemy and engaging in a genuine 'people's war' came as balm to the soul of the liberal ideologues who came to dominate the politics of the Patriot zone after the fall of Seville at the beginning of 1810 forced its headquarters to shift to the island-city of Cádiz, and they lost no opportunity to trumpet such examples of popular heroism to the heavens.[43]

Nor were even those forces in the interior that were genuinely engaged in fighting the French capable of meeting the challenge imposed by the Peninsular War. Between the autumn of 1809 and the winter of 1811–12, Napoleon had nothing to distract him from waging war in Spain and Portugal and, although he did not travel there himself, he in consequence poured many thousands of troops across the frontier and constantly urged his generals to take the offensive. In the face of this avalanche, the army did what it could, but, in the midst of a mixture of heroism and incompetence, it lost city after city – the most notable losses being Badajoz, Tarragona and Valencia – and with them thousands of men and guns. Far away in Aragón, Navarre and other provinces, Villacampa, Espoz y Mina, Díaz Porlier and the other heroes of the guerrilla struggle fought on, but all their efforts had little effect on checking the march of French conquest: it was, indeed, only the presence of the Anglo-Portuguese army and, more especially, its ability from the winter of 1811 onwards to take the offensive in effective fashion, that gave these forces their relevance.[44]

All this impacted very deeply on the army's psychology. Reduced to a secondary role in the ejection of the French, it had also been forced to endure the open scorn of many British soldiers (scorn that is echoed in much British writing on the Peninsular War to this very day). At the very time that it had been fighting the invaders with such devotion, moreover, it had seen itself stripped of most of the legal privileges that the military estate had enjoyed in 1808 by the *cortes* of Cádiz. Rather than a source of pride, the war against Napoleon therefore became one of humiliation – humiliation, moreover, that was in large part blamed on the civilian politicians who had actually run the war effort – and the result was a propensity towards military intervention in politics that was to mar the course of Spanish history until well into the twentieth century. In brief, the army became obsessed by the need to maintain law and order, the unity of Spain and the primacy of the armed forces, and in this fashion it was drawn deeper and deeper into the camp of political reaction. In consequence, it may be said that the victims of General Franco's firing squads in the Spanish Civil War of 1936–39 were the last casualties of the struggle against Napoleon.

NOTES

1. Cit. R. Fraser, *Napoleon's Cursed War: Spanish Popular Resistance in the Peninsular War* (London, 2008), p. xxiv.
2. For a general appraisal of the Spanish army prior to 1808, see C.J. Esdaile, *The Spanish Army in the Peninsular War* (Manchester, 1988), pp. 3–24. The two Spanish works that

provide much information on social aspects of the question are F. Andújar Castillo, *Los militares en la España del siglo XVIII: un estudio social* (Granada, 1991) and J.L. Terrón Ponce, *Ejército y política en la España de Carlos III* (Madrid, 1997).

3. For details of the war of 1793–95, see C.J. Esdaile, 'The Spanish army' in F.R. Schneid (ed.), *Armies of the French Revolutionary Wars* (Norman, Oklahoma, forthcoming).
4. Despite the publication of several highly favourable biographies in recent years, Godoy's efforts to reform the Spanish Army continue to go unremarked even in Spain. For an introduction to this topic, see Esdaile, *Spanish Army*, pp. 39–59.
5. For a recent Spanish language biography of Morla, see M.D. Herrero Fernández-Quesada, *Ciencia y milicia en el siglo XVIII: Tomás de Morla, artillero ilustrado* (Segovia, 1992).
6. The most accessible account in the English language of the campaigns of the Spanish Army in the Peninsular War is to be found in D. Gates, *The Spanish Ulcer: a History of the Peninsular War: a New History* (London, 1986). However, this should be supplemented by the more rounded C.J. Esdaile, *The Peninsular War: A New History* (London, 2002).
7. For a very good example of the way in which British accounts of the Spanish Army have been inclined both to conflate the pre-war army with that of the revolution and to write without reference to the social and political background, see C. Oman, *A History of the Peninsular War* (Oxford, 1902–30), pp. 89–102.
8. The most eloquent statement of this position in the anglophone historiography is to be found in J.L. Tone, 'The Peninsular War' in P.G. Dwyer (ed.), *Napoleon and Europe* (London, 2001), pp. 225–42.
9. For the social and political background to the events of 1808, see Esdaile, *Peninsular War*, pp. 1–32 *passim*.
10. The popular conviction that the French had come to Spain to punish Godoy is one that is frequently remarked on in French memoirs of the period. See, for example, L.F. Lejeune, *Memoirs of Baron Lejeune, Aide-de-Camp to Marshals Berthier, Davout and Oudinot*, ed. A. Bell (London, 1897), I, pp. 72–4.
11. Scholarly accounts of the Dos de Mayo are few and far between in English. However, perhaps the most detailed is that contained in G. Lovett, *Napoleon and the Birth of Modern Spain* (New York, 1965), pp. 131–50; for a recent Spanish account, see A. García Fuertes, *Dos de Mayo de 1808: el grito de una nación* (Madrid, 2007).
12. For an interesting discussion of popular perceptions of the political situation before and during the uprising, see R. Herr, 'Good and evil and the Spanish uprising against Napoleon' in R. Herr and H. Parker (eds), *Ideas in History* (Durham, North Carolina, 1965), pp. 157–81.
13. For an interesting case study of the origins of the revolt in one particular city, see M. Moreno Alonso, *La revolución 'santa' de Sevilla: la revuelta popular de 1808* (Seville, 1997).
14. In Seville, at least, as Fraser has pointed out (see Fraser, *Napoleon's Cursed War*, p. 128), some of the early proclamations issued by the provincial junta certainly support this hypothesis in that, instead of war actually being declared on France, Napoleon was rather simply threatened with war, the inference being that there was a strong hope that hostilities might be avoided.
15. For an expanded discussion of the organisation of the insurrection, see Esdaile, *Spanish Army*, pp. 79–83.
16. Even in these two latter instances, juntas appeared in both the provincial capitals and in the smaller towns, but, at least in principle, these bodies were subordinated to the military authorities as represented by Palafox and Cuesta.
17. For a detailed survey, see Fraser, *Napoleon's Cursed War*, pp. 125–7. See also Esdaile, *Peninsular War*, pp. 49–54.
18. For manpower levels in the Bourbon Army, see Oman, *History of the Peninsular War*, I, pp. 607–11. Meanwhile, a detailed discussion of the situation that pertained in the various regions of Spain may be found in C.J. Esdaile, 'Conscription in Spain in the Napoleonic

era' in D. Stoker (ed.), *Conscription in Napoleonic Europe* (London, 2008). Taking into account the many regiments that were caught in the French zone of occupation and in consequence either disintegrated or were interned or even, in the case of the Swiss, pressed into French service, the number of men actually available to the insurgents may have been as few as 100,000.

19. For an example, see Lovett, *Napoleon and the Birth of Modern Spain*, pp. 302–3.
20. B. Spencer to Lord Castlereagh, 21 June 1808, National Archives, War Office Papers, 1/226, f. 478.
21. Fraser, *Napoleon's Cursed War*, pp. 137–41; Oman, *History of the Peninsular War*, I, pp. 128–45 *passim*.
22. For the atmosphere in the immediate aftermath of the uprising, see Esdaile, *Peninsular War*, pp. 55–7, and Fraser, *Napoleon's Cursed War*, pp. 143–53.
23. For these figures, see Conde de Clonard, *Historia orgánica de las armas de infantería y caballería españolas* (Madrid, 1851–62), VI, p. 303.
24. There is no study in English of this propaganda campaign; for an introduction in Spanish, see E. de Diego García, 'La verdad construida: la propaganda en la Guerra de la Independencia' in A. Moliner Prada (ed.), *La Guerra de la Independencia en España, 1808–1814* (Barcelona, 2007), pp. 209–53.
25. The Cádiz militia – the Voluntarios Distinguidos de Cádiz – was a particularly nefarious force: very large, well uniformed and equipped and largely recruited from the city's substantial commercial community and its dependants, in February 1809 it secured a guarantee that it would never have to serve with one of the field armies by organising a riot and then proving the indispensability of its presence in the city by suppressing it with great verve and efficacy. See C.J. Esdaile, *Fighting Napoleon: Guerrillas, Bandits and Adventurers in Spain, 1808–1814* (London, 2004), pp. 75–6.
26. For a description of such a scene in Andalusia, see W. Jacob, *Travels in the South of Spain in Letters written A.D. 1809 and 1810* (London, 1811), pp. 189–91.
27. For all this, see Esdaile, *Fighting Napoleon*, pp. 67–78 *passim*; Fraser, *Napoleon's Cursed War*, pp. 234–45.
28. For some examples of attempts on the part of the authorities to avoid imposing conscription, see Esdaile, *Fighting Napoleon*, p. 86.
29. R. Semple, *A Second Journey in Spain in the Spring of 1809 from Lisbon through the Western Skirts of the Sierra Morena to Sevilla, Córdoba, Granada, Málaga and Gibraltar, and thence to Tetuan and Tangiers* (London, 1809), p. 178.
30. For the experiences of the army in the wake of the uprising, see Esdaile, *Spanish Army*, pp. 93–7 *passim*.
31. A. Ludovici (ed.), *On the Road with Wellington: the Diary of a War Commissary in the Peninsular Campaigns* (New York, 1925), pp. 174–5.
32. The best guide to the new regiments created in the course of 1808 is to be found in Clonard, *Historia orgánica*, VI, pp. 303–12.
33. In contrast to the 214 regiments of infantry mentioned above, 1808 saw the appearance of only 24 regiments of cavalry, many of them very weak.
34. A note on the uniforms worn by the soldiers may be of interest here. In 1808 the regular army seems already to have presented a fairly variegated appearance: in the line infantry, for example, some units were arrayed in the traditional white uniforms that had been re-introduced in 1807, whilst others were still dressed in the black-faced sky-blue that had been brought in by Godoy in 1803; equally, in the light infantry, whilst most regiments wore dark-blue coats cut in the same style as their counterparts in the line, a few still possessed 'tarleton' helmets and green hussar-style dolmans that were again a short-lived legacy of the royal favourite. As recruits flooded into the army in the wake of 1808 the situation got still worse: one regiment is recorded as having gone to war with half the men in bicornes and coats and the other half in forage caps and fatigue jackets. As for the new

levies, apart from a few 'troops of show' who obtained uniforms in all the colours of the rainbow, most of the men who got uniforms received round hats of various sorts and short jackets and breeches made of coarse brown cloth. Later in the war so a more 'French' style began to become common, complete with bell-topped shakoes: for some excellent depictions of soldiers dressed like this, see the paintings by Denis Dighton in the Royal Collection. Only in the period 1812–13, however, do the troops appear to have acquired the 'British' look that has so often been reproduced in books on the uniforms of the Peninsular War, and even then it is quite clear that it was by no means universal: in a summary list of 1814 many regiments appear in white or brown as well as the light and dark-blue typical of the uniforms sent from Britain. For details see J.M. Bueno Carrera, *El ejército y la armada en 1808* (Málaga, 1982) and J.M. Bueno Carrera, *Uniformes militares de la Guerra de la Independencia* (Madrid, 1989).

35. For the problem of desertion in Catalonia, see E. Canales, *Patriotismo y deserción durante la Guerra de la Independencia en Cataluña* (Coimbra, 1988). The immense difficulties faced by the army in the period 1808–9 in particular are discussed at length in Esdaile, *Spanish Army*, pp. 114–45. The travails of Spain's generals, however, should not be allowed to gloss over the fact that in many instances, the tactics they adopted on the battlefield were, at the very least, ill-advised.
36. Lord Wellington to Lord Wellesley, 24 August 1809, University of Southampton, Wellington Papers, 1/275.
37. G. Bankes (ed.), *The Autobiography of Sergeant William Lawrence, a Hero of the Peninsular and Waterloo Campaigns* (London, 1886), p. 53.
38. For an eloquent defence of the old regular army's efforts in the first year of the war, see A. García Fuertes, 'El ejército español en campaña en los comienzos de la Guerra de la Independencia, 1808–1809', *Monte Buceiro*, No. 13 (2008), 102–66. For the second siege of Zaragoza – an episode in which the lead was taken not by the armed civilians who had been prominent in the first siege but a large garrison of regular troops, albeit mostly regiments that had been raised since 1808 – see R. Rudorff, *War to the Death: the Sieges of Zaragoza, 1808–1809* (London, 1974), pp. 175–267.
39. For the conquest of Andalucía, see Oman, *History of the Peninsular War*, III, pp. 128–52.
40. The Duke of Wellington's struggles to rebuild the Spanish Army are chronicled in C.J. Esdaile, *The Duke of Wellington and the Command of the Spanish Army, 1812–1814* (London, 1990), pp. 108–35.
41. S. Cassells (ed.), *Peninsular Portrait, 1811–1814: the Letters of William Bragge, Third (King's Own) Dragoons* (London, 1963), p. 109; see also W. Thompson (ed.), *An Ensign in the Peninsular War: the Letters of John Aitchison* (London, 1981), pp. 255–6.
42. For a general discussion of the Spanish guerrillas, see Esdaile, *Fighting Napoleon*, pp. 90–192.
43. For the liberal view of the guerrillas and, indeed, the war in general, see Esdaile, *Spanish Army*, pp. 169–73.
44. This is not, however, to say that the guerrillas had no impact on the struggle at all. For a detailed discussion of the achievements of the guerrillas in Aragón and Navarre, see J.L. Tone, *The Fatal Knot: the Guerrilla War in Navarre and the Defeat of Napoleon in Spain* (Chapel Hill, North Carolina, 1994), and D. Alexander, *Rod of Iron: French Counter-Insurgency in Aragón during the Peninsular War* (Wilmington, Delaware, 1985).

Chapter Eight

The Portuguese Army

Malyn Newitt

INTRODUCTION

On 27 September 1810 Marshal André Masséna, commanding the French Army invading Portugal, decided to attack the position held by the British and Portuguese forces on the ridge of Busaco outside Coimbra. This position could have been easily outflanked but Masséna had been persuaded that the Portuguese brigades were only an 'army of peasants' and could be as easily defeated as their Spanish counterparts had been on so many previous occasions. However, the Portuguese not only held firm but repulsed the French attack. Although the battle itself was of little strategic importance, the performance of the Portuguese was such as to alter the whole balance of forces in the Iberian peninsula, for a Portuguese Army that eventually numbered around 60,000 men enabled Britain to overcome the lack of manpower that had hitherto hindered its military operations and to go on the offensive.

The structure of the Portuguese Army that fought in the Peninsular War was still recognisably that which had been created after the country had broken free from Spain in 1640 – a structure that was not to be fundamentally altered until 1836.[1] It was an army that was largely intended for defensive purposes. All able-bodied men were liable for military service and the regiments (*terços*) were raised and stationed in the provinces, and were officered by men of *fidalgo* status who traditionally resided in their own homes. The army was small, with a nominal strength of around 25,000 men, though in peacetime it only had half that number and special efforts had to be made to increase its manpower during time of war. This regular army was supplemented by militia regiments, known as the Segunda Linha, recruited by lot and commanded by a largely amateur officer corps of local gentry. There was also the Ordenança, a village guard that could be turned out in case of invasion and from whose numbers the militia and regular forces were recruited. This was an army that did not expect to have to fight outside Portugal, for the colonies had their own locally recruited armies and militias, supplemented from time to time by military convicts sent from Portugal.

The Portuguese Army of the *ancien régime* had been kept at a distance from the political centre by routinely appointing foreigners as commanders, men not linked to domestic factions and often appointed only for a specific campaign. The roll call of foreign commanders included Schomberg whose victories against Spain assured Portugal's independence, Lord Tyrawley, Schaumburg-Lippe who as Marshal-General between 1762 and 1765 carried through extensive reforms and introduced new military regulations, John Forbes of Skellater who commanded the forces during the war against the French in 1793 and Von Goltz.

In 1793 Portugal sent an expeditionary force of 5,052 men to fight on the Pyrennean frontier as part of the First Coalition against revolutionary France. The experience of fighting the French armies convinced a small group of young officers, which included the future Minister of War, Miguel Pereira Forjaz, that the army needed radical reform. In 1801 the country faced a Spanish invasion and in a campaign that lasted only three weeks (20 May–7 June) Portugal's frontier defences collapsed and the Prince Regent had to sue for peace, the town of Olivença being retained by Spain as a trophy of the war. As João Centeno wrote in 2008, 'this campaign of 1801 revealed the deplorable state in which the army found itself' and showed the shortage of experienced officers, the absence of effective central command and the lack of discipline.[2] In addition the army had only been able to mobilise 16,000 infantry and 2,000 cavalry, who were badly mounted and ineffective.

After the debacle of 1801 a review of Portugal's armed forces was undertaken by the new commander, Count von Goltz, and, in an atmosphere of bitter recrimination, various plans for the reorganisation and defence of Portugal were produced by John Forbes of Skellater, and the francophile officers Gomes Freire de Andrade and the Marquês de Alorna. In 1806–7 a radical restructuring of the army was at last begun. The regular army was divided into 3 divisions, each division having 4 brigades of infantry consisting of 2 regiments, 4 regiments of cavalry and 1 of artillery. The country was divided into 7 military governorships each of which had 24 brigades of Ordenança and 2 regiments of militia.[3] This was the army that Beresford inherited in 1809 but not before it had been thrown into considerable disarray by the first French invasion.

Meanwhile, a British military commission had concluded that the state of Portuguese frontier defences and the enfeebled state of the army meant that Portugal could not be defended against an attack from France and Spain.

THE FIRST FRENCH INVASION

This conclusion seemed to be born out when in October 1807 Napoleon decided to bring Portugal and the strategic port of Lisbon within the Continental System and despatched General Junot with an army to join the

Spanish in the occupation of the kingdom. While the Prince Regent and the Portuguese royal family left for Brazil, a Regency was appointed to negotiate with Junot. The armed forces were ordered not to resist the French and Junot duly entered Lisbon unopposed. The Portuguese Army and militia were then disbanded and the fortresses occupied by French or Spanish troops. The arrival of the French was welcomed by certain francophile elements, not least by Gomes Freire de Andrade and the Marquês de Alorna. Junot recruited these 2 officers to oversee the disbanding of the old army and the raising of a new force, to be called the Legião Portuguesa, made up of 4 infantry and 3 cavalry regiments totalling 9,000 men[4] which was despatched to join the Grande Armée in Germany.

In May 1808 popular insurrections broke out in Spain and in the north of Portugal and, although Junot moved swiftly to disarm his erstwhile Spanish allies, the French soon found themselves isolated in Lisbon. The Spanish forces that had occupied the north withdrew into Spain and on 6 June the Portuguese flag was raised in Porto. The north of Portugal was now under the effective control of the Bishop of Porto and a self-proclaimed Junta Provisional, while local juntas and volunteer forces formed spontaneously throughout the rest of the country. Meanwhile, the Portuguese ambassador in London, Domingos de Sousa Coutinho, aided by Colonel Carlos Frederico Lecor and with the encouragement of the British government, formed a corps of volunteers that became known as the Loyal Lusitanian Legion and which was placed under the command of Sir Robert Wilson.

The northern Junta sent a force south to assist Sir Arthur Wellesley who had landed with an army north of Lisbon and who defeated Junot on 21 August at Vimeiro, forcing him to sign the Convention of Cintra (now Sintra) by which the French evacuated the country.

Following the French evacuation the Portuguese Army was formally reconstituted (decree of 30 September) and new regulations were issued (beginning 14 October) which re-established the army along the lines of the 1807 reforms. The only major innovation was the creation of 6 battalions of *caçadores* (light infantry) with a strength of 3,700 men. Finally a decree of 11 December called the whole nation to arms '*para a defesa da patria*', which, as João Centeno points out, was no imitation of the French *levée en masse* but a return to 'a form of organisation of the defense of the kingdom almost as old as the kingdom itself'.[5]

In October 1808 Sir John Moore led most of the British army of occupation into Spain, while the few remaining British troops, under the command of General Craddock, collected in Lisbon ready to be embarked should the French invade again. Portugal was left to be defended by an army without arms, uniforms or horses and without an effective officer corps. It was in these circumstances that, at the end of December 1808, the Prince Regent asked Britain to appoint a general to train the new

Portuguese Army. Wellesley declined the appointment as the British government was already planning to send him with another expeditionary force to replace the army that had been lost during Moore's disastrous retreat to Corunna. Another general had to be found – junior enough to serve in Portugal under Wellesley – and the choice eventually fell on Major General William Carr Beresford. Beresford had commanded the British troops occupying Madeira early in 1808 and had been commandant of Lisbon at the time of the withdrawal of the French in September. He owed his appointment to his knowledge of Portuguese affairs, but also to his personal connections since, like Wellesley and Castlereagh, he came from the narrow group of aristocratic families that formed the Anglo-Irish Protestant Ascendancy.

BERESFORD TAKES COMMAND

Beresford received his appointment as commander of the Portuguese Army on 28 January 1809.[6] Although only a major general in the British Army, he was immediately promoted to the rank of Marshal so that he would have seniority over all the Portuguese generals. Beresford arrived in Portugal on 2 March and immediately set to work. As Soult had once again invaded Portugal and occupied Porto, Beresford was under extreme pressure from the Portuguese Regents to attempt the defence of the country. However, he failed to get Craddock, the British commander, to advance against Soult[7] and wrote to his half-sister Anne,

> the chaos and confusion in which I found everything here is not to be described, nor could I myself ... have believed that human ingenuity could have so perfectly confounded everything. Light is however beginning to appear and I hope we shall have shortly the pleasure of sending presents to England of at least a Marshal and Duke de l'Empire with a garnish of a few generals de plus.[8]

By May he was able to put 19,000 men of the old army (all either infantry or artillery) into the field to support Wellesley's campaign in the north. After the murder of General Bernardim Freire de Andrade (brother of the francophile Gomes) on 18 March, the Portuguese forces were led by Francisco da Silveira and Beresford himself, to whom Wellington wrote a stern warning: 'Remember that you are commander in chief of an army and must not be beaten'.[9] Beresford's corps of 6,000 Portuguese was sent to turn Soult's left flank, which it succeeded in doing, pursuing the retreating French. However, he failed to coordinate his movements with those of Wellesley and allowed the French to escape into Spain. Beresford received some of the blame for this and wrote to his half-sister:

> You know how sanguine I was of the expectation of quick success, and have only been mistaken in any of the French having escaped for

> which I need not be much criticised, as it is really wonderful how they escaped, tho' in so miserable a condition having abandoned everything, and trusting simply to their getting off by their lightness.[10]

THE REBUILDING OF THE PORTUGUESE ARMY

The Portuguese regiments had suffered badly during the 1809 campaign in the north, lacking supplies and basic equipment, experiencing widespread desertion and a collapse of discipline. As William Warre, one of Beresford's aides-de-camp, graphically described it,

> We quitted Spain ... partly from orders from Sir A.W., partly because we were absolutely starved, and the cursed Spaniards would do nothing for us, concealed all means of subsistence, and fled as fast as approached.... At Castello Branco also the army would not exist many days longer together, and our Commissariat, and even distribution of what little we had was infamous. There was no remedy left but to divide the army into corps ... and mean time employ ourselves in getting them clothed and disciplined.[11]

So, after the expulsion of Soult, Beresford began the task of retraining the Portuguese Army and revising the general regulations. His plan was to adopt the basic structure of the old army but to remodel it along British lines. To understand this decision, which received strong support from Wellesley and the British government, the manpower problems of the British Army have to be taken into account. Throughout the eighteenth century British regiments had continually to be supplemented by German and Swiss mercenaries, but manpower shortages persisted and it became clear that no campaign against Napoleon on the Continent could be successful unless the numerical strength of the British Army could be greatly increased. After the military debacles of Buenos Aires (1806–7) and Moore's retreat to Corunna (January 1809), defeats soon to be compounded by the still greater disaster of Walcheren, Britain saw in a new Portuguese Army a possible answer to its problems. However, for this solution to work, the Portuguese would have to be assimilated into the British military system, a process that was given some urgency by the fact that the Portuguese Regents could not afford to arm, clothe or supply an army of their own.

In the past the Portuguese armed forces had suffered from divided command, the office of Marshal General often being held by someone other than the commander in the field. So, from the start, Beresford was determined that he alone would make decisions concerning the army. This was to become an obsession that eventually brought about confrontation with the Regents. In the short term it led to a clash with Sir Robert Wilson, whose Loyal Lusitanian Legion operated very much as an independent army, and with Francisco da Silveira who published an account of the 1809 campaign taking credit for the successes of the Portuguese Army and who, because of his popularity in Portugal, felt free to act without Beresford's authorisation.[12] Divided command threatened divided loyalties and loyalty became a serious issue in 1810 when the Marquês de Alorna returned to Portugal on Masséna's staff. Some Portuguese militia who surrendered with the fall of Almeida in August 1810 entered French service, while others were paroled on Alorna's intercession so that they could spread pro-French propaganda in Portugal.[13]

On 29 April 1809 Wellesley was appointed Marshal General of the Portuguese army so that he had strategic control over all the allied forces, but he and Beresford always worked closely together. While Wellesley left all the day-to-day decisions to Beresford, the latter was happy to consult him on all major issues and benefited from the political muscle he was able to exert.[14]

During the five years that followed his appointment, Beresford rebuilt the Portuguese regular army raising its manpower to 60,000, more than double its pre-war numbers. He did not, of course, work in a vacuum and was materially helped by the Minister of War, Miguel Pereira Forjaz,[15] and by Charles Stuart, who was appointed to the Regency Council in 1810 and gave the Marshal his unqualified support. During the 1809 campaign Wellesley became convinced that the two armies had to be merged for operational purposes and to achieve this Beresford planned to recruit volunteer officers from the British Army to work alongside their Portuguese counterparts, and eventually to include Portuguese regiments within British divisions on campaign.[16] It took a long time to assemble an effective cadre of officers. At first those who volunteered for the Portuguese service were promised one step in promotion. However, when it became clear that this rank would only be effective in the Portuguese Army, a fifth of those who had originally volunteered resigned their commissions and William Warre declared he was 'astonished any British officer will come out on these terms'.[17] Most of the British officers could not speak Portuguese and further problems arose when the two armies had to operate together, for it was not clear whether an officer's rank in the Portuguese Army took precedence over his rank in the British. However, Beresford persisted with the experiment and by 1811, when Andrew Halliday published his account of Beresford's reforms, there were 213 British officers in Portuguese service.[18] Each unit had both British and Portuguese senior officers – all regiments having either a British colonel or lieutenant colonel. Beresford even recruited British sergeants to oversee drill and the maintenance of equipment.

The Portuguese infantry and *caçadores* units were grouped into ten brigades. Initially all but two of these were commanded by British officers but Portuguese officers gradually took over until all but two were commanded by Portuguese. In 1812 Beresford explained to Colonel Torrens that it was no longer possible to place British officers in command of Portuguese units as 'the Portuguese officers have now too just pretensions to be so treated ... [and] I cannot with any justice to the Portuguese officers, supercede them'.[19] Of the brigades, eight were attached to divisions of the British Army and only two, under the command of British officers, operated as independent units. To make this amalgamation of the two armies work, the Portuguese were to be drilled to the British system of bugle calls, commands were to be given in both languages and British training manuals were to be translated into Portuguese.

To accompany these changes, the old officer corps was purged and made increasingly professional. Warre had described the traditional Portuguese officer he had met in the north as 'detestable, mean, ignorant and self-sufficient'.[20] So, according to Halliday, 'the old and unfit officers were either dismissed from the service, or put upon the reformed list, and young men of merit actively promoted'.[21] A total of 107 officers, who had an average age of 57.7 years, were retired.[22] One of these had been in the army for 54 years, while Warre records that 3 non-commissioned officers who left the service had a combined age of 180 years.

Beresford reserved the right to decide on all promotions which, he made clear, would go to professionally competent officers not to men of high social rank, as had happened so often in the past and as still happened in the British Army. This was a principle that was hard to establish, as can be seen from a terse entry in the diary of Beresford's quartermaster general, Benjamin D'Urban, for 12 August 1810: 'Promotions from the Brazils, – the Marshal's resistance'.[23] 'Little by little he removed or neutralised those officers who by their prestige, ambition or combative nature offered resistance to his activities'[24] was the somewhat negative gloss that Fernando Pereira Marques put on this policy.

Beresford also increased army pay by 80–100 per cent to bring it into line with pay in the British Army. This was a measure that he had adopted during his short spell as Governor of Madeira in 1808 and Warre emphasised its importance in creating a sense of professionalism. 'Their [officers'] pay which has in some cases been more than doubled, gives them the means now of living like gentlemen and with respectability', and he went on to say he hoped that they would exert themselves so as not to 'be deprived of it, which they certainly will, without remorse, if they misbehave at all'.[25]

The decision to integrate the Portuguese Army with the British was opposed by the Regents who wanted their army to be used exclusively to defend the Portuguese frontiers, but the experience of the 1809 campaign had shown the problems the Portuguese Army would face if it tried to act independently. The Regents had been unable to pay, equip or supply their troops which in consequence suffered extreme hardships and desertions while on campaign. At the end of the campaign the army was in a disastrous state of disarray and had to be re-equipped and re-trained. The British subsidy, initially intended to pay for 10,000 men, was now increased to cover 30,000 and eventually the whole cost of the regular army – the Portuguese exchequer meeting the costs of the militia and Ordenança. In 1810 Britain also supplied uniforms, arms and equipment for 30,000 men (though at first much of it was scarcely fit for use) and eventually the whole army was clothed, armed and equipped by Britain.

One of the Portuguese Army's biggest problems was supply. Beresford appointed D'Urban to head his quartermaster's department but the commissariat arrangements, which were traditionally handled by the Junta das Viveres, continued to prove defective as the government of the Regents did not pay as well or as promptly as the British. As Halliday explained:

> Commissaries [are] appointed to the different brigades; but as those officers were almost always without money to pay for what was wanted, their presence was of little avail. The Storekeeper, to please his employer, endeavours to purchase the different articles of provision at the lowest rate; and as the poor farmer either cannot or will not sell at the prices offered military force is therefore had recourse to, and what can be found is dragged forth and given to the troops. What is seized in this way, and generally what is bought by the Portuguese Commissaries, is paid for by a bill upon the Junta in Lisbon; these bills, even in the best times, are seldom taken up till twelve months after they are due, and in the present state of the kingdom are considered as actually worth nothing.[26]

This left the Portuguese short of everything and, once the fighting moved into Spain, a joint commissariat department serving both armies was established.

Beresford also carried out a fundamental revision of military discipline. He himself acquired a reputation as a strict disciplinarian and, according to Halliday, was determined to reform the system he found in place:

> Marshal Beresford, early convinced of the horrid nature of this punishment [the *pancada*], ordered a small cane to be used instead of the sword, which, though still keeping up the national method of punishing, deprived it of its fatal consequences. When his Excellency took the command of the army, the officers and non-commissioned officers were in the habit of kicking and buffeting the poor soldiers on every occasion, and I believe, long custom had made striking the soldier lawful; he however set his face decidedly against this most abominable practice.[27]

Changes were made to the procedures for court martials, which were now conducted at regimental level with a much simplified set-up. All sentences were reviewed by Beresford himself instead of being referred to the Minister of War. The army suffered badly from desertion and from officers and men going absent without leave. In a memorandum written in October 1808 to General Bernardim Freire de Andrade, Beresford had identified the practice of allowing officers and men to reside in their own homes as a serious problem. After the experience of the 1809 campaign when many officers were, in Warre's words, 'troubled with *dores de barriga* [stomach pains], a disorder we have found very prevalent among the officers going to Spain, and for which we had numberless petitions to go to Caldas [to take the waters], till it became proverbial for not wishing to serve',[28] Beresford introduced a system of passports to regulate officers going on leave and medical boards to authorise absence on health grounds.[29] However, desertions continued and Beresford eventually began to deal with these by death sentences carried out in public.

In his reorganisation of the Portuguese Army Beresford found that the military traditions of Portugal gave him one great advantage. Ever since 1640 there had been a recognised duty on all adult males to serve in the armed forces. Although there were numerous exceptions to this general obligation, it meant that Beresford did not have to depend on volunteers to fill gaps in the regiments. A levy, said to have been of 50,000 men, was implemented in the summer of 1809 – not all of them very willing, for John Aitchison, serving with the 3rd Regiment of Guards, recorded having seen them 'marched under an escort of regulars chained to one another like French conscripts'.[30] Halliday described the old methods of recruitment that were still employed:

> The King ordains that the First Regiment of the Line shall consist of 2000 men. The Colonel finds upon examining his returns that 700 men are wanted to complete that number; he states this to the General of the province, who immediately issues an order to the Captain-Major of the district from which the First Regiment is recruited to send 700 young men to that corps; the Captain-Major, or his Deputy, passes a review of the district, picks out 700 young men, sends them to prison for a few days, *to tame them*, and as soon as the whole are collected, marches them off under an escort of his Ordenanza troops to the head-quarters of the First Regiment.[31]

The poor physical condition of many of the recruits thus obtained forced Beresford to require a minimum height of 4ft 9½in, which gives the impression of a somewhat diminutive army. However, by this method the ranks were filled and he was to use the same methods again in 1816, in very controversial circumstances, when Portugal was threatened by Spain with war.

A training depot for recruits was established at Peniche but, according to Halliday,

> it is to be regretted that a healthier place could not be procured with the other advantages of the Island of Peniche, as certainly a great

> number of the unfortunate recruits have fallen a prey to the epidemic of that swampy spot, which no doubt acted with double effect upon the depressed, half starved, and ill treated peasants sent as recruits to this depot.[32]

Although Mafra was also used: 'the depot will never be healthy, nor will it be possible to keep the army effective: the sick, the lame, and the lazy are all crouded into the same dungeon when recruited by the Captain-Major; contagion is generated, and very often those, and those alone, who were fit for the service are carried off by disease'.[33]

The army medical services also had to be restructured. According to Halliday, who was one of the army doctors recruited by Beresford, regimental surgeons in the old army could not prescribe medicine or draw teeth, never performed any duties and were absentees. The hospitals

> were infinitely more destructive to the army than the sword of the enemy, and they would have destroyed it much faster than it could have been recruited, had it not been for the exertion of Marshal Beresford ... for when the army took the field in 1809, there were not ten Assistant Surgeons with the whole of the forces, and even those deserted when they came to pass the frontier.[34]

One of Beresford's first acts was to establish fourteen military hospitals and to recruit twelve British Army doctors, who in February 1810 were placed under William Ferguson as inspector of hospitals, while medical supplies were sent to the units in the field.[35] Ferguson persuaded Beresford that a board with one British and two Portuguese surgeons should be appointed 'to examine all candidates for regimental appointments'. Surgeons and their assistants were given the rank of captain and lieutenant. Even so, 'it needed the positive command of Marshal Beresford to oblige the army Physicians to use mercury in syphilis; and when the British medical officers were introduced into their hospitals, they found patients who had been eight and ten months in hospital with the common itch'.[36]

After the expulsion of Junot in September 1808 the men who had served with the army in 1807 had been recalled to the colours even though not all possessed weapons or uniforms. Beresford never attempted to change the basic structure of the army, not least because he depended on the co-operation of Forjaz, who was the principal author of the 1806–7 reforms. There were twenty-four infantry regiments, most of them assigned to one of the provinces from which they drew their recruits. Each regiment had a single battalion of ten companies, including one of grenadiers. From an initial strength of around 21,000, the infantry numbers were increased to 36,000 by 1811.[37] These regiments were the core of the new Portuguese Army and they effectively doubled the manpower at Wellington's disposal. Before Beresford's appointment six battalions of light infantry known as *caçadores* (who wore distinctive brown uniforms) had been raised and eventually this number was doubled to twelve battalions. At the end of 1808 twelve cavalry regiments existed on paper but these lacked accoutrements and horses. Beresford reorganised them to have a regimental strength of 595 men (a total of 7,200) but as late as 1812 half the regiments still lacked proper mounts.

In addition there was a corps of Engineers which worked with the British on the Lines of Torres Vedras and other defensive works. Beresford inherited four artillery regiments which were largely assigned to garrison duties. He turned these into mobile field artillery batteries which were attached to the different divisions of the army on campaign. Their nominal strength stood at 3,900 men. There were other smaller units of the army – a battalion of 'Artificers', a corps of semaphore operators, officers assigned to the town garrisons, medical staff and police units. Together these brought the numbers of Portugal's 'first line' army to around 60,000 by 1811.[38]

In addition conscription filled the ranks of 48 militia regiments (numbering about 52,000 men) and a total of 1,500 companies of Ordenança, which were organised into 24 brigades. The Ordenança were a formal part of the armed forces of Portugal and in 1810 Wellington famously wrote to Masséna demanding that they be accorded the rights of combatants defending their country.[39] There were also various veteran and volunteer formations including the volunteer corps of the students of Coimbra University. In Lisbon, Moyle Sherer reported that, 'even the peaceful merchants formed themselves into corps, and volunteered to perform the duties of the garrison ... The commercial regiment of infantry furnished a grand guard, daily, near the exchange ... which was conducted in the most orderly and soldier-like manner'. And they had a band made up of professional musicians, 'all masters of the instruments on which they performed'.[40]

It is impossible to give any realistic numbers for these second and third-line forces but during the French invasions they were frequently in action and contributed substantially to the popular opposition to the French.

THE PORTUGUESE ARMY BECOMES EFFECTIVE

The Portuguese Army that reassembled in the autumn of 1808 did not impress British observers. Before the campaign against Soult in 1809 Wellington declared that the Portuguese troops looked terrible on parade and the 'officers were worse than anything I have ever seen',[41] while General Mackenzie, who commanded the troops in Lisbon, wrote in his diary that he did 'not like to have anything to do with the command of Portuguese troops'.[42] In his letters, William Warre charted the improvement in the army after it returned from the campaign. Whereas in

September he complained constantly of desertion, it being 'impossible to keep them together, while they know that they can return home with impunity when they like',[43] in December he wrote that,

> Lord W. as well as every British Officer have been very much, though agreeably, surprised at the state of our troops. I am inclined to think that had they justice done unto them in the common comforts, I may say necessaries of life, clothing and food, they would make as good soldiers as any in the world. None certainly are more intelligent or willing, or bear hardships and privation more humbly.[44]

During 1810 the improvement continued and he reported the general confidence of the army and its desire to be proved in a major action. Sherer agreed. In September he found himself camped near a Portuguese division and 'the grenadiers ... particularly attracted my notice: they were all fine-sized, soldier-like men; and their brown complexions, black mustachios, and large dark eyes, gave them a truly martial appearance'.[45] The opportunity came on 27 September at the Battle of Busaco (a battle that neither side need have fought) when 24,000 Portuguese infantry, cavalry and artillery were all engaged, a force equal in numbers to the British. It was the first clear indication of the manpower advantage Britain derived from the new Portuguese Army. Halliday records that

> the Eighth Regiment of Infantry of the Line was in such a wretched state when Marshal Beresford took the command of the army, that he ordered the few men which belonged to it to be drafted into other corps, so that it had no share in the campaign of 1809 ... At Busaco, this corps, composed almost entirely of young boys who had not been embodied for more than six months, charged the veteran troops of France in a most gallant manner, and put them to rout.[46]

The Battle of Busaco established the reputation of the Portuguese regiments. Victory over the French hugely boosted their self-confidence and morale and confirmed Beresford's authority. After the battle he was made Conde de Trancoso in the Portuguese peerage and all attempts by the Regency to have him replaced ceased.

After Busaco most of the Portuguese regular army was withdrawn behind the Torres Vedras Lines, where some 24,500 regular troops were supported by 20,000 militia and Ordenança.[47]

At the end of December 1810 Beresford was appointed by Wellington to command the forces watching Soult's advance south of the Tagus, and with the retreat of Masséna from northern Portugal in March 1811 the war moved to the frontier where the French held the key fortresses. On 10 March 1811 Soult secured the surrender of the key fortress of Badajoz and on 21 March took the Portuguese town of Campo Mayor. Beresford, in command of an Anglo-Portuguese Army, drove the French out of Campo

Mayor on 25 March and forced them to retreat on Badajoz, which he then besieged. To prevent Soult relieving the fortress and possibly invading southern Portugal, Wellington, who had strategic oversight of the operations, decided that Beresford should block Soult's advance at the village of Albuera. There on 15 May the most bloody battle of the whole war was fought. During the battle Beresford himself was in the thick of the fighting, famously unhorsing a Polish lancer by lifting him bodily out of the saddle. It is also clear that during the battle Beresford issued orders to protect the retreat of his army should it become necessary – a precaution that would later be held against him in the pamphlet warfare that re-fought the battle in the 1830s.[48]

Following his victory Beresford was made Marquês de Campo Mayor. Thereafter he usually signed his correspondence with his Portuguese title. However, the strains of the campaign led to a breakdown. He frankly told Wellington that he could not stand the pressure and the slaughter and went on leave till the end of the year. In a letter to Charles Stewart, Beresford explained his reaction to his victory:

> I was then not very well and in spite of the good fortune I had had, was very much out of spirits from the conviction of having acted unnecessarily in risking so immensely as would have been the consequences of misfortune ... my desire was against risking a battle which if unfortunate ... I saw plainly would overturn every thing that Lord Wellington had by his great talents and enterprise and patience joined ... so long in acquiring.[49]

The Portuguese Army was fully deployed in the campaigns of 1811. At the Battle of Fuentes d'Oñoro (5–7 May) the allied army included 10 Portuguese infantry regiments, 4 *caçadores* battalions, 2 cavalry regiments and an artillery battery, while Beresford had 7 infantry regiments, 1 battalion of *caçadores*, the Loyal Lusitanian Legion and 2 cavalry regiments at Albuera, totalling 10,200 men, the same number as in the British contingent.

In 1812 Portuguese units formed part of the storming parties that captured Ciudad Rodrigo (19 January) and Badajoz (6 April), while the Salamanca campaign saw a daring raid by the Portuguese cavalry under the command of Benjamin D'Urban behind French lines. In the subsequent battle 14 Portuguese infantry regiments took part supported by 9 *caçadores* battalions and 2 cavalry regiments. After the battle Sherer recalled seeing 'three thousand of the prisoners taken at Salamanca ... escorted by four hundred awkward-looking, ill-appointed Portuguese militia-men; whose air of pride and importance, as they regulated the motions of these "vainqueurs d'Austerlitz", was truly entertaining'.[50]

At Vitoria 28,000 Portuguese formed part of an allied army that numbered over 100,000 men and Portuguese forces – by now a fully integrated and trusted part of Wellington's army – were prominent in the campaigns in the Pyrenees and southern France in 1813–14.

THE MARSHAL

In order to make his control of the army effective Beresford created a large headquarters staff which amounted to over sixty-three officers. In addition, he was served by a Portuguese secretary, Manuel de Brito Mozinho, and a Military Secretary, António de Lemos Pereira de Lacerda, whose wife became Beresford's mistress and through whom he maintained direct contact with the Prince Regent in Brazil both during and after the war. Beresford created his own intelligence network and made sure that all matters relating to the army would be routed through his headquarters even when he was on campaign. He insisted that all regiments keep detailed records and daily issued his famous *Ordens do Dia* (Orders of the Day) by which all units knew of the new regulations that were being introduced and of the Marshal's views about their performance.[51] After the war Beresford's headquarters became in effect a shadow government as the Marshal tried to maintain his control over recruitment, the fortresses, arsenal, hospitals and the military budget.

Beresford gathered round him a body of trusted officers, men like Halliday, Warre and D'Urban, who clearly admired his commanding personality and administrative ability. Even General Long, who had been dismissed from his command on the eve of Albuera and had no reason to love the Marshal, described him as 'unreserved, affable, open, sociable, and obliging'.[52] Wellington's friendship with Beresford is a striking feature of their successful cooperation. Beresford was one of the few, possibly the only, senior general whom Wellington trusted and in whom he confided. He famously said of him that he was the only man he could trust to keep his army fed. During the war the two often dined alone and maintained a regular exchange of letters that lasted throughout their lives. They were portrayed in contemporary prints as the twin upholders of the Portuguese monarchy. Although Beresford was officially appointed Wellington's second-in-command in 1813, he was nevertheless hurt by the failure of Wellington to mention his contribution to the war in his official despatches and in August 1813 remarked plaintively to his half-sister Anne, 'it is the first time during the last three years that I am identified with the troops of which I am Commander in Chief'.[53]

One of the most remarkable testimonies to the important position that Beresford and the Portuguese Army occupied in Wellington's calculations occurred just before Waterloo. As the allied forces assembled in Belgium Wellington became concerned with what would happen should he be killed in action. It was reported to Earl Bathurst that 'the arrangement [he] ... would like of all others is the transport here of 15,000 Portuguese infantry under Lord Beresford, whose rank of Marshal on the Continent would supercede that of General which the Prince [of Orange] holds in the Dutch service'.[54] Beresford, it seems, would outrank all the other allied generals and would take over the command.

Portuguese opinion of the Marshal has been mixed. One of the Regents, Ricardo Nogueira, was later to write in his unpublished memoirs:

> He is a brave soldier and a great officer for disciplining the army. Portugal owes him a great deal in this respect and his ability in getting the military laws observed brought our troops to a state of perfection that in a short space of time placed them on a par with the best in Europe. A lot of this was due to his inflexibility of character and to his being a foreigner ... However, these good qualities of the Marshal were counterbalanced by great defects. He is extremely ambitious for power, obstinate and imprudent.[55]

Beresford's retention of the position of commander of the Portuguese Army after the war and his insistence on maintaining the wartime numbers of the army and their corps of British officers was seen by most Portuguese as a crippling burden on the country and his conduct of affairs as being dictatorial and tyrannical. Miguel Pereira Forjaz, his close collaborator during the war, became an irreconcilable opponent and by the time the 1820 Revolution broke out Beresford had become universally hated. Fernando Pereira Marques wrote of him in 1989: 'A foreigner he was not integrated into Portuguese society and did not experience the pressures and complicities born of common class interests.'[56] And his critique of Beresford went much further. 'Beresford wanted to *make* an efficient, functional army which would respond to the strategic, economic and political objectives of his mission in Portugal. He represented, let us remember, the agent of a metropolitan power acting in a dependent territory.'[57] João Centeno, in a scarcely veiled reference to Marques and other critics of Beresford, declared the criticism of Beresford's appointment to be 'totally unjust' for 'patriotism does not have to do with birth or nationality but with courage, dedication and self-denial in defence of the interests of the nation'.[58] These were qualities shown by many of the British officers but not by all those who were Portuguese by birth. 'Under the command of Beresford ... and under the administration of D. Miguel Forjaz, Minister of War, in an atmosphere of collaboration and mutual dependence, the army gained a discipline, cohesion and exemplary fighting spirit which was visible throughout the war'.[59]

WATERLOO AND AFTER

Beresford commanded the allied forces that occupied Bordeaux in March 1814 and played a decisive part, along with the Portuguese Army, in the

Battle of Toulouse in April. After the surrender of Napoleon, Beresford, who had been elected Member of Parliament for the family seat of Waterford in 1812, returned to Britain while Carlos Frederico Lecor, who had risen to be his second-in-command and who had been the only Portuguese to command a whole division in the allied army, returned with the Portuguese regiments to Lisbon. Portugal was now at peace but possessed a large and efficient veteran army which the Prince Regent intended to use to expand the frontiers of Brazil. In May 1815 he sent orders for 5,000 men from Beresford's army to be sent to Rio. On their arrival, commanded by Lecor, the soldiers, called by the locals Talaverans even though none of them had fought at Talavera, were marched south to occupy the Banda Oriental.

Meanwhile, Napoleon escaped from Elba. As an allied army began to assemble in the Netherlands, Wellington expected that Portugal would send a contingent. Transports were despatched and Beresford went to Portugal to prepare an expeditionary force. The Regents, however, refused to authorise the army's departure without explicit orders from Rio which had not arrived by the time the Battle of Waterloo was fought. Beresford was furious and mortified. He contemplated resignation and was encouraged in this by Wellington, who thereafter showed a scarcely disguised hostility towards Portugal. Instead, Beresford decided in July (when it was not yet clear that the war was over) to go in person to Rio to put his case to Dom João. Portugal paid the penalty for its non-participation in the Waterloo campaign, when the return of Olivença, which had been agreed in the peace preliminaries in 1814, was never implemented.

Beresford continued to command the Portuguese Army until 1820 when he and the other British officers were dismissed by the revolutionary Junta. In 1816 he was at last made Marshal General of all the Portuguese forces in Europe and in Brazil, revised the military regulations again and implemented a new levy of recruits to fill the depleted ranks. The army was maintained on a war footing, being involved in the confused fighting in the Banda Oriental and in defending the frontiers against the scarcely disguised hostility of Spain. It was later to play a major part in the history of Portugal, Brazil and the states of the Río de la Plata. From its officer corps emerged the elite who were to contest the civil wars of 1832–4 and 1847–8 and who were to dominate Portuguese and Brazilian politics until the 1850s, including the Dukes of Saldanha and Terceira, the Marquês Sá da Bandeira and, across the Atlantic, Carlos Lecor and João Bonifacio. The South American patriot José de San Martín also gained his military experience with this army. The aristocratic society of the Portuguese *ancien régime* had been transformed into a society in which the liberal and conservative factions both looked to its military cadres for leadership.

NOTES

1. For an account of the evolution of the Portuguese Army after 1640 see João Centeno, *O Exécito Português na Guerra Peninsular; vol 1 – Do Rossilhão ao fim da Segunda Invasão Francesa* (Lisbon, 2008), pp. 17–51.
2. Centeno, *O Exécito Português na Guerra Peninsular*, p. 67.
3. Ibid., pp. 82–3.
4. Ibid., pp. 102–4.
5. Ibid., p. 125.
6. The most detailed study of Beresford's career up to 1814 is S.E. Vichness, 'Marshal of Portugal. The Military Career of William Carr Beresford', unpublished PhD thesis (Florida State University, 1976).
7. W.F.P. Napier, *History of the War in the Peninsula and in the South of France* (6 vols, London, 1828–40), Vol. 2, pp. 91–2.
8. W.C. Beresford to Lady Anne Beresford, 23 April 1809, Public Record Office of Northern Ireland (PRONI) T3285\1\1.
9. Wellington Dispatches 11 May 1809, quoted in Vichness, 'Marshal of Portugal', p. 185.
10. W.C. Beresford to Lady Anne Beresford, 26 May 1809, PRONI T3285\1\1.
11. Sir William Warre, *Letters from the Peninsula 1808–1812*, ed. Edmond Warre (London, 1909), pp. 76–8.
12. I.J. Rousseau (ed.), *The Peninsular Journal of Major General Sir Benjamin D'Urban* (London, 1930), pp. 98–9.
13. Ibid., p. 137.
14. Beresford himself was made Marshal General in 1816 which gave him ultimate authority over all the Portuguese armies in Brazil as well as Europe.
15. For the role played by Miguel Pereira Forjaz in the rebuilding of the army see Francisco Arturo de la Fuente, 'Dom Miguel Pereira Forjaz: his early career and role in the mobilization and defence of Portugal during the Peninsular War, 1807–1814', unpublished PhD thesis (Florida State University, 1980).
16. There are numerous accounts of Beresford's reorganisation of the Portuguese Army. See in particular C.W.C. Oman, *Wellington's Army* (London, 1912; repr. London, 1968) and H.V. Livermore, 'Beresford and the Reform of the Portuguese Army', in Paddy Griffiths (ed.), *A History of the Peninsular War* (London, 1999), Vol. IX, pp. 121–44, Centeno, *O Exécito Português na Guerra Peninsular*; Vichness, 'Marshal of Portugal', René Chartrand and Bill Younghusband, *The Portuguese Army of the Napoleonic Wars* (3 vols, Oxford, 2000–1).
17. Warre, *Letters from the Peninsula 1808–1812*, p. 67.
18. Andrew Halliday, MD, *Observations on the Present State of the Portuguese Army as organised by Lieutenant-General Sir William Carr Beresford KB, Field Marshal and Commander in Chief of that army with an account of the different military establishments and laws of Portugal* (London, 1811), pp. 145–9.
19. Quoted in Livermore, 'Beresford and the Reform of the Portuguese Army', pp. 121–44; quotation p. 138.
20. Warre, *Letters from the Peninsula 1808–1812*, p. 78.
21. Ibid., p. 15.
22. Vichness, 'Marshal of Portugal', p. 228.
23. Rousseau (ed.), *The Peninsular Journal of Major General Sir Benjamin D'Urban*, p. 131.
24. Fernando Pereira Marques, *Exército e sociedade em Portugal* (Lisbon, 1989), p. 120.
25. Warre, *Letters from the Peninsula 1808–1812*, p. 116.
26. Halliday, *Observations on the Present State of the Portuguese Army*, p. 79.
27. Ibid., pp. 69–70.
28. Warre, *Letters from the Peninsula 1808–1812*, p. 81.
29. Vichness, 'Marshal of Portugal', p. 156.

30. W.F.K Thompson (ed.), *An Ensign in the Peninsular War. The Letters of John Aitchison* (London, 1981), p. 48.
31. Halliday, *Observations on the Present State of the Portuguese Army*, pp. 57–9.
32. Ibid., p. 59.
33. Ibid.
34. Ibid., pp. 83–5.
35. Vichness, 'Marshal of Portugal', p. 322.
36. Halliday, *Observations on the Present State of the Portuguese Army*, pp. 89, 96.
37. Numbers from Chartrand and Younghusband, *The Portuguese Army of the Napoleonic Wars* and Centeno, *O Exécito Português na Guerra Peninsular*, pp. 107–31.
38. For these units see Chartrand and Younghusband, *The Portuguese Army of the Napoleonic Wars.*
39. Letter in Centeno, *O Exécito Português na Guerra Peninsular*, p. 89.
40. Moyle Sherer, *Recollections of the Peninsula* (Staplehurst, 1996; first pub. 1824), p. 83.
41. Vichness, 'Marshal of Portugal', p. 181.
42. Quoted in ibid., p. 175.
43. Warre, *Letters from the Peninsula 1808–1812*, p. 84.
44. Ibid., p. 101.
45. Sherer, *Recollections of the Peninsula*, p. 104.
46. Halliday, *Observations on the Present State of the Portuguese Army*, p. 22.
47. Donald Horward (ed.), *The French Campaign in Portugal 1810–1811. An Account by Jean Jacques Pelet* (Minneapolis, 1973), p. 229.
48. Mark Thompson, *The Fatal Hill* (Sunderland, 2002).
49. PRONI D\LO\C18\63 I 238\2, W.C. Beresford to Charles Stewart, 25 May 1811.
50. Sherer, *Recollections of the Peninsula*, p. 184.
51. *Collecção das Ordens do Dia do Illustrissimo e Excellentissimo Senhor Guilherme Carr Beresford commandante em Chefe dos Exercitos de S.A.R. o Principe Regente Nosso Senhor. Annos 1809–1823* (12 vols, Lisbon, 1809–23). The *Ordens do Dia* are discussed in Centeno, *O Exécito Português na Guerra Peninsular*, especially pp. 151–2 and in Marques, *Exército e sociedade em Portugal*, pp. 119–30.
52. Quotation from a letter of General Long dated 21 March 1811 given in Lord Beresford, *A Second Letter to Charles Edward Long* (London, 1834), p. 3.
53. W.C. Beresford to Lady Anne Beresford, 27 August 1813, PRONI T3285\1\1.
54. Arthur Richard Wellesley, 2nd Duke of Wellington (ed.), *Supplementary Despatches and Memoranda of Field Marshal Arthur Duke of Wellington* (15 vols, London, 1858–72), Vol. 10, Torrens to Earl Bathurst, Ghent, 8 April 1815, pp. 41–3.
55. Biblioteca Nacional de Lisboa, Codice 6848-6853, Ricardo Raymundo Nogueira 'Memória das cousas mais notáveis que se tratarem nas conferencias do governo d'estes reinos desde o dia 9 de agosto de 1810, em que entrei a servir o logar de um dos governadores até a 5 de fervereiro de 1820'.
56. Marques, *Exército e sociedade em Portugal*, p. 120.
57. Ibid., p. 126.
58. Centeno, *O Exécito Português na Guerra Peninsular*, p. 147.
59. Ibid.

Chapter Nine

The Army of the Duchy of Warsaw

Jarosław Czubaty

'Poles! The great and invincible Napoleon is entering Poland with an army of 300,000. Your existence and Motherland depend on you. Your avenger, your creator has appeared ... Rise up in arms and prove to him that you are ready to shed your blood to regain your Motherland!' These words of an appeal issued on 3 November 1806 in Berlin lay at the beginning of the formation of the Army of the Duchy of Warsaw. Soon after the capture of the Prussian capital, it was obvious to Napoleon that the war was still far from over. While the vanguard of the Grande Armée was entering the Polish lands captured by the Prussians during the three partitions of Poland, the army of Frederick William III, almost destroyed during the first weeks of the war, was in the midst of being reinforced by its Russian ally, and thus a hitherto brilliant campaign could easily become a long drawn out and costly struggle. The prospect of conducting the war in a country far from his bases in France and Germany induced Napoleon to search for extraordinary means: to appeal to the patriotic enthusiasm of Poles – no inconsiderable force, as in 1806 they composed about 40 per cent of the inhabitants of the Kingdom of Prussia. Moreover, their military and financial support, their provision of food and the organisation of transport and military hospitals could facilitate the conduct of the war. The political implications of Polish participation on Napoleon's side could also strengthen the Emperor's position in the course of future negotiations with Prussia and Russia.

Such constituted the reasons behind Napoleon's decision to call to Berlin his proven adherents among the Poles so that they would appeal to the patriotism of their compatriots. General Jan Henryk Dąbrowski (1755–1818) was from 1797 the commander of the Polish Legions in Italy, organised on his own initiative. In 1806 he stayed with the remnants of his legions in the service of the King of Naples, as the rest had been destroyed in 1802–3 during the disastrous expedition to San Domingo in the West Indies. Józef Wybicki – an eminent political émigré after the Third Partition of Poland (1795) – was Dąbrowski's friend and the political representative of the Legions' interests with French and Italian authorities. Their appeal met with an enthusiastic reaction and soon after Dąbrowski's arrival in Poznań – the principal city in the western part of the Prussian partition – the first units of mounted volunteers entered the war on the French side. The progress of events in the other territories liberated by the Grande Armée was similar.

The Polish military effort was of great significance to the country's political future. On 19 November 1806, during an audience for the deputies of the Polish nobility, Napoleon declared: 'If I see 30 to 40,000 soldiers I shall proclaim your independence.' The Emperor's promise – although without any political guarantee – encouraged the leaders of the anti-Prussian movement to intensify the organisation of regular Polish forces; the first volunteer units were reinforced by conscripts, and new regiments were raised. On 27 November, French cavalry, forming part of Napoleon's vanguard, reached Warsaw. On 7 December, on the orders of Marshal Joachim Murat, Prince Joseph Poniatowski, King Stanisław August's nephew, was proclaimed the commander-in-chief of Polish forces, which seriously disappointed the very active and meritorious General Dąbrowski. On 18 December Napoleon entered the former capital of Poland, and after consultation with representatives of the Polish aristocracy and nobility, on 14 January 1807 he established the so-called Ruling Commission – a Polish provisional administration with Poniatowski as the Director of War. Spontaneous mobilisation was replaced by more precise principles – each of the departments of Poznań, Kalisz (Kalisch) and Warsaw was obliged to organise a legion (division) composed of four regiments of infantry, two regiments of cavalry (uhlans and chasseurs), an artillery battalion and a company of sappers. The assumed complement of each legion was 13,120 men.

The commanders of the legions were undoubtedly the most meritorious Polish generals of the time, though unfortunately the differences in their experiences, political attitudes and temperament hampered co-operation between them. The senior formation, I Legion, in the department of Poznań (the number of the division reflected its precedence in the organisation) was commanded by Dąbrowski, who until 1792 had been in Saxon service. He was well known as a successful commander during the Kościuszko Insurrection (1794), and then as the competent and charismatic leader of Polish forces in Italy. As a commander, Dąbrowski was not a brilliant tactician but his courage and organisational abilities were unquestionable – he was a typical patriarch to his soldiers. The admiration of his patriotic virtue shared by many of his compatriots was reflected by the popularity of the so-called 'Dąbrowski's Mazurka' – which became the Polish national anthem.

The commander of II Legion (Kalisz), General Józef Zajączek (1752–1826), had been connected with the group contemptuously dubbed as

'Polish Jacobins' during the Kościuszko Insurrection. Imprisoned after the collapse of the uprising by the Austrians as a dangerous radical, after his release he joined then the (French) Army of Italy in 1797. He served there and in Egypt under Bonaparte and later became a divisional commander of the Grande Armée. The former Jacobin became a faithful adherent of the Emperor: 'I am a French general and I command the Polish troops now because the Emperor ordered me to do so,' he declared in 1807. Although a brave and experienced commander, Zajączek was not as popular among the Poles as Dąbrowski due to his difficult character, which often entangled him in conflicts with his superiors and colleagues. In particular, his attitude towards Poniatowski was a blend of jealousy, caused by the Prince's higher rank in the army, and the idiosyncrasy of the former radical towards the aristocracy.

Prince Joseph Poniatowski (1763–1813), commander of the III Legion (Warsaw), gained his first military experience in Austrian service, but after some years he was asked by King Stanisław August to join the Polish army. In 1792 he commanded the Polish forces during the war with Russia. Russian numerical superiority rendered the struggle unwinnable, but Prince Joseph was able to score some tactical successes that marked him out as a competent commander and a man of great personal courage. The Kościuszko Insurrection put Poniatowski in a delicate position as the radical insurgents accused the prince of being a secret agent of the king, who was in fact debarred from power. Yet Poniatowski proved his patriotism by joining Kościuszko's army as a volunteer, and after 1795 he kept away from any kind of political activity, such that many Poles merely perceived him as a rather light-headed aristocrat. In 1806 Poniatowski became the divisional commander of longest service, though he possessed no war experience similar to that of Dąbrowski and Zajączek. Nor could he compete with them in the field of 'patriotic sacrifices' after 1806. The prince was the representative of an influential group of the aristocracy – Napoleon's decision to offer him the post of commander-in-chief of the Polish Army was explained as an act of political calculation and provoked much tension among the three generals and their adherents in the army over the next few years.

After 2 months' organisation Polish troops amounted to about 24,000 men. There were various ways of filling the ranks, the first being the *pospolite ruszenie* (*levée en masse*) of the nobles, which had once been employed in the Polish-Lithuanian Commonwealth as a source of supplementary military power. This tradition was revived with a proclamation calling for a draft of mounted volunteers to be equipped at their own expense. Every nobleman who possessed one village or more was also expected to furnish at least one 'substitute' with a uniform and horse. The second method of raising troops was the regular conscription of men aged

18–24 from every tenth household. Conscription – mostly in the nobles' estates – also provided the horses for cavalry units, artillery, ambulances, wagons and transport. In November and December 1806 this 'army without a state' (for the outcome of war and the Emperor's final decision respecting the 'Polish question' were still unknown) was strengthened by about 3,000 Polish deserters from the Prussian Army – the officers who had decided to make a career in Prussian uniform before 1806 and ordinary soldiers forced to wear them by dint of conscription.

The expenses generated by this hasty organisation were covered by the nobility and townspeople. In spite of conscription the owners of landed estates and the municipal authorities were obliged to cover part of the costs connected with equipping and provisioning the forces, but the patriotic enthusiasm among Poles induced many of the landowners to participate in organising the troops in spite of the obligatory charges. While the wealthiest noblemen – such as Prince Antoni Sułkowski and Counts Stanisław Mielżyński and Stanisław Poniński – formed their own regiments. Napoleon provided indispensable financial support, such that in November 1806 alone Dąbrowski received 40,000 francs from the Emperor's treasury.

The usually difficult problem of arming the troops proved in fact quite easy to solve in the conditions of the 1806–7 campaign, for during the first months of organisation Napoleon ordered the delivery to the Poles of about 35,000 Prussian muskets (the 1750, 1780 and 1805 models), taken from the arsenals of captured fortresses and from the manufactories in Potsdam. There were also some troops armed with French infantry muskets (the 1777 Charleville). Artillery pieces were of Prussian manufacture, as well, as were most of the sabres, swords and pistols, although small arms of these kinds were more varied due to the individual officers' predilections.

The problem of selecting the officer cadre for the army seemed to be more difficult to sort out, as the lack of competent commanders could lead to problems in maintaining order among the newly raised troops or their heavy losses in action. There were in any case few units that could provide suitable candidates. The most valuable of them came from the Polish Legions in Italy and Germany (the so-called Danube Legion was organised by General Karol Kniaziewicz in the German theatre of operations in 1799–1801). From these units about thirty officers, still serving with Dąbrowski in the Kingdom of Naples, were immediately recalled home. There were also numerous former legionaries who decided to leave military service after the peace settlement with Austria in 1801, and settled in the territory of the Prussian Partition. Their war experience gleaned from the 1797–1800 campaigns and their knowledge of French regulations and tactics rendered them appropriate candidates for the higher commissioned ranks in the army. Thus, in 1807 former legionaries comprised about 45 per cent of battalion and squadron commanders. Almost half of the officers who gained general's epaulettes in the Army of the Duchy of Warsaw from 1807 came from this group. Strongly connected with General Dąbrowski and committed to the idea of rebuilding Poland under the Emperor's protection, they were perceived by the majority of their compatriots as ardent patriots, but by some of the pro-Russian malcontents as Napoleon's mercenaries.

The second reservoir of candidates for officer rank were those veterans of the 1792 war against Russia and the Kościuszko Insurrection who after the Third Partition did not join the Polish military formations abroad but decided to remain in the country. Soon after his nomination to the post of Director of War, Poniatowski issued an appeal to these 'former colleagues and officers', encouraging them to join the army. Although they had had no military service for twelve years and were less experienced in the changing mode of warfare than the legionaries, their engagement was required by the necessity of immediately forming an army. Many of them were in any case meritorious and competent commanders.

The organisation of the army was also supported by some officers transferred from Napoleon's service. Some of them were Polish legionaries, who after 1801 enlisted in the French Army; a few of them – like Colonel Jean Pelletier – were French artillery specialists or engineers. The need for experienced officers was also met by Poles drawn from the Prussian Army. This way of creating a cadre of officers was also applied in subsequent years. After the war with Austria in 1809, many Polish officers in Habsburg service joined the Army of the Duchy of Warsaw. On the orders of the Minister of War, Prince Poniatowski, 30 per cent of vacant lieutenancies and captaincies were reserved for such men, with the rank of lieutenant usually offered to volunteers, mostly of noble birth. An exception was made for the few aristocrats and noblemen who founded their own regiments and became their respective commanders. As they possessed no military experience, it was decided that their staff officers and commanders of battalions or squadrons should be selected from among the elder officers with long military service.

The leaders of the Polish national movement expected that it would be possible to raise their forces to a strength of about 40,000 men, but organising them and providing food, supplies and quarters for a corps of the Grande Armée in the winter season – and in a country ravaged by war – proved a difficult task. The process of organisation was also retarded by Napoleon's order to bring forward as rapidly as possible all those battalions and squadrons that were deemed ready for action. At the end of the 1807 campaign there were in fact about 24,000 soldiers in the ranks – the number that Napoleon had predicted to be the most probable figure to be achieved during his conferences with Dąbrowski and other Poles in

November 1806. Taking into account all the difficulties that the authorities faced, the formation of the troops constituted a success, accomplished by the enthusiasm of the Poles, their civic sacrifices and their ability to improvise.

The first Polish units fought in skirmishes and battles from November 1806 onwards. They were usually divided into small formations among the divisions of the Grande Armée and also served as scouts and guides. The more numerous Polish units from Zajączek and Dąbrowski's legions began active service in February 1807, when a few hundred mounted volunteers under the French general Lasalle took part in the Battle of Eylau (7–8 February). On the 23rd, 10,000 men under Dąbrowski's command captured Tczew. From April to June several thousand Polish troops took part in operations north-east of Warsaw, in the sieges of Kolberg (now Kołobrzeg) and Danzig (now Gdańsk), where Polish troops lost about 2,000 killed, wounded and taken prisoner. Dąbrowski's legion also fought at the Battle of Friedland (14 June), in which the Polish regiments in Marshal Mortier's corps operated on the left wing of Napoleon's army and lost 540 men.

According to the Treaties of Tilsit (7–9 July 1807) between France and Russia and Prussia, the Duchy of Warsaw was created from the territories of the Prussian Partition. Although the choice of the King of Saxony, Frederick Augustus III, as its ruler was acceptable to Poles (two representatives of the Wettin dynasty had ruled Poland as elected kings between 1697 and 1763), the boundaries and the name of the new state provoked disappointment and criticism among them. The newly created Duchy was a tiny state in comparison to the Kingdom of Poland as it had existed before the First or even the Second Partition (1772, 1792) and its name did not contain the word 'Poland'. Such an act of political compromise by Napoleon with Russia and Prussia gave rise to a suspicion that the project of restoring the Polish state with the Emperor's support amounted merely to a political daydream. The terms of the Treaty of Tilsit concerning the Poles weakened the enthusiasm of their officer corps towards Napoleon to such an extent that the Director of Police, Aleksander Potocki, alarmed the Council of the State of the Duchy with the comment that 'the Polish officers and gentlemen, who, forgetting their oath of loyalty towards His Majesty the Emperor, dare to use improper words that outrage the respect owing to this monarch.' The wave of discontent soon subsided, as the Poles appreciated the consequences of destabilising the European political situation. In short, the chance of another war between Napoleon and Russia or Austria, which could convert the Duchy of Warsaw into a resurrected 'Kingdom of Poland', seemed quite high. Thus, maintaining the army in as strong a state as possible was perceived as a Polish *raison d'état*.

According to the constitution conferred by Napoleon (22 July 1807), the Duchy of Warsaw was to maintain an army of 30,000 men. The traditional Polish form of the military uniforms, as well as the four-cornered 'czapka' headdress and the official name of the forces, 'Polish Army of the Duchy of Warsaw', met with the enthusiasm of Poles and were understood as a clear promise that the state created at Tilsit was only a transitory form on the way to the rebuilding of Poland.

Supreme command of the army was nominally the prerogative of the king. In fact the post of commander-in-chief rested dually with the Minister of War, Prince Poniatowski. Respecting the competence of Frederick Augustus, Prince Joseph sent him periodic reports concerning the state of the army, its budget, conscription, engineers' work on fortresses and other matters, which were agreed to by the monarch, but such approval usually constituted a mere formality. Poniatowski's real superior was Napoleon himself. He executed his power via Marshal Davout, who stayed in the Duchy of Warsaw until August 1808 and thereafter in Prussia. He was responsible for the current situation of the army – recruitment, organisation of the regiments, military intelligence and other matters, but all strategic plans and decisions concerning the most important matters were made in Paris. The role of Davout was also important, for owing to his senior position he could easily block almost all of Poniatowski's initiatives. The marshal initially did not trust Prince Joseph, regarding him as a member of the group of aristocrats secretly devoted to Russia. Davout's suspicions were encouraged by former Polish Jacobins, a group barred from power but nonetheless influential, thanks to their close contacts with French generals and Etienne Vincent, Napoleon's diplomatic representative in the Duchy. Their critical opinions about Prince Joseph derived from their ill-disposition towards the aristocracy and their attempts to weaken the position of this faction who, by dint of decisions made by Napoleon, headed the government of the Duchy. Davout's attitude towards Poniatowski diametrically changed when he became more familiar with the politics of the Duchy and its most prominent figures.

The French marshal was not the only one who distrusted the Minister of War or criticised him. In spite of the Jacobins, who would have preferred their former colleague Zajączek at the head of the Duchy's military hierarchy, Dąbrowski's adherents shared the opinion that chief command ought to belong to the most meritorious commander of the Polish Legions in Italy. Both groups were united in their criticism of Poniatowski's lack of patriotic activity in the years 1795–1806, his sybaritic habits and the largesse he afforded his friends and clients in the distribution of officers' promotions and military decorations after 1806. The prince was not without blame in stimulating the rivalry of the three generals' factions in the army – e.g. his decision to change the numbering of the legions provoked an explosion of discontent among the officers and men of Dąbrowski's division which – although formed as the first one in 1806 – lost its prestigious number to the division under the direct command of the Minister of War.

In spite of his opponents' opinions, Poniatowski as a Minister of War was sufficiently competent to implement some reforms and changes in the structure of the army. The haste with which the first stage of the organisation of the army was carried out in 1806–7 negatively affected the quality of the men who had been called up to the ranks. Moreover, the health of the soldiers was harmed by the difficult conditions prevailing in the provisional quarters established during the winter, where the men found themselves afflicted by hunger, disease and lack of medical care. The combined effect of all these factors, in addition to casualties, rendered it necessary to replace part of the new cadre when the campaign ended. During 1808 about 8,000 soldiers – ill, wounded or too old for active service – were replaced by new recruits. According to the principle of equality before the law, introduced by the constitution of the Duchy, conscription was obligatory for men aged 21–28 from all classes of society. The number conscripted was fixed every year by the King according to proposals tabled by the Ministry of War. Particular candidates for the army had been chosen from among the mass of young men conscripted by lot. Those not keen to fight were allowed to deliver substitutes – usually young men from poorer families. Priests, rabbis, teachers and members of the bureaucracy were excluded from conscription. The King's decree of 1812 relieved the Jews from the duty of military service in return for a special tax paid by Jewish communities. This resolution was in recognition of principles of religion and customs that differentiated Jews from other classes of society and which made their adaptation to army life difficult. The other reason was more pragmatic – the weak results of the earlier conscriptions among the Jewish population proved its almost universal abomination of military service.

The whole military force of the Duchy of Warsaw was divided into three divisions. The First Division (commanded by Poniatowski himself) consisted of the 1st, 2nd, 3rd and 4th Regiments of infantry and two regiments of cavalry, the 1st Chasseurs and 2nd Uhlanen. The Second Division (Zajączek) was formed by the 5th, 6th, 7th and 8th Regiments of infantry and two regiments of cavalry, the 3th Uhlanen and 4th Chasseurs. The Third Division (Dąbrowski) was formed by the 9th, 10th, 11th and 12th Regiments of infantry and two regiments of cavalry, the 5th Chasseurs and 6th Uhlanen.

According to a decree of 30 March 1810, the infantry regiments consisted of 3 battalions, with 6 companies each. There were 3 grenadier, 3 voltigeur and 12 fusilier companies in the unit, the whole regiment numbering about 2,500 officers and men, though in fact usually between 1,500 and 2,900. The cavalry regiments were composed of 4 squadrons, with 2 companies each, including 1 elite grenadier company in the regiment. The number of troopers in the unit exceeded 800. The chronic financial problems of the Duchy's treasury influenced the types of cavalry regiments deployed, for the high cost of equipment and the shortage of suitable horses accounted for the single unit of heavy cavalry – a two-squadron cuirassier regiment.

Each division was completed by 1 battalion of foot artillery, consisting of 3 companies (batteries), each of 6 guns, plus 1 battalion of sappers and 1 company of wagons. During 1808–9 2 companies of horse artillery, each with 4, then 6, guns were organised thanks to the financial sacrifices of Roman Sołtyk and Włodzimierz Potocki (by whose benefaction the latter, being the son of the ill-famed leader of the pro-Russian confederacy of Targowica in 1792, hoped to restore the reputation of his family). Both men also became the commanders of the newly founded units.

The characteristic feature that differentiated the Army of the Duchy of Warsaw from most other contemporary forces in Europe was the significant percentage of cavalry, such that the ratio of infantry regiments to cavalry formed in 1808 stood at 2:1, falling to almost 1:1 in 1810. This tendency reflected national tradition and appealed to the sentiments of Poles who remembered with fondness past glories achieved by their famed horsemen. Although more than a hundred years had passed since the victories of Żółkiewski's, Chodkiewicz's or Sobieski's troops over the Muscovite, Swedish and Turkish armies, respectively, the cavalry was still the most popular kind of unit among nobles, who willingly participated in the cost of forming such regiments or filled their ranks as volunteers. The most important reason for organising so many Polish cavalry regiments was Napoleon's high opinion of their value in combat based upon his observation of the Polish regiments of the Chevaulégers of the Imperial Guard and the lancers of the Vistula Legion fighting in Spain. In time, with the growing possibility of conflict on the vast plains of Eastern Europe, another argument appeared – the high number of Polish light cavalry units could assure the corps of the Grande Armée indispensable support in reconnaissance.

The fundamental structure of the army based on three divisions was made essentially for administrative purposes, for the units that composed the divisions acted individually or within other military structures. At the beginning of 1808, for instance, the Army of the Duchy was composed of 31,000 men, more than 6,000 horses and 242 guns, but only about 14,000 troops stayed in the country. In 1808 Napoleon, aiming to strengthen his forces and to ease the difficulties of the Duchy's treasury, decided to take into his pay the 4th, 7th and 9th Infantry regiments which formed the so-called 'Division of the Duchy of Warsaw' sent to Spain. In addition, three other infantry regiments and two cavalry regiments garrisoned Prussian fortresses.

Such a dislocation of forces caused serious problems in April 1809 when the Austrian Archduke Ferdinand with a corps of 30,000 entered the Duchy of Warsaw, the main Austrian campaign plan consisting of capturing Warsaw and isolating the Polish army so as to block its retreat both to Saxony and Danzig. The occupation of the Napoleonic protectorate was meant to appease the pro-French sympathies of the Polish subjects of the Habsburg monarchy (living in Galicia) and provide Austrian diplomacy a stronger position in negotiations with Prussia and Russia concerning their possible support for an anti-Napoleonic coalition. After the first five days of the campaign Archduke Ferdinand was close to achieving the first objective of his plan. On 19 April Austrian forces approached the outskirts of Warsaw but found themselves blocked at Raszyn by 12,000 men under Poniatowski. The struggle was not decisive, but its result was advantageous for Polish forces which, having offered strong resistance, persuaded the Austrians not to risk an immediate storm of Warsaw. As Poniatowski was convinced that there was no strategic sense in defending the capital and that Ferdinand was not eager to continue the attack, both sides signed a convention respecting the evacuation of the city. Thanks to its conditions – favorable to the Polish forces – Poniatowski could cross the Vistula and operate on its right bank, thus preserving his ability to manoeuvre and enabling him to enlarge his army through conscription proclaimed in a region free from Austrian occupation.

At the beginning of May, Poniatowski assumed the initiative by moving his forces south along the right bank of the Vistula and entered the territories occupied by Austria in 1795 (so-called New Galicia). Archduke Ferdinand, entangled in occupying Warsaw and trying to advance towards the north of the Duchy, was not able to counteract his opponent. During the next few weeks Polish troops, operating in areas inhabited by their compatriots, conquered vast territories in Galicia – including much of the territory lost in 1772 – with the important towns of Lwów, Lublin and Sandomierz, as well as the fortress of Zamość. Using experience gained in 1806–7, new Polish regiments were founded. The danger of isolation from his base in Austria forced Archduke Ferdinand to turn his corps back towards Galicia. The character of operations in this theatre had little in common with Napoleon's style of warfare – despite desiring a decisive battle, in practice both the Poles and the Austrians preferred manoeuvre that aimed to put the enemy in a vulnerable or exposed position. Poniatowski's army ultimately prevailed, without a pitched battle, for when an armistice was announced after the Battle of Wagram, the Duchy was free of Austrian troops and a significant part of Galicia stood under the control of Polish troops. The 'first victorious war since the time of King Sobieski' evoked a wave of national enthusiasm and completely altered opinion about Prince Poniatowski, for the commander-in-chief of the army became the personification of national honour and glory: 'Brave rider on the brave horse, of inflexible courage, brilliant honour, beautiful form and black moustache, he was an ideal of Polish commander. If, standing on the edge of Hell, he had shouted: ''Follow me, children!'' he would have been followed without hesitation!' – wrote one of his officers. The image of Poniatowski carrying a musket and nonchalantly smoking a pipe while leading an infantry counterattack during the Battle of Raszyn became the most famous Polish image of the imperial era.

By the terms of the Treaty of Schönbrunn (14 October 1809) the territory of the Duchy of Warsaw was increased by about 50 per cent and the number of its inhabitants grew to 4,300,000. In March 1810 its army was composed of 18 regiments of infantry (11 garrisoned on home soil), 16 regiments of cavalry (11 regiments of uhlans, 2 of chasseurs, 2 of hussars and 1 of cuirassiers), 1 regiment of foot artillery, 4 companies of horse artillery (6 guns each), 1 battalion of sappers and a company of craftsmen. The artillery of the Duchy was increased by sixty-eight Austrian guns captured in 1809 and an additional fifty guns delivered on Napoleon's orders from the arsenal in Stettin (now Szczecin). The number of men in the ranks grew from 60,000 in 1810 to 75,000 in 1812.

Military expenses grew over time: 13 million zlotys in 1807, 40 million in 1810 and 50 million in 1811. Almost 70 per cent of the expenses of the state in the years 1810–11 were assigned to the army's needs. Although the amount of money was fixed, the regimental treasuries were empty: the army had no money to cover current expenses due to the desperate situation of the state's finances owing to damage suffered during war and as a result of Napoleon's continental blockade, which denied both access to British goods and the export of Polish products and commodities to Britain. While the enormous cost of maintaining and strengthening the fortresses at Modlin and Zamość, the organising of new regiments and the establishment of magazines on the roads to the eastern frontier of the Duchy continued to be covered thanks to further subsidies from Napoleon, the critical financial situation of the army forced Poniatowski to agree to transfer the 5th, 10th and 11th Regiments of infantry from the garrison of Danzig to the Emperor's pay. Apart from the formation and training of new units, gathering military intelligence formed an important task performed by the army in 1810–12. This was carried out by individual officers travelling in the territories of the old Poland annexed by Russia during the Partitions or by regiments of cavalry patrolling the frontier with Russia.

During the 1812 campaign, which initially seemed to fulfil Polish dreams of rebuilding the Kingdom of Poland, the military forces of the Duchy of Warsaw were divided among the corps of the Grande Armée, with 37,000 soldiers forming V Corps commanded by Poniatowski himself. This formation consisted of 3 divisions, each composed of 2 brigades of infantry and 2 regiments of cavalry: the 16th Division, commanded by Zajączek, contained the 3th, 15th and 16th Regiments of infantry and the 4th and 12th of cavalry; the 17th division, commanded by Dąbrowski, consisted of the 1st, 6th and 14th of infantry, and the 1st and 15th of cavalry; and the 18th Division, commanded by Ludwik Kamieniecki, then Karol Kniaziewicz, comprised the 2nd, 8th and 12th of infantry, and the 5th and 13th of cavalry. The rest of the Duchy's regiments were attached to other corps. A few regiments of cavalry formed the 4th Light Cavalry Division in IV Corps of the Cavalry Reserve. The division commanded by General Aleksander Rożniecki (the 2nd, 3rd, 7th, 11th, 16th Cavalry regiments) boasted a strength of 5,600. The so-called Division of the Duchy of Warsaw, transferred from Spain, was included in IX Corps under Marshal Victor. The 5th, 10th and 11th Infantry regiments from the garrison of Danzig, plus the 9th Cavalry regiment served in I Corps under Davout. The 6th, 8th and 10th Cavalry regiments served in I Corps of the Cavalry Reserve. The total Polish military effort in 1812, including units of the Vistula Legion, the Chevaulégers of the Guard and new regiments organised in Lithuania, exceeded 100,000, making it the second largest national contingent of the Grande Armée.

If Napoleon had led the campaign according to the common expectations of Poles he would have directed Poniatowski's V Corps to Volhynia (Wołyń) and Podolia (Podole) – southern territories of the Russian Empire incorporated following the Second and Third Partitions of Poland. The presence and activity of Polish forces there could have easily repeated the success of the Galician campaign of 1809. Instead, the Emperor preferred to divide his Polish troops among the units of his main striking force. During the first stage of the campaign Poniatowski's corps acted on the left wing of Napoleon's army, commanded by Prince Jerome Bonaparte. In the course of pursuing General Bagration it lost about 30 per cent of its strength in only eight weeks – not by action but by exhausting marches. At the end of July the corps joined Napoleon's main body and on 17 August took part in the storm of Smolensk, attacking the Ratchynskoe and Nikolskoe suburbs of the town. The determination of its attack and the heavy losses sustained (about 1,500 killed and wounded) by V Corps earned for its soldiers and officers 88 crosses of the *Légion d'honneur*.

During the following months, Poniatowski's corps and other units of the army of the Duchy shared the vicissitudes of the whole force marching to Moscow and then retreating west, in the course of which the Poles took part in every major battle from Mozhajsk to the Berezina. Only the 17th Division, commanded by Dąbrowski, operated separately near Minsk against the growing forces of Admiral Chichagov (acting in the capacity of a general). Dąbrowski's defeat on 21 November, which resulted in the loss of the bridge over the Berezina at Borisov, forced Napoleon to change his plan for crossing the river.

The remnants of V Corps that reached Warsaw consisted of only about 400 officers and men, who were however able to bring back all of their guns. The losses of the other regiments from the Army of the Duchy were also very severe. The reconstruction of the army began immediately in December 1812 in a process encompassing the survivors from the defeat in Russia, fortress garrison troops, detached soldiers who gradually returned to the ranks, including units of the National Guard serving as regular regiments, and new conscription. Rejecting the proposal by Tsar Alexander to abandon Napoleon and proclaim neutrality, Poniatowski left the Duchy in May 1813 and joined his ally in Saxony. The regiments of the Duchy – about 18,000 soldiers – were distributed between VIII Corps and IV Cavalry Corps, except for Dąbrowski's division, which acted as an independent unit. A further few thousand soldiers of the Duchy remained in the country as garrisons of the fortresses in Modlin, Częstochowa, Toruń, Zamość and Danzig (Gdańsk). During the 1813 campaign Duchy forces suffered heavy losses, especially at the Battle of Leipzig (16–19 October). On the last day of the struggle a significant part of the Polish troops shielding the retreat of Napoleon's army was intercepted due to the untimely destruction of the bridge over the River Elster. The Poles lost about 10,000 men – wounded, killed or prisoners of war – including the wounded Prince Poniatowski, who drowned while trying to cross the Elster.

On 28 October, during a meeting on the way to Schlüchtern, Napoleon persuaded senior Polish officers that in spite of the last defeat, the rebuilding of Poland was still possible with his protection. The remnants of the Army of the Duchy of Warsaw – about 5,500 – decided to follow the Emperor and continue the fight. However, Polish commanders demonstrated the necessity of maintaining the national character of their army during the campaign of 1814 by deploying them in separate units from the French in the form of 3 regiments of cavalry, 1 regiment of infantry, a company of horse artillery, 4 companies of foot artillery and a company of sappers, plus a few hundred soldiers directed to the new 3rd Regiment of the Éclaireurs (Scouts) of the Imperial Guard. All regiments, especially cavalry, fought in the battles of the 1814 campaign in France, including Vauchamps (14 February), Craonne (7 March), Laon (9–10 March), Arcis-sur-Aube (20 March) and Paris (30 March).

After Napoleon's abdication, the remnants of Polish military forces found themselves in a difficult and delicate situation. The country had been under Russian occupation since the previous year, and King Frederick August was interned by the Allies. The political future of the Polish question seemed rather gloomy, especially as the Poles appeared to be the last faithful ally of Napoleon. Polish officers led by General Dąbrowski decided to 'secure the national honour' first. Napoleon was asked officially to declare that Polish soldiers had fulfiled their duty as allies of France. On 11 April the Emperor issued a declaration stressing that he 'was always just to the loyalty and bravery of the Army of the Duchy of Warsaw, which were witnessed by so many battlefields'. The second decision of the Polish generals and officers was to ask Tsar Alexander, known among many Poles for his liberal attitudes, to allow the remnants of the Army of the Duchy to return to the country. The answer of the Russian monarch was more than satisfactory. Alexander, beginning his great task of strengthening the position of Russia in Europe, decided to use the question of the rebuilding of Poland as one of his means: Polish regiments were allowed to return to the Duchy with their arms and commanders and were put under the authority of the Tsar's brother, Grand Duke Constantine, while the Military Organisation Committee, consisting of Polish generals, was established to undertake fundamental changes to the structure of the army and to begin its reconstruction. On 20 June 1815, when the Kingdom of Poland with Alexander I as its king was proclaimed, the army of the newly created state numbered 22,000 men.

The new Kingdom, a Russian satellite, consisted of an even smaller area than the Duchy, but after the defeats of 1812–14 even many Poles believed it a better solution to the Polish question than the alternative – the complete disappearance of the Polish state. Pro-Napoleonic sympathies were appeased by placing hopes in Alexander's liberal policies and for the future reunification of the Kingdom, ultimately to include the Polish territories of the Russian partition, as promised by the Tsar. But the next fifteen years would bring growing disappointment to Polish public opinion, and in 1830–31 the Polish Army, still based around a nucleus of Napoleonic veterans, would again resort to war with Russia, seeking, yet failing again to achieve, an independent nation.

Chapter Ten

The Army of the Kingdom of Italy

Frederick C. Schneid

Late in the afternoon of 24 October 1812 the Italian divisions of Prince Eugène de Beauharnais' IV Corps crossed the worn bridge over the Luja River and moved through the smoke-filled town of Maloyaroslavets. The previous evening a brigade of the 13th French Division entered the town, but a determined Russian attack during the morning succeeded in driving them back. Fighting raged as Eugène fed his decimated French regiments into the fray. By noon stubborn Russian resistance and continued reinforcement threatened the bridgehead. At noon the Prince sent General Domenico Pino's 15th Italian Division forward, followed shortly thereafter by the serried ranks of the Italian Royal Guard. The weight of numbers told, as the Italians pushed the Russians from Maloyaroslavets to the heights beyond. The impetus of the Italian assault waned after sustained combat. The timely arrival of Marshal Davout's I Corps on the opposite bank meant reinforcements were at hand. Prince Eugène and the IV Franco-Italian Corps, the Armée d'Italie, had unexpectedly collided with the Russian army, seeking to block Napoleon's retreat from Moscow.[1]

The Battle of Maloyaroslavets was the high watermark of Napoleon's Italian army. Its regiments served from Spain to Russia, and its role in the 1812 campaign represented the culmination of almost two decades of military development. The battle also served as the turning point – as was the entire Russian campaign. The Army of the Kingdom of Italy lost many of its veterans in Russia, never to reach the level of professionalism and *esprit de corps* that it had achieved through the glory years of empire.

The Army of the Kingdom of Italy was unique. No previous Italian kingdom existed, and there was little if any commonality to provide cohesion to this military institution. Clemens von Metternich, the future Austrian Foreign Minister and Chancellor, referred to Italy as a 'geographic expression'. Prior to 1796, it was divided into roughly a dozen independent states. They had, since the Middle Ages, spent much of their time competing with each other, rather than accepting any sort of cultural or linguistic uniformity. There was no common dialect, although Tuscan served as the language of the Italian educated. Beyond that, the overwhelming majority of Italian merchants, farmers, peasants and urban workers saw their neighbours as rivals or enemies.

Napoleon's conquest of Italy in 1796 was a revolution in the geo-politics of the peninsula. The French came as both conquerors and liberators, depending on perspective, but the rapid overthrow of the Kingdom of Piedmont-Sardinia, Lombardy, Venetia and the central Italian states in less than a year and the retention of northern Italy under French hegemony for the next decade, provided a slate from which General Bonaparte could lay the foundations of an Italian kingdom. The Cisalpine and Cispadane Republics were established as French satellites shortly after the conquest of Italy. General Bonaparte authorized the formation of Italian revolutionary legions as auxiliary forces. The Cisalpine and Cispadane Legions and the Lombard Legion comprised volunteers from various parts of Italy; they resembled more a National Guard than a national professional army. They fought in central Italy in 1797 and again during the War of the Second Coalition (1798–1802).

The Legions and their officer corps formed the cadre of the future Army of the Kingdom of Italy. By the conclusion of the 1797 campaign the two Italian Legions consisted of no more than 7,000 men. Within two years, however, there were eight Cisalpine Legions, the Lombard Legion and a regiment of cavalry, the Cavalleria Cisalpina. By the conclusion of Napoleon's first campaign in Italy (1797) the Cisalpine and Cispadane Legions were amalgamated into unified regiments for the nascent Italian republic. This transformation pre-figured the official creation of the Italian Republic in 1802.[2]

In anticipation of a national army the revolutionary legions were reorganized into seven infantry regiments and two of cavalry. Following the revolutionary tradition regimental formations were designated *mezza-brigati* (demi-brigades), until 1803 when 'regiment' returned to favour. The Italian Republic possessed 5 *mezza-brigata di linea* (demi-brigade of the line) and 2 *mezza-brigata di leggiere* (demi-brigade light), each composed of two battalions. The Cavalleria Cispalpina became the 1st Cacciatore a cavallo (Chasseurs à cheval), and in 1802, the 1st Reggimento di Ussaro (Hussars) was raised. As no historical state existed prior to the establishment of the Italian Republic, its army had no predecessor on which to base its tradition and organization. The French model thus served as the model for the new Italian army. With the creation of the Italian Republic in 1802, Napoleon – in his capacity as President of the Republic – established 2 battalions of Guardia delle Presidente (Presidential Guard), 1 of Grenadiers (Granatieri) and 1 of Chasseurs (Cacciatori) and added a regiment of artillery to the army.[3]

The military administration developed during the Revolution as well, and its men were drawn largely from Lombardy. Napoleon overran the

Habsburg-ruled Italian duchy in 1796, and Milan thereafter became the capital of the new republic. Milanese and Lombards became the largest group represented in the ranks of the Italian Army and its administration between 1796 and 1806. The Ministero della Guerra (Ministry of War) of the Italian Republic – later kingdom – consisted of four divisions: army, marine, logistics and military infrastructure. Two additional divisions, the Office of the Director of Military Conscription and the Deposito della Guerra were under the administrative aegis of the ministry but remained largely autonomous. The Deposito della Guerra closely resembled Napoleon's Grande Quartier Générale. The bureau was divided among topography (planning), military intelligence and official histories. The ministry and its subordinate departments grew in size and complexity as the Italian Army expanded and its responsibilities increased. By 1811, the military administration employed 1,387 officers and men.[4]

ORGANIZATION AND EXPANSION

The evolution of the Italian Army paralleled the development and expansion of the French Army under Napoleon. In 1804, the cavalry increased with the raising of a 2nd Regiment of Hussars. The following year, however, Napoleon, in his new capacity as King of Italy, converted the two Hussar regiments into the Dragoni Napoleone and Dragoni Regina respectively.[5] This brigade became the battle cavalry of the Italian Army through the Napoleonic Wars. The Presidential Guard became the Guardia Reale (Royal Guard), and the Cacciatori Bresciani, an independent light battalion, had 'Reale' added to its name. All told, by 1805, the Army of the Kingdom of Italy consisted of 5 line regiments, 2 light, 1 light cavalry, 2 dragoon and 1 artillery regiment – roughly 20,000 men out of a population of 4 million.

In the aftermath of the victorious War of the Third Coalition, the Italian Army expanded. Italian infantry regiments were organized around two combat battalions and a third depot battalion. Between 1806 and 1809 a third combat battalion was added, bringing the strength of an Italian regiment on a par with its French counterparts. The cavalry were organized around four squadrons and remained at that strength throughout the wars. In 1806, Napoleon established the Veliti Reale (Royal Velites). This regiment was attached to the Italian Royal Guard with the purpose of recruiting sons of the middle class. Service in this elite regiment meant a fast track as officers or non-commissioned officers in the line. Similarly, the Guardia del onore was created to cater for the sons of the Italian nobility. No more than two squadrons were raised, and they failed to draw significant numbers.[6]

During the course of 1807, the Cacciatori Reale Bresciani expanded to three battalions and was designated 3rd Leggiere. The Cacciatori Istriani, a light battalion, and the Reggimento Dalmazia Reale (Royal Dalmatian

Regiment) were recruited from ethnic Italians who lived in the formerly Austrian territories of Istria and Dalmatia. The growing demands of war in Spain in 1808, and the increased scope of Napoleon's Empire led to further expansion of the line regiments. The 6th and 7th Line and the 2nd Cacciatori a cavallo were raised by the end of the year. This provided a substantial increase in manpower to an army that now boasted 60,000 combat troops. The 7th Line was drawn largely from troops serving with the Papal Army in the Romagna, which was annexed to the Italian kingdom in 1808.[7] Indeed, in anticipation of the impending war with Austria in 1809, the companies of the Cacciatori Istriani were divided between the 1st and 2nd Leggiere.[8]

The final growth of the Italian Army came in the two years preceding the Russian campaign. A fourth combat battalion was added to the light infantry and a fifth for the line. Moreover, Prince Eugène added another light regiment, 4th Leggiere in 1810, and two cavalry regiments the following year, 3rd and 4th Cacciatori a cavallo. The Royal Guard received the addition of the Reggimento del Coscritti della Guardia (Conscripts of the Guard) in 1810.[9] By 1812, the Italian Army numbered more than 80,000 combat troops spread from Spain to Russia.

OFFICERS AND NCOs

The officers of the army came from all corners of Italy. They were drawn initially from volunteers who had military service in the varied armies of the Italian principalities prior to 1799. Later, officers were promoted from the ranks, from the Veliti Reale or graduates of the military school at Modena. The officer corps overwhelmingly comprised ethnic Italians: 61 per cent came from regions within the kingdom and another 23 per cent were born in Tuscany, the Papal States or Piedmont-Sardinia, Naples, Corsica or the Italian cantons of Switzerland.[10] The remainder came from French departments, and had first been assigned to the Italian revolutionary legions prior to 1802.

The Italian Army required 1,100 officers during its first years (1801–6).[11] At its height in 1811, it needed 5,000 officers for all branches. This was a figure never achieved, and the loss of valuable men in 1812 made it impossible to replace them. More than 1,100 officers were killed and wounded over the 9 years of war.[12] Napoleon was not inclined to replace losses among the Italian officer corps with Frenchmen. He had followed this practice briefly during his first campaign in Italy, but that was when the scope of the campaign and his ambitions were limited. The Italian Army muddled through despite the shortage.

CONSCRIPTION AND DESERTION

Volunteers populated the revolutionary legions, but as with the French Army, the ranks were fed by conscription. The Conscription Law of

1803 (based upon the French Jourdan Law of 1798), established annual conscription on the French model.[13] Each department was responsible for contributing a percentage of conscripts concomitant with its population base. The kingdom was divided into twenty-five civil departments at its height in 1810, and five military divisions. Males between the ages of 20 and 25 could be called for service, although recruits were largely drawn from the youngest of this age group. During any conscription year 7 per cent of males were called for service.[14] In 1809, 1812 and 1813 supplementary conscription expanded the ranks further. In these cases, the percentage of conscripts in each department could double. This was particularly so in 1813 when the Italian Army had been decimated during the Russian campaign. Between 1803 and 1814 more than 170,000 Italians were conscripted for military service from a population of 6 million.[15] Technically, conscripts were separated between the active army and the reserve. During the first years of the Italian Republic, reservists received training at their depots and then returned home until called. By 1805, however, the reserve became a bureaucratic distinction and in reality all conscripts, whether designated active or reserve, served.

Conscription was not terribly popular and desertion was a problem from the start. During the peacetime years of the Italian Republic (1802–5) desertion was minimal, but thereafter the kingdom's territorial expansion and growing military demands led to increased rates of desertion. From 1805–9 approximately 50 per cent of conscripts called failed to appear for military service.[16] Desertion was classified in two forms: failure of conscripts to appear at their depots and desertion. The former category conscripts did not arrive at their assigned depots by the deadline established by the administration. Generally, this was November of the conscription year, but in cases of supplementary conscription, it could be any month decreed. Italian Gendarmerie (military police) and departmental and cantonal authorities were required to 'round up' those who lagged or tried to 'hide in the hills'. *Refrattari* companies (penal units) were formed from those caught, but only temporarily when these men could be distributed to their assigned regiments. The frequency of actual desertion was directly related to whether the kingdom was at war. Soldiers disappeared from their regiments in Italy and on campaign. The level of desertion on campaign, however, was equivalent to that of the French Army. It was a

Table 10.1 Conscription 1803–13[17]

1803–5	31,200
1806–9	38,090
1810–12	56,447
1813	33,779

problem in Spain and in Russia, but again, the desertion rates of Italians were lower that that of other satellite and allied armies, and roughly equivalent to the French. In Russia, desertion rates did not exceed 15 per cent in General Pino's 15th Italian Division, and was much less in the Guardia Reale Division.[18] The Italian divisions in Russia were in far better shape when the army left Moscow in October than any other satellite divisions excluding the Poles. For this reason Napoleon ordered Prince Eugène's IV Corps to form the advance guard of the Grande Armée during the initial stages of the retreat.

DEPLOYMENT AND PERFORMANCE

The Army of the Kingdom of Italy saw service in virtually every campaign of the Napoleonic Wars. As one of the first French satellites established during the Revolution, its soldiers were considered an auxiliary of France's military power. During the wars of the Revolution the Italian legions and *mezza-brigati* remained in the Italian peninsula, but afterwards, beginning in 1804, the regiments were regularly dispatched to military theatres for duty beyond the borders of Italy. Unlike other satellite troops, however, the individual regiments were often broken up, with several battalions serving in one part of Europe, while the remaining troops fought in another. This peculiarity made the proper administration of the army even more difficult.

The majority of infantry, cavalry and artillery of the Italian Army spent much of the Napoleonic Wars under the banner of the Armée d'Italie. This was the theatre army for northern Italy. In 1805 it was under the command of Marshal André Masséna. Thereafter, Napoleon's stepson and Viceroy of Italy, Prince Eugène de Beauharnais, led it. Generally, two Italian divisions were attached to this army, in addition to the Guardia Reale. As a rule, half to two-thirds of the Italian Army remained in Italy while the rest served abroad.

Napoleon's reliance on the Italian Army depended upon the respective campaign. During the War of the Third Coalition, Napoleon ordered to the camp at Boulogne the Guardia Reale and the 1st and 2nd Leggiere (light) and 1st Linea (line). When he abandoned plans for the invasion, the Guardia Reale were attached to his Imperial Guard division and marched with the Grande Armée, while the other brigade held position on the Channel coast. As the scope of the wars increased, Italian troops were scattered throughout the Empire, but with the majority remaining within the kingdom's frontiers. Unlike their French contemporaries, regiments after 1808 were often divided among different campaign theatres. For example, in January 1809, three battalions of the 1st Leggiere were in Spain, and the remaining two in Italy. In 1810, the 6th Line had three battalions in Spain, and two in garrison on Elba.[19] This odd allocation of military

Table 10.2 Italian Infantry battalions deployed 1806–13

	1806	1807	1808	1809	1810	1811	1812	1813
A. Nord	6							
A. Naples	8	4						
Gr. Armée		8					16	6
A. Italie				10	12			
A. Espagne			2	12	12	21	16	11
Italy	5	8	22	20	23	19	11	17
Other garrisons	2	6	10	13	9	8	6	6

Adapted from Piero Croaciani, Virgilio Illari and Ciro Paoletti, *Storia militare del Regno Italico (1802–1814)* (Rome, 2004), Vol. II, p. 603.

resources was unique to the Italian Army, and not similarly applied to any other satellite force. Table 10.2 provides a vivid illustration of the army's diverse responsibilities.

In 1806 an Italian division joined Marshal Masséna's Armée du Naples for the invasion of that southern Italian kingdom. It operated in Apulia, and participated in counter-insurgency operations in Calabria through 1807. The Italian brigade deployed along the Channel coast in 1805, was reinforced and sent to Germany during the Prussian campaign. Under the command of General Pietro Teulié, it played a key role during the siege of Kolberg. During the course of 1807, Napoleon allocated several corps for the pending invasion of Spain. One Italian division (truly brigade strength), under General Giuseppe Lecchi, was attached to Duhesme's Corps d'Observation du Pyrenées Orientale. In October a second division (full strength) under General Domenico Pino arrived in Spain. The two Italian divisions were attached to Gouvion St Cyr's VII Corps, and participated in the siege of Gerona in 1809.

Italian divisions allocated to the respective French imperial armies prior to 1809 comprised an infantry brigade, a cavalry brigade and artillery. In 1809, however, the war with Austria, and the consolidation of Napoleon's Empire led to the establishment of formal divisions, and their employment as a coherent military and administrative unit. Divisional commanders served with their divisions for more than one campaign and this created greater cogency within the Italian Army. Despite these developments, the Italian Army was never deployed in corps strength. Napoleon and Prince Eugène preferred to allocate one or two Italian divisions to a French corps under French command, as in 1812, or deploy the divisions independently for specific operations. This was particularly the case when used in counter-insurgency operations in Calabria (1806–9) and the Tyrol (1809–10). Indeed, Napoleon never organized the Armée d'Italie into official corps, but preferred the temporary '*lieutenance*' as ad hoc corps formations.

The war of 1809 against Austria tested the survivability of the Kingdom of Italy. Poor initial deployment by Eugène led to defeat at Sacile. For this campaign four Italian divisions were concentrated in northern Italy, with Fillipo Severoli and Achille Fontanelli's divisions, the Guardia Reale and a division of Italian cavalry attached to Eugène's army. Severoli's regiments, initially held in reserve, fought at Sacile and successfully threw the Austrians out of the vital village of Porcia. Fontanelli's division was ready for campaign a few weeks later, and held in reserve at the battle on the Piave. He was later committed against Austrian forces around Tarvis and replaced by General Jean-Baptiste Rusca for the advance into Hungary. The division guarded the line of supply and communication to Italy and was later dispatched to the Tyrol to aide in operations against Andreas Hofer.[20]

In June 1809, Severoli's division fought at Raab. It was committed early in the day; its first brigade shattered during an Austrian counterattack. The second brigade, reinforced with a French division, made a successful assault on the Austrian flank by early afternoon. Severoli's division suffered substantial casualties and remained in garrison at Raab, not following on to Wagram two weeks later. The Guard remained in reserve during both battles, but was committed at Wagram on the afternoon of the second day. Accompanied by the Dragoni de la Reine and Napoleone, the Guard formed the second wave of the assault upon the Russbach plateau, just east of Wagram. The attack succeeded in ejecting the Austrians from the town and its environs compromising the Austrian centre.[21]

The immense scale of the Russian campaign led Napoleon to create overstrength regiments for the Grande Armée. The French Emperor drew men and material from across Europe. A total of five divisions of the Armée d'Italie became IV Corps of the Grande Armée. Under Prince Eugène, IV Corps comprised the Guardia Reale, 2 French divisions, the 15th Italian division under General Pino and 3 brigades of cavalry, 1 French, 2 Italian. The strength of an Italian division between 1809 and 1812 varied between 7,000 and 9,000 men. General Pino's division with IV Corps numbered almost 12,000 men, while the Guardia Reale increased to almost 6,000. The total commitment of the Army of the Kingdom of Italy to IV Corps, including cavalry, artillery and support troops, exceeded 25,000 men, or one-third of the Italian Army.[22]

The Italian divisions marched to Moscow with the Grande Armée. Pino's division was detached to chase Russian flying columns threatening the line of supply prior to the climactic Battle of Borodino. Eugène recalled the division, but it did not arrive on the field until late in the day after a forced march. The Guardia Reale were held in reserve and did not see combat until late October at Maloyaroslavets. It continued to fight along with the Grande Armée during the disastrous retreat. Both Pino and the Guard were engaged at Krasnyi and the Berezina.

The Italian divisions suffered enormous casualties during the Russian campaign. Valuable veterans of seven years' campaigning formed the majority of soldiers lost. Eugène had the painful task of rebuilding the Italian Army upon his return to Italy in May 1813. His task was further complicated because the Italian regiments that stayed behind in 1812 were called to Germany to reinforce the Emperor. An Italian brigade fought under General Paul Grenier in the spring campaign, and General Henri Bertrand's corps boasted an entire Italian division. What was left included depot battalions and a host of conscripts. The distribution of Italian troops in Europe included 21,000 in Germany, all the survivors of IV Corps; 10,000 in Spain and 6,000 in Italy, Illyria and assorted garrisons.[23]

The reconstruction of the army became a priority. Austria mobilized for war under the cover of 'peace diplomacy', but it had been evident to both Napoleon and Eugène that war was coming. Over the course of the spring of 1813, emergency conscription and an active Gendarmerie provided for 7,000 additional Italian recruits. Eugène requested Napoleon recall Severoli and Giuseppe Palombini's Italian divisions from Spain. It was already clear that the war in the Iberian Peninsula was lost. These veterans added experience to the inexperienced army. They did not, however, arrive until the autumn campaign was well under way.

Prince Eugène conducted a successful defence of the kingdom through the autumn. He decreed a supplementary conscription of 15,000 men in October to strengthen his dwindling ranks. Three Italian infantry divisions including the Guard and a cavalry division took the field against Austria. By January a fourth Italian division, reinforced from Spain, joined in the campaign. The Kingdom of Italy was the last French satellite to surrender to the Sixth Coalition. The Treaty of Schiarino-Rizzino, concluded on 17 April 1814, ended the war in Italy, almost three weeks after the fall of Paris. The Italian Army however, was not entirely disbanded. In June 1814 *Feldmarshall* Heinrich Bellegarde, Austrian military commander in Italy, ordered the remaining battalions of the army be amalgamated and absorbed into the Austrian Army as 9 regiments (8 infantry, 1 cavalry) of the Austro-Italian corps.[24]

ASSESSMENT

The Kingdom of Italy provided the largest contingent of satellite troops for Napoleon's imperial armies. Their participation in virtually every campaign of the Napoleonic Wars made the Italian Army vital to Napoleon's military ambitions. The question remains as to the extent to which the army was a national force. The lack of any unitary state prior to 1797 meant that propaganda, administration and military service provided the backbone of a national identity. Historians differ on the extent to which Napoleon succeeded in creating an 'Italian' identity in the army. It is clear that this was a purposeful part of building an *esprit de corps*, and while many of the officers were 'Italian patriots', we do not know how much this filtered down to the rank and file.

The army provided an effective source of manpower. It was led by professional officers, and as the conscripts served in multiple campaigns, they too became professional soldiers. The French marshals and generals who commanded Italian troops always spoke well of their performance. They were considered reliable and respectable. The Army of the Kingdom of Italy was perhaps one of the most successful institutions created by Napoleon, although its legacy remains a question for debate.

NOTES

1. Prince Eugène de Beauharnais, *Mèmoires et Correspondence Politique et militaire du Prince Eugène* (Paris, 1858–60), VIII, pp. 18–21.
2. Piero Croaciani, Virgilio Illari and Ciro Paoletti, *Storia militare dell'Italia Giacobina (1796–1802)* (Rome, 2001), Vol. I, pp. 436–8.
3. Frederick C. Schneid, *Soldiers of Napoleon's Kingdom of Italy: Army, State and Society, 1800–1815* (Boulder, CO, 1995), p. 27.
4. '*Situazione Generale Dell'Effetivo al primo di Gennaio 1811*', Beauharnais Archives, Firestone Library, Princeton University (hereafter BA) 48/1 Military Reports 1807–13. In comparison, Napoleon's GQG boasted 4,500 men.
5. Schneid, *Soldiers of Napoleon's Kingdom of Italy*, p. 27.
6. Ibid., p. 36.
7. Piero Croaciani, Virgilio Illari and Ciro Paoletti, *Storia militare del Regno Italico (1802–1814)* (Rome, 2004), Vol. I, tome 2, p. 579.
8. Decree by Prince Eugène, 28 March 1809, Archivio di Stato Milano, Ministero della Guerra (hereafter ASMMG) 793, Leva- disposizione generale 1809.
9. Croaciani, Illari and Paoletti, *Storia militare del Regno Italico*, Vol. I, tome 2, p. 504.
10. Schneid, *Soldiers of Napoleon's Kingdom of Italy*, p. 37.
11. '*Complet de l'armée italienne en 1806*', BA 47/3.
12. Schneid, *Soldiers of Napoleon's Kingdom of Italy*, p. 48.
13. A second conscription law was enacted in 1806, providing for the expansion of the army. It remained in effect until the fall of the kingdom in 1814.
14. Conscription Reports for 1807, 1808, 1809, 1811, BA 45/25.
15. A further 8,000 were conscripted for the Italian Navy and 9,500 were conscripted from Dalmatia and Istria. Adapted from Croaciani, Illari and Paoletti, *Storia militare del Regno Italico*, Vol. I, tome 2, p. 263
16. Ibid., Vol. I, tome 2, p. 52.
17. Table adapted from Croaciani, Illari and Paoletti, *Storia militare del Regno Italico*, Vol. I, tome 2, p. 263. Figures include supplementary conscription; does not include conscription for Istria or Dalmatia.
18. '*Situation de IV Corps, 1812*', bi-weekly status reports of the divisions of IV Corps in Russia. Archives de la Guerre, Service Historique de l'armee du terre (hereafter AGSHAT) C2 527.
19. Croaciani, Illari and Paoletti, *Storia militare del Regno Italico*, Vol. I, tome 2, pp. 606–7.
20. Frederick C. Schneid, *Napoleon's Italian Campaigns, 1805–1815* (Westport, CT, 2002), chapter 6. More recently, John H. Gill, *1809: Thunder on the Danube* (London, 2009), II, chapters 4 and 5.
21. Schneid, *Napoleon's Italian Campaigns*, pp. 90–1.
22. '*Situation de IV Corps, 1812*', AGSHAT C2 527.
23. '*Situazione dell Armata di terra 11 Aprile 1813*', BA 47/11.
24. Schneid, *Napoleon's Italian Campaigns*, chapter 8; Croaciani, Illari and Paolletti, *Storia militare del Regno Italico*, Vol. I, tome 2, p. 600.

Further Reading

The literature of the Napoleonic Wars is vast, surpassed in number only by books on the Second World War and the American Civil War. Books specifically on aspects of the armies of this period are listed below, though readers may also wish to consult the plethora of campaign and battle studies, as well as the biographies of commanders, that abound on the subject.

GENERAL STUDIES OF NAPOLEONIC ARMIES OR SPECIFIC ARMS OF SERVICE

Crumplin, Michael. *Men of Steel: Surgery in the Napoleonic Wars*, Shrewsbury, Quiller Press, 2007.

Dawson, Anthony, Paul Dawson and Stephen Summerfield. *Napoleonic Artillery*, Marlborough, Crowood Press, 2007.

Fletcher, Ian. *Fortresses of the Peninsular War, 1808–14*, Oxford, Osprey, 2003.

Funcken, Liliane and Fred Funcken. *The Napoleonic Wars: Arms and Uniforms*, 2 vols, New York, Prentice-Hall, 1984.

Haythornthwaite, Philip. *Napoleonic Cavalry: Weapons and Warfare*, London, Weidenfeld & Nicolson, 2001.

——. *Napoleonic Infantry: Weapons and Warfare*, London, Weidenfeld & Nicolson, 2001.

——. *Weapons and Equipment of the Napoleonic Wars*, London, Arms and Armour Press, 1999.

——. *Uniforms of the Peninsular War, 1807–1814*, London, Weidenfeld Military, 1996.

——. *Uniforms of Waterloo*, London, Weidenfeld Military, 1996.

——. *The Napoleonic Source Book*, London, Cassell, 1990.

——. *Uniforms of the Napoleonic Wars, 1796–1814*, Poole, Blandford Press, 1985.

——. *Uniforms of the Retreat from Moscow*, New York, Hippocrene, 1976.

Kiley, Kevin. *Artillery of the Napoleonic Wars*. London, Greenhill, 2004.

McNab, Chris. *Armies of the Napoleonic Wars: An Illustrated History*, Oxford, Osprey, 2009.

Muir, Rory. *Tactics and the Experience of Battle in the Age of Napoleon*, New Haven, Yale University Press, 2000.

Nosworthy, Brent. *With Musket, Cannon and Sword: Battle Tactics of Napoleon and his Enemies*, New York, Sarpedon, 1996.

Over, Keith. *Flags and Standards of the Napoleonic Wars*, London, Bivouac, 1976.

Partridge, Richard and Michael Oliver. *Napoleonic Army Handbook*, 2 vols, London, Constable and Robinson, 1999.

Rothenburg, Gunther. *The Art of Warfare in the Age of Napoleon*, Bloomington, Indiana University Press, 1980.

Smith, Digby (Otto von Pivka). *Uniforms of the Napoleonic Wars: An Illustrated Encyclopedia*, London, Lorenz, 2006.

——. *The Greenhill Napoleonic Wars Data Book*, London, Greenhill, 1998.

——. *Armies of the Napoleonic Era*, New York, Taplinger, 1979.

Wise, Terence. *Flags of the Napoleonic Wars*, 2 vols, London, Osprey, 1978.

FRENCH ARMY

Augoyat, Antoine. *Aperçu Historique sur les fortifications, les ingéneurs et sur le corps du génie en France*, 3 vols, Paris, Dumaine, 1860–4.

Bowden, Scott. *Napoleon's Grande Armée of 1813*, Chicago, Emperor's Press, 1990.

Brice, Leon. *Le corps de santé militaire en France: sa evolution, ses campagnes, 1708–1882*, Paris, Berger-Levrault, 1907.
Chandler, David (ed.). *Military Maxims of Napoleon*, London, Greenhill, 2002.
——. *The Campaigns of Napoleon*, London, Weidenfeld & Nicolson, 1995.
—— (ed.). *Napoleon's Marshals*, London, Macmillan, 1987.
Chartrand, Renée. *Napoleon's Guns, 1792–1815. Vol. 1: Field Artillery*, Oxford, Osprey, 2003.
——. *Napoleon's Guns, 1792–1815. Vol. 2: Heavy and Siege Artillery*, Oxford, Osprey, 2003.
Crowdy, Terry. *French Napoleonic Infantryman, 1803–15*, Oxford, Osprey, 2002.
Dempsey, Guy. *Napoleon's Mercenaries: Foreign Units in the French Army under the Consulate and Empire, 1799–1814*, London, Greenhill, 2002.
Elting, John. *Swords Around a Throne: Napoleon's Grande Armée*, London, Weidenfeld & Nicolson, 1997.
Escalle, Charles-Pierre. *Des marches dans les armées de Napoléon*, Paris, Chapelot, 1912.
Forrest, Allan. *Napoleon's Men: The Soldiers of the Revolution and Empire*, London, Hambledon, 2002.
——. *Conscripts and Deserters: The Army and French Society during the Revolution and Empire*, Oxford, Oxford University Press, 1989.
Griffith, Paddy. *French Napoleonic Infantry Tactics*, Oxford, Osprey, 2007.
Haythornthwaite, Philip. *The Waterloo Armies: Men, Organization and Tactics*, London, Pen & Sword Military, 2007.
——. *Napoleon's Commanders. Vol. 2: c. 1809–15*, Oxford, Osprey, 2002.
——. *Napoleon's Commanders. Vol. 1: c. 1792–1809*, Oxford, Osprey, 2001.
——. *Weapons and Equipment of the Napoleonic Wars*, London, Arms and Armour Press, 1998.
——. *Napoleon's Military Machine*, Staplehurst, Spellmount, 1995.
——. *Napoleonic Source Book*, London, Cassell, 1990.
——. *Napoleon's Specialist Troops*, London, Osprey, 1988.
——. *Napoleon's Line Infantry*, London, Osprey, 1983.
Howard, Martin. *Napoleon's Doctors*, Staplehurst, Spellmount, 2006.
Johnson, David. *Napoleon's Cavalry and Its Leaders*, Charlottesville, Howell, 1999.
Lachouque, Henry. *The Anatomy of Glory: Napoleon and His Guard*, trans. Anne S.K. Brown, London, Greenhill, 1997.
Lucas-Dubreton, Jean. *Soldats de Napoléon*, Paris, Flammarion, 1948.
Lynn, John. 'Toward an Army of Honor: The Moral Evolution of the French Army, 1789–1815', *French Historical Studies* 16, no. 1 (Spring), 152–73.
Macdonald, A.G. *Napoleon and His Marshals*, London, Prion, 1996.
Markham, David. *Imperial Glory: The Bulletins of Napoleon's Grande Armée*, London, Greenhill, 2003.
Nafziger, George. *Imperial Bayonets: Tactics of the Napoleonic Battery, Battalion and Brigade as Found in Contemporary Regulations*, London, Greenhill, 1996.
Nosworthy, Brent. *With Musket, Cannon and Sword: Battle Tactics of Napoleon and his Enemies*, New York, Sarpedon, 1996.
Partridge, Richard and Michael Oliver. *Napoleonic Army Handbook. Vol. 2: The French Army and Her Allies*, London, Constable and Robinson, 2002.
Pawly, Ronald. *Mounted Grenadiers of the Imperial Guard*, Oxford, Osprey, 2009.
——. *Napoleon's Mounted Chasseurs of the Imperial Guard*, Oxford, Osprey, 2008.
——. *Napoleon's Polish Lancers of the Imperial Guard*, Oxford, Osprey, 2007.
——. *Napoleon's Mamelukes*, Oxford, Osprey, 2006.
——. *Napoleon's Scouts of the Imperial Guard*, Oxford, Osprey, 2006.
——. *Napoleon's Carabiniers*, Oxford, Osprey, 2005.
——. *Napoleon's Imperial Headquarters. Vol. 1: Organization and Personnel*, Oxford, Osprey, 2004.
——. *Napoleon's Imperial Headquarters. Vol. 2: On Campaign*, Oxford, Osprey, 2004.
——. *Napoleon's Guards of Honour, 1813–14*, Oxford, Osprey, 2002.

Philip, Raymond de. *Etude sur le Service d'Etat Major pendant les guerres du premier empire*, Paris, Chapelot, 1900.
Quimby, R.R. *The Background of Napoleonic Warfare*, New York, Columbia University Press, 1957.
Riley, Jonathan. *Napoleon as a General: Command from the Battlefield to Grand Strategy*, London, Hambledon Continuum, 2007.
Rogers, H.C.B. *Napoleon's Army*, Barnsley, Leo Cooper, 2005.
Rothenburg, Gunther. *The Art of Warfare in the Age of Napoleon*, Bloomington, Indiana University Press, 1980.
Six, Georges. *Les généraux de la révolution et de l'empire*, Paris, Bordas, 1947.
——. *Dictionnaire biographique des généraux et amiraux français de la révolution et d'empire*, 2 vols, Paris, Saffroy, 1934.
Smith, Digby (Otto von Pivka). *The Prussian Army – To 1815*, Atglen, Schiffer Publishing, 2004.
——. *Napoleon's Regiments: Battle Histories of the Regiments of the French Army, 1792–1815*, London, Greenhill, 2000.
——. *The Greenhill Napoleonic Wars Data Book*, London, Greenhill, 1998.
——. *Armies of the Napoleonic Era*, London, Taplinger, 1979.
Tarnstrom, Ronald. *French Arms*, Linsborg, Trogen, 2001.
Thoumas, C.A. *Les transformations de l'armée français*, 2 vols, Paris, Berger-Levrault, 1887.
Uffindell, Andrew. *Napoleon's Immortals: The Imperial Guard and its Battles, 1804–1815*, Staplehurst, Spellmount, 2007.
Vachée, J.B. *Napoleon at Work*, Minneapolis, PDI, 1995.
Wilkinson-Latham, Robert. *Napoleon's Artillery*, London, Osprey, 1975.
Wise, Terence. *Artillery Equipments of the Napoleonic Wars*, London, Osprey, 1979.

RUSSIAN ARMY

Begunova, Alla. *Povsednevnaia zhizn' ruskogo gusara v tsarstvovanie Aleksanndra I*, Moscow, Molodaia gvardiya, 2000.
Bogdanov, L. *Russkaia armiya v 1812 godu: organizatsiya, upravlenie, vooruzhenie*, Moscow, Ministerstvo Oborony SSSR, 1979.
Hartley, Janet M. *Russia, 1762–1825: Military Power, the State and the People*, Westport, Praeger, 2008.
Kagan, Frederick. 'Russian Military Reform in the Age of Napoleon', in *Reforming the Tsar's Army: Military Innovation in Imperial Russia from Peter the Great to the Revolution*, ed. David Schimmelpenninck van der Oye and Bruce W. Menning, Cambridge, Cambridge University Press, 2003, pp. 189–203.
Kagan, Frederick and R. Higham (eds). *The Military History of Tsarist Russia*, Basingstoke, Macmillan, 2002.
Keep, J.L.H. *Soldiers of the Tsar: Army and Society in Russia 1462–1874*, Oxford, Clarendon Press, 1985.
LeDonne, J.P. *The Grand Strategy of the Russian Empire, 1650–1831*, Oxford, Oxford University Press, 2004.
——. *Absolutism and Ruling Class: The Formation of the Russian Political Order, 1700–1825*, New York, Oxford University Press, 1991.
Lieven, Dominic. *Russia Against Napoleon: The Battle for Europe, 1807 to 1814*, London, Allen Lane, 2009.
Mikaberidze, Alexander. 'For Faith, Tsar and Fatherland: Conscription in Russia in the late Eighteenth and Early Nineteenth Centuries', in *Conscription in Napoleonic Europe, 1798–1815: A Revolution in Military Affairs?*, eds Donald J. Stocker and Harold Blanton, London, Routledge, 2009, pp. 46–65.
——. *The Russian Officer Corps in the Revolutionary and Napoleonic Wars, 1792–1815*, New York, Savas Beatie, 2005.

Seaton, Albert. *The Russian Army of the Napoleonic Wars*, London, Osprey, 1979.
Spring, Laurence. *The Cossacks, 1799–1815*, Oxford, Osprey, 2003.
——. *Russian Grenadiers and Infantry, 1799–1815*, Oxford, Osprey, 2002.
Ulyanov, Ilya. *1812. Russkaya pekhota v boyu* (*1812. Russian Infantry in Battle*), Moscow, Eksmo, 2008.
——. *Istoriya Rossiiskikh voisk. Regulyarnaya pekhota* (*History of the Russian Troops: Regular Infantry*), Vols 1 and 2, Moscow, Eksmo, 1998.
Zhmodikov, Alexander and Yuri Zhmodikov. *Tactics of the Russian Army in the Napoleonic Wars*, West Chester, Nafziger Collection, 2003.

AUSTRIAN ARMY

Angeli, Moritz Edler von. *Erzherzog Carl von Osterreich als Feldherr und Heeresorganisator*, 5 vols, Vienna, K.u.K. Hofuniversitäts-Buchhändler, 1896–98.
Castle, Ian. *Eggmühl 1809*, London, Osprey, 1996.
——. *Aspern & Wagram 1809*, London, Osprey, 1994.
Criste, Oscar. *Erzherzog Carl von Osterreich*, 3 vols, Vienna, Braumüller, 1912.
Demian, Johann. *Darstellung der österreichische Monarchie nach den neuesten statistischen Beziehungen*, Vienna, Carmesina, 1804.
Dolleczek, Anton. *Geschichte der österreichischen Artillerie*, Graz, Akademische Drück und Verlag, repr. 1970.
——. *Monographie der kuk öst-ung blanken und Handfeuerwaffen*, Graz, Akademische Drück und Verlag, repr. 1970.
Duffy, Christopher. *Instrument of War*, Chicago, Emperor's Press, 2000.
Gallina, Johann. *Beitrage zur Geschichte des öst. Heerwesens*, Vienna, n.p., 1872.
Haythornthwaite, Philip. *Austrian Specialist Troops of the Napoleonic Wars*, London, Osprey, 1989.
——. *Austrian Army of the Napoleonic Wars (2) Cavalry*, London, Osprey, 1986.
——. *Austrian Army of the Napoleonic Wars (1) Infantry*, London, Osprey, 1983.
Hirtenfeld, Jaromir. *Der Mariatheresienorden und seine Mitglieder*, Vienna, Staatsdruckerei, 1856–7.
Hollins, David. *Austrian Frontier Troops, 1740–1798* Oxford, Osprey, 2005.
——. *Austrian Commanders of the Napoleonic Wars*, Oxford, Osprey, 2004.
——. *Austrian Napoleonic Artillery, 1792–1815*, Oxford, Osprey, 2003.
——. *Hungarian Hussar, 1756–1815*, Oxford, Osprey, 2003.
——. *Marengo 1800*, Oxford, Osprey, 2000.
——. *Austrian Grenadiers & Infantry, 1788–1816*, London, Osprey, 1998.
——. 'Finest Autocrats of all Europe', in *Military Illustrated* (No. 106: March 1997), 20–4.
——. *Austrian Auxiliary Troops, 1792–1816*, London, Osprey, 1996.
Kaindl, Dr Franz. 'Die KK Militärgrenze – zur Einführung in ihrer Geschichte', in *Die KK Militärgrenze – Beiträge zu ihrer Geschichte*, Vienna, HGM, 1973.
——. 'Von den gemalten zu den gewebten Feldzeichen', in *Schriften des Heeresgeschichtliches-museum in Wien Band 4*, Vienna, HGM, 1969.
Karger, Johann. *Die Entwicklung der Adjustierung, Rüstung und Bewaffnung der österreich-ungarische Armee, 1700–1809*, Hamburg, LTR, 1998.
Karl, Erzherzog von Osterreich (ed. F. Malcher). *Ausgewählte Schriften*, Vienna, Braumüller, 1893–94.
Kriegsarchiv, Wien. *Osterreichische Militärische Zeitschrift*, Vienna, Streffleur, 1806–1910.
Kriegsgeschichtliche Abteilung des k.u.k. Kriegsarchivs. *Befreiungskriege 1813–14*, 5 vols, Vienna, Staatsdruckerei, 1911–13.
——. *Krieg 1809*, 4 vols, Vienna, Staatsdruckerei, 1906–10.
——. *Kriege gegen die französische Revolution*, 2 vols, Vienna, Staatsdruckerei, 1905.
——. *Krieg unter Josef II*, 2 vols, Vienna, Staatsdruckerei, 1905.

Kunisch, Johannes. *Der Kleine Krieg (Band 4 of the Frankfurter Historische Abhandlungen)*, Wiesbaden, Steiner, 1973.

Macartney, Christopher. *The Habsburg Empire, 1792–1918*, London, Weidenfeld & Nicholson, 1969.

Oesterreichischer Militaer-Almanach (1790–1803), continues as *Schematismus der kais. königl. Armee (1804–1808)*, then *Schematismus der Oesterreichisch-kaiserlichen Armee (1810–1815)*.

Rauchensteiner, M. *Kaiser Franz und Erzherzog Carl*, Vienna, Verlag für Geschichte und Politik, 1972.

Regele, Oscar. *Generalstabschefs aus vier Jahrhunderten*, Vienna, Herold, 1966.

Rothenberg, Gunther. *Napoleon's Great Adversaries: The Archduke Charles and the Austrian Army, 1792–1814*, London, Batsford, 1982.

——. *The Military Border in Croatia 1740–1881*, Chicago, University of Chicago Press, 1966.

Sagvari, Gyorgy. *Das Buch der Husaren*, Budapest, Magyar Könyvklub, 1999.

Smola, Karl. *Handbuch für k.k. österreichische Artillerie-Offiziere: mit Benützung der hinterlassenen Schriften des k.k. Generalmajors in der Artillerie Joseph Freiherrn von Smola*, Vienna, Beck, 1839 (2nd edn of the *Taschenbuch*).

——. *Taschenbuch für die kk öst. Artillerie-Officiere. Teilweise nach dem hinterlassen Schriften des Joseph Freiherrn von Smola*, Vienna, Beck, 1822.

Veltze, Alois (ed.). *Das Kriegsjahr 1809 in einzelen Darstellungen*, Vienna, Stern, 1909.

Wagner, Walter. *Von Austerlitz bis Königgratz: Osterreichische Kampftaktik im Spiegel Der Reglements,1805–1864*, Osnabrück, BiblioVerlag, 1978.

Wolf-Schneider, Oskar. 'Der öst-ung. Generalstab' (unpublished essay), Vienna, Kriegsarchiv Nachlässe B197/12, 1965.

Wrede, Alphons von. *Geschichte der kk Wehrmacht*, 5 vols, Vienna, Staatsdruckrei, 1898–1903.

Würzbach, Constant von. *Biographisches Lexicon des Kaisertums Osterreich*, Vienna, Hofdrückerei, 1856–91.

Zehetbauer, Ernst. *Landwehr gegen Napoleon*, Vienna, öbv, 1999.

Zimmerman, J. *Militärverwaltung und Heeresaufbringung in Osterreich bis 1806*, Frankfurt, Bernard und Graefe, 1965.

PRUSSIAN ARMY

Chandler, David. *Jena 1806: Napoleon Destroys Prussia*, New York, Berg, 1993.

Das Preussische Heer der Befreiungskriege, 3 vols, Berlin, Ernst Siegfried Mittler und Sohn, 1912–14 (1920).

Die Reorganisation der Preußischen Armee nach dem Tilsiter Frieden, 2 vols, Ernst Siegfried Mittler und Sohn, Berlin, 1862–6.

Fiedler, Siegfried. *Taktik und Strategie der Revolutionskriege, 1792–1848*, Bonn, Bernhard and Graefe, 2002.

Haythornthwaite, Philip. *The Waterloo Armies: Men, Organization and Tactics*, London, Pen & Sword Military, 2007.

Hofschroer, Peter. *Prussian Staff and Specialist Troops, 1791–1815*, Oxford, Osprey, 2003.

——. *Prussian Reserve, Militia and Irregular Troops, 1806–15*, London, Osprey, 1987.

——. *Prussian Cavalry of the Napoleonic Wars Vol. 1: 1792–1807*, London, Osprey, 1985.

——. *Prussian Cavalry of the Napoleonic Wars. Vol. 2: 1807–15*, London, Osprey, 1985.

——. *Prussian Light Infantry, 1792–1815*, London, Osprey, 1984.

Jany, Curt. *Geschichte der Königlich Preußischen Armee*, 3rd and 4th vols, Berlin, Karl Siegismund, 1929 and 1933.

Ortenburg, Georg. *Waffen der Revolutionskriege, 1792–1848*, Bonn, Bernhard and Graefe, 1988.

Paret, Peter. *Yorck and the Era of Prussian Reform, 1807–1815*, Princeton, Princeton University Press, 1966.

Schmidt, Oliver. *Prussian Regular Infantryman, 1808–15*, Oxford, Osprey, 2003.

Shanahan, William. *Prussian Military Reforms, 1786–1813*, New York, Columbia University Press, 1945.
Vaupel, Rudolf. *Das Preussische Heer vom Tilsiter Frieden bis zur Befreiung 1807–1814*, Vol. 1 (second never published), Leipzig, S. Hirzel, 1938.
Walter, Dierk. *A Military Revolution? Prussian Military Reforms before the Wars of German Unification*, Forvarsstudier 2/2001, Oslo, Norwegian Institute for Defence Studies, 2001.
Young, Peter. *Blücher's Army, 1813–15*, London, Osprey, 1972.

BRITISH ARMY

Barthorp, Michael. *Wellington's Generals*, London, Osprey, 1990.
Blackmore, Howard L. *British Military Firearms, 1650–1850*, London, Greenhill, 1994.
Brett-James, Anthony. *Life in Wellington's Army*, London, Donovan, 1995.
Burnham, Robert and Ron McGuigan. *The British Army against Napoleon: Facts, Lists and Trivia, 1805–1815*, Barnsley, Frontline Books, 2010.
Chappell, Mike. *Wellington's Peninsular Regiments. Vol. 2: The Light Infantry*, Oxford, Osprey, 2004.
——. *Wellington's Peninsular Regiments. Vol. 1: The Irish*, Oxford, Osprey, 2003.
Esdaile, Charles. *The Peninsular War: A New History*, London, Penguin, 2003.
Fletcher, Ian. *Galloping at Everything: The British Cavalry in the Peninsular War and at Waterloo, 1808–15*, Staplehurst, Spellmount, 1999.
——. *Wellington's Regiments: The Men and Their Battles, 1808–1815*, Staplehurst, Spellmount, 1994.
Fortescue, Sir John. *History of the British Army*, vols 6–10, Uckfield, Naval and Military Press, 2004.
——. *The County Lieutenancies and the Army, 1803–1814*, Uckfield, Naval and Military Press, 2002.
Fosten, Brian. *Wellington's Infantry*, Vol. 1, London, Osprey, 1992.
——. *Wellington's Infantry*, Vol. 2, London, Osprey, 1992.
——. *Wellington's Heavy Cavalry*, London, Osprey, 1982.
——. *Wellington's Light Cavalry*, London, Osprey, 1982.
Franklin, Carl. *British Napoleonic Uniforms: A Complete Illustrated Guide*, London, History Press, 2009.
——. *British Napoleonic Field Artillery*, Staplehurst, Spellmount, 2007.
——. *British Rockets of the Napoleonic and Colonial Wars, 1805–1901*, Staplehurst, Spellmount, 2005.
Glover, Michael. *The Peninsular War, 1807–14: A Concise Military History*, London, Penguin, 2001.
——. *Wellington as Military Commander*, London, Penguin, 2001.
——. *Wellington's Army in the Peninsula, 1808–1814*, New York, Hippocrene, 1977.
Glover, Richard. *Britain at Bay: Defence against Bonaparte, 1803–14*, London, Allen and Unwin, 1973.
——. *Peninsular Preparation: The Reform of the British Army, 1795–1809*, Cambridge, Cambridge University Press, 1963.
Guy, Alan J. (ed.). *The Road to Waterloo: The British Army and the Struggle against Revolutionary and Napoleonic France, 1793–1815*, London, National Army Museum, 1990.
Hallows, Ian S. *Regiments and Corps of the British Army*, London, Arms and Armour Press, 1991.
Haythornthwaite, Philip. *British Napoleonic Infantry Tactics*, Oxford, Osprey, 2008.
——. *The Waterloo Armies: Men, Organization and Tactics*, London, Pen & Sword Military, 2007.
——. *British Rifleman, 1797–1815*, Oxford, Osprey, 2002.
——. *Weapons and Equipment of the Napoleonic Wars*, London, Arms and Armour Press, 1999.
——. *The Armies of Wellington*, London, Arms and Armour Press, 1996.

——. *The British Infantry of the Napoleonic Wars*, London, Weidenfeld & Nicolson, 1996.
——. Wellington's Military Machine. London, Guild, 1989.
——. Wellington's Specialist Troops. London, Osprey, 1988.
Henry, Chris. *British Napoleonic Artillery, 1793–1815. Vol. 2: Siege and Coastal Artillery*, Oxford, Osprey, 2003.
——. *British Napoleonic Artillery, 1793–1815. Vol. 1: Field Artillery*, Oxford, Osprey, 2002.
Holmes, Richard. *Redcoat: The British Soldier in the Age of Horse and Musket*, London, HarperCollins, 2001.
Howard, Martin. *Wellington's Doctors: The British Army Medical Services in the Napoleonic Wars*, London, History Press, 2008.
Hughes, B.P. *Firepower: Weapons Effectiveness on the Battlefield, 1630–1850*, London, Arms and Armour Press, 1974.
Lawford, James. *Wellington's Peninsular Army*, London, Osprey, 1973.
Muir, Rory, Robert Burnham and Howie Muir. *Inside Wellington's Peninsular Army, 1808–1814*, London, Pen & Sword Military, 2006.
Myatt, Frederick. *British Sieges of the Peninsular War*, Staplehurst, Spellmount, 1987.
Oman, Charles. *Wellington's Army, 1809–1814*, London, Greenhill, 1912.
Page, E.C.G. *Following the Drum: Women in Wellington's Wars*, London, Deutsch, 1986.
Partridge, Richard and Michael Oliver. *Napoleonic Army Handbook: The British Army and Her Allies*, London, Constable and Robinson, 1999.
Reid, Stuart. *Wellington's Army in the Peninsula, 1809–14*, Oxford, Osprey, 2004.
——. *British Redcoat. Vol. 2: 1793–1815*, Oxford, Osprey, 1997.
——. *Wellington's Highlanders*, Oxford, Osprey, 1992.
Rogers, H.C.B. *Wellington's Army*, London, Ian Allan, 1979.
——. *Weapons of the British Soldier*, London, Seeley Service, 1960.
Strawson, John. *Beggars in Red: The British Army, 1789–1889*, London, Hutchinson, 1991.
Uffindell, Andrew. *National Army Museum Book of Wellington's Armies*, London, Pan, 2005.
Urban, Mark. *Rifles: Six Years with Wellington's Legendary Sharpshooters*, London, Faber, 2004.
Ward, S.G.P. *Wellington's Headquarters*, Oxford, Oxford University Press, 1957.
Weller, Jac. *Wellington in the Peninsula*, London, Greenhill, 1999.
——. *Wellington at Waterloo*, London, Greenhill, 1991.

ARMIES OF THE CONFEDERATION OF THE RHINE

Angelelli, Jean and Alain Pigeard. *La Conféderation du Rhin*, Paris, Quator, 2002.
Bowden, Scott. *Napoleon's Grande Armée of 1813*, Chicago, Emperor's Press, 1990.
Costa de Serda, Emile. *Les Troupes Sociales sous le Ier Empire*, Paris, Dumaine, 1874.
Gill, John H. 'Vermin, Scorpions and Mosquitoes: The Rheinbund in the Peninsula', in *The Peninsular War: Aspects of the Struggle for the Iberian Peninsula*, ed. Ian Fletcher, Staplehurst, Spellmount, 1998.
——. *With Eagles to Glory: Napoleon and His German Allies in the 1809 Campaign*, London, Greenhill, 1992.
Holzhausen, Paul. *Die Deutschen in Russland*, Berlin, Morawe & Scheffelt, 1912.
Kraft, Heinz. *Die Württemberger in den Napoleonischen Kriegen*, Stuttgart, Kohlhammer, 1953.
Nafziger, George. *Poles and Saxons of the Napoleonic Wars*, Chicago, Emperor's Press, 1991.
Partridge, Richard and Michael Oliver. *Napoleon Army Handbook: The French Army and Her Allies*, Vol. 2, London, Constable and Robinson, 2002.
Sauzey, Camille. *Les Allemands sous les Aigles Françaises*, vols I–VI, Paris, Terana, 1987–8.
Smith, Digby (Otto von Pivka). *1813: Leipzig: Napoleon and the Battle of the Nations*, London, Greenhill, 2001.
——. *Napoleon's German Allies. Vol. 1: Westfalia and Kleve-Berg*, London, Osprey, 1992.
——. *Napoleon's German Allies. Vol. 2: Nassau and Oldenburg*, London, Osprey, 1991.

——. *Napoleon's German Allies. Vol. 3: Saxony*, London, Osprey, 1979.
——. *Napoleon's German Allies. Vol. 4: Bavaria*, London, Osprey, 1980.
——. *Napoleon's German Allies. Vol. 5: Hesse*, London, Osprey, 1992.

SPANISH ARMY

Alexander, Donald. *Rod of Iron: French Counter-Insurgency in Aragón during the Peninsular War*, Wilmington, Scholarly Resources Press, 1985.

Andújar Castillo, Francisco. *Los militares en la España del siglo XVIII: un estudi o social*, Granada, Universidad de Granada, 1991.

Borreguero Beltrán, Cristina. *El reclutamiento militar por quintas en la España del siglo XVIII: origenes del servicio militar obilgatorio*, Valladolid, Universidad deValladolid, 1989.

Bueno Carrera, José María. *El ejército y la armada en 1808*, Málaga, private publication, 1982.

Bueno Carrera, José María. *Uniformes militares de la Guerra de la Independencia*, Madrid, Aldaba Militaria, 1989.

Chartrand, René. *Spanish Army of the Napoleonic Wars. Vol. 1: 1793–1808*, Oxford, Osprey, 1998.

——. *Spanish Army of the Napoleonic Wars. Vol. 2: 1808–1812*, Oxford, Osprey, 1999.

Esdaile, Charles. 'The Spanish Army', in Frederick Schneid (ed.), *Armies of the Revolutionary Wars*, Norman, University of Oklahoma Press, forthcoming.

——. 'Conscription in Spain in the Napoleonic era', in Donald Stoker, Frederick Schneid and Harold Blanton (eds), *Conscription in Napoleonic Europe, 1789–1815: A Revolution in Military Affairs?*, London, Routledge, 2008, pp. 102–21.

——. *Peninsular Eyewitnesses: the Experiences of War in Spain and Portugal, 1808–1814*, Barnsley, Pen & Sword, 2008.

——. *Fighting Napoleon: Guerrillas, Bandits and Adventurers in Spain, 1808–1814*, London, Yale University Press, 2004.

——. *The Peninsular War: a New History*, London, Allen Lane, 2002.

——. *The Duke of Wellington and the Command of the Spanish Army, 1812–1814*, London, Macmillan, 1990.

——. *The Spanish Army in the Peninsular War*, Manchester, Manchester University Press, 1988.

Fraser, Ronald. *Napoleon's Cursed War: Popular Resistance in the Spanish Peninsular War*, London, Verso, 2008.

Lovett, Gabriel. *Napoleon and the Birth of Modern Spain*, 2 vols, New York, New York University Press, 1965.

Ministerio de Defensa. *La Guerra de la Independencia, 1808–1814: el pueblo spañol, su ejército y sus aliados frente a la ocupación napoleónica*, Madrid, Ministerio de Defensa, 2007.

Moliner Prada, Antonio (ed.). *La Guerra de la Independencia en España, 1808–1814*, Barcelona, Nabla Ediciones, 2007.

Oman, Charles. *A History of the Peninsular War*, Oxford, Clarendon Press, 1902–30.

Smith, Digby (Otto von Pivka). *Spanish Armies of the Napoleonic Wars*, London, Osprey, 1975.

Terrón Ponce, José Luis. *Ejército y política en la España de Carlos III*, Madrid, Ministerio de Defensa, 1997.

Tone, John. *The Fatal Knot: the Guerrilla War in Navarre and the Defeat of Napoleon in Spain*, Chapel Hill, University of North Carolina Press, 1994.

PORTUGUESE ARMY

Centeno, João. *O Exécito Português na Guerra Peninsular; vol. 1 – Do Rossilhão ao fim da Segunda Invasão Francesa*, Lisbon, Prefácio, 2008.

Chartrand, René and Bill Younghusband. *The Portuguese Army of the Napoleonic Wars*, 3 vols, Oxford, Osprey, 2000–1.

Cole, John William. *Memoirs of British Generals distinguished during the Peninsular War*, 2 vols, London, Richard Bentley, 1856.

Collecção das Ordens do Dia do Illustrissimo e Excellentissimo Senhor Guilherme CarrBeresford commandante em Chefe dos Exercitos de S.A.R. o Principe Regente Nosso Senhor. Annos 1809–1823, 12 vols, Lisbon, António Nunes dos Santos, 1809–23.

F.F.M.C.D. (Frade Fortunato Monge Cisterciense). *Notícias Biográficas do Marechal Beresford*, Lisbon, 1811.

Fuente, Francisco Arturo de la. 'Dom Miguel Pereira Forjaz: his early career and role in the mobilization and defence of Portugal during the Peninsular War, 1807–1814', unpublished PhD thesis, Florida State University, 1980.

Glover, Michael. 'Beresford and his Fighting Cocks: the Regeneration of the Portuguese Army', *History Today*, April 1976.

Halliday, Andrew. *Observations on the Present State of the Portuguese Army as organised by Lieutenant-General Sir William Carr Beresford KB. Field Marshal and Commander in Chief of that army with an account of the different military establishments and laws of Portugal*, London, John Murray, 1811.

Horward, Donald (ed.). *The French Campaign in Portugal 1810–1811. An Account by Jean Jacques Pelet*, Minneapolis, University of Minnesota Press, 1973.

Livermore, H.V. 'Beresford and the Reform of the Portuguese Army', in *A History of the Peninsular War*, ed. Paddy Griffith, Vol. IX, London, Greenhill, 1999, pp. 121–44.

Marques, Fernando Pereira. *Exército e sociedade em Portugal*, Lisbon, Alfa, 1989.

Napier, W.F.P. *History of the War in the Peninsula and in the South of France*, 6 vols, London, Warne, 1828–40.

Newitt, Malyn and Martin Robson (eds). *Lord Beresford and British Intervention in Portugal, 1807–1820*, Lisbon, ICS, 2004.

Oman, C.W.C. *Wellington's Army*, London, Arnold, 1912, repr. Edwards, London, 1968.

Rousseau, I.J. (ed.). *The Peninsular Journal of Major General Sir Benjamin 'Urban*, London, Longmans, 1930.

Sherer, Moyle. *Recollections of the Peninsula*, Staplehurst, Spellmount, 1996.

Smith, Digby (Otto von Pivka). *The Portuguese Army of the Napoleonic Wars*, London, Osprey, 1977.

Thompson, Mark. *The Fatal Hill*, Chapelgarth, Mark Thompson Publishing, 2002.

—— (ed.). *The Letters of Charles Edward Long and General Lord Viscount Beresford*, Chapelgarth, Mark Thompson Publishing, 1993.

Thompson, W.F.K. (ed.). *An Ensign in the Peninsular War: The Letters of John Aitchison*, London, Michael Joseph, 1981.

Vichness, S.E. 'Marshal of Portugal: The Military Career of William Carr Beresford', unpublished PhD thesis, Florida State University, 1976.

Warre, Sir William. *Letters from the Peninsula, 1808–1812*, ed. Edmond Warre, London, John Murray, 1909.

Wellesley, Arthur Richard, 2nd Duke of Wellington (ed.). *Supplementary Despatches and Memoranda of Field Marshal Arthur Duke of Wellington*, 15 vols, London, 1858–72.

ARMY OF THE DUCHY OF WARSAW

Askenazy, S. *Książę Józef Poniatowski*, Warsaw, Państwowy Instytut Wydawniczy, 1978.

Białkowski, Antoni. *Wspomnienia starego żołnierza*, Gdynia, Armagedon, 2003.

Broekere, Stanisław. *Pamiętniki z wojny hiszpańskiej 1808–1814*, Gdynia, Armagedon, 2004.

Correspondance du prince Joseph Poniatowski avec la France 1807–1813, Poznań, Poznańskie Towarzystwo Przyjaciół Nauk, vols I–VI, 1921–9.

Czubaty, Jarosław. *Wodzowie i politycy. Generalicja polska lat 1806–1815*, Warsaw, Viator, 1993.

Dał nam przykład Bonaparte. Wspomnienia i relacje żołnierzy polskich 1796–1815, Krakow, Wydawnictwo Literackie, vols I–II, 1984.

Gembarzewski, Bronisław. *Wojsko polskie. Księstwo Warszawskie 1807–1814*, Warsaw, Gebethner i Wolff, 1905.

Jaszowski, Józef. *Pamiętniki dowódcy rakietników konnych*, Warsaw, Pax, 1968.
Kukiel, Marian. *Dzieje oręża polskiego w epoce napoleońskiej*, Poznań, Rzepecki i ska, 1912.
Łukasiewicz, Mariusz. *Armia księcia Józefa 1815*, Warsaw, Wydawnictwo MON, 1986.
Lukowski, Jerzy. *Liberty's Folly*, New York, Routledge, 1991.
Małachowski, Stanisław. *Pamiętniki*, Lwów, A. Rogosz, 1876.
Morawski, Ryszard and Adam Paczuski. *Wojsko Księstwa Warszawskiego. Ułani*, Warsaw, Karabela, 2009.
Morawski, Ryszard and Henryk Wielecki. *Wojsko Księstwa Warszawskiego. Generalicja I sztaby*, Warsaw, Bellona, 1996.
Nadzieja, Jadwiga. *Generał Józef Zajączek*, Warsaw, Wydawnictwo MON, 1975.
Nafziger, George *et al. Poles and Saxons of the Napoleonic Wars*, Chicago, Emperor's Press, 1991.
Nieuważny, Andrzej and Ryszard Morawski. *Wojsko Księstwa Warszawskiego. Artyleria, inżynierowie, saperzy*, Warsaw, Pelta, 2004.
Pachoński, Jan. *Generał Jan Henryk Dąbrowski*, Warsaw, Wydawnictwo MON, 1981.
Pawłowski, Bronisław. *Wojna polsko-austricka 1809 r*, Warsaw, Volumen – Bellona, 1999.
Smith, Digby (Otto von Pivka). *Napoleon's Polish Troops*, London, Osprey, 1974.
Sołtyk, Roman. *Relation des opérations de l'armée aux ordres du prince Joseph Poniatowski pendant la campagne de 1809 en Pologne contre les Autrichiens*, Paris, Gaultier-Laguionie (Maison Anselin), 1841.
Staszewski, Janusz. *Wojsko polskie na Pomorzu w roku 1807*, Gdańsk, Gdańskie Towarzystwo Naukowe, 1958.
Sułkowski, Antoni Paweł. *Listy doo żony z wojen napoleońskich*, Warsaw, Czytelnik, 1987.
Von Brandt, Heinrich. *In the Legions of Napoleon: The Memoirs of a Polish Officer in Spain and Russia, 1808–1813*, London, Greenhill, 1999.
Zych, Gabriel. *Armia Księstwa Warszawskiego*, Warsaw, Wydawnictwo MON, 1961.

ARMY OF THE KINGDOM OF ITALY

Beauharnais, Prince Eugène de. *Mèmoires et Correspondence Politique et militaire du Prince Eugène*, 10 vols, Paris, Michel Levy Frères, 1858–60.
Connelly, Owen. *Napoleon's Satellite Kingdoms*, New York, Free Press, 1965.
Crociani, Piero, Virgilio Ilari and Ciro Paoletti. *Storia Militare del Regno Italico, 3 vols (1802–1814)*, Roma, Stato Maggiore dell'Esercito, 2004.
Grab, Alex. 'Conscription and Desertion in Napoleonic Italy, 1802–1814', in Donald Stoker and Frederick C. Schneid (eds), *Conscription in the Napoleonic Era: A Revolution in Military Affairs?*, London, Routledge, 2009.
Ilari, Virgilo, Piero Crociani and Ciro Paoletti. *Storia Militare dell'Italia Giacobina (1796–1802)*, Roma, Stato Maggiore dell'Esercito, 2001.
Pivka, Otto von (Digby Smith). *Napoleon's Italian Troops*, London, Osprey, 1992.
Schneid, Frederick C. *Napoleon's Italian Campaigns, 1805–1815*, Westport, Praeger, 2002.
——. *Soldiers of Napoleon's Kingdom of Italy: Army, State and Society, 1800–1815*, Boulder, Westview/HarperCollins, 1995.

Index

Please note: at the request of the compiler, Napoleon Bonaparte has not been indexed, as references occur *passim*.

Abensberg 5, 155
Abercromby, Sir Ralph 128
Adriatic 62
Aitchison, John 220
Alba de Tormes 204
Albuera 206, 224–5
Alexander I 2–9, 36–42, 47–55, 75, 156, 242–3
Alicante 199
Almonacid de Toledo 204
Alorna, Marquês de 213–14, 217
Alps 2, 5, 11
America
  Civil War 14, 200, 208
  War of Independence 127, 134
Andalucía 198, 205
Andrade, General Bernardim Freire de 213–15, 220
Ankudinov 47
Ansbach 75, 82–3, 112, 122
Antwerp 59
Apulia 250
Aragón 197–8, 208
Arakcheyev, General Aleksey 50–2, 55
Arcis-sur-Aube 12, 242
Arenberg 154, 159, 176, 182
Armée du Nord 13, 26–7, 32
Aspern-Essling 5, 27, 74
Asturias 197–8
Augereau 19–20
Augusta Amelia, Princess 152
Augustus III, Frederick 235–6
Austerlitz 2, 14–15, 21, 26, 28, 55, 69, 74, 95, 151, 157
Austrian Netherlands, *see also* Belgium 60, 64
Austrian Succession, War of the 65

Badajoz
  fortress of 8, 140, 223
  Siege of 8, 145, 166, 208, 224
Baden 19, 24, 152–5, 159, 163–6
Baden, Margrave Wilhelm of 184
Bagration, General Peter 9, 51, 95, 241
Bailén 6, 189, 191–2, 203
Baker rifle 136
Balearic Islands 188, 198
Banda Oriental 227
Barclay de Tolly, Field Marshal Mikhail Andreas 9
Barrosa 8
Bashkirs 44
Bathurst, Henry, 3rd Earl of 225
Bautzen 10, 27, 33, 163, 170
Bavaria 2–4, 11, 19, 24, 152–63, 172
Bayonne 20, 165–6, 177, 193
Bayreuth 75, 122
Beauharnais, Prince Eugène de 5, 9, 152, 244, 249
Belchite 204
Belgium, *see also* Austrian Netherlands 12, 18, 20, 23, 27, 32, 59, 60, 75–9, 93–4, 156, 225
Bennigsen, General Levin August Theophil 3–4
Beresford, Major General William Carr 7, 206, 213–27
Berezina
  Battle of 163–7, 241, 251
  River 9
Berg, Grand Duchy of 126, 152, 173–5
Bergen-op-Zoom 145
Berlin 3, 112, 176, 230
Bernadotte, Marshal Jean Baptiste 3, 10–11, 125, 156, 168–9, 183
Bertrand, General Henri 252
Bidassoa 165
Blake, General Joaquín 206
Blücher, Field Marshal Gebhard Leberecht von 10–13, 32, 104, 112
Board of Ordnance 144–5
Bohemia 10, 57, 59–60, 74–81, 88, 91–2, 158

Bonaparte, Jerome 4, 158, 171–3, 241
Bonaparte, Joseph 6–7, 12, 205
Bonifacio, João 227
Bordeaux 226
Borodino 9, 160, 170, 173, 251
Boulogne 1–2, 249
Bourbon dynasty, the 12
Brandenburg 102–5
Braunau 157
Brazil 6, 214, 225–7
Breslau 168
Brest 1
Brunswick, Duke Friedrich Wilhelm (*d.* 1815) 181
Brunswick, Duke Wilhelm Ferdinand (*d.* 1806) 3
Brussels 12
Bryansk 43
Bukovina 60, 77
Burgos 8, 145
Busaco 7, 212, 223
Buxhöwden, Fedor 50

Cádiz 1, 8, 200, 205, 208
Calabria 15, 133, 250
Caldiero 2, 57
Campo Mayor 223–4
Canada 130, 145
Canaries 198
Cape Finisterre 1
Cardedeu 204
Carinthia 76, 91
Carniola 59, 75–6, 91
Carpathian Mountains 62, 91
Caspian Sea 44, 53
Castalla River, Battle of 206
Castello Branco 216
Castile, Old 197
Castiles 193, 198
Catalonia 20, 25, 172–80, 193, 199–200, 204
Catherine II (the Great) 37–42
Caucasus 36, 41
Cenis, Mount 69
Centeno, João 213–14, 226
Champaubert 11
Charles (Karl Ludwig), Archduke 2, 4, 58–9, 69–70, 81, 91, 93, 95
Charles III 190, 193, 201
Charles IV 188, 190, 193, 195
Charter of Liberties, *see also* Peter III 37, 49
Chasteler, Johann 69–70
Château-Thierry 11
Chernigov Province 44
Chichagov, Admiral 241
Cintra, Convention of 6, 214
Cisalpine Republic 245
Cispadane Republic 245
Ciudad Rodrigo
  fortress of 8, 140
  Siege of 143–5, 224
Clausewitz, Carl von 52
coalitions
  First Coalition 63, 78–9, 86, 93, 213
  Second Coalition 63, 67–8, 78, 84, 128, 245
  Third Coalition 2, 58, 63, 74, 246, 249
  Fourth Coalition 2, 98
  Fifth Coalition 4
  Sixth Coalition 10, 252
  Seventh Coalition 12
Coimbra University 222
Colberg, Siege of 240
Conde de Belveder, the 190
Condé, Prince 49, 53
Confederation of the Rhine 3–4, 10–11, 15, 19, 125–6, 148–67, 170, 176–8, 181–5
Congreve, Sir William 140
Constantine, Grand Duke 83, 243
Copenhagen 129, 140
Corunna 7, 215–16
Cossacks 9, 44
Craddock, General 214–15
Craonne 12, 242
Croatia, Kingdom of 60–2, 91
Cuesta, Captain General Gregorio García de la 7, 197
Częstochowa 242

d'Erlon, Marshal Jean-Baptistse Drouet 20
d'Este, Archduke Ferdinand 71, 82–5
Dąbrowski, General Jan Henryk 230–7, 241–2
  Dąbrowski's Mazurka 231
Dalberg, Carl von 180
Dalmatia 18, 60, 80–1, 247
Danube 2, 5, 22, 62, 90, 91, 168, 233
Danzig (Gdańsk) 124, 160–4, 168, 171–4, 178, 180–1, 235, 239–42
Davidov, Denis 45
Davout, Marshal Louis 3, 5, 18, 23, 166, 185, 236, 241, 244
Denmark 183, 188, 191

Dennewitz 11, 161
de Sousa Coutinho, Domingos 214
Díez, Juan Martín 207
Dmitriev-Mamonov, Count 47
Dolgoruky, Prince Peter 48
Dos de Mayo 194–6
Dresden 10–11, 31, 34, 85, 170–3, 180
Drouot, General Antoine 32
Duhesme, General Philibert-Guillaume 94, 250
Duka, Peter 69–70, 76, 95
Dundas, Sir David 135
Dupont, General 6
Dürnstein 2
Dutch Army 12, 18, 23, 29, 33

Ebelsberg 164
Eckmühl (Eggmühl) 5, 78
Egypt 128, 232
Ekaterinoslavl 42
Elba 12, 32, 34, 227, 249
Elbe, River 4, 101, 103, 109, 122–3
Elchingen 2
Elisabeth, Tsarina 49
Elster, River 11, 242
Emil, Prince of Hesse 184
Erfurt 181
Ertel, General Lieutenant Fedor 44, 80
Espinosa de los Monteros 191
Extremadura 190, 198, 204
Eylau 4, 158, 235

Ferdinand VII 194–5
Ferdinand, Grand Duke 178
Fifth Coalition, *see* coalitions
Finland 46
First World War 58, 112, 144
Flanders 128, 134
Fontainebleau 30
Fontanelli, Achille 251
Forbes, John 213
Forjaz, Miguel Pereira 213, 217, 221, 226
Fourth Coalition, *see* coalitions
Franco, General 208
Frankfurt 154, 159, 180–1
Franz II, Emperor 75, 82–5, 151
Frederick Augustus III 235
Frederick the Great 3, 21, 87, 158
Frederick William I 85, 112, 116
Frederick William III 4, 230
Friedland 235
Friedrich August, Elector (King of Württemberg) 153, 155, 161–3, 167, 170
Fuentes d'Oñoro 224

Galicia, New 239
Galicia, Polish 60–2, 75–80, 86, 239, 241
Galicia, Spanish 198
Gamonal 190, 204, 207
Gebora River, Battle of the 206
George III 3, 147
Georgia 36, 38
Gerona, Siege of 172–4, 178, 191, 205, 250
Gibraltar 130, 145
Glinka, Sergey 49, 51
Glogau 165, 171, 181
Glukhov 43–4
Godoy, Manuel de 190–7
Goltz, Count von 213
Gorizia 91
Gouvion St Cyr, Marshal Laurent 19, 24, 160, 250
Gradisca 91
Graham, Sir Thomas 8
Granada 202
Graudenz
  fortress of 107, 109
  Siege of 166, 174, 178
Graz, cadet school at 65
Grenier, General Paul 252
Gribeauval, General Jean-Baptiste Vacquette de 87–9
Grossbeeren 11
Grouchy, Marshal Emmanuel 13, 24
Grünne, Generalmajor 58

Habsburg dynasty 5, 57–9, 91, 97, 178, 239
Hadik, Karl 87
Haiti 128
Hanger, Colonel George 133
Hanover 3, 129, 147–8, 156, 181
Heilsberg 4, 158
Hellwig, Major von 125
Hesse, Prince Emil of 184
Hesse-Darmstadt 19, 24, 152–4, 159, 165–6
Hofer, Andreas 251
Hohenlohe, Prince 3, 75, 84
Hohenzollern dynasty 176–7

Hollabrunn 2
Holland, Kingdom of 15, 18, 20, 29, 144–5, 156
Holy Roman Empire 3, 57, 60, 64, 92, 151, 178
Hungary 59, 64, 75–81, 85, 166, 251
Hüningen 88

Iashvili, General Vladimir 50
Iberia 174–5
Igualada 199
Imperial Guard, Napoleon's 13–14, 26–35, 48, 167, 174–5, 238, 242, 249
India 128, 130, 144
Ireland 127, 130
Isenburg 154, 176–7
Italy, Kingdom of 15, 81, 156, 244–6, 249–53

Jacobins 232, 236
Jena 3, 165–7, 176
Jews 60–1, 237
Johannes Lichtenstein, Prinz 85–7
John, Archduke 5, 59, 76, 82–4, 91
Joseph II 60, 91
Joseph, Archduke 91
Junot, General Jean-Andoche 6, 24, 173, 184, 213–14, 221

Kakhovsky, General Mikhail 50
Kalisch, Convention of 10, 231–2
Kaluga 42
Kamensky, Mikhail 50
Kamieniecki, Ludwik 241
Katzbach, River 11
Kharkov 42
Kherson 47
Kniaziewicz, General Karol 233, 241
Kolberg (now Kołobrzeg)
  fortress of 107, 109
  Siege of 168, 176, 179, 235
Kolin 63
Königsberg 106
Korsakov, General Aleksey 50
Kościuszko, General Tadeusz 231–4
Kosel, fortress of 109
Krasnyi 9, 167, 251
Krockow, Captain 124
Kulm 11, 180
Kurmark 103
Kursk 42
Kutuzov, Admiral Ivan 50
Kutusov, Field Marshal Mikhail 2, 9, 50

La Haye Sainte 149
Lacerda, António de Lemos Pereira de 225
La-Fère-Champenoise 12
Landshut 5
Lannes, Marshal Jean 3
Laon 12, 242
Lasalle, General Antoine-Charles-Louis 235
Latour-Maubourg, General 24, 82, 84
Lawrence, William 136, 205
Lecchi, General Giuseppe 250
Lecor, Colonel Carlos Frederico 214, 227
Lefebvre, Marshal François 158
Leipzig 11, 20, 25, 31, 35, 57–8, 73, 163, 167, 173, 178, 242
Lemberg 59
Leuthen 158
Liberties, Charter of, *see also* Peter III 37, 49
Liechtenstein 176
Lichtenstein, Prinz Johannes 85–7
Liège 109
Ligny 13
Lippe-Detmold, principality of 154, 179–80
Lithuania 241
  Polish-Lithuanian Commonwealth 232
  Tartars 33
  volunteer recruits in 46
Littoral, the 59, 91
Lobau, Marshal, *see* Mouton, Marshal Georges
Lobau Island 5
Lodermaria 60, 81
Lomanov-Rostovsky, General Dmitri 44
Lombardy 60, 76–7, 85, 245
London 6, 214
Louis Ferdinand, Prince 3, 118, 193
Louis XVIII 12
Louise, Queen of Prussia 112
Low Countries, *see also* Netherlands 68
Löwen 95
Lublin 239
Ludwig, Crown Prince 155
Ludwig, Duke Prosper 182
Luja, River 244

Lützen 10, 27, 33, 173, 181
Lützow, Major von 124
Lwów 59, 239

Macdonald, Marshal Jacques Etienne 11, 19, 24, 160, 165
McGrigor, Dr James 144
Mack, General Karl 2, 58, 64, 68–74, 82, 83, 86, 94
Mackenzie, General 222
Madrid 6–8, 150, 191–5
Magdeburg 112, 180
Maida 133
Maloyaroslavets 9, 244, 251
Mansfeld 122
Mantua 60, 77
Marengo 57, 69, 78, 87, 95
Maria Theresa
  Academy 64
  Order of 63, 65
'Marie-Louises' 19
Markgrafneusiedl 96
Marques, Fernando Pereira 218, 226
Masséna, Marshal André 2, 7–9, 212, 217, 222–3, 249–50
Max I, Elector of Bavaria 153
Mayer, Anton 69–72, 93
Mecklenburg 154–5, 159, 181–4
Medellín 203
Mediterranean 1, 148
Melissino, General Peter 50
Meshcheriaks 44
Mesko, Staff Major 68
Metternich, Prince Clemens Wenzel Lothar von 73, 244
Metz 179
Mielżyński, Count Stanisław 233
Milan 59, 246
Mina, Francisco Espoz y 207–8
Modena 76, 82, 84, 247
Modlin, fortress of 171, 178, 240, 242
Molins de Rey 204
Mont St Jean, *see also* Waterloo 13
Montbrun, General Louis-Pierre 24
Montmirail 11
Moore, Lieutenant General Sir John 7, 127–9, 135, 147, 214–16
Moravia 2, 15, 59–64, 75–81, 88, 91, 156
Morla, Tomás de 191
Morón de la Frontera 199
Moscow 9, 42, 150, 160, 163, 167, 173, 182, 241, 244, 249, 251
Mouton, Marshal Georges 26
Mozhajsk 241
Mozinho, Manuel de Brito 225
Mozyr 44
Müller-Zakomelsky, General Lieutenant Egor 44
Müller-Zakomelsky, General Peter 50
Munich 160
Murat, Marshal Joachim 6, 22, 167, 174, 194, 231
Murray, George 146

Nansouty, General Etienne-Marie-Antoine-Champion 24
Napier, George 143
Napier, William 190–1
Naples 15, 129, 174, 230, 233, 247, 250
Nassau 159, 172–82
National Guard 11, 14, 20, 30, 159, 242, 245
Neerwinden 57, 95
Neipperg, Staff Major 68
Neiße 118
Nelson, Vice Admiral Lord Horatio 1
Netherlands, *see also* Low Countries 11, 60, 64, 76, 227
Neuchâtel 111
Neumark 103, 106
Neville, J.F. 132
New Galicia 239
New Orleans 140
Ney, Marshal Michel 11–13, 18, 23, 165
Niemen, River 9–10, 18, 173, 184
North Sea 156, 180
Nostitz-Rieneck, Graf 58, 85
Novgorod 42–3

Ocaña 7, 203
Oder, River 103, 184
Old Castile 197
Oldenburg, Duchy of 152–6, 159, 181
Olivença 213, 227
Olmütz, cadet school at 65
Oppermann, General 52
Ordnance, Board of 144–5
Orel 42
Oudinot, Marshal Nicholas 11, 23, 160
Oviedo, University of 197

Pajol, General Claude-Pierre 26
Palafox, General José de 197
Palombini, Giuseppe 252
Pamplona 197
Paris 8–13, 20, 29, 97, 123, 174, 196, 236, 242
  Convention of 101, 107, 111
  Treaty of 12–13
Paul I (Tsar) 42, 51
Pelletier, Colonel Jean 234
Peninsular War 6–8, 128, 130, 137–9, 142, 148, 188, 191, 199, 208, 212
Peter I (the Great) 42, 51
Peter III (Tsar) 37, 49
Petrozavod 42
Pfuel, Carl 52
Piave, Battle on the 251
Piedmont-Sardinia, Kingdom of 18, 23, 79–81, 245, 247
Pino, General Domenico 244, 249–51
Pitt, William 2, 128
Plata, Río de la 227
Platov, Matvei 51
Podolia 241
Poland
  Duchy of Warsaw 4, 9, 15, 18, 33, 230, 234–42
  First Partition 60
  Polish-Lithuanian Commonwealth 232
  Second Partition 235
  Third Partition 60, 230, 234, 241
Polotsk 160
Poltava 44
Pomerania 102–3, 107–9, 115
Poniatowski, Prince Joseph 18, 23, 231–2, 234–42
Poniatowski, King Stanisław August 231
Poniński, Stanisław 233
Porcia 251
Porlier, Juan Díaz 207–8
Portugal 6–10, 127–33, 137, 141, 146, 148, 188, 208, 212–17, 220–7
Posen (Poznań) 103, 231
Potocki, Aleksander 235
Potocki, Włodzimierz 238
Potsdam 100, 233
Prague 59, 81
Pressburg, Treaty of 2, 151
Preußen, Prince August von 118
Prochaska, Johann 64, 69, 86
Prozorovsky, Alexander 50
Prussia 3–4, 15–16, 22, 53, 58, 85, 98, 111, 126–8, 151–2, 155, 158–9, 162, 165–7, 174, 179–82, 230, 235–6, 239
  Partition of 98, 102
Pskov 43
Pultusk 3, 158
Pyrenees 8, 11, 166, 172–81, 184, 189, 225

Quatre Bras 12, 149

Raab 5, 91, 251
Radetzky, Johann 69, 72–3, 85
Rastatt 84
Raszyn 239–40
Ratisbon 5
Ratkau 112
Reiche, Captain von 109, 125
Reille, Marshal Honoré-Charles-Michel-Joseph 20
Repnin, General Peter 50
Reuß, Lieutenant Colonel von 125
Revolutionary Wars 58, 65, 79, 83, 93–4, 137, 151
Reynier, General Jean Louis 169–70
Rhine, River 2, 4, 11, 20, 25, 31, 103, 127, 150–1, 174–6, 181, 184
Rhineland 103, 134
Ried, Treaty of 161
Rivoli 69
Rochefort 1
Rouyer, General Marie François 177–9
Royal Artillery 138–9, 145–6
Royal Engineers 144–6
Royal Navy 1, 6–7, 127, 191
Royal Staff Corps 145
Rożniecki, General Aleksander 241
Rüchel, Lieutenant-General von 106, 117
Rumyantsev, General Field Marshal Peter 48
Rusca, General Jean-Baptiste 251
Russia
  Anglo-Russian alliance 2
  Franco-Russian relations 3, 9, 16, 18, 230, 235
  Napoleon's invasion of 27–9, 36–7, 47–8, 59, 97, 175, 178–81, 184
  Napoleon's losses in 10, 19

Saalfeld 3
Sacile 5, 251

St Domingue, *see* Haiti
St George's Cross 136
St Helena 13
Salm-Kyrburg 154, 176
Salm-Salm 154, 176
Salzburg 77, 91
San Domingo 230
San Marcial 206
San Martín, José de 227
San Sebastian, Siege of 8, 145
Sánchez, Julián 207
Sandhurst, Royal Military College at 146
Sandomierz 239
Saragossa, *see* Zaragoza
Saratoga 127
Saxony, Kingdom of 3, 15, 30, 64, 103, 115, 126, 152–4, 159–60, 167–72, 232, 239, 242
Scharnhorst, General Gerhard Johann David von 73
Schaumann, Augustus 202
Schaumburg-Lippe 154, 179, 213
Schels, J.B. 72
Schiarino-Rizzino, Treaty of 252
Schill, Major Ferdinand von 114, 124–5, 182
Schlüchtern 242
Schmitt, Heinrich 69–70
Schönbrunn, Treaty of 5, 97, 240
Schwarzburg 179–80
Schwarzenberg, Field Marshal Karl Philipp, Prince zu 10–12, 73, 86, 96
Second Coalition, *see* coalitions
Second World War 14
Serbia 81
Seslavin, General Alexander 50
Seven Years War 41, 58, 67, 89, 136, 167
Seventh Coalition, *see* coalitions
Severoli, Fillipo 251–2
Seville 196–8, 208
Sherer, Moyle 128, 222–4
Siberia 41, 54
Sicily 148
Siebenbürgen 59–63, 73–7, 81, 85, 91
Silesia 75, 91, 103, 106–21, 125, 162
  1807 campaign in 173
  Austrian 59
  Lower 102, 114
  Prussian fortresses in 158
  Upper 102
Silveira, Francisco da 215–16
Sixth Coalition, *see* coalitions
Slavonia 60–3, 77, 80–1, 91
Smola, Josef 64, 89, 95
Smolensk 9, 43–4, 50, 241
Sołtyk, Roman 238
Somerset, Lord Fitzroy 147
Somosierra 204
Soult, Marshal Nicolas Jean-de-Dieu 7–8, 20, 25, 205, 215–16, 222–3
Spanish Civil War 208
Spanish Succession, War of the 199
Spencer, Sir Brent 198
Stadion, Johann Philipp Karl Joseph 59
Stewart, Charles 224
Stewart, William 146
Stockach 57
Stralsund, Siege of 166, 174–8
Stuart, Charles 217
Stuttgart 157
Styria 59, 75–7, 91–2
Suchet, Marshal Louis Gabriel 8, 20, 25, 172, 177
Sukhtelen, General Paul 52
Sułkowski, Prince Antoni 233
Sweden 2, 125

Talavera 7, 134, 137, 165, 177, 191, 204–5, 227
Targowica, confederacy of 238
Tarragona 8, 208
Tarvis 251
Tauroggen, Convention of 10
Tczew 235
Teulié, General Pietro 250
Third Coalition, *see* coalitions
Thuringia 126, 178–9
Tilsit, Treaty of 4, 6, 16–17, 103, 122, 235–6
Titel 90
Toll, General Karl 50, 73
Torgau 167, 170, 178, 181
Toropetz 43–4
Torrens, Colonel 217
Torres Vedras, Lines of 7–8, 145, 222–3
Toruń 242
Toulon 1
Toulouse 8, 227
Trachenberg Plan 10, 73
Trafalgar 1
Transylvania, *see also* Siebenbürgen 85
Trieste 59, 81
Tudela 204
Tula 42

Turkey 58–60
Tver 42
Tyrawley, Lord 213
Tyrol 5, 60, 77–81, 125, 156–8, 162, 179, 250–1

Uclés 203
Ukraine 38, 44, 59
Ulm 2, 11
Ural Mountains 44

Valencia 8, 196–8, 208
Valls 204
Vandamme, General Dominique 11, 25, 161–2, 172–3
Vauchamps 11, 242
Venetia 60, 75–7, 80, 245
Victor, Marshal Claude 7, 19, 24, 241
Vienna 2, 5, 12, 59, 64–74, 81, 90–2, 126
Villacampa, Pedro 158, 177, 179
Villeneuve, Admiral Pierre-Charles-Jean-Baptiste-Silvestre 1
Vimeiro 6, 214
Vincent, Etienne 236
Vistula Legion 29, 238, 241
Vistula, River 101, 103, 160, 239
Vitoria 8, 165, 177, 206, 224
Volga, River 44
Volhynia (Wołyń) 241
Volkonsky, Field Marshal General Peter 48
Vorarlberg 60, 76, 155, 162, 164
Vorontsov, General Mikhail 50, 52
Vyazemsky, General V. 51

Wagram 5, 27, 57, 69, 73, 75, 91, 96, 155, 158, 164, 166, 168–9, 239, 251
Walcheren Island 4, 144, 148, 216
Waldeck 82, 84, 154, 159, 179–80
Warre, William 216–25
Warsaw 3, 158, 170, 235, 239, 241
Warsaw, Duchy of 4, 9, 15, 18, 33, 230–42
Waterloo 13–14, 20–1, 25–7, 32, 35, 115, 122–3, 128–9, 133, 136–7, 140, 145–9, 170, 225, 227
Wavre 13, 21, 26–7
Weilmarn, General Ivan 50
Wellesley, Lieutenant General Sir Arthur (later the Duke of Wellington) 6–8, 11–13, 20, 32, 127, 129–33, 135, 138–41, 144–7, 204–6, 215, 221–7, 214–17
Weser, River 103, 148
West Indies 1, 128, 144–5, 230
Westphalia, Kingdom of 4, 19, 24, 31, 81, 86, 103, 148, 150, 154, 156, 195, 171–3, 184
Weyrother, Franz 69–70
Wilhelm, Margrave of Baden 184
Wilson, Sir Robert 214–16
Wimpffen, Max 69, 72, 75
Wittgenstein, General Ludwig Adolf Peter 10
Wolzogen, Ludwig 52
Woolwich, College at 129, 144
Wrede, General Carl Philip Freiherr von 11, 156, 158, 160–1, 184
Württemburg 18, 23, 76, 82–5, 152–64
Würzburg 24, 57, 75, 78, 87, 94–5, 154, 159, 172, 174, 178–9
Wybicki, Józef 230

Yorck, Major-General Hans David Ludwig von 101
Yorktown 127

Zach, Anton 64, 70–2, 75
Zajączek, General Józef 231–2, 235–7, 240
Zamość, fortress of 239
Zaragoza (Saragossa) 6–7, 196, 205
Znaim 158, 164, 166